REVIEW OF
RESEARCH IN
EDUCATION

Review of Research in Education is published annually on behalf of the American Educational Research Association, 1430 K St., NW, Suite 1200, Washington, DC 20005, by SAGE Publications, 2455 Teller Road, Thousand Oaks, CA 91320. Send address changes to AERA Membership Department, 1430 K St., NW, Suite 1200, Washington, DC 20005.

Member Information: American Educational Research Association (AERA) member inquiries, member renewal requests, changes of address, and membership subscription inquiries should be addressed to the AERA Membership Department, 1430 K St., NW, Suite 1200, Washington, DC 20005; fax 202-238-3250. AERA annual membership dues are $150 (Regular and Affiliate Members), $110 (International Affiliates), and $40 (Graduate and Undergraduate Student Affiliates). **Claims:** Claims for undelivered copies must be made no later than six months following month of publication. Beyond six months and at the request of the American Educational Research Association, the publisher will supply missing copies when losses have been sustained in transit and when the reserve stock permits.

Subscription Information: All non-member subscription inquiries, orders, back-issue requests, claims, and renewals should be addressed to SAGE Publications, 2455 Teller Road, Thousand Oaks, CA 91320; telephone (800) 818-SAGE (7243) and (805) 499- 0721; fax: (805) 375-1700; e-mail: journals@sagepub.com; http://www.sagepublications.com. **Subscription Price:** Institutions: $163; Individuals: $56. For all customers outside the Americas, please visit http://www.sagepub.co.uk/customercare.nav for information. **Claims:** Claims for undelivered copies must be made no later than six months following month of publication. The publisher will supply missing copies when losses have been sustained in transit and when the reserve stock will permit.

Abstracting and Indexing: Please visit http://rre.aera.net and, under the "More about this journal" menu on the right-hand side, click on the Abstracting/Indexing link to view a full list of databases in which this journal is indexed.

Copyright Permission: Permission requests to photocopy or otherwise reproduce copyrighted material owned by the American Educational Research Association should be submitted by accessing the Copyright Clearance Center's Rightslink® service through the journal's website at http://rre.aera.net. Permission may also be requested by contacting the Copyright Clearance Center via its website at http://www.copyright.com, or via e-mail at info@copyright.com.

Advertising and Reprints: Current advertising rates and specifications may be obtained by contacting the advertising coordinator in the Thousand Oaks office at (805) 410-7763 or by sending an e-mail to advertising@sagepub.com. To order reprints, please e-mail reprint@sagepub.com. Acceptance of advertising in this journal in no way implies endorsement of the advertised product or service by SAGE or the journal's affiliated society(ies). No endorsement is intended or implied. SAGE reserves the right to reject any advertising it deems as inappropriate for this journal.

Change of Address: Six weeks' advance notice must be given when notifying of change of address. Please send old address label along with the new address to ensure proper identification. Please specify name of journal.

International Standard Serial Number ISSN 0091-732X
International Standard Book Number ISBN 978-1-4129-9706-5 (Vol. 35, 2011, paper)
Manufactured in the United States of America. First printing, March 2011.

Printed on acid-free paper

REVIEW OF RESEARCH IN EDUCATION

Youth Cultures, Language, and Literacy

Volume 35, 2011

Stanton Wortham, Editor

University of Pennsylvania

American Educational Research Association

Review of Research in Education

Youth Cultures, Language, and Literacy

Volume 35

EDITOR

STANTON WORTHAM
University of Pennsylvania

AMERICAN EDUCATIONAL RESEARCH ASSOCIATION
Tel: 202-238-3200 Fax: 202-238-3250
http://www.aera.net/pubs

FELICE J. LEVINE
Executive Director

TODD REITZEL
Director of Publications

Contents

Cover images © iStockphoto.com.

Introduction

Youth Cultures and Education

STANTON WORTHAM
University of Pennsylvania

Educators, policymakers, and the public are often deeply interested in youth cultures and practices. Young people nowadays, we are told, behave in selfish, deviant, apathetic, irrational, creative, altruistic, engaged, tolerant, and various other, often-contradictory ways. Popular accounts label and characterize generations "X," "Y," and now "Z," the "net" generation, the "Peter Pan" generation, the "silent" generation, and so on. Such accounts of youth often have little to do with youth themselves, but instead express adult concerns about the nature and trajectories of social groups. Some adult accounts of youth nonetheless also reflect legitimate hopes and worries for and about them. Educators should attend to widely circulating accounts of youth, because these often yield or buttress attitudes and policies that influence young people. If we take for granted misleading popular accounts of contemporary youth, we may fail to understand young people and treat them in counterproductive ways. On the other hand, insightful accounts of youth and attempts to understand their views can help educators work more successfully with them.

Most popular conceptions of youth culture oversimplify. Many youth beliefs and practices change rapidly and draw on heterogeneous resources that move across the contemporary world. Because of migration, the ease of travel, and new media and communications technologies, youth culture crosses social and national borders, often yielding complex hybrids that include both components rooted in local histories and globally circulating forms. Despite this complexity, it is important for both scholars and educators to understand youth cultural practices. These practices infiltrate and mediate other important processes—appearing in schools, for instance, as distractions and sometimes as components of lesson plans, and deeply influencing students' social and personal identities. Many youth practices also involve remarkable creativity and skill, and youth are often more motivated to engage in these

Review of Research in Education
March 2011, Vol. 35, pp. vii–xi
DOI: 10.3102/0091732X10391735
© 2011 AERA. http://rre.aera.net

practices than in traditional educational activities. If we could understand and incorporate aspects of youth practices into our pedagogy, as many educators have imagined, perhaps we could educate youth more effectively.

Most adults, however, fail to appreciate the full complexity of youth practices—not just their heterogeneity and rapid emergence but also their reflexivity. At the same time as adults create and circulate accounts of young people, youth create and transform the practices and conceptions that make up "youth cultures." They do not simply engage in activities that we adults might be able to construe for them. They give accounts of their own activities, often in ways that run counter to adult accounts. Furthermore, youth cultural practices usually contain tacit or explicit accounts of the adult world, resisting common norms and stereotypes or celebrating alternative identities and goals. They give accounts of us, as we give accounts of them. Productive theories of and engagements with youth culture will require a deeper understanding of how adult cultures and youth cultures construe each other.

Both adult accounts of youth, and youth cultures themselves, are reflexive: They involve characteristic signs, ideals, and practices that groups circulate and engage in, and they involve meta-level accounts of those signs, ideals, and practices. Adults create and enforce educational scripts and standards, for instance, and they also construe these as appropriate ways to behave and reasonable goals to have. Youth create and consume contemporary musical genres and multimedia products, for instance, and they often construe these as powerful, engaging, and effective. Furthermore, both adults and youth give accounts of each other's signs, ideals, and practices—and, in fact, a central part of each group's ideals and practices is based on its accounts of the other. Youth define themselves and organize their action partly in response to their accounts of adult ideals and practices, and adults do the same thing as we develop educational practices that we apply to youth and as we imagine the future of our societies. Of course, both "adults" and "youth" are heterogeneous sets, and so various subsets are offering their own accounts of the signs, ideals, and practices of various subsets, such that the full situation is even more complex.

This volume reviews contemporary research on the interplay between youth cultures, educational practices, and the accounts that adults and youth tacitly and explicitly give of each other. The chapters examine varying types of practice—ranging from computer programming to verbal rap battles to canonical literacy activities—that take place in various settings around the world—from schools to playgrounds, homes, clubs, and through the Internet. Most chapters describe the historical and material conditions within which these practices occur, exploring the distribution of material and symbolic resources among different types of youth and adults. Each chapter also tells a story about how adult accounts and youth accounts intersect with some domain of youth practice and with each other. Sometimes this intersection yields hope for mutual understanding and more productive education, as when laudable aspirations embedded in youth practices can intertwine with curricular goals to yield powerful learning experiences. At other times, the intersection yields misunderstanding and attempts by both youth and adults to undermine the other's goals.

Three central themes appear in the chapters' accounts of youth culture: Youth cultural practices are often creative, global, and counterhegemonic. Almost all the chapters describe youth being highly creative in various types of activities, often in the face of material constraints. Yasmin Kafai and Kylie Peppler describe creative computer programming and "do-it-yourself" multimedia activities that large numbers of youth engage in—both reviewing others' accounts and describing some of their own work on virtual worlds and "wearable computing." Lesley Bartlett, Dina López, Erika Mein, and Laura Valdiviezo describe creative out-of-school youth literacy practices in Latin America and the Caribbean, arguing that many policymakers and educators limit themselves to a narrow definition of "literacy" and thus fail to recognize and take advantage of youth engagement and creativity. Maisha Winn and Nadia Behizadeh describe critical literacy practices that many youth engage in, arguing that youth creativity in such practices is undervalued but a crucial resource that we can use to counteract the epidemic of incarcerated urban youth.

Many of the chapters also describe how globalization has transformed youth cultures, bringing resources from around the world into practices that are nonetheless tied to local cultures, histories, and material constraints. Shalini Shankar describes how diasporic South and East Asian youth draw on heterogeneous signs, ideals, and practices from various parts of the world as they navigate mainstream expectations and develop social identities. She argues that youth do not find the heterogeneity of these resources unsettling, as many adults do, but instead embrace multiplicity and rapid change as they position themselves in increasingly complex Western societies. H. Samy Alim traces how hip-hop songs and practices circulate around the world, describing hybrid styles in East Asia and elsewhere that can include multiple languages and that connect local histories and resources with global patterns. In these youth cultures, multiplicity is valued as the norm and those trying to impose a monoglot standard are portrayed as backward. Thea Abu El-Haj and Sally Bonet argue that Muslim youth from transnational communities creatively fashion senses of belonging by drawing on ideals and practices from various religious, ethnic, and national communities. They describe how youth have reacted to stereotypes of Muslims after 9/11 by producing more complex senses of transnational selves and by trying to communicate these more nuanced accounts to others.

Most of the chapters also describe how youth cultural practices struggle against and sometimes invert hegemonic ideas and practices. Betsy Rymes shows how contemporary media provide youth pathways to collective self-expression that are often opaque not only to adults but also to youth who are not part of highly specialized peer groups. Intense involvement in hip-hop or online fan-fiction writing, for example, requires heterogeneous sets of knowledge and depth of involvement not found in traditional schooling, which often attempts to tie youth culture down by matching it with mainstream agendas. Jennifer Cole describes how African youth often see themselves as part of a generational rupture or dramatic transformation in how young people enter adulthood, in which they cannot follow the pathways taken by their parents—though she argues that this notion of rupture oversimplifies. Her chapter shows how youth culture in some parts of the world is not a simple lifestyle choice, not something to do in leisure time, but is instead central to youths' struggle to count as "adult" in the contemporary world. Alim juxtaposes the intense love of language exhibited by participants in hip-hop cultures with the failure of most educators to recognize or engage these young people's abilities and affinities. He shows how, in response to mainstream construals of them, youth involved in hip-hop invert traditional value hierarchies—for instance, pointing out the irony of what they call "illiterate" adults who do not even recognize nonmainstream literacies but nonetheless believe that they are empowered to judge who is "literate."

The counterhegemonic nature of many youth practices means that they invert influential adult ideals. In some cases, adults respond in kind, casting youth cultures as deficient. Bartlett, López, Mein, and Valdiviezo show how many policymakers across Latin America and the Caribbean use an oversimplified view of literacy and label many youth as "at risk," deviant, and even dangerous. Official attempts to remedy the situation too often rely on literacy programs that ignore the technologically mediated, often multilingual, and culturally hybrid literacy practices that contemporary youth engage in. Winn and Behizadeh describe how many poor urban youth in the United States are subjected to surveillance in schools that sometimes focuses more on discipline than instruction—because adults construe these youth and their practices as deviant and threatening. They show how such accounts of youth, embedded in the educational and juvenile justice systems, facilitate the "school-to- prison pipeline" that begins with school discipline and ends with a disproportionate number of urban minority youth being incarcerated.

Almost all the chapters ask how educators could more productively relate to creative, global, and counterhegemonic youth practices. Instead of construing youth as different and misguided, could educators learn from and work with youth culture? Many of the chapters argue that schooling has a dual nature: It usually reinforces unjust social hierarchies, but it can also give young people the resources to challenge those hierarchies. Often schools do both at once, and the contact zone between schools and youth cultures thus contains both significant risk and potential reward. There is risk if educators' accounts of youth cultures lead them to stereotype or not effectively serve youth who refuse to reproduce mainstream ideals and practices. There could be reward if educators incorporate aspects of youth cultures that align with educational goals.

Most of the chapters argue that youth cultures need not be opposed to educational practices and institutions. Both Alim and Winn and Behizadeh propose that schooling can take advantage of alternative literacies embedded in youth cultural practices. Alim argues that youth often respond to pedagogies that are "intimate, lived, and liberatory." Educators can incorporate youth cultural practices that have these characteristics and work toward the liberatory goals that they share with many youth. Kafai and Peppler argue that youth develop creative, ethical, and technical competencies while producing multimedia objects, and they suggest that educators could teach these competencies more effectively if schools engaged with such technologies and if educators positioned youth as producers of knowledge instead of as consumers of the curriculum. Both Shankar and Abu El-Haj and Bonet argue that schools could broaden their account of citizenship—moving beyond the idea of allegiance to one nation-state—and help youth develop senses of belonging to multiple relevant communities, by drawing on youths' own creative connection of self to various communities.

We should not imagine, however, that some final rapprochement between youth and adult accounts is possible or desirable. It would be best if educators, policymakers, and education researchers could avoid stereotypical and deficit-based accounts of youth. It would be productive if educators could connect their pedagogy, and their civic and ethical goals for schooling, to youth cultural ideals and practices. But many youth will nonetheless continue to construe mainstream educational ideals and practices as archaic, unproductive, or unjust. Youth cultures and educational practices are also heterogeneous, as Cole argues, and they change over time. In fact, both youth cultures and educational practices should gain strength from their ability to change as ideals and social realities change—it seems, in fact, that educators might learn something from youth about productive change.

Instead of envisioning a convergence between youth and adult accounts of each other, we should shift to what Rymes calls a "repertoire" model. Educators' and youths' ideals and practices are heterogeneous sets of partly overlapping signs, ideas, and activities. Any individual and any community recognizes or participates in only a subset of these, and any two individuals and communities—even if we typically oppose them, as with "youth" and "adults" or "mainstream" and "marginalized"— overlap in their repertoires. As Cole argues, we must embrace heterogeneity both descriptively and normatively. Descriptively adequate accounts of youth culture will acknowledge their heterogeneity, and as we envision more productive ways to educate youth, we should build on that heterogeneity by expecting and incorporating it. Progress will involve expanding the repertoires of both adults and youth, negotiating partial rapprochements and productive synergies in local settings, and then renegotiating as other factors intervene and repertoires change.

ACKNOWLEDGMENTS

I would like to thank the contributing authors for their insights and persistence and the consulting editors for their advice and timeliness. Vivian Gadsden envisioned this volume and asked me to edit it—and both she and Ritty Lukose helped with the initial planning—for which I am grateful. Todd Reitzel, Felice Levine, and the AERA Publications Committee have been supportive throughout the process, and Sara Sarver from Sage has handled the production skillfully. This work was completed while I was a William T. Grant Foundation Distinguished Fellow, and I appreciate the Foundation's support.

Chapter 1

Asian American Youth Language Use: Perspectives Across Schools and Communities

SHALINI SHANKAR
Northwestern University

Recent studies of Asian American youth language practices have presented compelling insights about the identities and migration experiences of young people
of Asian descent. This chapter offers a detailed examination of the relationship
between language use and select issues concerning Asian American youth, including
social life, schooling, acculturation, and intergenerational relationships. Specifically,
how do Asian American youth negotiate aspects of their migration experience
through their language practices? And, what insights about race, ethnicity, class, and
gender can be learned about migration and diaspora through a focus on youth language use? The chapter covers three main topics about the language practices of
Asian American youth: identity, style, and stereotypes. The first portion of the chapter discusses performances of Asian American youth identity through language
practices. Studies of bilingualism, heritage language learning, language socialization,
and the role of language in intergenerational relationships are explored. Engagements
with media, new media, and consumption offer further examples of how language
use enables youth to make diasporic connections and to express aspects of language
and culture in their everyday lives. Heritage language shift, in some cases an inevitable outcome of generational change, underscores the dynamic nature of languages
and their usage in migration contexts. The next section delves into ethnographic case
studies of "style," a linguistic anthropological and sociolinguistic framework that
foregrounds the everyday speech practices of Asian American youth. Youth perform
regionally available styles of speaking as well as locally created, group-specific styles,
along with varieties of English that provide exemplification not only of identity
formation but also of gender, ethnicity, and race.

Review of Research in Education
March 2011, Vol. 35, pp. 1–28
DOI: 10.3102/0091732X10383213
© 2011 AERA. http://rre.aera.net

The latter portion of the chapter is concerned with how Asian American youth language practices are received in the White public sphere. Stereotypes that Asian American youth contend with create expectations not only for academic achievement but also for language use. Youth of various class backgrounds negotiate ideologies about heritage languages and varieties of English differently, even within the same ethnic group. In this vein, variation within the category of "Asian American" will be examined to understand how language use may create social differences within as well as between ethnic groups. Ideologies of English monolingualism shape the ways in which youth manage ESL (English as a Second Language) and other language learning classes, the language choices they make during social time at school, and how peers, school faculty, and others regard and judge particular linguistic choices. Language choices that Asian American youth make thus not only shape their identities but also contribute to processes of racialization in school environments.

To explore the ways in which language use is linked to the identities and subjectivities of Asian American youth, research from several bodies of literature—including linguistic anthropology, international migration studies, and immigrant education—are discussed. Case studies of Asian American youth language practices in nonclassroom environments, including social time at school, with their families, and in their communities, will be a central focus. Looking across these domains, Asian American youth will be considered as social actors who make choices about language use that shape identity, community, and generational change. Select studies of Asian youth in the United Kingdom and Canada, as well as of Latino youth in the United States, provide additional ways of considering the language practices of Asian American youth. Taken together, the chapter considers how ideologies of language and culture that prevail in the lives of Asian American youth may shape their orientations toward their own language use as well as that of others, and how they manage linguistic challenges particular to migration and diaspora. It thus extends studies of immigrant education by considering how youth actively shape identities through language use while they also negotiate their subjectivity in schools and communities.

ETHNOGRAPHIC APPROACHES TO YOUTH AND LANGUAGE

Since 1965, when the United States began to solicit immigrants actively after decades of restrictive policies, social scientists have sought to understand how individuals and families of the "new immigration," particularly those from Asia and Latin America, have built lives for themselves in America. Youth in the category "Asian American" are immigrants or children of immigrants from East Asia, South Asia, Southeast Asia, and the Pacific Islands. The category also includes young people whose ancestors immigrated before 1965, primarily from China, Japan, and in lesser numbers, from India and the Philippines. In a 2008 update to the 2000 Census (report CB08-FF.05), the U.S. Census Bureau estimates a population of 14.9 million

Asians (alone or in combination with other races). Although numerous aspects of culture, heritage, and language retention have been studied, relatively little attention has been paid to understanding everyday language use among youth of the new immigration. Rather, the predominant focus has been on intergenerational tension, feelings of displacement, and clashes of cultural values. Both in migration studies, which groups youth by generational categories of first, second, and 1.5 (referring to youth who migrated during late childhood or early adolescence), and in minority education studies, the focus is on how "immigrant" youth are culturally conflicted outsiders because of the disjuncture of their migration experience. At times this focus can be overwhelming, and it is also important to focus on the performative cultural and linguistic practices that youth use to create a sense of belonging.

Youth-centered perspectives on migration that consider them as more than simply "immigrants" can also be productive. A revision in terminology from *immigrant* to *diasporic* reorients focus from youth as subjects of assimilation to youth as agents who engage in everyday cultural and linguistic practices. Lukose (2007) argues that the concept of diaspora and insights from diaspora studies can productively complicate the otherizing status of "immigrant education" and problematize some of the underlying assumptions on which the U.S. education system is based. Considering the diasporic connections of second-generation youth is an important counterpoint to the more limited, relational connotations of the term *minority* in an educational context. Lam (2006) likewise advocates for an approach that extends beyond the terminology of *nation-state* and *immigrant* to consider diasporic connections that shape social and educational participation. She shifts focus from "minority" issues to a "transcultural" perspective that integrates a wider range of social and learning experiences. In doing so, she critiques "deficit" approaches in which culture is viewed as holistic in favor of a cultural affirmation model that takes into account diverse practices of youth (Lam, 2006, pp. 215–216).

Youth-centered approaches to Asian American language use can demonstrate how the cultural and linguistic choices young people make are linked to and shaped by different migration contexts. Considering diasporic youth as social actors can broaden the purview of questions beyond classic migration areas of intergenerational tension and entry into adulthood to the everyday mechanisms youth develop to handle changes linked to migration. About such adaptation, Bucholtz (2002) contends,

Rapid social change need not be experienced as dramatic or unsettling by the young people living through it . . . it is important to bear in mind that youth are as often the agents as much as the experiencers of cultural change. (p. 530)

Language use is a central arena through which youth enact identities, and understanding these practices in context can speak to broader migration concerns. Ethnographic studies of youth have emphasized the importance of looking at youth concerns in and of themselves rather than solely in relation to adult issues.

Ethnographic perspectives on the study of language use and migration can extend questions of retention and loss by looking at emic categories that youth use to organize their social lives. Long-term in situ observation, in addition to self-report, provides additional perspectives not available from survey and interview-based studies. Ethnographic approaches to youth language use demonstrate how language in context shapes meanings of race, class, and gender (Smitherman, 1999). Alim and Baugh (2007) demonstrate how schools position minority youth as speakers and the ways in which young people both challenge and work within linguistic constraints. Goodwin's (2006) extensive work on girls' identity construction through play during recess and after school illustrates the complex social negotiations that can occur between young people themselves. The ways in which girls verbally interact, take turns, and perform particular stances is shaped by, and shapes, meanings of gender and ethnicity. Also focusing on gender, Fordham (2008) discusses how youth use linguistic and material signifiers to index, or indirectly refer to, Black identities other than those of low-income Black neighborhoods. These and other studies of youth language use provide extensive insights about youth educational orientation and performance, social life, and engagements with popular culture.

Examinations of youth language use outside of formal pedagogical contexts can address central questions of migration and diaspora, including generational change, racial and ethnic formation, gender, and class. Informal environments—such as social spaces at school, time with peers, and family and community settings—are sites where youth can use language in creative and social ways. Models for research both inside and outside the classroom are offered by the field of "linguistic anthropology of education" (LAE), which includes nonpedagogical dimensions of youth education alongside formal classroom instruction (Wortham, 2008). LAE's focus on youth linguistic practices outside of pedagogical contexts, including social time at school, afterschool programs, and community-based organizations, emphasizes the importance of these spaces in youth lives as well as their linkages to more formal educational settings and tasks (Ball & Heath, 1993; Rymes, 2001; Vadeboncoeur, 2006). With its ethnographic focus, LAE can expand migration and immigrant education topics of language retention and loss to look at a range of context-specific uses of language, including language socialization, identity, and style. The following sections delve into these issues for Asian American youth.

LANGUAGE AND IDENTITY

Linkages between language and identity can demonstrate not only youth affiliations and preferences but also the everyday tactics youth use to negotiate subjectivities (Bucholtz & Hall, 2004). In addition to self-report about language use, language-based studies of identity-making practices show how youth negotiate aspects of their migration experience through modalities such as bilingualism, heritage language use, code switching, language socialization, and translation. Linguistic dimensions of youth engagements with media, popular culture, and consumption can show how youth connect to heritage languages as well as to other languages, and how these communicative forms play a role in social interactions with peers and family. Language shifts and changes in usage are a routine part of generational change in diaspora and can also speak to questions of acculturation and identity.

Bilingualism and Heritage Languages

Studies of bilingualism among Asian Americans and other youth of the new immigration take both macro- and micro-level approaches to understanding the significance of speaking heritage languages and English. Migration studies explore the comparative bilingual abilities of first-, second-, and third-generation immigrants. In their "children of immigrants longitudinal study" (CILS) consisting of survey and interview data, Portes and Rumbaut (2001) consider English proficiency as a way of measuring acculturation. The rate at which second-generation youth acquire English is correlated with the same for their parents, and these measures are used to quantify acculturation. Based on youth ethnic identification and self-report, they conclude that English-speaking ability is an important component of youth identity. Their analysis of "selective acculturation" reveals that youth who "retain" their parents' culture and language feel less of a generational clash than those "youths who have severed bonds with their past in the pursuit of acceptance by their native peers" (Portes & Rumbaut, 2001, p. 274).

The role of bilingualism is also significant insofar as it aids immigrant families in entering and thriving in the labor market and participating more substantially in a multilingual global economy. Bilingualism is especially important to the transnational activities of the second generation (M. Levitt & Waters, 2002). The success of transnationalism relies heavily on heritage language retention, so much so that attachments to homelands may be renewed or curtailed based on the linguistic abilities of the second generation. Rumbaut (2002) argues that language retention and loss are important to understanding second-generation relationships to homelands and that bilingual ability is a key component of these connections. This is especially the case as scholars look past the second-generation to third-generation youth to assess the viability of social, economic, and political ties that their parents maintain to homelands (P. Levitt & Jaworsky, 2007). Bilingualism has also been noted to facilitate connections between teens and their parents and enables youth to take advantage of social connections in their ethnic communities (Zhou & Bankston, 1998).

Bilingualism can be useful in understanding how children learn cultural codes from their heritage culture as well as American society. Lee (2005) examines bilingualism among Hmong youth as a way of investigating their subjectivity as minority students. As they acquire English literacy, they also learn select aspects of American culture and codes. The teachers in Lee's study seem to consider this socialization to be a part of the broader ESL mission. Lee (2005, p. 55) uses the term *Americanized* for those youth who have adopted these values and may be more particular about their ethnic identification, versus those "traditional" youth who are primarily 1.5

generation and more optimistic about their prospects in the United States. Looking at bilingualism among Latino youth, Zentella (1997) investigates intergenerational politics of bilingualism on *el bloque* among three generations of Puerto Ricans in New York City. She reports how a range of linguistic processes—language socialization, code switching, bilingualism, and language shift—are significant to shaping the identities of Latino youth. In addition to Spanish, Zentella also draws attention to youth use of New York City varieties of English and African American Vernacular English (AAVE).

Heritage language learning enables youth to develop linguistic proficiency and deepen connections with others in their language community, and Asian American youth have been documented in their efforts to learn Chinese, Japanese, and Korean (He & Xiao, 2008; Jo, 2001; Kondo-Brown, 2006). Those who are heritage language proficient vary in their ability to pass it along to their children, and such differences shape how Asian American youth regard their ethnic identification (Ching & Kung, 1997). The value placed on English also plays a role in bilingual practices and language learning. Song (2010) identifies Korean American communities' language ideologies that situate English as a cosmopolitan language that may be leveraged as a marketable commodity. Song contrasts families who migrate to the United States on a short-term basis for their children's education with long-term Korean immigrants. Examining the language ideologies and practices of these two groups, she interviews mothers who arrange for and assist their children in acquiring English proficiency. Although English is highly valued, the mothers express feelings of regret about children who have not learned Korean and thus cannot easily communicate with others in their Korean social networks. Code switching among Asian Americans provides further exemplification about the contexts and means by which speakers alternate between a heritage language and English. Speakers' use of two or more codes has been examined in several heritage languages, including Japanese (Ervin-Tripp, 1964; Kozasa, 2000), Korean (Kang, 2003; Lo, 1999; Shin & Milroy, 2000), Vietnamese (Kliefgen, 2001; Tuc, 2003; Wolfram, Christian, & Hatfield, 1986), and Hawai'ian Creole (Romaine, 1999). Code switching can also focus on how speakers alternate between nonheritage languages. For instance, Lo (1999) documents how Chinese Americans make use of Korean and AAVE.

Intergenerational studies of heritage language use can demonstrate the ways in which youth learn kinship terms and social structures linked to their heritage culture (Kang, 2003; Shin, 2005). Song (2009) investigates how Korean American children manipulate interpersonal terms of address that they are socialized into using. Youth choice about the use of Korean or English terms of address is demonstrated through the ways in which they manipulate respectful and familiar modes of address. Like other studies of language socialization (i.e., Schieffelin & Ochs, 1986), Song traces how youth learn not only language but also social norms, gender relations, and a sense of self vis-à-vis others in a community setting. In a bilingual context, these norms may not translate across languages, and Song demonstrates the creativity that youth use to manage intergenerational and peer social relationships.

Providing another perspective on intergenerational communication, "language brokering" describes the process by which young people translate for older members of their communities. Language brokering and translation work position children and youth as active participants in the migration process (Orellana, Thorne, Chee, & Lam, 2001). Orellana (2009) describes the rewards as well as the challenges of this type of language work, as seemingly straightforward translation can quickly become complicated when youth are asked to communicate about sensitive topics, legal matters, and financial issues that typically do not involve children. Especially awkward are events such as parent–teacher conferences in which youth struggle to translate both positive and negative feedback about themselves, each of which poses a distinct difficulty. As they bridge the gap between adults in positions of authority and their immigrant parents, youth must negotiate power dynamics of a largely English-speaking White public sphere (Reynolds & Orellana, 2009). Tse (1996) documents this process for both Chinese American and Vietnamese American communities and notes that these youth translators differ from those in Latino communities. With the latter, youth English-speaking ability may not be accurately assessed by the school, even though these youth are vital to translation processes (Tse, 1995). Drawing attention to the largely unacknowledged work that youth do as translators and interpreters, Valdes (2003) contends that youth who may be labeled as "high risk" should be evaluated more closely with regard to their bilingual accomplishments to better understand the ways in which they may be "gifted." These youth can inadvertently become involved in family matters concerning finance, the law, and their own education in ways that noninterpreter youth seldom do. Such linguistic practices shape the identities of Asian American and other diasporic youth.

Heritage languages and English varieties are linked to ethnic and racial identity (Kang & Lo, 2004), and ethnic identification and identity are negotiated through language choice (Fought, 2006; Heller, 1986). Foner (2002) regards language to be a part of ethnic identity that mediates intergenerational connections for second-generation youth. Looking at Asian American youth of different ethnicities, Kibria (2003) investigates youth relationships with their heritage culture and language. She contextualizes her study in a broader look at the racial and ethnic experiences of youth of the new immigration from Asia and Latin America to understand how youth become "ethnic Americans" or "racial minorities." Kibria includes heritage language along with culture as part of what she calls "ethnic identity capital" to draw attention to differences of ethnic experiences among Asian American youth. Ethnic identity capital is a useful concept for considering how youth make choices about how and when to perform their heritage culture and language. Ethnic identity capital illustrates the agentive ways in which youth use language, along with other aspects of their heritage, to shape their racial and ethnic identities.

Heritage language use can illustrate processes of diasporic belonging and generational change. Kang (2009) explores this theme by studying discursive constructions of identity to differentiate between "ethnic groups" and "ethnic identity." Looking at first-, second-, and 1.5-generation Korean American camp counselors, she discusses how youth self-classify themselves and make judgments about others. Emphasizing the importance of locally inflected meanings of ethnicity, Kang notes the perceived disjuncture between "being" Korean at the camp and "feeling" Korean American through particular uses of language. Language use and ethnicity show how youth within an ethnic group connect with their specific heritage culture. Ek (2009) offers a case study of language and identity for a second-generation Latina young woman who is able to develop a distinct Guatemalan identity despite not identifying with dominant Mexican American/Chicana groups in her region. Ek discusses "multiple socializations," including "Americanization" and "Mexicanization," to which this Guatemalan teenager is subject and explores how this shapes her language choice and use. By choosing to use a Guatemalan variety of Spanish, she indexes her ethnic and national affiliation while also positioning herself as Latina in a school context where students of this background maintain cultural and linguistic values that at times conflict with school norms.

These studies underscore the centrality of heritage languages in the formation of diasporic youth identities. Asian American youth use their heritage languages to express a sense of belonging and connection to their heritage cultures as well as their communities. These language practices can also be linked to other aspects of social life, especially engagements with media and practices of consumption.

Youth Language Practices, Media, and Consumption

Asian American youth engagements with media, consumption, and other aspects of popular culture are important tools for identity formation, and an eye toward language use in these realms can further understandings of diaspora and generational change. Gadsden (2008) emphasizes that youth engage with media in ways that shape their linguistic practices of story telling, literacy, and learning. About media-based language practices, she asserts, "Youth draw on and revise existing language and linguistic genres to construct their own language(s) and linguistic codes" (Gadsden, 2008, p. 51) and emphasizes that they come to bear on their experiences in school. Reyes (2007) examines how Southeast Asian American youth negotiate ethnic stereotypes through video production in an afterschool program in Philadelphia. This media-making activity is one through which youth explore their status as "the Other Asian" in ways that differentiate them from wealthier, higher-achieving Asian American youth. In this realm, Reyes contends that youth borrowings from AAVE are positive for youth who wish to create a more urban subjectivity. Linguistic elements drawn from hip-hop enable diasporic youth to create connections with other youth worldwide (Alim, Ibrahim, & Pennycook, 2009). For instance, youth of Latin American descent in Montreal use hip-hop to connect with Canadian youth as well as those in Latin America, thus emphasizing the potential of linguistic and expressive culture in shaping diasporic identities (Sarkar & Winer, 2006).

Youth sustain linguistic connections with heritage languages through their engagements with media. Looking at heritage language media consumption, Rubinstein-Ávila (2007) presents a case of a teenage Dominican American girl who uses her transnational connections to keep her interest in Spanish language media active, including viewing and discussing telenovelas (Spanish language soap operas) as well as books about the Dominican Republic. In my investigation of media-based language practices, I document how youth engage with Bollywood films in everyday peer interactions as well as intergenerational relationships (Shankar, 2009). Ethnographic research with Desi teens in Queens, New York, and Silicon Valley, California, illustrates how these youth incorporate Hindi film dialogue into their peer interactions and how family viewing practices facilitate bilingualism between generations. Even youth whose heritage language is not Hindi may watch subtitled films and turn to their parents and grandparents for translation assistance. Memorable lines from popular films offer boys and girls prescripted ways to flirt with one another, and youth use "*filmi*" (a Hindi word referring to conventions and content of Bollywood films) styles of speaking, such as those linked to villains, heroes, or other archetypal characters to create jokes and humorous utterances among themselves. During the film viewings, youth speak in Hindi, Punjabi, and other heritage languages as well as English with their parents and grandparents. These language practices provide a more complex sense of how Desi youth use Bollywood as a cultural and linguistic resource in constructing identities.

New media, especially online communities, offer multilingual domains for youth that may not be easily found in their everyday lives. Youth can participate in online social environments that their schools may not provide and use them as alternative means of identification and socializing (McGinnis, Goodstein-Stolzenberg, & Costa Saliani, 2007). Lam (2004) documents Asian American youth affiliations with particular online cultures in which they create linguistic networks that surpass those of their school and communities. She describes ways in which Chinese immigrant teenagers acquire English to connect with a global anime youth culture in ways that transcend mainstream American language practices. Lam and Rosario-Ramos (2009) also investigate how Chinese American youth create linguistic resources to develop social relationships and networks through instant messaging (IM). Making connections with linguistic communities elsewhere, especially through a "wider migrant diaspora," shapes self-presentation and identity for youth in the United States (Lam & Rosario-Ramos, 2009, p. 187). Similarly, Yi's (2009) investigation of Korean American teenagers' online activities reveals that youth participants use a mix of English and Korean to discuss both Korean and American cultural preferences and practices. These cases demonstrate how first- and second-generation Asian American youth use online spaces such as personal profiles and social networking sites to maintain linguistic connections with youth elsewhere.

Like media, consumption is another fertile area in which to examine diasporic youth language practices, especially how verbal and material cultures intersect in youth lives. Although it has been widely argued that consumption is an integral part of youth culture and of diaspora, the specific ways in which it is linguistically informed in the context of diasporic youth invites more detailed examination. Looking beyond traditional areas of ethnic consumption can reveal intergenerational engagements with a wide range of material forms. Among Desi youth and their families in Silicon Valley, I document a process I call "metaconsumption," which refers to forms of talk that enable teenagers and their families to create and circulate narratives about objects they may own or wish to own (Shankar, 2006). High-end cars, sound systems, and other objects are highly valued in these communities, and the ways in which teens affiliate with them through verbal practices can confer status and prestige. Especially noteworthy is the intergenerational nature of such values, and how youth as well as their parents collaborate about choices and jointly participate in consumption practices. The ways in which Desi youth and their families create and circulate verbal narratives about material culture provide a shared practice that challenges the notion that intergenerational conflict is the dominant relationship dynamic in a migration situation. Rather than considering material and linguistic investment in these objects to simply be a sign of assimilation, I consider how they allow Desi teens and their families to become further socially and linguistically invested in their own tightly knit ethnic communities.

In all these cases, language use is an integral part of how youth create identities and connections with their communities. Tools such as media allow youth to participate in language communities beyond those available to them in their everyday lives. Consumption of both media and material culture allow youth to mediate intergenerational relationships and forge relationships in their immediate as well as broader diasporic communities. Another relevant dimension of language use is heritage language shift and the transition to English and other languages.

Heritage Language Shift and Loss

In as much as heritage language use and bilingualism are important aspects of Asian American youth language use, so too are processes of heritage language shift and loss. Decades of assimilation research have examined how immigrants retain or lose aspects of their heritage culture and language while acquiring new social modes and greater use of American English. Although assimilation is still a dominant theoretical framework, recent migration studies have veered away from straight-line, ethnocentric models in which immigrants are thought to relinquish all aspects of their heritage language and culture in favor of understanding it as a selective process in which individuals choose particular aspects of American culture. In her work on South Asian American youth, Gibson (1988) calls this model "multilinear acculturation" and argues that youth selectively adopt aspects of American culture and language while retaining valued elements from their heritage culture and language (see also Gibson & Ogbu, 1991). Gibson applies this approach in examining South Asian American teenagers of Sikh heritage in California. In her study, Sikh youth are able to participate in their school activities while also maintaining an active religious and cultural life in their communities.

Youth heritage language use is linked to processes of linguistic assimilation, which can occur differently according to socioeconomic status. Alba and Nee's (2003) "segmented assimilation" builds on Gibson's approach and suggests a number of outcomes for how immigrants may become new Americans. They identify several assimilation trajectories in which heritage language is a variable that may be lost or retained, and assert that language is a significant component of the assimilation process. Either bilingualism or heritage language loss is the likely outcome of generational change; the latter, which they call "full linguistic acculturation," is a near inevitability for third-generation and some second-generation youth (Alba & Nee 2003, p. 219).

Scholars have examined processes of language shift as speakers move generationally from being bilingual to monolingual English speakers (Shridhar, 1988). The heritage language interference prevalent in first-generation youth may not carry over between generations (Mendoza-Denton & Iwai, 1993). Ng, Lee, and Pak (2007, p. 107) indicate that language loss and generational differences in heritage language-speaking abilities may have "negative effects on family relations" because of differences in acculturation. Heritage language loss generally occurs within three generations because of pressures surrounding assimilation, including "linguistic inferiority internalized by minority individuals" (Ng et al., 2007, p. 107), among other factors such as building relationships with other English speakers and a monolingual English public sphere. Despite this trend, linguistic assimilation may not occur by the third generation because transnational ties and new immigrant arrivals can change patterns of language transmission and shift (Tse, 2001). Dicker (2006) demonstrates that for Dominican Americans who live in Washington Heights in New York City and maintain ties with their homeland, cultural and linguistic orientation can vary from typical patterns. The young Dominican Americans in her study enjoy Hispanic music, media, and being practicing bilinguals with family and friends. Dicker's (2006, p. 715) case shows how transnational ties of Dominican Americans disrupt expected language shift.

Other perspectives illustrate how cultural changes that affect youth can be traced through subtle shifts in language. Duranti and Reynolds (2009) study intergenerational differences in linguistic ability and assert that 1.5-generation Samoan youth are the most balanced bilinguals of Samoan and English. They look at the social norms that inform language choice and note that children prefer to choose the code they speak and resent being "forced" to use one or the other. Pronunciation, especially important in distinguishing "good" from "bad" Samoan language, can vary according to English fluency. They thus illustrate how subtle cultural changes occur through linguistic shift; in this case, a "child's point of view" not common in Samoan culture is developed and exercised through the adoption of English kinship terms in favor of traditional Samoan "*matai*" titles and proper names (Duranti & Reynolds, 2009, p. 250).

Asian American youth experience linguistic acculturation in different ways, and heritage language shift and loss can be an emotional process for youth. In her examination of the loss of heritage languages among Asian American youth, Hinton (2009) counters the xenophobic sentiment that immigrants refuse to learn English. Through 250-plus language "autobiographies," Hinton explores the issues youth manage regarding their heritage languages, including learning English through ESL, "language rejection" due to accent discrimination and heritage language ridicule from non–Asian American peers, and the gradual loss of heritage language. Not only does this process fill some youth with regret, but it also forms the basis of intergenerational communication difficulties and criticism from relatives and community members. Hinton's research also indicates that youth may be embarrassed about their heritage language use until they reach college and realize their desire to be fluent in it. Ultimately, many of these youth struggle to reconcile what appear to be conflicted aspects of their identity due to the process of heritage language loss.

In these ways, heritage language use and bilingual practices are an integral part of understanding identity for Asian American youth. These language practices can demonstrate ethnic identity formation, generational shifts, and community membership for youth. Language-based practices of media and consumption extend and expand the ways in which youth use their heritage languages to connect with their heritage cultures and with local and diasporic communities. Heritage language shifts tell another part of this story and trace how youth create and manage linguistic identities differently than their parents and other adults in their communities. Some youth regret not being able to speak their heritage language, whereas others use varieties of English and distinct styles that reflect aspects of their ethnic and racial identity.

STYLES OF SPEAKING AND RACIALIZATION

Just as heritage language use and aspects of bilingualism inform Asian American youth identities, style is another perspective from which to understand how youth negotiate linguistic aspects of the migration experience. Style draws attention to socially relevant ways in which speakers use phonetic, lexical, and other linguistic resources to create distinctive ways of speaking (Eckert, 2008; Irvine, 2001; Woolard, 2008). Coupland (2007) discusses style as a type of sociolinguistic variation that indexes particular social values and one that draws attention to the social judgments that people attach to them. Expanding this definition, linguistic anthropological understandings of style situate variation in the context of other cultural practices. Style draws attention to how diasporic youth regard heritage languages and varieties of English, and how these choices can be linked to clothing, social cliques, musical preferences, and other relevant aspects of youth culture (Eckert, 2000).

Style complements the youth-centered approach taken here because it draws attention to everyday performances of language. Beyond documenting whether or not youth use heritage languages, style is a way of understanding how youth perform locally recognizable identities that inform regional meanings of race, ethnicity, gender, and class. In this vein, considering not only heritage language use but also how youth use varieties and styles of English is a relevant component of understanding youth in migration contexts. Looking at youth in the United Kingdom, Hewitt (1986) identifies racially coded talk as a way youth perform ethnicity by using locally available styles. Youth enact Caribbean and South Asian identities by using certain language varieties—a process that underscores the fluidity of language as a resource in constructing diasporic identities.

Concerned with similar themes, Rampton's (1995) sociolinguistic study of language practices among youth of South Asian and Caribbean descent documents and analyzes microinteractions that occur between youth, especially their ethnically marked performances. Rampton offers the concept of "crossing" as a way to understand how youth inhabit and perform styles not usually linked with their own ethnicity so that they may gain membership into particular speech communities. Crossing, passing, and appropriation are all ways in which speakers use styles typical of other language communities. Rampton (2006) further explores these themes by looking at how youth speech practices push class boundaries and index regional social values. South Asian and Caribbean youth adopt distinctive accents and ways of speaking in their peer groups. Locally prevalent styles of "posh" and "cockney" serve as resources for youth as they aim to construct socially recognizable selves and identities.

Looking at hybridity is another way of understanding how youth construct ethnic identities and styles from language practices, and useful examples can be found in work on Asians in the United Kingdom. Building on research about diasporic Asian language use in the United Kingdom that looks at adult language use and community building (Saxena, 1994, 2000; Wei, 1994), studies of youth have focused on connections between language practices and ethnic formation. Harris's (2006) research on the language practices of "Brasians" or British South Asians in the late 1990s substantively examines linkages between language use and new ethnicities. Harris extends this paradigm—which itself critiques earlier cultural studies to formulate a less essentialist approach to ethnicity—to consider language use among Punjabi- and Gujarati-speaking youth in the United Kingdom. Linkages between language choice and ethnic identification are examined through analysis of recorded speech and interviews to present empirically grounded analyses of hybridity and change for youth in this diasporic location.

Also concerned with language and ethnicity, Baumann (1996, p. 47) notes how South Asian men and women in Southall use different greeting styles and lexical items from "Indian-English" and "Afro-American or Caribbean" English, and how their children adopt distinct styles and accents from West London in their social interactions with one another. Baumann (1996, p. 155) also describes "*Southalli*," a Southall language variety that combines Punjabi, Urdu, and Hindi; in contrast, "pure" Punjabi can both draw respect as well as ridicule for its "*pindhu*" or "peasant" connotations. Being "*bilati*" or a South Asian living in Britain, then, is indexed by use of this language variety, which Baumann's interviewees note as being recognizable in India as well as in the United Kingdom.

Examples of style from studies of Latinos also illustrate how youth use heritage languages as well as English to affiliate with social groups and claim social distinction in school settings. Bailey (2001) documents the multiple linguistic forms youth use from English and Spanish to construct their identities. He challenges the perceived uniformity of the category of African American by drawing attention to the linguistic heterogeneity of Spanish-speaking youth who identify as Hispanic, American, and African American. Youth construct "non-White" linguistic identities by drawing on African American English and mocking White English forms, as well as by performing "non-Black" identities by claiming Spanish and distinguishing themselves from African Americans. Bailey (2001, p. 214) demonstrates how this occurs through everyday talk that enables Dominican American teenagers to differentiate themselves from one another and challenge a White linguistic hegemony.

Investigating the language practices of Latina gang girls, Mendoza-Denton's (2008) fine-grained sociolinguistic study couples linguistic constructions of style with material expressions, such as distinctive makeup and photographs that circulate among gang girls. She notes stylistic differences in phonology and documents how phonetic differences in the Spanish and English speech of rival Norteño and Sureño gangs are readily recognizable to each other and serve as further markers of group membership and affiliation.

Youth also use varieties of English to construct styles; indeed, the use of varieties of English is a significant aspect of understanding Asian American language use (Lo & Reyes, 2009). AAVE has been shown to be a vital resource for Asian American youth constructions of style. Lee (2005) observes that "Americanized" youth in her study adopt AAVE as a way of performing a sense of belonging and differentiate themselves from more newly arrived youth. Reyes (2009) links language and racialization by observing how Southeast Asian American youth use elements of AAVE to participate in an urban youth style. Youth use features of this language to create distinctive identities that index meanings differently for certain speakers and listeners. Whereas adults may more greatly value Mainstream American English, youth place a premium on using AAVE slang terms such as *aite* ("all right") and *na mean* ("do you know what I mean") correctly among themselves. Through successful performances and recognitions, these urban Asian American youth participate in their racial formation by linguistically affiliating with African Americans. Similarly, Chun (2001) looks at how language indexes racial meaning and how youth use racially marked varieties of language in their performances of identity. Chun examines how some Asian American youth appropriate AAVE terms such as *whitey* (White person) and *boody* (booty) to index an urban youth culture. Using this language variety enables these youth to perform aspects of their identity, but as Chun notes, not necessarily to affiliate with African Americans or Black subjectivity.

Youth use of particular English language varieties can also illustrate stylistic differences within an ethnic group. In her research with Laotian American youth in Northern California, Bucholtz (2009) follows how two teenage girls each use English to form affiliations with different racially marked social groups at school. Both girls are aware of the local, gang-related stereotypes about Laotian Americans, and each creates a different strategy to cope with not being a "model minority." Bucholtz illustrates how style both creates and exploits linguistic stereotypes and traces the linguistic styles and social affiliations of two girls, "Nikki" and "Ada." Nikki seeks membership into African American social circles and accordingly uses resources from AAVE to perform in-group membership. In contrast, Ada uses hypercorrect English to affiliate herself with White nerds and to distance herself from what she considers to be the negative connotations of her ethnic group. Although Nikki's linguistic style challenges the model minority stereotype, Ada's attempts position her closer to it and away from the prevalent gang-based image. Bucholtz also notes that bivalency, or simultaneous membership in more than one linguistic community, allows these teens to participate in multiple linguistically organized speech communities rather than being contained to one. Such a distinction is helpful to illustrate how Asian American youth may move between different social groups and speech communities at school and in their communities.

Desi Teens: A Case Study in Style

Language use can help illustrate how differences within an ethnic group become crystallized into socially popular and marginal youth social cliques. In my research on Desi (South Asian American) teens, I look at styles of language as a lens to broader processes of racial and gender formation (Shankar, 2008b). I investigate the class-informed differences that separate cliques of "FOBs" (Fresh off the Boat) from "popular" teens in a diverse Silicon Valley high school.[1] Language use is a key social differentiator among teens within this ethnic group. Whereas some cliques of popular Desi teens only speak English at school, other cliques of socially marginalized second-generation youth called FOBs use Punjabi and Hindi during their social time at school. Even among teens who can speak their heritage language, differences emerge between popular teens who opt to only speak English and FOBby teens who choose to incorporate Punjabi and Hindi in their conversations with one another.

In their constructions of style, speakers in each clique choose distinctive resources from language varieties to index locally relevant constructions of diasporic identity and group belonging. FOBs draw linguistic elements from Punjabi, Hindi, and varieties of English, including hip-hop language and California slang to construct styles that provide a sense of solidarity in an otherwise alienating school environment. The varieties of English each group uses not only overlap but also vary enough for one group to distinguish itself from the other. Popular Desi teens use "Valley Girl" and types of regional California slang and avoid profanity and other language that would be considered "marked" or differing from school norms. Popular style relies heavily on cultural and linguistic attributes that are desirable and preferred in a school context, and such choices are paired with youth participation in school events, minimal profanity use, and rarely speaking a heritage language at school; clothing and comportment also complement these choices. FOBs, in contrast, base their styles more heavily on gang culture prevalent in their neighborhoods and incorporate linguistic elements that are dispreferred in a high school environment. They construct styles using lexical and phonetic elements from hip-hop, gang terminology, and profanity from Punjabi and English.

The content of specific styles undoubtedly vary as different speakers perform them, but the ways in which they index locally relevant values illustrate connections between language, race, and class for Desi youth. Youth who perform FOB styles index their working-class neighborhoods and to the blue-collar jobs that their parents hold; they are socially marginalized in the school and tend to not be as academically successful as their popular peers from upper-middle-class families. This latter group generally has the advantage of their parents' advocacy in schools, and their interactional styles mirror those of the wealthy residential communities and neighborhoods in which they live. FOBby teens construct styles that display their displeasure about the school, and boys openly perform "tough language" (see Eckert, 2000) within earshot of school faculty.

One FOB clique that consisted mostly of boys regularly discussed fights they had witnessed, participated in, or heard about through school gossip. A distinctive feature of the way boys talk about fights is that they consistently claim a position of power and victory for themselves. In describing events that they witnessed, boys were sure to indicate that they would have handled altercations better than those who lost. In one exchange, 16-year-old Harbinder spoke to his friends about a fight he had witnessed. Routinely engaging in fights himself, Harbinder expressed notable disdain for the way one boy in the fight carried himself. He exclaimed, "Smoky beat the shit out of his punk ass. That boo was cryin' and shit." Harbinder's use of the term "boo," usually an affectionate term used for a significant other, is here used to underscore the lack of toughness displayed by the boy who was beaten. Through his use of profanity, Harbinder offers his negative judgment of the victim's stance and positions himself as someone who would have handled the situation very differently.

In this example, styles of speaking are linked to class-based processes of racialization. Harbinder's toughness makes him and his FOB friends racially marked and positions these Desi youth with other working-class Latinos and Vietnamese American teens at their school. Their tough language practices make them stand out in comparison with their popular peers. In this case, as with the others discussed in this section, style can draw attention to how language use is linked to racialization for diasporic youth, including how those within the same ethnic group may be racialized differently. Racialization can be further understood by examining language practices in the context of ideologies and stereotypes.

STEREOTYPES, LANGUAGE IDEOLOGIES, AND THE WHITE PUBLIC SPHERE

Asian American youth contend with numerous stereotypes in schools that have an impact on their educational expectations, social positioning, and language choices. Although introduced decades ago, the model minority stereotype has persisted in shaping experiences of schooling for Asian American youth. The stereotype developed subsequent to its introduction in 1966, when *U.S. News and World Report* magazine and the *New York Times* both featured major articles identifying Asian Americans, especially Chinese and Japanese Americans, as economically self-sufficient and driven in terms of education and social adaptability. Critics of this stereotype argue that this characterization not only failed to account for the diversity within this population but also positioned Asian Americans against other minority groups considered to be a social and economic problem for the U.S. government, especially African Americans and some Latinos (Prashad, 2000).

Despite its sensationalist underpinnings, the model minority stereotype has endured in part because many who answered America's call for educated professionals came from Asia and were able to enter the American job market in medicine, law, engineering, and other white-collar professions. In 1965, an earlier quota system that had limited immigration from certain countries was replaced by the Hart-Cellar Act, which set a quota of 20,000 immigrants from each country and outlined a system of preferred categories for immigration, including highly skilled labor that the United States needed, as well as family unification. This resulted in a rapid and substantial growth of immigrants from Asia, nearly 7 million between 1970 and 2000; contemporary immigration from Asia is largely family sponsored (80%) or employer sponsored (20%; Zhou, 2004, p. 36). This socioeconomic status differs starkly from earlier in the century when Asian immigrants held predominantly blue-collar jobs in the service industry, as farmers, or worked on railroads. Because of this shift from blue collar to professional, and because many Asian Americans have achieved considerable socioeconomic success, the stereotype continues to be embraced by some Asian Americans while it also persists in the American educational system.

Youth and the Model Minority Stereotype

Recent research has illustrated the negative effects of the model minority stereotype for youth in educational and social environments. Lee (1996) has extensively studied how it creates undue pressure for those youth poised to meet its expectations and poses a host of problems for those who cannot perform at this elevated level. Students suffer at the hands of this stereotype, especially when they do not accomplish the high standards associated with the term (Lee, 2004, p. 123). Inkelas's (2006, p. 14) study of higher education challenges the "whiz kid" stereotype plaguing Asian American youth and suggests that casting Asian Americans as "success stories" can obscure the real educational challenges that some of them face. In their research on Asian American youth, Zhou and Lee (2004, p. 8) distinguish between second-generation youth who grow up in affluent middle-class suburbs and maintain little contact with coethnics in urban enclaves, and those who live in urban ethnic communities. They report that Asian American parents may push their children to perform academically and may overemphasize education over leisure, and this is especially the case for upper-middle-class youth (Zhou & Lee, 2004, p. 15). Zhou and Lee are particularly concerned with the disjuncture between how youth see themselves versus how outsiders view them as a group. In this vein, the model minority myth has kept them from being considered "normal" in an educational context.

Understanding the diversity of students who inhabit the ethnically and linguistically varied category of "Asian American" has led to critiques of the model minority stereotype and a more careful consideration of the needs of at-risk Asian American youth (Lee & Kumashiro, 2005). Disaggregating the category of "Asian American" into smaller groups is one way to complicate expectations and performances. Some Asian American youth—especially refugees from Vietnam and Cambodia or lower socioeconomic groups such as Hmong and Pacific Islanders—may not be able to academically perform as well as some of their peers from East and South Asia (Ima, 1995). Even within populations that are thought to be high-achieving, individual case studies show that this may not always be the case. Lew (2004) follows a cohort of second-generation Korean American youth who have dropped out of their New York City high schools. Like the African American youth in Fordham's (2008) work, these dropouts also associate "success" with "acting White" and relate their own challenging experiences with Blackness. Yet their model minority status complicates any simple alignment, and Lew indicates that aspects of their ethnic background facilitate social mobility in ways not available to many Black urban youth. Korean dropouts are nonetheless well aware of how they differ from affluent, high-achieving Korean American students (Lew, 2004, p. 318). This heterogeneity is a reminder of the variance that exists among youth within the same ethnic group, and that class and other differences require more nuanced attention. A look at language practices in conjunction with the model minority stereotype will expand this inquiry.

Language Ideologies and English Monolingualism

Meanings linked to languages and their contexts of use vary according to diasporic community, and may also differ from dominant social institutions such as schools. Language ideologies are important because they can draw attention to historical and political economic dimensions of Asian American youth language use. Language ideologies about heritage languages and English shape youth language use in migration contexts. Language ideologies refer to implicit and explicit ideas about languages and language use and can shape speakers' dispositions about and choices surrounding language varieties and styles (Schieffelin, Woolard, & Kroskrity, 1998). Ideologies of language travel with speakers, and the valuation of heritage languages and English, as well as norms of language use, are particular to each population. Language ideologies can also be transfigured across transnational contexts (Park, 2009), and local norms can further complicate dynamics of heritage language use in schools.

In their schools, Asian American youth negotiate bilingualism and heritage language use in the context of the monolingual English public sphere. The White public sphere privileges English monolingualism and heritage languages can be viewed as inferior to English. Hill (2008) has written extensively about a variety of discriminatory language she calls "mock Spanish" and acts as a vehicle for prejudice against Latinos. Hill contends that Spanish malapropisms and lexical misuse are ways that non-Spanish speakers maintain power in a White public sphere. Likewise, Urciuoli (1999) describes a similar dynamic in her research with Puerto Rican communities in New York City. Although Spanish may be the preferred language for speakers, those outside the community can perceive it negatively. Urciuoli makes the distinction between how Spanish language use, along with marked displays of culture, may racialize speakers negatively, whereas English use maintains a nonthreatening sense of ethnicity. Zentella (1997) offers similar observations of the challenges of Spanish English youth bilingualism in the context of the English Only movement (see also Santa Ana, 2005). Bilingualism thus creates dynamics of belonging and exclusion at home and school respectively, even though it is an important social tool for young people (Hakuta, 1986).

Research on language use in schools demonstrates that certain languages and language varieties are "marked" and stand out compared with unmarked varieties that operate as unspoken standards or norms (Bucholtz & Hall, 2004). Mainstream American English (MAE) prevails in schools as an unmarked variety, making some other varieties of English, along with heritage languages, marked and contradictory to school expectations. Benjamin Bailey (2007) documents the reception of bilingual language practices of Dominican American teenagers in schools. Youth use Spanish in their close friendships at school and consider it a positive aspect of their identity. These speech practices, however, can be negatively judged in a school context that privileges English. Coupled with the already low expectations of these Latino youth, Spanish language practices can be viewed as further evidence of youth disinterest in school and inability to competently speak English. Like other Latino youth, those in Bailey's study are often caught between their own linguistic practices and the judgments about them, about which they may not be aware. In contrast, the Latina gang girls in Mendoza-Denton's (2008) research are well aware of their social and linguistic marginality. Speaking Spanish can be a way of demonstrating insider membership to fellow members of a gang, whereas poetry written and circulated in English and Spanish is an important linguistic tool that these Latina girls use to cope with their challenging lives.

Research among Desi (South Asian American) teens in Silicon Valley high schools investigates how socioeconomic variance within this group differently shapes their social and linguistic practices at school (Shankar, 2008a). The prominent success of some Desis in the Silicon Valley high-tech industry obscures the working-class struggles of others in this ethnic group, and this divide is evident in the ways in which Desi teenagers negotiate expectations placed on them in high school. Upper-middle-class teens experience model minority pressure to excel from parents, school faculty, and peers, whereas working-class youth can be criticized and marginalized for academic performances that may fall short of meeting the stereotype. In both cases, Desi youth have a difficult time managing the inflated expectations placed on them as Asian Americans. Despite the tremendous diversity in this Northern California high school, differences expressed outside the confines of "multicultural" and "international" day celebrations become marked, racializing discourses (Shankar, 2004). Norms of speaking MAE are maintained not only by school faculty and teachers but also by popular Desi youth. Popular Desi teens uphold the model minority expectations of English monolingualism and speak MAE because it benefits their academic goals and participation in school activities. FOBby teens, however, can draw the unwanted attention of faculty and teachers who can regard their heritage language use in schools as evidence that they may not speak English well. Like their Latino peers, Desi youth who speak their heritage language in school are often overlooked by faculty for school enrichment activities and leadership positions.

These cases demonstrate how class and language use together influence processes of racialization for diasporic youth. The explicit focus on language practices provides further exemplification about how youth negotiate stereotypes and expectations, and how some youth are more advantageously positioned to do so than others. These dynamics can also persist in ESL classrooms and other contexts of English language learning.

English as a Second Language

The process of English language learning reveals the fraught relationship between heritage languages and English use for youth. Studies of immigrant education have extensively examined pedagogical and social dimensions of language learning in ESL, English Language Learning, and bilingual education programs. These studies consider how formal learning environments affect academic success and student feelings of inclusion and belonging in a school environment for Asian American youth (Louie, 2005). Since the 1974 Supreme Court case of *Lau v. Nichols*, U.S. schools have been required to provide an education to non–English speaking students equal to that of fluent English speakers. Recent state-level policies, such as California's proposition 227, which did away with bilingual education, have worked against English Language Learners (Gándara, Moran, & Garcia, 2004).

Studies of ESL and bilingual education programs indicate that despite the prevalence of seemingly progressive ideologies such as multiculturalism, school teachers and faculty may not take such a pluralistic approach in calibrating their expectations of how immigrant youth should assimilate culturally and especially linguistically (see, e.g., Fine, Jaffe-Walter, Pedraza, Futch, & Stoudt, 2007; García, 2009; Gutiérrez, Baquedano-Lopez, & Asato, 2000). Studies of literacy practices document the challenges and pitfalls for Asian Americans learning English (Chiang & Schmida, 1999; Kliefgen, 2001), and this hardship is especially pronounced for Asian American youth from working-class and at-risk groups, including Hmong Americans (Weinstein-Shr, 1993), Khmer (Hardman, 1998; Needham, 2003, Skilton-Sylvester, 2002), Laotian Americans (Fu, 1995), and Samoan Americans (Duranti & Reynolds, 2009; Reynolds, 1995).

English learning environments can bring to the fore another prejudice that Asian American youth must manage, namely, the "forever foreigner" stereotype. Tuan's (1998) influential formulation contrasts this outsider position with "honorary White," underscoring the difficulty of creating positive Asian American identities. Such challenges are highlighted in ESL classes, where learning English and transitioning from ESL to mainstream English classes can be a stigmatizing social experience for some youth. Talmy (2009) notes that ESL students may be permanently labeled "linguistic Others" because of the attitudes toward them. Although the pedagogy and instruction of the course reifies their status as forever foreigners, students resist judgments that label them "FOB." Some students' attempts to shed this pejorative label take the form of transferring it to a peer whom they believe better exemplifies the term's negative connotations. By doing so, some students reproduce the linguistic discrimination from which they themselves suffer. Asian American youth are not alone in this marginalization. Latino youth experience difficulties as well, and teachers can compare ESL students with those in special education and suggest that because students struggle with English, they may also have trouble speaking and writing in Spanish (Wortham, Mortimer, & Allard, 2009, p. 398). Cammarota (2004) identifies the ways in which Latino youth become disinterested in their education because of problems at school, issues with language, and cultural differences between the home and school environments. Boys and girls manage these challenges differently, and both contest marginalization through particular stances against the school. All these cases emphasize the difficulties youth face in managing stereotypes that set particular expectations for them, and in using language to express identity and belonging in a White public sphere that may not accommodate such practices.

DIRECTIONS FOR FURTHER RESEARCH

This review of Asian American youth language practices has sought to offer alternative ways of considering familiar questions of identity, school orientations, and generational change by foregrounding language use. Looking at language use in the context of other cultural and educational practices shows its central role in shaping youth ethnic identities and racial subjectivities. Youth make choices about their heritage language and varieties of English in their everyday practices of bilingualism, code switching, and engagements with media. Changes in these usages can be seen by looking at shifts in heritage language use over generations, including modifications to pragmatic aspects of language, modes of address, and lexical innovation. Speaking abilities of second- and third-generation youth also draw attention to how language can underscore the types of cultural changes that can occur in migration contexts. Heritage language shift or loss need not mean a disassociation with aspects of one's heritage culture, and studies of style show how youth construct linguistic identities using aspects of their heritage language as well as varieties of English. The use of varieties of English linked to other racial groups, such as AAVE, as well as the use of locally created, distinctive styles of speaking that operate at the school level demonstrate the creativity of youth in their language practices with one another. Differences of language use within an ethnic group are especially important to understanding how racialization and ethnic identity formation occur. Style draws attention to this variance and expands questions of language use beyond bilingual ability, retention, and loss to provide a fuller sense of how language use is a meaningful part of identity, subjectivity, and generational change in migration contexts.

The ways in which Asian American youth are positioned by language ideologies and class shape how they think about and use their heritage languages. In the White public sphere, heritage languages are largely unwelcome outside of events and contexts that celebrate multiculturalism and ethnic diversity, and heritage languages can be vehicles for anti-immigrant sentiment. One such criticism is that immigrants cling to their heritage languages and refuse to learn English. Research indicates just the opposite. In one study, 85% of the U.S.-born second-generation respondents indicated that they are able to speak English very well (Rumbaut, 2002), even outperforming both the first- and third-generation youth (Kao & Tienda, 1995; Portes & Rumbaut, 2001). Furthermore, high rates of shift from bilingualism to English monolingualism are occurring among the second generation, and these findings confirm that immigrant families are certainly learning English (Alba & Nee, 2003). Nonetheless, language-based prejudice and accent discrimination remain a central part of linguistic life for adults and youth of the new immigration alike (Lindeman, 2003; Lippi-Green, 1997; Zhou & Bankston, 1998). This can happen differently for youth whose language practices are marked in a school context—whether it is Spanish, Punjabi, AAVE, or a hybrid style that stands out as different from MAE. The specific reception of each varies according to context, but the overall dynamic draws attention to how language use can be a contentious aspect of diasporic youth acculturation, and that the White public sphere does not readily accommodate linguistic variation.

Such a reaction underscores the challenges as well as opportunities Asian American youth face as they use heritage languages and varieties of English to construct identities and negotiate meanings of race, class, and gender in America. Further research on uses of heritage languages and varieties of English is needed to provide a broader range of case studies that can shed light on aspects of diaspora and migration for Asian American youth. An increased emphasis on spaces outside of formal pedagogical contexts can expand understandings of language use in immigrant education studies to consider the other ways in which schools regard youth language use. Likewise, family- and community-based research on language use can offer alternative perspectives to that of intergenerational tension by considering linguistic aspects of socialization, humor, emotion, and everyday interaction alongside cultural clashes. Taken together, the language practices of Asian American youth can be considered as a dynamic and integral part of understanding identity, diaspora, and generational change.

ACKNOWLEDGMENTS

Many thanks to my consulting editor Stanton Wortham for his comments and guidance with this chapter, as well as to Stacey Lee and Angela Reyes for their reviewer comments. I am also grateful to Ana Aparicio and Jillian Cavanaugh for their helpful suggestions. I am grateful to the Spencer Foundation for Research Related to Education as well as the Social Science Research Council International Migration Program for funding portions of my research discussed in this chapter.

NOTE

[1]Of the approximately 2,200 students during the 1999–2000 school year, nearly 50% were Asian American (about 30% Desi), 25% Latino, 12% White, 6% African American, and less than 1% Native American.

REFERENCES

Alba, R., & Nee, V. (2003). *Remaking the American mainstream: Assimilation and contemporary immigration.* Cambridge, MA: Harvard University Press.

Alim, H. S., & Baugh, J. (2007). *Talkin black talk: Language, education, and social change.* New York, NY: Teachers College Press.

Alim, H. S., Ibrahim, A., & Pennycook, A. (2009). *Global linguistic flows: Hip hop cultures, youth identities, and the politics of language.* New York, NY: Taylor & Francis.

Bailey, B. (2001). The language of multiple identities among Dominican Americans. *Journal of Linguistic Anthropology, 10,* 190–223.

Bailey, B. (2007). Heteroglossia and boundaries. In M. Heller (Ed.), *Bilingualism: A social approach* (pp. 257-274). New York, NY: Palgrave Macmillan.

Ball, A., & Heath, S. B. (1993). Dances of identity: Finding an ethnic self in the arts. In S. B. Heath & M. W. McLaughlin (Eds.), *Identity and inner-city youth: Beyond ethnicity and gender* (pp. 69–93). New York, NY: Teachers College Press.

Baumann, G. (1996). *Contesting culture: Discourses of identity in multi-ethnic London.* Cambridge, England: Cambridge University Press.

Bucholtz, M. (2002). Youth and cultural practice. *Annual Review of Anthropology, 31,* 525–552.

Bucholtz, M. (2009). Styles and stereotypes: Laotian American girls' linguistic negotiation of identity. In A. Reyes & A. Lo (Eds.), *Beyond Yellow English: Toward a linguistic anthropology of Asian Pacific America* (pp. 21–42). New York, NY: Oxford University Press.

Bucholtz, M., & Hall, K. (2004). Language and identity. In A. Duranti (Ed.), *A companion to linguistic anthropology* (pp. 369–394). Malden, MA: Wiley-Blackwell.

Cammarota, J. (2004). The gendered and racialized pathways of Latina and Latino youth: Different struggles, different resistances in the urban context. *Anthropology and Education Quarterly, 35,* 53–74.

Chiang, Y. D., & Schmida, M. (1999). Language identity and language ownership: Linguistic conflicts of first-year university writing students. In L. Harklau, K. M. Losey, & M. Siegal (Eds.), *Generation 1.5 meets college composition: Issues in the teaching of writing to US-educated learners of ESL* (pp. 81–96). Mahwah, NJ: Erlbaum.

Ching, M., & Kung, H. (1997). Ethnic identity, Americanization, and survival of the mother tongue: The first- vs. second- generation Chinese professionals in Memphis. In C. Bernstein, T. Nunnally, & R. Sabino (Eds.), *Language variety in the South revisited* (pp. 163–170). Tuscaloosa: University of Alabama Press.

Chun, E. W. (2001). The construction of white, black, and Korean American identities through African American Vernacular English. *Journal of Linguistic Anthropology, 11,* 52–64.

Coupland, N. (2007). *Style: Language variation and identity.* Cambridge, England: Cambridge University Press.

Dicker, S. (2006). Dominican Americans in Washington Heights, New York: Language and culture in a transnational community. *International Journal of Bilingual Education and Bilingualism, 9,* 713–727.

Duranti, A., & Reynolds, J. (2009). Phonological and cultural innovations in the speech of Samoans in Southern California. In A. Reyes & A. Lo (Eds.), *Beyond Yellow English: Toward a linguistic anthropology of Asian Pacific America* (pp. 233–252). New York, NY: Oxford University Press.

Eckert, P. (2000). *Linguistic variation as social practice: The linguistic construction of identity at Belten High*. Malden, MA: Blackwell.

Eckert, P. (2008). Variation and the indexical field. *Journal of Sociolinguistics, 12,* 453–476.

Ek, D. (2009). "It's different lives": A Guatemalan American adolescent's construction of ethnic and gender identities across educational context. *Anthropology & Education Quarterly, 40,* 405–420.

Ervin-Tripp, S. (1964). An analysis of the interaction of language, topic, and listener. *American Anthropologist, 66,* 86–102.

Fine, M., Jaffe-Walter, R., Pedraza, P., Futch, V., & Stoudt, B. (2007). Swimming: On oxygen, resistance, and possibility for immigrant youth under siege. *Anthropology & Education Quarterly, 38,* 76–96.

Foner, N. (2002). Second-generation transnationalism, then and now. In P. Levitt & M. Waters (Eds.), *The changing face of home* (pp. 242–252). New York, NY: Russell Sage Foundation.

Fordham, S. (2008). Beyond capital high: On dual citizenship and the strange career of "acting white." *Anthropology & Education Quarterly, 39,* 227–246.

Fought, C. (2006). *Language and ethnicity: Key topics in sociolinguistics*. Cambridge, England: Cambridge University Press.

Fu, D. (1995). *My trouble is my English: Asian students and the American dream*. Portsmouth, NH: Boynton/Cook.

Gadsden, V. (2008). The arts and education: Knowledge generation, pedagogy, and the discourse of learning. *Review of Research in Education, 32,* 29–61.

Gándara, P., Moran, R., & Garcia, E. (2004). Legacy of Brown: Lau and language policy in the United States. *Review of Research in Education, 28,* 27–46.

García, O. (2009). *Bilingual education in the 21st century: A global perspective*. Oxford, England: Wiley-Blackwell.

Gibson, M. (1988). *Accommodation without assimilation: Sikh immigrants in an American high school*. Ithaca, NY: Cornell University Press.

Gibson, M., & Ogbu, J. (Eds.). (1991). *Minority status and schooling*. New York, NY: Garland.

Goodwin, M. (2006). *The hidden life of girls: Games of stance, status, and exclusion*. Oxford, England: Blackwell.

Gutiérrez, K., Baquedano-Lopez, P., & Asato, J. (2000). "English for the children": The new literacy of the old world order, language policy and educational reform. *Bilingual Research Journal, 24,* 87–112.

Hakuta, K. (1986). *Mirror of language: The debate on bilingualism*. New York, NY: Basic Books

Hardman, J. (1998). Literacy and bilingualism in a Cambodian community in the USA. In A. Durgunoglu & L. Verhoeven (Eds.), *Literacy development in a multilingual context: Cross-cultural perspectives* (pp. 51–81). Mahwah, NJ: Erlbaum.

Harris, R. (2006). *New ethnicities and language use*. New York, NY: Palgrave Macmillan.

He, A. W. & Xiao, Y. (Ed.). (2008). *Chinese as a heritage language: Fostering rooted world citizenry*. Honolulu: University of Hawai'i Press.

Heller, M. (1986). The role of language in the formation of ethnic identity. In M. J. Rotherman & J. Rotheram (Eds.), *Children's ethnic socialization: Pluralism and development* (pp. 180–200). Newbury Park, CA: Sage.

Hewitt, R. (1986). *White talk, black talk*. Cambridge, England: Cambridge University Press.

Hill, J. (2008). *The everyday language of white racism*. Malden, MA: Wiley-Blackwell.

Hinton, L. (2009). Loss of heritage languages in the United States. In A. Reyes & A. Lo (Eds.), *Beyond Yellow English: Toward a linguistic anthropology of Asian Pacific America* (pp. 331–346). New York, NY: Oxford University Press.

Ima, K. (1995). Testing the American dream: At-risk Southeast Asian refugee students in secondary schools. In R. Rumbaut & W. Cornelius (Eds.), *California's immigrant children:*

Theory, research, and implications for educational policy (pp. 191–209). San Diego: University of California, Center for U.S.-Mexican Studies.

Inkelas, K. (2006). *Racial attitudes and Asian Pacific Americans: Demystifying the model minority.* New York, NY: Routledge.

Irvine, J. (2001). "Style" as distinctiveness: The culture and ideology of linguistic differentiation. In P. Eckert & J. Rickford (Eds.), *Style and sociolinguistic variation* (pp. 21–43). Cambridge, England: Cambridge University Press.

Jo, H. (2001). "Heritage" language learning and ethnic identity: Korean Americans' struggle with language authorities. *Language, Culture, and Curriculum, 14,* 16–41.

Kang, M. A. (2003). Negotiating conflict within the constraints of social hierarchies in Korean American discourse. *Journal of Sociolinguistics, 7,* 299–320.

Kang, M. A. (2009). Constructing ethnic identity through discourse: Self-categorization among Korean American camp counselors. In A. Reyes & A. Lo (Eds.), *Beyond Yellow English: Toward a linguistic anthropology of Asian Pacific America* (pp. 131–147). New York, NY: Oxford University Press.

Kang, M. A., & Lo, A. (2004). Two ways of articulating hetereogeneity in Korean American narratives of ethnic identity. *Journal of Asian American Studies, 7,* 93–116.

Kao, G., & Tienda, M. (1995). Optimism and achievement: The educational performance of immigrant youth. *Social Science Quarterly, 76,* 1–19.

Kibria, N. (2003). *Becoming Asian American.* Baltimore, MD: Johns Hopkins University Press.

Kliefgen, J. A. (2001). Assembling talk: Social alignments in the workplace. *Research on Language and Social Interaction, 34,* 279–308.

Kondo-Brown, K. (Ed.). (2006). *Heritage language development: Focus on East Asian immigrants.* Philadelphia, PA: John Benjamins.

Kozasa, T. (2000). Code-switching in Japanese/English: A study of Japanese-American WWII veterans. In M. Nakayama & C. J. Quinn, Jr. (Eds.), *Japanese/Korean linguistics* (pp. 209–222). Stanford, CA: Center for the Study of Language and Information.

Lam, W. S. E. (2004). Second language socialization in a bilingual chat room: Global and local considerations. *Language Learning & Technology, 8*(3), 44–65.

Lam, W. S. E. (2006). Culture and learning in the context of globalization: Research directions. *Review of Research in Education, 30,* 213–237.

Lam, W. S. E., & Rosario-Ramos, E. (2009). Multilingual literacies in transnational digitally mediated contexts: An exploratory study of immigrant teens in the United States. *Language and Education, 23,* 171–190.

Lee, S. (1996). Unraveling the "model minority" stereotype: Listening to Asian American youth. New York, NY: Teachers College Press.

Lee, S. (2004). Up against whiteness: Students of color in our schools. *Anthropology and Education Quarterly, 35,* 121–125.

Lee, S. (2005). *Up against whiteness: Race, school, and immigrant youth.* New York, NY: Teachers College Press.

Lee, S., & Kumashiro, K. (2005). *A report on the status of Asian Americans and Pacific Islanders in education: Beyond the "model minority" stereotype.* Washington, DC: National Education Association of the United States.

Levitt, P., & Jaworsky, B. N. (2007). Transnational migration studies: Past developments and future trends. *Annual Review of Sociology, 33,* 129–156.

Levitt, M. & Waters, P. (2002). Introduction. In P. Levitt & M. Waters (Eds.), *The changing face of home* (pp. 1-32). New York, NY: Russell Sage Foundation.

Lew, J. (2004). The "other" story of model minorities: Korean American high school dropouts in an urban context. *Anthropology and Education Quarterly, 35,* 303–323.

Lindeman, S. (2003). Koreans, Chinese, or Indians? Attitudes and ideologies about non-native English speakers in the United States. *Journal of Sociolinguistics, 7,* 348–364.

Lippi-Green, R. (1997). *English with an accent: Language, ideology, and discrimination in the United States.* London, England: Routledge.

Lo, A. (1999). Codeswitching, speech community membership, and the construction of ethnic identity. *Journal of Sociolinguistics, 3,* 461–479.

Lo, A., & Reyes, A. (2009). Introduction: On Yellow English and other perilous terms. In A. Reyes & A. Lo (Eds.), *Beyond Yellow English: Toward a linguistic anthropology of Asian Pacific America* (pp. 3–20). New York, NY: Oxford University Press.

Louie, V. (2005). Immigrant newcomer populations, ESEA, and the pipeline to college: Current considerations and future lines of inquiry. *Review of Research in Education, 29,* 69–105.

Lukose, R. (2007). The difference that diaspora makes. *Anthropology and Education Quarterly, 38,* 405–418.

McGinnis, T., Goodstein-Stolzenberg, A., & Costa Saliani, E. (2007). "indnpride": Online spaces of transnational youth as sites of creative and sophisticated literacy and identity work. *Linguistics and Education, 18,* 283–304.

Mendoza-Denton, N. (2008). *Homegirls: Language and cultural practice among Latina youth gangs.* Malden, MA: Wiley-Blackwell.

Mendoza-Denton, N., & Iwai, M. (1993). "They speak more Caucasian": Generational differences in the speech of Japanese-Americans. In R. Queen & R. Barrett (Eds.), *Proceedings of the First Annual Symposium about Language and Society-Austin* (pp. 58–67). Austin: University of Texas Press.

Needham, S. (2003). "This is active learning": Theories of language, learning, and social relations in the transmission of Khmer literacy. *Anthropology and Education Quarterly, 34,* 27–49.

Ng, J. C., Lee, S. S., & Pak, Y. K. (2007). Contesting the model minority and perpetual foreigner stereotypes: A critical review of literature on Asian Americans in education. *Review of Research in Education, 31,* 95–130.

Orellana, M. F. (2009). *Translating childhoods: Immigrant youth, language, and culture.* New Brunswick, NJ: Rutgers University Press.

Orellana, M. F., Thorne, B., Chee, A. E., & Lam, W. S. E. (2001). Transnational childhoods: The participation of children in the processes of family migration. *Social Problems, 48,* 572–591.

Park, J. S. Y. (2009). *The local construction of a global language: ideologies of English in South Korea.* Paris, France: Mouton De Gruyter.

Portes, A., & Rumbaut, R. (2001). *Legacies.* Berkeley: University of California Press.

Prashad, V. (2000). *The karma of brown folk.* Minneapolis: University of Minnesota Press.

Rampton, B. (1995). *Crossing: Language and ethnicity among adolescents.* New York, NY: Longman.

Rampton, B. (2006). *Language in late modernity: Interaction in an urban school.* Cambridge, England: Cambridge University Press.

Reyes, A. (2007). *Language, identity, and stereotype among Southeast Asian American youth: The other Asian.* Mahwah, NJ: Erlbaum.

Reyes, A. (2009). Asian American stereotypes as circulating resource. In A. Reyes & A. Lo (Eds.), *Beyond Yellow English: Toward a linguistic anthropology of Asian Pacific America* (pp. 43–62). New York, NY: Oxford University Press.

Reynolds, J. (1995). *Tautalaititi and Tags: A study of Samoan American child language socialization as syncretic practice.* Los Angeles: University of California.

Reynolds, J., & Orellana, M. F. (2009). New immigrant youth interpreting in white public space. *American Anthropologist, 111,* 211–223.

Romaine, S. (1999). Changing attitudes toward Hawai'i Creole English: Fo' get one good job, you gotta know ho fo; talk like one haole. In J. Rickford & S. Romaine (Eds.), *Creole genesis, attitudes and discourse* (pp. 287–301). Amsterdam, Netherlands: John Benjamins.

Rubinstein-Ávila, E. (2007). From the Dominican Republic to Drew High: What counts as literacy for Yanira Lara? *Reading Research Quarterly, 42,* 568–589.

Rumbaut, R. (2002). Severed or sustained attachments? In P. Levitt & M. Waters (Eds.), *The changing face of home* (pp. 43–95). New York, NY: Russell Sage Foundation.

Rymes, B. (2001). *Conversational borderlands: Language and identity in an alternative urban high school.* New York, NY: Teachers College Press.

Santa Ana, O. (Ed.). (2005). *Tongue-tied: The lives of multilingual children in public education.* New York, NY: Rowman & Littlefield.

Sarkar, M., & Winer, L. (2006). Multilingual code-switching in Quebec rap: Poetry, pragmatics and performativity. *International Journal of Multilingualism, 3,* 173–192.

Saxena, M. (1994). Literacies among Punjabis in Southall. In M. Hamilton, D. Barton, & R. Ivanic (Eds.), *Worlds of literacy* (pp. 195–214). Clevedon, England: Multilingual Matters.

Saxena, M. (2000). Taking account of history and culture in community-based research on multilingual literacy. In M. Martin-Jones & K. Jones, (Eds.), *Multilingual literacies: Reading and writing different worlds* (pp. 275–298). Amsterdam, Netherlands: John Benjamins.

Schieffelin, B., Woolard, K., & Kroskrity, P. (Eds.). (1998). *Language ideology: Practice and theory.* New York, NY: Oxford University Press.

Schieffelin, B. B., & Ochs, E. (1986). Language socialization. *Annual Review of Anthropology, 15,* 163–191.

Shankar, S. (2004). FOBby or tight? 'Multicultural day' and other struggles in two Silicon Valley high schools. In M. Checker & M. Fishman, (Eds.), *Local actions* (pp. 184–207). New York, NY: Columbia University Press.

Shankar, S. (2006). Metaconsumptive practices and the circulation of objectifications. *Journal of Material Culture, 11,* 293–317.

Shankar, S. (2008a). *Desi land: Teen culture, class, and success in Silicon Valley.* Durham, NC: Duke University Press.

Shankar, S. (2008b). Speaking like a model minority: "FOB" styles, gender, and racial meanings among Desi teens in Silicon Valley. *Journal of Linguistic Anthropology, 18,* 268–289.

Shankar, S. (2009). Reel to real: Desi teen linguistic engagements with Bollywood. In A. Reyes & A. Lo (Eds.), *Beyond Yellow English: Toward a linguistic anthropology of Asian Pacific America* (pp. 309–324). New York, NY: Oxford University Press.

Shin, S. (2005). *Developing in two languages: Korean children in America.* Clevedon, England: Multilingual Matters.

Shin, S., & Milroy, L. (2000). Conversational code-switching among Korean-English bilingual children. *International Journal of Bilingualism, 4,* 351–383.

Shridhar, K. (1988). Language maintenance and language shift among Asian-Indians: Kannadigas in the New York area. *International Journal of Sociology of Language, 69,* 73–87.

Skilton-Sylvester, E. (2002). Literate at home but not at school: A Cambodian girl's journey from playwright to struggling writer. In G. A. Hull & K. Schultz (Eds.), *School's out! Bridging out-of-school literacy with classroom practice* (pp. 61–90). New York, NY: Teachers College Press.

Smitherman, G. (1999). *Talkin that talk: Language, culture and education in African America.* New York, NY: Routledge.

Song, J. (2009). Bilingual creativity and self-negotiation: Korean American children's language socialization into Korean address terms. In A. Reyes & A. Lo (Eds.), *Beyond Yellow English: Toward a linguistic anthropology of Asian Pacific America* (pp. 213–232). New York, NY: Oxford University Press.

Song, J. (2010). Language ideology and identity in transnational space: Globalization, migration, and bilingualism among Korean families in the USA. *International Journal of Bilingual Education and Bilingualism, 13,* 23–42.

Talmy, S. (2009). Forever FOB?: Resisting and reproducing the other in high school ESL. In A. Reyes & A. Lo (Eds.), *Beyond Yellow English: Toward a linguistic anthropology of Asian Pacific America* (pp. 347–365). New York, NY: Oxford University Press.

Tse, L. (1995). Language brokering among Latino adolescents: Prevalence, attitudes, and school performance. *Hispanic Journal of Behavioral Sciences, 17,* 180–193.

Tse, L. (1996). Language brokering in linguistic minority communities: The case of Chinese- and Vietnamese-American students. *Bilingual Research Journal, 20,* 485–498.

Tse, L. (2001). Resisting and reversing language shift: Heritage-language resilience among U.S. native biliterates. *Harvard Educational Review, 71,* 676–707.

Tuan, M. (1998). *Forever foreigners or honorary whites?* New Brunswick, NJ: Rutgers University Press.

Tuc, H. (2003). *Vietnamese-English bilingualism: Patterns of code-switching.* London, England: Routledge Curzon.

Urciuoli, B. (1999). *Exposing prejudice: Puerto Rican experiences of language, race, and class.* Boulder, CO: Westview Press.

Vadeboncoeur, J. A. (2006). Engaging young people: Learning in informal contexts. *Review of Research in Education, 30,* 239–278.

Valdes, G. (2003). *Expanding definitions of giftedness: The case of young interpreters from immigrant communities.* New York, NY: Routledge.

Wei, L. (1994). *Three generations, two languages, one family: Language choice and language shift in a Chinese community in Britain.* Clevedon, England: Multilingual Matters.

Weinstein-Shr, G. (1993). Literacy and social process: A community in transition. In B. Street (Ed.), *Cross-cultural approaches to literacy* (pp. 272–293). Cambridge, England: Cambridge University Press.

Wolfram, W., Christian, D., & Hatfield, D. (1986). The English of adolescent and young adult Vietnamese refugees in the United States. *World Englishes, 5,* 47–60.

Woolard, K. (2008). Why dat now? Linguistic-anthropological contributions to the explanation of sociolinguistic icons and change. *Journal of Sociolinguistics, 12,* 432–452.

Wortham, S. (2008). Linguistic anthropology of education. *Annual Review of Anthropology, 37,* 37–51.

Wortham, S., Mortimer, K., & Allard, E. (2009). Mexicans as model minorities in the new Latino diaspora. *Anthropology & Education Quarterly, 40,* 388–404.

Yi, Y. (2009). Adolescent literacy and identity construction among 1.5 generation students: From a transnational perspective. *Journal of Asian Pacific Communication, 19,* 100–129.

Zentella, A. C. (1997). *Growing up bilingual.* Malden, MA: Blackwell.

Zhou, M. (2004). Coming of age at the turn of the twenty-first century: A demographic profile of Asian American youth. In J. Lee & M. Zhou (Eds.), *Asian American youth: Culture, identity, and ethnicity* (pp. 33–50). New York, NY: Routledge.

Zhou, M., & Bankston, C. L. (1998). *Growing up American: How Vietnamese children adapt to life in the United States.* New York, NY: Russell Sage Foundation.

Zhou, M., & Lee, J. (2004). Introduction: The making of culture, identity, and ethnicity among Asian American youth. In J. Lee & M. Zhou (Eds.), *Asian American youth: Culture, identity, and ethnicity* (pp. 1–30). New York, NY: Routledge.

Chapter 2

Education, Citizenship, and the Politics of Belonging: Youth From Muslim Transnational Communities and the "War on Terror"

THEA RENDA ABU EL-HAJ
SALLY WESLEY BONET
Rutgers University

I was kind of like oh my short skirts and my tank tops and I was kind of embarrassed. Like I'm Muslim too. So, it was September 11th. It was the war on Iraq. It was the *intifada*. And I, I wanted to be—I wanted to be Arab. I wanted visibly to be Arab and Muslim. And I covered my hair. And I prayed for a while. And I got really religious for a while, like I won't even pluck my eyebrows. And then I got to a point where it didn't—it just stopped making sense completely. 'Cause I started to, like I have a very deep conviction that some form of a God whatever it is, some form of that thing exists. And it was like that God does not, is not going to burn me if I don't pray or if I don't cover my hair or if I have a drink once in a while. I just like I just realized a lot of Muslims around me were paying really careful attention to that, but like at the same time throwing away insane amounts of food and being racist and being classist. And so I was like I, I think God cares more about—whatever like God is—cares more about how you're, how you're treating everyone and, and how you're like how you're reacting with what's around you and are you hurting or are you just like do you not care? You know and I was like I deeply care and I think that's really important too, I should take that into account. Covering my hair stopped meaning anything. I was—I was Arab and Muslim and everyone—like I was more Arab and Muslim than a lot of people that covered their hair. And so to me it was like that doesn't matter anymore. So it was no longer a part of my identity . . . And the fact that I'm American also means that I, I can participate in and change American society in a really profound way, you know? I hope.

—Zayna (Palestinian American, age 23 years)

So [after 9/11] I wouldn't tell anybody that I was Arab. I went throughout my entire middle school career without telling anybody I was Arab. If people assumed I was Spanish, I was Spanish. If they asked I would just blow off the question. I would—whatever—I had a few schemes. It's embarrassing to me now, that I, you know now that I'm older now that I have the ideas that I have. I'm embarrassed of that period, but I

Review of Research in Education
March 2011, Vol. 35, pp. 29–59
DOI: 10.3102/0091732X10383209
© 2011 AERA. http://rre.aera.net

think it's important that I tell you that . . . I completely understood how alienated I might be, right, if I told people I was Arab. I remember like after September 11 my mother and, I guess, the family were in the car and another car pulls up beside us and people just start pointing and laughing. You know? And it was after September 11th, and I remember that it was probably because of, you know, my mom she wore the *hijab* and things like that. And it's like a humiliation I felt. So in order not to feel that feeling in order not to go through that every single day for the next 3 years of middle school, you know I just sort of I wasn't Arab, I wasn't Muslim, I was whatever; you know, I was American, I was Spanish, whatever . . . To me to be a Palestinian, or, or just, not, not to be a Palestinian, but the idea of me being a Palestinian means that in some way or other I have to fight for the freedom of Palestine and the freedom of Palestinians. So, and often times I have, I have socialist leanings. And so often times these two things come into conflict with being an American. So when, when these two are in conflict I am a Palestinian, not an American. But at other times when you ask me about Barack Obama, when you ask me about, about [city] public schools, when you ask me about these, these types of things I am wholly an American. So it's, I'm, I'm, my identity's sort of flipping between these two constantly.

—Kamal (Palestinian American, age 19 years)

Zayna and Kamal, sister and brother, describe the different trajectories they took in the post-9/11 context as they developed their sense of identity and belonging in relation to multiple imagined communities in their high school years and beyond. Although, according to Zayna, her parents are secular, Zayna's initial response (one that was not uncommon for young Muslim women) was to embrace and publicly mark a religious identity. Kamal took a different path, to hide his status as a Muslim and a Palestinian. Over time, though, each came to approach these identities in new ways and drew on their multiple affiliations as Palestinians, Americans, and Muslims to fashion forms of cultural, civic, and political participation. As children of refugee-status Palestinian parents, Kamal and Zayna had been fundamentally influenced by their parents' struggle to gain citizenship and they understood well the power that legal U.S. citizenship affords. They had also directly experienced the effects of war. Born in the United States, as young children they moved to Iraq in order to stay united with their father who, as the child of Palestinian refugees himself, had no legal citizenship status. When the war landed in their backyard in the form of a bomb, they returned to the United States with their mother, who had been able to obtain a green card through the sponsorship of relatives. After years apart, their father was able to obtain a green card and join his family. Although they were finally united under the banner of a shared citizenship, Zayna, Kamal, and their parents continued to live lives at the crossroads of several political conflicts. Long before September 11, 2001, they were often confronted with the common, blanketing image of Palestinians as terrorists. After September 11, 2001, Zayna and Kamal found themselves positioned as outsiders to the U.S. nation—a position symbolized by the type of street-level encounter that Kamal found so humiliating.

Although their stories illustrate lives buffeted by migration and war, their narratives emphasize the ways that, as adolescents and young adults, Zayna and Kamal were actively engaged in social, cultural, and political realms that reflected their con-nections to multiple communities. In what she described as her earliest political activism, as a 14-year-old high school student, Zayna joined a dance troupe that performed *dabkeh* (a folkdance) to raise money for Palestinian children in need of medical care and other resources. In high school and college, Zayna took on a leader-ship role as an educator and political activist for peace and justice in Palestine and Iraq. And, as an artist who drew on Palestinian cultural resources, she taught others Palestinian *dabkeh* while working with an Arab American community arts organiza-tion; and she was the curator of a local art show about Palestinian embroidery. Although it took Kamal longer, by the time he was a senior in high school and on into his college years, Kamal eagerly embraced his multiple affiliations by educating others about Palestine, becoming involved in the campaign to elect President Barack Obama, and carving out a vision of a future in which he imagined working as a doc-tor in the service of Palestinians living under occupation or in refugee camps. In high school, college, and beyond, Zayna and Kamal were actively involved in both the antiwar and the antioccupation movements. As they moved from adolescence to adulthood, Zayna and Kamal drew on the knowledge, experiences, histories, and cultural resources circulating through the Palestinian diaspora to develop a sense of belonging, and cultural, civic, and political commitments, to multiple communities in the United States and abroad. But, they did so while also maintaining—some-times uncomfortably—their status as "Americans," and they consciously worked to challenge and reshape U.S. culture and politics.

Kamal and Zayna are representative of many youth today who live their lives across multiple real and imagined national terrains. We begin with these brief case studies to illustrate concretely the ways that youth from Muslim[1] transnational com-munities[2] living in the United States are fashioning themselves as social, cultural, and political actors in the face of the post-9/11 climate. We argue that their experiences challenge us to think in fresh ways about belonging and citizenship and demand that we ask new questions about the role of education in forging democratic citizenship in current times. As we describe in more detail below, we take citizenship to encom-pass much more than a person's legal status and the political and civil rights and responsibilities this entails (Banks, 2004; 2008; Castles & Davidson, 2000; Kymlicka, 1995; Marshall, 1964; Rosaldo, 1994). To be substantive, citizenship must also include social and cultural rights that allow people to participate as full members of their communities. In this article, we are particularly concerned with examining the ways that youth from Muslim transnational communities are enacting active citizenship practices in cultural, civic, economic, and political realms.

Importantly, citizenship is always tied up with questions of belonging. Historically, citizenship has often been delimited to people who are defined as belonging to an imagined national community that is discursively constructed (Anderson, 1983/1991). This imagined community simultaneously sets the parameters for exclusion. Yuval-

Davis, Anthias, and Kofman (2005), citing Crowley (1999), argue that "belonging is a thicker concept than that of citizenship" (p. 526), because democratic participation is related to the emotional experiences of inclusion and exclusion. In the wake of September 11, 2001, youth from Muslim transnational communities in the United States have faced particular challenges in forging a sense of belonging to this society (Abu El-Haj, 2005, 2007; Maira, 2004, 2009). Positioned as inassimilable outsiders to the imagined national community, and threatened by government policies and practices that compromise the civil and human rights of their communities (Akram & Johnson, 2004; Murray, 2004), young people from Muslim transnational communities often find neither the sense of belonging nor the political conditions for substantive inclusion into this society. As a consequence of both discursive practices, and political policies, Muslims—especially, but not exclusively those from transnational communities—often struggle to exercise their rights and to forge pathways to active citizenship (Castles & Davidson, 2000; Yuval-Davis et al., 2005).

In this chapter, we argue for examining more deeply the ways that youth from Muslim transnational communities are defining and engaging (or not engaging) in active citizenship practices, articulating a sense of belonging within and across national borders, and frequently developing and acting on critical perspectives on the politics of nationalism and the "war on terror."[3] Whereas much of the work to date examines how youth from Muslim transnational communities negotiate their religious and ethnic identities, we argue for shifting the focus of research from an emphasis on youth identities to an account of how these social identities are intimately bound up with questions of citizenship, which Levinson (2005) has usefully described as "the rules and meanings of political and cultural membership" (p. 336). Moreover, we suggest that we need robust accounts of the role that schools play in shaping the parameters of social membership and political participation for these youth (Abu El-Haj, 2007; Hall, 2002; Levinson, 2005). As the key institutions of social incorporation for youth from transnational communities, schools are centrally involved in the processes through which young people develop their sense of belonging and learn (explicitly but also, perhaps more important, implicitly) the meanings and practices of citizenship. We argue that the experiences of these youth in the post-9/11 context illustrate that educating young people for active citizenship—for meaningful inclusion and participation in their societies—must account for lives lived figuratively and materially across the borders of nation-states.

UNDERSTANDING THE IMPACT OF GLOBALIZATION, NATIONALISM, AND IMPERIALISM

Our understanding of how youth from Muslim transnational communities are negotiating belonging and citizenship is informed by consideration of two critical processes: globalization and imperialism. These nested contexts hold important implications for research that explores the relationship between youth identities, education, and democratic participation.

Globalization, Transnationalism, and the Nation-State

The lives of youth from transnational communities must be understood in relation to critical questions about national belonging raised by contemporary global migration patterns. Transnational communities, along with modern technologies that facilitate the flow of goods, people, and information across borders, limit the salience of nation-states as organizing boundaries for people's personal and political sense of belonging (Appadurai, 1996; Castles & Davidson, 2000; Suárez-Orozco, 2001; Yuval-Davis et al., 2005). However, even as the everyday experience of belonging is becoming more complex for young people who live their lives both imaginatively and physically across borders, nation-states remain intractable, powerful forces in their lives.

Nation-states regulate people's belonging, both materially, by determining their access to a range of rights, and discursively, by linking these rights to inclusion in the imagined national community (Castles & Davidson, 2000; Hall, 2004; Soysal, 1998). Even as global migration challenges the salience of these imagined national communities, the boundaries of national belonging are continually being contested and remade through political and cultural discourses. The boundaries of national belonging change as different groups of people are included or excluded from the imagined community (Anderson, 1983/1991; Billig, 1995; Calhoun, 2005; Hall, 2002; Yuval-Davis et al., 2005). The work of maintaining an imagined national community is carried out, in part, through the practices of everyday nationalism that organize people's sense of belonging to particular nation-states (Billig, 1995; Calhoun, 2005). Billig (1995) argues that nations reproduced themselves daily though practices he calls "banal nationalism . . . the ideological habits which enable established nations of the West to be reproduced in everyday life" (p. 6). After September 11, 2001,[4] these everyday habits took on new significance for youth from Muslim transnational communities living in the United States, as they had to consciously decide how to align themselves in relation to practices such as displaying flags or pledging allegiance in schools. At the same time, it is not only ideological habits that assert the boundaries of belonging to nation-states. Nation-states continue to exert significant power over people's lives through governmental policies that regulate the rights of entry, work, and political participation. Our point is that even as youth from Muslim transnational communities live lives that cross real and imagined global boundaries, they do so in relation to the ongoing power of nation-states to regulate inclusion and exclusion through discursive constructions of belonging and through governmental policies and everyday practices of discrimination (Abu El-Haj, 2007; Hall, 2002; Maira, 2004, 2009).

Imperialism

In this chapter, we also expand the frameworks within which youths' lives have been understood to include imperial power (Abu El-Haj, 2010; Maira, 2009). It is beyond the scope of this chapter to discuss the extensive debates about imperialism. For our purposes, we are referencing the ways that the United States and European nations have exercised and continue to exercise military, economic, and political power on a global stage (see Justice, 2010; Khalidi, 2004; Maira, 2009; Mamdani, 2004). There has been little literature that uses imperialism as a framework for understanding the education of youth from Muslim transnational communities in today's schools (see, for exceptions, Abu El-Haj, 2010; Maira, 2009). Imperialism must be considered in relation to both state policies (power and authority) and the cultural discourses that justify, and thus are intimately intertwined with, these state policies.

Understanding the war on terror as an expression of a new form of U.S. and European imperial power, we take its reach to be simultaneously global and local. Youth from Muslim transnational communities in the United States, as well as Canada and Europe, often are affected dually by the war on terror in the Middle East and Asia and by local manifestations of state surveillance, restrictions on civil liberties, detentions, and deportations. These young people are cognizant of, and some are affected directly by, the military and economic policies of Western nations globally. As they consume alternate media sources, speak with relatives and friends in the Middle East and South Asia, and travel, they often develop perspectives that are critical of Western policies. At the same time, they experience the local effects of governmental surveillance and disciplining of their communities. Thus, the lives of youth from Muslim transnational communities are influenced by imperial policies.

These state imperial policies are bolstered by a cultural discourse developed—as Said (1978) carefully explicated in his seminal work, *Orientalism*—over centuries of encounter between the West and the "Orient." In its most recent iteration, the "clash of civilizations" hypothesis (Huntington, 1996; Lewis, 2002) argues that Islam and its putative "culture" are inimical to "Western" values. This thesis purports a fundamental difference between the liberal, democratic, and pluralist values of "Western" societies and antidemocratic, patriarchal, and even violent tendencies attributed to Islam. As a result of this pervasive cultural discourse, youth must navigate their everyday lives in families, communities, and schools in relation to these images of Islam, the Arab World, and South Asia as fundamentally repressive, antidemocratic, violent, and so forth.

We suggest that to understand the experiences of youth from Muslim transnational communities—in schools and society—we must examine how the processes of globalization and imperialism take shape in their everyday lives. This does not mean positioning youth as simply acted on by these forces; rather, it implies exploring how young people negotiate membership, produce cultural forms, participate in politics, and so on, in relation to the local manifestations of these broader processes (Appadurai, 1996; Lukose, 2009).

EXPLORING THE LIVES OF YOUTH FROM MUSLIM TRANSNATIONAL COMMUNITIES

We are concerned primarily with the impact of the post-9/11 environment in the United States, and as such, this chapter focuses on studies with youth (school age through early adulthood) from Muslim transnational communities living in this country that have been published since 2001. However, we also draw selectively from the English language literature about youth from Muslim communities living in Canada and Great Britain to illustrate several themes that reverberate across these various contexts. The attacks of September 11, the bombings in Madrid and London, and the unfolding war on terror on both sides of the Atlantic lend some common ground to the experiences of youth from Muslim transnational communities living in Western countries. At the same time, there are important differences between these contexts. The postcolonial contexts and the fact that European countries have been slower than the United States to grant citizenship to immigrants mean that Muslim communities living in Europe struggled with political, social, and economic inclusion well before the advent of the war on terror. Given these contextual differences, it is beyond the scope of this chapter to do a comprehensive comparative analysis across these national contexts. Instead, we draw on only a few of the research studies from Canada and Great Britain to highlight themes that are echoed in the small but growing body of U.S. literature. In what follows, we review the major focal themes that emerge within the recent research: identity, gender, citizenship, and school experiences.

Negotiating Multiple Identities

The ways that youth from Muslim transnational communities forge their sense of identity across multiple cultural worlds has been a primary focus in the research literature. An evaluation of this literature must consider the theoretical understandings of culture and identity that undergird the research design and analysis. Although, for the most part, the recent literature has recognized that the post–Cold War cultural politics of the "clash of civilizations" thesis and the current context of the war on terror create an environment in which one's identity as a Muslim, Arab, or South Asian is likely to be experienced as being in conflict with one's American, Canadian, or British identity, the research often take these identities at face value, exploring how youth make sense of their lives in relation to these multiple identities. Some of the literature adopts a view of these identities as tied into cultural systems that are treated as separate and bounded, positioning young people as navigating between often incompatible cultural divides (Sarroub, 2001, 2005; Zine, 2001). Even as these accounts describe how youth are actively constructing new identities at these crossroads, the research risks reinforcing notions of a fundamental clash between cultural systems. Other research attends to the post–September 11, 2001, political context in accounting for the ways that young people construct their religious/cultural identifications (Ewing & Hoyler, 2008; Ghaffar-Kucher, 2009; Mondal, 2008; Sirin & Fine, 2008). This shift toward examining how identities come into being and take on meaning within particular historical, political contexts is of critical import to youth studies. We argue, however, that across the literature, the research often is designed such that it takes young people's sense that they are negotiating *between* separate identities at face value rather than investigating the specific ways that claims of identity come to be taken up in particular local contexts in relation to the cultural politics of the war on terror.

The notion that youth are navigating cultural *divides* is most pronounced in recent literature that relies on research conducted before 9/11 (Sarroub, 2001, 2005; Zine, 2001). Although our concern here is to understand the impact of the post-9/11 context, we include these studies because they are illustrative of the frameworks that have dominated research on immigrant education, which focus primarily on processes of assimilation and acculturation for new communities (Hall, 2004; Suárez-Orozco, 2001). Zine's (2001) research with Muslim Canadian youth and Sarroub's (2001, 2005) ethnographic study with Yemeni American girls offer portraits of teenagers creatively negotiating the conflicting values, norms, and expectations of their religious/ethnic communities and those of the dominant Canadian and U.S. societies, respectively. Sarroub conducted an ethnographic study of Yemeni American girls and their literacy practices as they crossed the contexts of home, school, and the mosque. Sarroub argues that the girls found themselves living in "two worlds," struggling to chart a course between "different ways of being": the cultural world of their Yemeni homeland and the new world of the United States. Sarroub (2005) argues that the girls' lives "illustrate that *an inevitable clash* [italics added] occurs at the intersection of U.S. republican values and the sociocultural practices of the Southend" (p. 44) in which families' expectations, rituals and religious practices, early marriages, ongoing ties to Yemen, and the father's lineage create a set of expectations at odds with the promises of academic achievement and careers in the United States. Connected to both worlds, but living fully in neither, Sarroub describes these young women as "sojourners" who carve out new imagined spaces between these conflicting cultures.

In an early study, Zine (2001) explores how 10 Muslim youth and their parents worked to sustain a Muslim identity within secular, Canadian public schools. Her research illustrates how these young people struggled to maintain *siratal mustaqeem* (the straight path)—an "Islamic lifestyle"—within dominant contexts in which expectations for teen behavior (such as drinking and dating) were at odds with those of their religious community. Similar to Sarroub (2001, 2005), Zine (2001) understands the boundaries of youth identities as contested and constructed, and she argues that young Muslims actively negotiated their identities in relation to the conflicting parameters of dominant (i.e., Canadian) and ethnic, religious, and cultural frameworks. Zine proposes that the work young Muslims did, individually and collectively, to actively commit to maintaining Islamic lifestyles reinforced their religious identifications that, in turn, helped them resist pressures for assimilation to dominant Canadian teenage norms. Zine's work is sensitive to the discriminatory contexts of the public schools and the broader Canadian society, and she argues that Islamophobia—discrimination against Muslims—as well as racial discrimination interact to put these youth at risk for academic disengagement through, for example, placement in low-stream tracks. Zine argues that youths' commitments to an "Islamic lifestyle" supported them to resist feelings of alienation and exclusion within these discriminatory contexts. Although she understands the assertion of Muslim identity to be an active form of resistance to these young people's position as religious and racial/ethnic minorities in Canadian society, Zine implies that the boundaries of Islamic religious practices are clearly defined, unmediated by historical time, place, particular local practices, and so forth. She refers, for example, to "Islamic tradition" and "Islamic lifestyle" in ways that suggest these are given. The struggles of young Canadian Muslims to negotiate their identities are analyzed in terms of an active reaffirmation of their religious commitments, which protects against the influences of dominant Canadian culture.

Research that focuses on how youth from Muslim transnational communities fashion identities in relation to what are taken, a priori, to be clearly delineated, often conflicting cultural and religious values and traditions risks contributing to essentializing views of cultures. Moreover, this stance can inadvertently play into the "clash of civilizations" thesis that takes a static view of Islamic culture and society—a thesis that we must remember has held political sway since the end of the Cold War (Mamdani, 2004; Said, 2001). Research that explores the identities of youth from Muslim communities must be careful to acknowledge the dynamic and variable nature of all religious and cultural beliefs and practices. More important, the research must theorize the cultural politics—writ large and small—through which a sense of divide is created, resisted, and bridged in everyday discourse and practice. We must investigate youths' struggles to establish or maintain a sense of cultural or religious authenticity or their feelings that they are negotiating between two different, sometimes conflicting, cultures, as *products* of sociohistorical processes and cultural politics—as ways that youth are positioning themselves and being positioned in relation to questions of identity, nation, and belonging (see also Kibria, 2007; Mamdani, 2004).

Hall's (2002) research with British Sikh youth—a non-Muslim community—illustrates a different approach to studies of youth identities and offers us a useful theoretical perspective to bring to research conducted with youth from Muslim transnational communities. Hall argues that British Sikh youth described themselves as torn between cultures, even as they produced cultural forms that reflected the dynamic processes of cultural production. Her work cautions us against reading the conflicts that youth feel between cultures as simply or primarily an outcome of actual differences between cultures. Hall argues that youths' felt sense of conflict between cultural identities must be understood as an outcome of the politics of nation formation in the United Kingdom and postcolonial relations. Hall investigates British Sikh youths' lives across multiple contexts (home, school, and community) in relation to broader governmental policies of social incorporation for new immigrant communities from former colonial countries. In doing so, she shows how youths' sense of contrast between identities is related to conflicts over belonging to an imagined British national community. By including the process of nation formation in her analysis, Hall employs a framework of cultural production that shifts away from a picture of youth forming identities within and against static cultural planes, toward a critical account of how youth identities are forged in the crucible of the politics of migration, globalization, and imperialism.

Several recent studies of Muslim youth identities align with Hall's (2002) more dynamic theoretical framework, examining how September 11, 2001, reshaped religion as a primary focus for identification for these young people (Ewing & Hoyler, 2008; Ghaffar-Kucher, 2009; Mondal, 2008; Sirin & Fine, 2008). These studies illustrate the ways that "Muslim American" or "Muslim British" are identity categories around which Muslim youth from different ethnic, racial, and linguistic groups have recently been coming together for support and civic and political engagement. Thus, this work importantly acknowledges the ways that youth identities are flexible and emergent and are constructed within a particular sociopolitical context.

U.S. studies demonstrate that for youth from Muslim American transnational communities, post-9/11 encounters with discrimination and state surveillance of their communities often formed the backdrop against which they wrestled with the meaning of their multiple identities (Abu El-Haj, 2007; Ewing & Hoyler, 2008; Ghaffar-Kucher, 2009; Maira, 2004, 2009; Sirin & Fine, 2008). The tensions emerged from several sources. Many youth reported feeling the September 11, 2001, attacks as Americans, yet despite their resonance with the feelings of sadness and shock experienced across the country, they found their communities immediately marginalized and positioned as threatening outsiders. At the same time, many were critical of the United States' decision to go to war in Afghanistan and Iraq with dire consequences for the majority Muslim populations in those countries. Several studies show that, as they responded to a context of heightened discrimination and the war on terror, youth from many different transnational communities felt compelled to identify more consciously as Muslim, highlighting religion above national or ethnic affiliations (Ewing & Hoyler, 2008; Ghaffar-Kucher, 2009; Kibria, 2007; Sirin & Fine, 2008). Young people emphasized their identities as Muslims for multiple purposes, including creating collective safe spaces against a political climate that positioned them as threatening outsiders and educating the public about Islam and its positive contributions to a multicultural pluralist nation.

Overall, youth from Muslim transnational communities have also continued to identify as Americans despite the ways their communities have been positioned as outsiders to the imagined national community. However, there appears to be much more variability in the ways young people experienced and wrestled with their identities as Americans. Sirin and Fine (2008) conducted the largest research study with young Muslim Americans from immigrant communities in the New York metropolitan region (surveying 204 youth aged 12–25 years, leading focus groups, creating identity maps with a subset of those surveyed, and conducting six life history interviews). Examining how youth navigate hyphenated identities, their analysis concludes that a majority developed what they call "integrated paths—skillfully melding their 'Muslim' and 'mainstream U.S.' cultures" (Sirin & Fine, 2008, p. 141). A smaller group lived in 'parallel worlds' traversing between two compartmentalized lives as Muslims and American but comfortably were figuring how to build bridges between them. Only a small number of their participants expressed conflict between their identities as Muslims and as Americans. In contrast, a study with South Asian Muslim youth from professional families living in the Raleigh–Durham, North Carolina, area reported that many of the young people experienced significant struggle and ambivalence around the possibility of inhabiting both Muslim and American identities (Ewing & Hoyler, 2008). Importantly, the youth did not view their struggles as an outcome of the kind of cultural divide described by Sarroub (2001, 2005) and Zine (2001). The young people did not feel conflict between what they perceived to be dominant American, and their religious and ethnic cultural practices; rather, they wrestled with their experiences of social exclusion and drew self-consciously on their identities as both Muslims and as Americans to claim a public space for themselves in the social and political landscape. In fact, across the literature, there is evidence that many youth from Muslim transnational communities draw on their identities as Americans to demand inclusion and justice—a point to which we will return in our discussion of youth citizenship (Abu El-Haj, 2007; Ewing & Hoyler, 2008; Sirin & Fine, 2008).

However, there is also evidence that for some communities, particularly working-class Pakistani and Bangladeshi immigrants, youth are asserting Muslim/ethnic identities *in opposition* to American identities (Ghaffar-Kucher, 2009; Kibria, 2007). Importantly, both studies show that young people are actively constructing a sense of an "authentic" Muslim/ethnic identity in response to the ways that they have been positioned as outsiders to the imagined national community. These young people's sense of conflict between their religious/cultural identities and the broader American community is analyzed in relation to the cultural politics through which this conflict is constructed and mediated rather than being attributed to fundamental cultural clashes. Thus, again young people's forms of identification are intimately linked with citizenship practices, which we discuss in detail below.

Studies of British Muslim youths' identities offer a useful comparison with studies of Muslim youth in the United States, showing similar tensions and resolutions (Lewis, 2007; Mondal, 2008). British Muslims have faced long-term struggles for social, economic, and political inclusion in the context of decolonization; nevertheless, the September 11, 2001, attacks on the United States, the July 7, 2005, bombings of the London Underground, and the United Kingdom's participation in the war on terror intensified questions about inclusion for their communities. Similar to their counterparts in the United States, British Muslim youth appear to be asserting the importance of their religious identities over and above their ethnic affiliations, in comparison with their parents' generation (Kibria, 2007; Lewis, 2007; Mondal, 2008). The literature on British Muslim youth identities emphasizes the range of ways that these young people are defining and negotiating the meaning and parameters of what it means to be Muslim through expressions of pop culture, online communities, and religious practices. Through these expressions of religious identity, many young British Muslims are joining across ethnic lines to develop a collective identity from which, as we discuss below, they are demanding greater participation in the democratic polity.

Read collectively, these studies suggest that, overall, young Muslims in the United States and United Kingdom are navigating a sense of belonging to these societies, not without conflict but with more facility than often described in the popular imagination. Many Muslim youth see no conflict between their identities as Muslims and as Americans or Britons. In fact, for these young Muslims, it is precisely their sense of being American or British—part of a democratic polity—that drives many to speak out against the injustices that their communities have faced since 9/11. The two studies that do find Bangladeshi (Kibria, 2007) and Pakistani (Ghaffar-Kucher, 2009) youth asserting a religious identity in opposition to British or American identities show that these forms of identification are allowing young people to respond to experiences of racialized marginalization they face in their schools and communities. Although both studies describe an uncomfortable fit between Muslim and mainstream identities, they argue that the sense of opposition between what it means to be Muslim and American or British is constructed within the cultural politics of globalization, decolonization, and the war on terror.

To avoid slipping into perspectives that reinforce the "clash of civilizations" thesis, then, it is critical that research on youth identities investigates how these identities get enacted and inhabited locally in relationship to particular broader sociopolitical contexts and processes. Moreover, it is useful to resist a picture of Muslim and American, British, or other identities as existing on two ends of a continuum rather than thinking of them as overlapping fields within which young people position themselves differently, at different moments in time. In addition, it is important to examine how youth who identify as Muslims are actively engaging in a *range* of discourses and practices about the parameters of what being Muslim entails.

We suggest two considerations for future research about Muslim youth identities. Research must be careful not to presume that Muslim and mainstream national identities should be the primary axes for investigation. This dualist framework misses other important identifications that youth from transnational Muslim communities enact. As one example, Sirin and Fine (2008) focused their analysis on the dimensions of "Muslim" and "mainstream American" identities, and in doing so, they left open questions about other dimensions of identity that were salient to the youth. In fact, a careful read of their data indicates other important lines of identification, as young people talked about being "Palestinian" or "Pakistani" or "Arab American" and drew identity maps that featured flags and symbols of other kinds of national unity. These identifications warrant further investigation as we seek to understand how young people navigate belonging and citizenship in contemporary times. Abu El-Haj (2007), for example, has shown that for Palestinian American Muslim youth, their national identity—as members of an imagined Palestinian diasporic community—is highly salient, and it is their relationship with the struggle for a national homeland that centrally shapes their lives. Moreover, by framing research around questions of Muslim American identities, we may also fail to capture the experiences of youth who might have chosen nonreligious responses to the context of the war on terror. Overall, we call for more research that takes a grounded look at how discourses and practices around particular forms of identification emerge in specific local contexts, intimately bound up with national and global contexts. We need more ethnographic accounts that examine the complex ways that youth inhabit particular identities in specific contexts and interactions, and across time, not only through talk but also through actions and forms of cultural production (see, e.g., Abu El-Haj, 2007, 2009; Ghaffar-Kucher, 2009; Hall, 2002; Lukose, 2009; Maira, 2009).

Gender and Islam

Much focus has been paid to the question of gender identities for Muslim youth. This focus cannot be divorced from the role that gender discourse plays in the cultural politics surrounding the war on terror. The dominant public political narratives about Islam frame gender relations among Muslims as primarily repressive and regressive—a product of outmoded cultural traditions. Importantly, these discourses coconstruct Muslim women as silent, passive, and victimized and "Western" women as agentic, free subjects. The pervasive claim that Muslim women need to be emancipated from their patriarchal societies has been mobilized to justify the U.S. war in Afghanistan and Iraq (Abu-Lughod, 2002; Haddad, Smith, & Moore, 2006; Zine, 2006). Zine (2006) shows how contemporary discourses are related to early Orientalist representations that rationalized imperial domination as a means to bring freedom for Muslim women. In the Orientalist imagination, the Muslim veil is the primary symbol of women's oppression and subjugation (Haddad et al., 2006; Zine, 2006). Thus, the female body often becomes the icon around which the "clash of civilizations" hypothesis rallies (Abu El-Haj, 2010; Abu-Lughod, 2002; Haddad et al., 2006; Zine, 2006).

The practices through which gender relations are produced, negotiated, and contested in Muslim communities must be examined in relation to processes of imperialism, nationalism, and diaspora (Abu-Lughod, 1998). The bodies of women have often been sites through which, for example, the politics of nationalism (in anticolonialist struggles) or ethnic preservation (in the context of migration) have been contested. Women (and their bodies) have often been the terrain on which colonized and oppressed people have reclaimed cultural rights, in part, through an assertion of an "authentic" identity. For example, as we discuss below, restrictions on girls' sexuality can become a cultural boundary to create and maintain a distinction between Arab American culture and mainstream American culture, as a means to avoid assimilation (Ajrouch, 2004). However, women are also not simply pawns in anticolonial and antiassimilationist struggles. Muslim women, for example, have used the veil as a form of political identification and a means of resisting Eurocentric norms (Ben-Habib, 2002; Mushaben, 2008; Zine, 2006).

The research about gender and youth from Muslim communities can be characterized in terms of three, sometimes overlapping, themes that echo the patterns found in the literature on youth identities that we discussed above. One theme suggests that gender is a site through which youth are negotiating between "traditional Muslim" and "modern Western" cultural demands. Although this perspective investigates how youth construct new identities in relation to these two cultures, it also highlights cultural differences between "Muslim" and "Western" gendered practices (Sarroub, 2001, 2005; Zine, 2001). As noted above, this perspective is most pronounced in research that was conducted before September 11, 2001. Sarroub's (2001, 2005) study of Yemeni American girls examines how the gendered practices of Yemeni culture, such as arranged marriages at a young age, the inability to pursue a college education, and the experience of being under surveillance by Yemeni boys and men in the community, were in direct conflict with school expectations for academic achievement and future education for girls. Similarly, Zine's (2001) early study with eight Muslim Canadian students and their parents highlights how youth negotiated the different and conflicting expectations for gender interactions in Islam and the dominant culture. Both Zine (2001) and Sarroub (2001, 2005) show that the girls manage conflicting cultural expectations in creative ways, setting boundaries for public interaction to maintain their position as Muslim girls, even as they imagine alternate possibilities for their lives. Interestingly, Sarroub found that classrooms allowed for more interaction between girls and nonrelated boys because of the mediating role of teachers and the curriculum; however, ultimately the girls rejected postsecondary education and remained within the confines of their families' cultural expectations. Importantly, these studies take girls' agency seriously, exploring how they strategically navigate differing cultural expectations for gender relations. As we showed above, however, this approach fails to examine the cultural politics through which a sense of divide is created (and undone) in relation to broad sociohistorical processes and within particular everyday practices in local contexts.

A second theme in the research on Muslim gender identities explores the ways that young people are negotiating and enacting gender identities and practices in relation to the attempts by new immigrant communities to carve out forms of authenticity in these new contexts (Ajrouch, 2004; Zine, 2006). Ajrouch's (2004) focus group study with Arab American youth highlights the roles of girls as the bearers of an "authentic" cultural identity. Youth maintained their sense of Arab American identity through a distinction they made between the ways that "White girls" and "Arab girls" act. Interestingly, these young men and women distanced themselves from recent immigrants whom they called "boaters"; nevertheless, they claimed a kind of authentic Arab American identity through the construction of particular forms of femininity and appropriate female behavior that were posited in opposition to the actions of White girls. In Ajrouch's framework, restrictions on girls' behavior must be understood as a social practice through which the boundaries of in-group membership emerge. Importantly, these social practices do not go unchallenged as some girls push back against these norms and expectations. Thus, Ajrouch shows how youth are actively constructing and contesting gendered practices as they work to resist assimilation and create a sense of identity and belonging in the United States.

A third approach reflected in Zine's (2006) recent work (see also Mushaben, 2008) offers a more robust perspective, expanding beyond the theme of cultural identity to examine how Muslim girls' gendered practices reflect struggles for citizenship in mainstream society. Analyzing data that she collected before 9/11 and showing how the emergent themes are echoed in the post-9/11 climate, Zine argues that Canadian Muslim adolescent girls attending Islamic school constantly worked against public discourses that positioned themselves outside the boundaries of Canadian citizenry and found ways to "negotiate the burden of representation and negative essentialism" (p. 246). At the same time, they wrestled with the dominant expectations within their Muslim school community that required the *hijab* as an expression of piety. Zine shows that most of the girls consciously chose to adopt the *hijab* as an expression of faith and spiritual freedom—a choice that held particular salience in the face of the broader context of Islamophobia. However, she argues that Muslim girls are constructing their gendered identities in relation to both the challenges of Canadian citizenship and patriarchal forms of social control within their religious community. Read together, the literature suggests that Muslim girls are simultaneously carving out legitimate cultural and political spaces for themselves— in school and society—and actively negotiating the parameters of what it means to be Muslim and female within their own families and communities.

Thus, studies of gender in relation to youth from Muslim transnational communities must be careful to analyze how young people's gendered discourses and practices are embedded within the field of contemporary cultural politics through which questions about the role of Muslim communities—their inclusion and participation—in North American and European democracies are being actively negotiated. As we argued above, if we fail to understand the ways that gendered identities are being constructed and enacted in relation to broader processes of globalization and imperialism, we often end up with a portrait of youth torn between cultures—a perspective that ossifies cultures and risks reinforcing the idea that there is a basic incompatibility between Muslim and Western ways of doing gender.

Youth Citizenship: Active Practice Within and Across Borders

We are suggesting, moreover, the importance of shifting from a narrower focus on how youth from Muslim transnational communities are straddling their multiple identities to an explicit exploration of how they are negotiating belonging and citizenship in contexts of globalization and imperialism. This means understanding youths' cultural, civic, political, and economic practices as modes of active citizenship through which they are fashioning a place for themselves in their societies. It also means paying attention to how these young people are participating in diasporic communities—exploring how global processes are intimately imbricated with lives lived locally (Abu El-Haj, 2007, 2009; Maira, 2004; 2009; see also Appadurai, 1996; Lukose, 2007).

As we discussed in the introduction, we are referencing expanded notions of citizenship that take seriously questions of identity and belonging. This expanded conceptualization of citizenship considers how identity and belonging influence individuals' capacities for substantive inclusion into society and affect the ways people participate in local, national, and global contexts. Broad conceptualizations of citizenship implicate not only legal status but also the capacity to exercise a range of rights and responsibilities: civil, political, social, and cultural (Banks, 2004, 2008; Castles & Davidson, 2000; Kymlicka, 1995; Marshall, 1964; Rosaldo, 1994). Modern forms of citizenship evolved initially to include civil rights, which guarantee individual rights (such as free expression and equality before the law), and political rights, which grant people political power. These initial rights were expanded to include social rights that offer citizens benefits such as education and health care that are necessary to guarantee their capacity to participate fully in their societies. More recently, cultural rights—the right to maintain linguistic, cultural, and group affiliation—have emerged as a key aspect of modern citizenship (Castles & Davidson, 2000; Kymlicka, 1995; Rosaldo, 1994).

Cultural citizenship acknowledges that people's capacities to participate as full and equal citizens are often limited by their position in a nation's racial/ethnic hierarchy (Ong, 1996; Rosaldo, 1994). Cultural citizenship also references the ways that cultural forms and practices contribute to political and civic participation (Flores & Benmajor, 1997; Rosaldo, 1994). Cultural citizenship is an expansive concept that includes the everyday cultural productions through which people forge membership and actively participate in their societies. At the same time, global migration has led to citizenship practices that allow people to maintain connections across national boundaries, strategically acquiring economic, social, and political rights—what Ong (1999) coined "flexible citizenship" (p. 6). The concepts of cultural and flexible citizenship offer perspectives through which to understand the range of ways that youth from Muslim transnational communities construct group affiliations and act on their societies. Although not all the research consciously addresses young people's citizenship practices, much of the literature points to the ways that youth from Muslim transnational communities are leveraging their membership as religious and ethnic minorities to challenge exclusionary and discriminatory practices and are demanding inclusion and equity.

Although the belief that Muslims are inassimilable outsiders is rooted in longstanding imperial politics of the United States in the Middle East and Asia (Khalidi, 2004; Mamdani, 2004), it was September 11, 2001, that dramatically changed the landscape for Muslim youth in the United States. This sudden shift in their position in U.S. society crystallized the salience of religious affiliation as a site not only for many young people's identification but also for their citizenship practices (Ewing & Hoyler, 2008; Ghaffar-Kucher, 2009). A range of studies (Ewing & Hoyler, 2008; Ghaffar-Kucher, 2009; Sirin & Fine, 2008) showed that youth responded to the climate of the war on terror by engaging their identities as Muslims in a more politically conscious way, often transcending ethnic and national affiliations for an encompassing sense of belonging to a transnational Muslim community, the *ummah*. Ghaffar-Kucher (2009) argues that post-9/11, "the 'religification' of urban, working class Pakistani American youth, that is, the ascription and co-option of a religious identity, trumps all other forms of categorization, such as race and ethnicity" and "significantly influences the youths' identities, notions of citizenship, and feelings of belonging" (p. 164). Ghaffar-Kucher (2009) shows how Pakistani American Muslim youth leverage their religious identities to build social relationships with other Muslims, push back against dominating images of their community, and make demands on their school communities (e.g., for recognition of religious holidays); but, for these young people, belonging to "American" society seems out of reach. The middle-class South Asian youth in Ewing and Hoyler's (2008) study also became more self-consciously religiously identified in the wake of September 11, 2001; however, this did not mean they abandoned a sense of belonging to the United States. For some, the challenges of full inclusion in the United States led them toward a strategy of "flexible citizenship" (Ong, 1999) through which they anticipated drawing on the educational and political resources of U.S. citizenship to be able to relocate to other countries if necessary. The differences in how the young people in these two studies forged a sense of belonging to U.S. society, and the ability of the youth in Ewing and Hoyler's (2008) study to imagine engaging in flexible citizenship practices may be an outcome of the differences in their social class status. This suggests a need to do more research that explicitly examines the impact of social class on how these youth navigate the struggles for belonging in the post-9/11 context.

Sirin and Fine (2008) examined how young Muslims in the United States drew on their religious affiliations to challenge discrimination and oppression. Interestingly, they found that there was a gender difference in the ways that the youth engage in what they call "contact zones"—spaces in which Muslim Americans encounter people from diverse communities. The young women often took a stance of educator, feeling an obligation to teach others about Islam, to counter stereotypes and misinformation. These young women were optimistic about the promises of a pluralist multicultural America. Young men, on the other hand, were more skeptical and embittered about the possibilities of inclusion and belonging and as a consequence were less committed to civic engagement and social action. Sirin and Fine (2008) speculate that these differences may be related both to the deeper exclusions experienced by Muslim men, given pervasive images they face as terrorists and oppressors of women, and to the fact that their encounters tended to be with people in positions of authority. Women, they suggest, may be more willing and able to be civically engaged precisely because the spheres in which they operate offer more possibility for movement and action. Thus, looking across the U.S. literature, we see that many young Muslims are leveraging their religious identifications as a means for active participation and civic engagement across the boundaries of ethnicity and nationality (Ewing & Hoyler, 2008; Kibria, 2007; Sirin & Fine, 2008). However, we need more research that investigates how other factors, such as gender or socioeconomic class, may be mediating citizenship practices for these youth.

The context for the growing religious affiliation among youth from transnational communities is different in Great Britain where economic, social, and political exclusion has been decades in the making; however, recent history has heightened the status of Muslims as inassimilable outsiders. The rise in religious affiliation among second- and third-generation Muslim British youth is related to their efforts to forge social inclusion and engage in active citizenship practices (Kibria, 2007; Lewis, 2007; Mondal, 2008). Through explorations of young British Muslims, Lewis (2007) and Mondal (2008) seek to dispel the popular narrative that Muslim youth are increasingly alienated from British society, at risk of becoming violent extremists. Both studies show that, for the majority, increasing religious affiliation is not primarily a sign of alienation from British society. In fact, many young British Muslims are strengthening their commitments to Islam to collectively combat the social and economic marginalization their communities have traditionally faced and to claim full participation as British citizens. Kibria's (2007) research with Bangladeshi youth offers a somewhat different perspective. Although her research concurs that young people are embracing Islam and its connection to the *ummah*—the global Muslim community—as a means of resisting social, economic, and political exclusion, she also finds they are taking up religious identities as a way to resist what they imagine to be the corrupting moral influence of dominant British culture. Despite these differences, the research has found that religiosity is one path through which second- and third-generation Muslim youth seek to achieve social, cultural, and economic empowerment in the face of the discriminatory social and economic contexts in which they find themselves. Mondal (2008) found that, unlike their parents who still view the countries from which they migrated as "home," second- and third-generation Muslim youth see themselves as British and are, in fact, carving out a sense of belonging to British society. Importantly, for this generation, "being British" does not reference some imagined cultural ideal; rather, it is about a "lived practice" of "integration that demonstrates a commitment to living and working in a particular locality, being interested in local politics or volunteer activities or social work, and having friends from other social groups" (Mondal, 2008, p. 95). Mondal challenges dominant definitions of social integration that are assimilationist in nature and suggests that Muslim youths' commitments and sense of belonging to British society do not depend on giving up their religious and ethnic affiliations. Moreover, unlike Kibria (2007), Mondal (2008) finds that young Muslims' strengthening commitments to the *ummah* are not in conflict with their commitments to Britain; rather, they suggest that young people today are actively engaged with local, national, and global contexts at the same time.

Resonating with these findings in Great Britain, Zine's (2004, 2006) studies with Muslim Canadian youth show how religious affiliation is a source of resistance to the dominant Canadian context (especially its discriminatory aspects) without signaling a rejection of the goals of inclusion and belonging to Canadian society. Across these studies, we see youth developing forms of social integration that do not depend on conformity to an imagined national ideal (as American, British, or Canadian). Thus, despite the different historical and political contexts, across the United States, Canada, and Britain, religious affiliation among Muslim youth has become a resource for cultural citizenship through which they challenge exclusionary practices and seek full participation in the social, cultural, economic, and political spheres of these democratic societies. Through a range of activities including forms of cultural production and consumption (such as pop music, fashion, online forums, and educational and political activism), young people from Muslim transnational communities are asserting their right to belong and participate as full members of their societies.

Whereas the studies above illustrate how youth are engaging their religious affiliations to combat exclusion and forge a place for their communities in the countries in which they reside, a small, but growing literature attends to the ways that youth from Muslim transnational communities experience the post-9/11 context not only in relation to the United States but also in relation to their lived experiences and imagined relationships across the boundaries of nation-states (Abu El-Haj, 2007, 2009; Maira, 2004, 2009). These studies complicate the picture of religion as the only source of affiliation for these young people. Abu El-Haj's (2007) research with Palestinian American youth from a working-class immigrant community illustrates the ways that transnational affiliations shape their relationship to citizenship and belonging. Palestinian American youth distinguished between citizenship and national belonging. They described "having" U.S. citizenship but "being" Palestinian—part of a diasporic and, in their case, transnational migratory, Palestinian community. Their sense of national (Palestinian) identity was forged through direct and mediated experiences with the Israeli occupation of Palestine and in relation to the exclusionary definitions of "American" national identity they encountered in schools and communities, particularly after September 11, 2001. Practicing "flexible citizenship" (Ong, 1999) these youth drew on the rights afforded them as U.S. citizens to be actively engaged in the social, cultural, economic, and political spheres both in the United States and in Palestine. Importantly, they understood that the power afforded them by their U.S. citizenship enabled the youth and their families to exercise rights (e.g., to travel, work, and dissent) that they did not have living under occupation.

Maira's (2004, 2009) ethnographic study of South Asian Muslim youth also explores the ways that young people fashion citizenship and belonging in relation to local, national, and global politics. Maira is critical of multicultural discourses that attempt to fit Muslims into a frame of racialization rather than parsing the ways that these communities are politically profiled in relation to U.S. imperial power. Similar to the Palestinian community in Abu El-Haj's (2007) study, the families of the youth in Maira's (2004, 2009) research engaged in the practice of flexible citizenship through transnational migration to attain economic and educational resources unavailable in their countries of origin. U.S. citizenship—or the desire for it—did not erase their strong sense of belonging to the national community of the countries from which their families migrated. Young people maintained affective ties to their imagined national community through the consumption of popular culture, participation in cultural events, and creation of strong relationship with other South

Asian families. At the same time, the demands of work and school changed the shape of cultural practices: for example, more girls and women worked outside of the home in response to the economic demands of the family, and working youth found little time to engage in activities with other members of their community. Against a picture of two binary cultures in conflict, Maira shows how transnational affiliations take particular local shape in the everyday practices of youth and families in complex affective and material ways. Maira also shows how the knowledge of, and connection to, South Asia, coupled with their communities' experiences with the policies of the war on terror, shaped powerful discourses of dissent in relation to the United States' position as an imperial power. Thus, like Abu El-Haj (2005, 2007), Maira's (2004, 2009) work illustrates the ways that youth from transnational communities articulate political commitments that take into account people's lives near and far. Maira's (2004, 2009) and Abu El-Haj's (2005, 2007) research suggests that youth from transnational communities are creating everyday practices through which they engage in cultural, economic, and political actions across the borders of nation-states.

We have argued for consciously shifting our analytic focus from questions of identity to young people's discourses and practices in relation to rights, citizenship, and belonging in the post-9/11 era. The multifaceted discourses and practices of new forms of citizenship that youth from Muslim transnational communities are forging offer a grounded critique of national belonging as the primary basis for affording inclusion and citizenship rights. Looking across the complex and variable ways that youth from Muslim transnational communities are fashioning different ways to belong within and across the literal and imagined borders of nation-states challenges our understanding of citizenship and civic participation and raises critical questions about the education of young people today.

Schooling and Youth Citizenship

As the primary institutions through which youth from transnational communities encounter the state, schools are a key site for shaping citizenship and democratic participation for young people. As Levinson (2005) reminds us, schools "play a preponderant role in projecting the discourses that define the limits and necessary qualities of political participation and social belonging" (p. 334). Given the cultural politics that position members of Muslim transnational communities as inassimilable outsiders, accounts of the lived experiences of youth from these communities in U.S. schools is of critical import; however, there are few such studies (Abu El-Haj, 2005, 2007, 2010; Ghaffar-Kucher, 2009; Maira, 2009; Sarroub, 2001, 2005; Sarroub, Pernicek, & Sweeney, 2007). These studies take two primary approaches to their investigations: (a) focusing on processes of acculturation and assimilation by examining how differences in cultural norms and practices affect academic engagement and achievement (Sarroub, 2001, 2005; Sarroub et al., 2007) or (b) investigating how racial/ethnic and religious discrimination and the politics of the war on terror shape the everyday experiences and academic achievement of these young people (Abu El-Haj, 2005, 2007, 2010; Ghaffar-Kucher, 2009; Maira, 2009).

Sarroub and her colleagues (Sarroub, 2001, 2005; Sarroub et al., 2007) explore educational attainment for immigrant youth from Middle Eastern communities in relation to the disjuncture between their home and host cultures. In her ethnographic study conducted before September 11, 2001, Sarroub's focus is on questions of immigrant acculturation and assimilation. She argues that, for Yemeni American girls, academic achievement was constrained by the conflicting social and cultural expectations of their families and their schools. Certain school practices (e.g., gym class) caused social anxieties for their families and led to increased surveillance of the girls by the boys from their community. Girls felt conflicted about these practices, even as they enjoyed school as a space for being with their peers and imagining college aspirations. Often married young, some girls struggled with the purposes of school given that they did not expect to go on to college. Sarroub argues that Yemeni values and practices often function in binary opposition to the goals and purposes of public schooling in the United States, hindering the possibilities for academic achievement for these girls in the immediate future. Sarroub (2005) writes,

The ambiguity with which the *hijabat* [girls who wear a head scarf] faced their futures conflicted with their school's goal of producing educated citizens who will contribute to society . . . As long as the *hijabat* are constrained by the expectations of the Southend and Yemen, they are unlikely to benefit from or contribute to American society. (p. 117)

As we discussed above, Sarroub (2005) posits a fundamental cultural conflict—a conflict between the republican values of the United States and those of the Yemeni community—as the undergirding reason for the Yemeni girls' failure to pursue higher education.

Drawing on more recent research with Iraqi refugee high school students conducted after September 11, 2001, Sarroub et al. (2007) maintain a similar theoretical framework. They examine the struggles that one Kurdish refugee teen, Haydar, faced in relation to literacy learning. Working to explain how this student, who was successful in work-related literacy practices, was failing in school, the authors point to the disjuncture Haydar experienced in relation to his identity as a male and a worker upon moving to the United States. They attribute Hadyar's difficulty learning to read in school to his struggles to reimagine himself as a male and a worker in this new context that seemed worlds away from the forms of masculine identity as an independent farmer that he had forged in Kurdistan and refugee camps before his arrival in the United States. Determined to support his family financially, Haydar could not find the relevance of academic literacy to his work prospects. Sarroub et al. argue that Haydar is "representative of a new type of immigrant (a refugee) whose home life is incompatible with school expectations, and as such he and others like him are likely to fail and drop out of school" (p. 668), and they propose that teachers work to build bridges between school literacy and the multiple literacies that students practice out of school—a point with which we agree.

However, the argument that academic underachievement is an outcome of a disjuncture between home and school literacies is not a new one (see Heath, 1983), and the limitations of this framework have been widely discussed (see Erickson, 1987; Ogbu, 1987; Varenne & McDermott, 1998). For the purposes of our argument, this framework of cultural disjuncture has two primary limitations. First, as we discussed above, this perspective that youth are caught between two different cultural systems reinforces the notion that Muslim (in this case Yemeni and Kurdish) and "Western" cultural values and practices are inimical, rather than accounting for the dynamic ways that people shape and reshape cultural practices in everyday interactions. For example, Haydar's struggles over masculinity revolved around the recurring themes of work, cars, and girls: Do these struggles reflect disjunctures between Kurdish forms of masculinity and "American" ones, as Sarroub and her colleagues (Sarroub et al., 2007) argue, or might they be read as ongoing struggles learned, at least in large part, here in the United States? As Appadurai (1996) has argued eloquently, in the context of globalization, "culture becomes less of Bourdieu's habitus and more an arena for conscious choice, justification and representation" (p. 44). Young people, like Haydar, are not simply caught between cultures; they are drawing on multiple cultural forms to create new identities and cultural practices. In fact, Sarroub's (2001, 2005) ethnography of the Yemeni American youth offers a thoughtful, nuanced portrait of the girls engaged in processes of cultural production—actively constructing the parameters and meaning of cultural practices through, for example, their consumption of pop music and their fantasies about romance and relationships. Interestingly, Sarroub (2005) also notes that some parents were strongly supportive of the girls' education; and Sarroub was hopeful that this support might help the young women to realize their college aspirations in the future. These observations do not fit with the picture Sarroub paints of what, as we noted earlier, she calls "an inevitable clash" (p. 44) between U.S. republican values and Yemeni cultural norms. As we suggested earlier, the second limitation of a framework that explains academic achievement in terms of cultural disjunctures is that we cannot take people's experiences of cultural conflict at face value but must analyze explicitly the cultural politics through which these accounts of cultural clash are developed. This means that to understand more fully the educational experiences of youth from Muslim communities, we must turn our attention to the ways that broader sociopolitical processes that regulate the boundaries of participation and inclusion in democratic societies are being actively negotiated in the everyday practices of U.S. schools.

This brings us to the second approach to research about the education of youth from Muslim transnational communities, which directly addresses the ways that globalization, imperialism, and particularly the cultural politics of the war on terror have shaped the experiences of these students inside their schools (Abu El-Haj, 2005, 2007, 2010; Ghaffar-Kucher, 2009; Maira, 2004, 2009). Ethnographic studies with

Palestinian American (Abu El-Haj, 2005, 2007) and Pakistani American (Ghaffar-Kucher, 2009) youth find remarkably similar patterns in how the cultural politics of the war on terror infuse the everyday practices in schools, with serious consequences for the education of these young people. In the wake of September 11, 2001, male students often found themselves confronted with teachers and peers who viewed them as terrorists, whereas female students were, more often, viewed as oppressed. Thus, these young people's educational experiences, connections to school environments, and academic aspirations were shaped in relation to the politicized context of the war on terror. Within these contexts, young people fashioned responses in complex ways. Whereas some youth gave up on the promise of academic attainment, most continued to pursue educational achievement with the conscious understanding that it would open up economic possibilities for their families in the United States and abroad (Abu El-Haj, 2007; see also Maira, 2009). Youth responded in variable ways to the daily expressions of "banal nationalism" (Billig, 1995) inside schools. For example, Abu El-Haj (2007) shows that although, in response to the U.S. invasions of Afghanistan and Iraq, some Palestinian American youth refused to stand and recite the Pledge of Allegiance (risking disciplinary action), others felt that, particularly as visible Muslims, it was critical to stand and show others that they respected the United States. Some youth, especially boys, engaged in self-defeating strategies, taking up the roles they were offered and acting out in ways that reinforced images of Muslim violence (Ghaffar-Kucher, 2009). Some students responded to their status as inassimilable outsiders by educating their teachers and peers about the "truth" about Islam, carving out space for entry into a pluralist society. This strategy shows how the concept of a true or authentic Islam is developed in particular sociohistoric contexts and illustrates our point that we must explore the range of ways that young people take up cultural discourses and practices that make claims about identity in relation to broader political processes, such as the war on terror.

We suggest that, to understand the education of youth from Muslim transnational communities as related to processes of nation formation, we must move beyond analyses that focus on questions of achievement, acculturation, and assimilation. That is, research on the education of youth from Muslim transnational communities must analyze processes of nation formation—the ways that national belonging and inclusion are continually reshaped and reasserted in relation to these new communities (Abu El-Haj, 2007, 2010; Hall, 2004). Abu El-Haj (2010) pushes this paradigm further to illustrate that school is a site at which the cultural politics of U.S. imperial power play out in everyday practices that discipline youth from Muslim communities. In her research with Palestinian American youth, she shows that teachers and administrators drew on beliefs about Islam as oppressive to women or as advocating violence, and they imagined U.S. education as a site for "liberalizing" Muslim girls or curtailing the putative aggressive or violent beliefs and behaviors of Muslim boys. For example, shortly after September 11, 2001, two Palestinian American boys were suspended for drawing pictures of planes crashing into buildings. The teacher who reported them simply assumed the drawings indicated some kind of threat rather than exploring the meaning with the young men. (After 9/11, many children drew planes crashing into buildings, and we can assume this held various meanings for different children.) In fact, time and again, the Palestinian American boys in the school were suspended or expelled because of conflicts that resulted from the presumption that they were prone to violence and aggression. Interestingly, another response to the presumption of male violence was a belief that U.S. education could pacify this tendency. Returning to the example of the drawings of the planes, in an interview that occurred 2 years after the incident, the teacher who had reported the students continued to assume that the boys intended the drawings as either a threat or as support for the 9/11 attacks; however, she had decided that she should have reasoned with them rather than having had them suspended. This teacher argued for the power of U.S. education to turn the boys away from violent extremism. In this and other incidents, educators' strongly held beliefs in the liberating nature of U.S. education directly affected the Palestinian American students' experiences in school. Abu El-Haj's study (2010) suggests an urgent need to understand better how the cultural politics of U.S. imperial power (as a putative democratizing, liberal force in the world) is affecting the daily experiences of youth from many different communities.

Our accounts of education for youth from Muslim transnational communities must go well beyond the questions of acculturation and assimilation that have traditionally dominated the literature on immigrant education. Research needs to focus on how belonging and citizenship—particularly as lived experiences—are being regulated through schooling and on the processes through which education positions young people for democratic participation or exclusion. Moreover, we need research that explores schools as institutions within which processes of globalization and imperialism are negotiated locally.

BEYOND IDENTITIES: TOWARD AN UNDERSTANDING OF YOUTH CITIZENSHIP

The existing literature about youth from Muslim transnational communities living in North America and Europe suggests a need for further investigation of the ways that the processes of globalization and the war on terror enter the everyday lives of young people, shaping discourses and practices of citizenship and belonging, which are, in turn, being reshaped by the youth themselves. As countries across the globe wrestle with the contours of citizenship and belonging, the question of how young people learn to become active participants—and what forms of participation they take up—in their local, national, and global contexts is arguably one of the most important educational questions. Understanding these processes requires research that considers the following three issues.

Examine Claims Around Culture and Identity in Relation to Cultural Politics That Regulate Inclusion and Exclusion

Since September 11, 2001, Muslims living in the United States have often found themselves drawn into a kind of banal multicultural discourse in which they are asked to speak as "good Muslims" (Mamdani, 2004) showing that Muslim religious beliefs and practices can be incorporated into the patchwork quilt of pluralist democracies. This move—a completely understandable one for communities under attack—often depends on a subtle reassertion of essentialized notions of a "good" Islamic culture that averts our attention away from cultural and governmental policies that render these communities "enemies within."

It is, we suggest, within this political context that we must consider how our research paradigms reinforce or resist these frameworks for defining culture. Research that investigates the cultural practices of Muslim communities—even while acknowledging the changing nature of these practices—runs the risk of reifying cultures and cultural practices if the research is not framed to investigate the discourses and practices through which culture gets invoked, in particular places at particular times. The insight is not new (Eisenhart, 2001; Gonzalez, 2005; Hall, 2002; Pollock, 2008; Varenne & McDermott, 1998); and yet, as we have shown in this chapter, much of the research on youth from Muslim transnational communities has not fully explored its implications. We need more research that examines how and under what circumstances youth are making claims about culture and what resources they draw on to fashion cultural forms. And we need to explore the range of forms these cultural practices are taking among youth from various Muslim transnational communities.

Moreover, the primary research focus on identity—and how young people negotiate multiple identities—also contributes to this analytic problem. Investigations that explore young people's experiences through the lens of identity—even as they may acknowledge these are fluid, hybrid, and multiple—often do not pay enough attention to understanding the everyday work through which local, national, and global processes shape youth identifications, discourses, and actions in particular, unpredictable ways at specific historical moments. This means that we need to theorize how and why certain forms of identification have become salient in relation to processes of globalization and imperialism. For example, much of the research with youth from Muslim transnational communities has shown that religion is becoming a more salient form of affiliation in the post-9/11 environment. However, the reasons for this increased salience and the ways that young Muslims organize and engage in citizenship practices are different, for example, in the United States and Britain; and we need more comparative and nuanced accounts of the contexts within which youth are organizing around religious affiliation (see, e.g., Kibria, 2007). Moreover, especially in the post-9/11 environment in which we are primed by the cultural politics of the war on terror to see Islam as the most salient dimension for investigation, we must not lose sight of other forms of affiliation that are highly significant to the youth—for example, the national aspirations of Palestinian American youth (Abu El-Haj, 2007, 2010) or the working-class consciousness of the South Asian youth in Maira's (2009) research. The processes of globalization and imperialism yield complex and multifaceted fields within which young people forge identities and a sense of belonging, which must be fully explored. Importantly, the post-9/11 environment creates a new context in which we cannot afford to investigate culture or identity outside of a careful, grounded account of how these notions are constituted in relation to the cultural politics of the war on terror. This is precisely because culture is being explicitly invoked as a rationale for the putative inassimilable nature of Muslim communities.

Investigate How Youth Participate in Local, National, and Global Contexts

Whereas in recent years, much discussion about youth from transnational Muslim communities has focused on the question of integration or lack of integration into the nation-states in which they reside, this question itself implicates national identification and assimilation as normative and the failure to feel this primary sense of belonging to one nation-state as problematic. This assumption does not reflect the realities of how many youth from these (and other) communities fashion a sense of belonging in today's world. As this chapter has shown, youth from Muslim transnational communities are enacting a much more complex and multifaceted sense of belonging that encompasses, for example, their affiliations with the country in which they reside; with the global community of Muslims—the *ummah*; and with other imagined national communities.

This new reality means that we must shift the questions we ask in educational research, particularly in relation to transnational communities. Research on immigrant education often focuses on questions of social incorporation, which, important as those are, need to be accompanied by a deeper understanding of the ways that education is involved in ongoing processes of nation building and citizenship formation (Abu El-Haj, 2007; Hall, 2002; Levinson, 2005). More important, we also need to pay attention to how youth position themselves, produce cultural forms, engage in civic action, and so on, within *and* across the borders of nation-states. For young people from transnational communities, their sense of belonging to multiple communities suggests that citizenship is a more complicated affair than we often assume. Although citizenship, taken at face value, suggests commitment to and action within the boundaries of one nation-state, many young people are actually finding themselves acting in relation to multiple nation-states and imagined communities (Anderson, 1983/1991). We need more research that pays careful attention to how young people are engaged in everyday practices through which they interact with local, national, and global forces (Abu El-Haj, 2007; Hall, 2002; Lukose, 2007, 2009; Suaréz-Orozco, 2000).

Conduct Ethnographies in Schools and Communities

We also need more studies that document the actual everyday experiences of youth from Muslim transnational communities in their schools, families, and communities to understand how their experiences, discourses, and practices are shaped by, and in turn respond to, processes of globalization, nationalism, and imperialism. Moreover, we need research that pays particular attention to the ways that schools are involved in the processes of nation formation and imperialism. That is, we need to see how these processes actually unfold within educational discourses and practices and how young people actively take up the challenges of inclusion and citizenship within these contexts. This means that we need more multisite and comparative ethnographies that explore young people's lives across a range of settings and track how globalization and imperialism are at work at the local level.

YOUTH CITIZENSHIP IN THE GLOBAL CONTEXT

The September 11, 2001, attacks in the United States and the bombings in Madrid and London have focused much public discourse around questions of alienation and anger among Muslims—particularly youth—living in the United States and Europe. These conversations are often concerned with whether Muslim and American or European identities are fundamentally incompatible with each other. Thus, the primary questions in the popular imagination circulate around debates about the ostensible "clash of civilizations" and around questions about whether this clash makes social, cultural, and political integration for these relatively new communities an unlikely outcome. We suggest that the more relevant question is to understand how young people from Muslim transnational communities are actually fashioning new forms of citizenship and belonging in relation to local, national, and global contexts—forms that require us to rethink our expectations and understandings of these terms in our times. And it suggests that we need to explore the processes through which these young people develop commitments to—or alternatively feel alienated from—active participation in the civic, economic, cultural, and political lives of their various communities.

These concerns raise new considerations for citizenship education in our schools. In recent years, even in the face of new migration trends, citizenship education in U.S. schools, unfortunately, has taken a back seat in the press for economic productivity. A vigorous democracy, however, depends on the full participation of its young people, and schools cannot afford to ignore educating youth for active citizenship. However, the new demographic facts on the ground mean that we cannot reinvigorate citizenship education without problematizing the paradigms that dominate current educational approaches—frameworks that continue to emphasize loyalty to the nation-state as the basis for citizenship and belonging (Abowitz & Harnish, 2006). The experiences of youth from Muslim transnational communities suggest a need for new educational approaches to developing engaged and active young citizens working for a more just and peaceful future for nations across the globe. Developing these new approaches will depend on a richer understanding of how young people are constructing "glocal" lives.

NOTES

[1]Although we focus this chapter on youth from Muslim transnational communities, it is critical to note that the post–September 11, 2001, context has created a discriminatory climate that affects all Muslims and also communities—for example, Arab Christians and Sikhs—who have been taken for Muslims. At the same time, it is important to note that the cultural discourses that justify the "war on terror" often are directed not solely at Islam but also at Arab, Pakistani, and other ethnic groups. Moreover, we write of youth from Muslim communities while also acknowledging that this choice of delineation is problematic because it risks slipping into presumptions that all people within those groups identify themselves as Muslims, are religious, or share similar experiences.

[2]There is, of course, ongoing debate about the use of the terms *immigrant, diasporic,* and *transnational* (see Lukose, 2007). We choose to refer to transnational communities to suggest the ways that people often move back and forth across the globe and the ways they maintain material, affective, and imagined ties to multiple nation-states, even several generations after migration.

[3]We put this phrase in scare quotes the first time we introduce it to emphasize the problematic nature of this constructed term. It should also be noted that President Obama's administration retired the term *war on terror*; however, the two wars begun under the Bush administration, and many of the governmental policies developed in response, remain in place at this time.

[4]Although September 11, 2001, is often marked as the beginning of a new era for these communities, in fact, the view of Islam as a threat to the "West" was firmly entrenched at the moment of the bombings in the United States.

REFERENCES

Abowitz, K. K., & Harnish, J. (2006). Contemporary discourses of citizenship. *Review of Educational Research, 76,* 653–690.

Abu El-Haj, T. R. (2005). Global politics, dissent and Palestinian-American identities: Engaging conflict to re-invigorate democratic education. In L. Weis & M. Fine (Eds.), *Beyond silenced voices: Class, race and gender in United States schools* (Rev. ed., pp. 119–215). Albany: State University of New York Press.

Abu El-Haj, T. R. (2007). "I was born here but my home it's not here": Educating for democratic citizenship in an era of transnational migration and global conflict. *Harvard Educational Review, 77,* 285–316.

Abu El-Haj, T. R. (2009). Imagining postnationalism: Arts, citizenship education and Arab American youth. *Anthropology & Education Quarterly, 40,* 1–19.

Abu El-Haj, T. R (2010). "The beauty of America": Nationalism, education and the "war on terror." *Harvard Educational Review, 80,* 242–274.

Abu-Lughod, L. (1998). Feminist logics and postcolonial conditions. In L. Abu-Lughod (Ed.), *Remaking women: Feminism and modernity in the Middle East* (pp. 3–31). Princeton, NJ: Princeton University Press.

Abu-Lughod, L. (2002). Do Muslim women really need saving? Anthropological reflections on cultural relativism and its Others. *American Anthropologist, 104,* 783–790.

Ajrouch, K. J. (2004). Gender, race, and symbolic boundaries: Contested spaces of identity among Arab American adolescents. *Sociological Perspectives, 47,* 371–391.

Akram, S. M., & Johnson, K. R. (2004). Race and civil rights pre-September 11, 2001: The targeting of Arabs and Muslims. In E. C. Hagopian (Ed.), *Civil rights in peril: The targeting of Arabs and Muslims* (pp. 9–25). Chicago, IL: Haymarket Books.

Anderson, B. (1991). *Imagined communities: Reflections on the origin and spread of nationalism.* New York, NY: Verso. (Original work published 1983)

Appadurai, A. (1996). *Modernity at large: Cultural dimensions of globalization.* Minneapolis: University of Minnesota Press.

Banks, J. A. (2004). Introduction: Democratic citizenship education in multicultural societies. In J. A. Banks (Ed.), *Diversity and citizenship education: Global perspectives* (pp. 3–15). San Francisco, CA: Jossey-Bass.

Banks, J. A. (2008). Diversity, group identity and citizenship education in a global age. *Educational Researcher, 37,* 129–139.

Ben-Habib, S. (2002). *The claims of culture: Equality and diversity in the global era.* Princeton, NJ: Princeton University Press.

Billig, M. (1995). *Banal nationalism.* London, England: Sage.

Calhoun, C. (2005). *Nations matter: Culture, history and the cosmopolitan dream.* New York, NY: Routledge.

Castles, S., & Davidson, A. (2000). *Citizenship and migration: Globalization and the politics of belonging.* New York, NY: Routledge.

Crowley, J. (1999). The politics of belonging: Some theoretical considerations. In A. Gedess and A. Favil (Eds.), *The politics of belonging: Migrants and minorities in contemporary Europe* (pp. 15–41). Aldershot, England: Ashgate.

Eisenhart, M. (2001). Changing conceptions of culture and ethnographic methodology. In V. Richardson (Ed.), *Handbook of research on teaching* (4th ed., pp. 209–225). Washington, DC: American Educational Research Association.

Erickson, F. (1987). Transformation and school success: The politics of educational achievement. *Anthropology & Education Quarterly, 18,* 335–356.

Ewing, K. P. & Hoyler, M. (2008). Being Muslim and American: South Asian Muslim youth and the war on terror. In K. P. Ewing (Ed.), *Being and belonging: Muslims in the United States since 9/11* (pp. 80–103). New York, NY: Russell Sage

Flores, W. V., & Benmajor, R. (1997). *Latino cultural citizenship: Claiming identity, space and rights.* Boston, MA: Beacon Press

Ghaffar-Kucher, A. (2009). Citizenship and belonging in an age of insecurity: Pakistani immigrant youth in New York City. In F. Vavrus & L. Bartlett (Eds.), *Critical approaches to comparative education: Vertical case studies from Africa, Europe, the Middle East and the Americas* (pp. 163–180). New York, NY: Palgrave.

Gonzalez, N. (2005). Beyond culture: The hybridity of funds of knowledge. In N. Gonzalez, L. C. Moll, & C. Amanti (Eds.), *Funds of knowledge: Theorizing practices in household, communities and classrooms* (pp. 29–46). Mahwah, NJ: Erlbaum.

Haddad, Y. Y., Smith, J. I., & Moore, K. M. (2006). *Muslim women in America.* New York, NY: Oxford University Press

Hall, K. D. (2002). *Lives in translation: Sikh youth as British citizens.* Philadelphia: University of Pennsylvania Press.

Hall, K. D. (2004). The ethnography of imagined communities: The cultural production of Sikh ethnicity in Britain. *The Annals of the American Academy of Political and Social Science, 59,* 108–121.

Heath, S. B. (1983). *Ways with words: Language, life and work in communities and classrooms.* Cambridge, England: Cambridge University Press.

Huntington, S. (1996). *The clash of civilizations and the remaking of the world.* New York, NY: Simon & Schuster.

Justice, B. (2010). *Education and the American empire.* Manuscript in preparation.

Khalidi, R. (2004). *Resurrecting empire: Western footprints and America's perilous path in the Middle East.* Boston, MA: Beacon Press.

Kibria, N. (2007). The 'new Islam' and Bangladeshi youth in Britain and the US. *Ethnic and Racial Studies, 31,* 243–266.

Kymlicka, W. (1995). *Multicultural citizenship: A liberal theory of minority rights.* New York, NY: Oxford University Press.

Levinson, B. A. U. (2005). Citizenship, identity, democracy: Engaging the political in the anthropology of education. *Anthropology & Education Quarterly, 36,* 329–340.

Lewis, B. (2002). *What went wrong? Western impact and Middle Eastern response.* London, England: Oxford University Press.

Lewis, P. (2007). *Young, British and Muslim.* London, England: Continuum International.

Lukose, R. A. (2007). The difference that diaspora makes. Thinking through the anthropology of immigrant education in the United States. *Anthropology & Education Quarterly, 38,* 405–413.

Lukose, R. A. (2009). *Liberalization's children: Gender, youth and consumer citizenship in globalizing India.* Durham, NC: Duke University Press

Maira, S. (2004). Imperial feelings: Youth culture, citizenship and globalization. In M. M. Suárez-Orozco & D. B. Qin-Hilliard (Eds.), *Globalization: Culture and education in the new millennium* (pp. 203–234). Berkeley: University of California Press.

Maira, S. M. (2009). *Missing: Youth, citizenship and empire after 9/11.* Durham, NC: Duke University Press.

Mamdani, M. (2004). *Good Muslim, bad Muslim: America, the Cold War and the roots of terror.* New York, NY: Pantheon.

Marshall, T. H. (1964). *Class, citizenship, and social development: Essays of T. H. Marshall.* Westport, CT: Greenwood.

Mondal, A. A. (2008). *Young British Muslim voices.* Oxford, England: Greenwood World.

Murray, N. (2004). Profiled: Arabs, Muslims and the post-9/11 hunt for the "enemy within." In E. C. Hagopian (Ed.), *Civil rights in peril: The targeting of Arabs and Muslims* (pp. 27–68.). Chicago, IL: Haymarket Books.

Mushaben, J. C. (2008). Gender, hip-hop and pop-Islam: The urban identities of Muslim youth in Germany. *Citizenship Studies, 12,* 507–526.

Ogbu, (1987). Variability in minority school performance: A problem in search of an explanation. *Anthropology & Education Quarterly, 18,* 312–334.

Ong, A. (1996). Cultural citizenship as subject making. *Current Anthropology, 37,* 737–751.

Ong, A. (1999). *Flexible citizenship: The cultural logics of transnationality.* Durham, NC: Duke University Press.

Pollock, M. (2008). From shallow to deep: Toward a thorough cultural analysis of school achievement patterns. *Anthropology and Education Quarterly, 39,* 369–380.

Rosaldo, R. (1994). Cultural citizenship and educational democracy. *Cultural Anthropology, 9,* 402–411.

Said, E. (2001). The clash of ignorance. *The Nation, 273,* 11–13.

Said, E. W. (1978). *Orientalism.* New York, NY: Vintage Books.

Sarroub, L. K. (2001). The sojourner experience of Yemeni American high school students: An ethnographic portrait. *Harvard Educational Review, 71,* 390–412.

Sarroub, L. K. (2005). *All American Yemeni girls: Being Muslim in public schools.* Philadelphia: University of Pennsylvania Press

Sarroub, L., Pernicek, T., & Sweeney, T. (2007). "I was bitten by a scorpion": Reading in and out of school in a refugee's life. *Journal of Adolescent & Adult Literacy, 8,* 668–679.

Sirin, S., & Fine, M. (2008). *Muslim American Youth: Understanding hyphenated identities through multiple methods.* New York: New York University Press.

Soysal, Y. N. (1998). Toward a postnational model of membership. In G. Shafir (Ed.), *The citizenship debates: A reader* (pp. 189–217). Minneapolis: University of Minnesota Press.

Suárez-Orozco, M. (2001). Globalization, immigration, and education: The research agenda. *Harvard Educational Review, 71*, 345–365.

Varenne, H., & McDermott, R. (1998). *Successful failure: The school America builds.* Boulder, CO: Westview Press.

Yuval-Davis, N., Anthias, F., & Kofman, E. (2005). Secure borders and safe haven and the gendered politics of belonging: Beyond social cohesion. *Ethnic and Racial Studies 28*, 513–535.

Zine, J. (2001). Muslim youth in Canadian Schools: Education and the politics of religious identity. *Anthropology & Education Quarterly, 32*, 399–423.

Zine, J. (2004). Anti-Islamophobia education as transformative pedagogy: reflections from the educational front lines. *American Journal of Islamic Social Sciences, 21*, 110–119.

Zine, J. (2006). Unveiled sentiments: Gendered Islamophobia and experiences of veiling among Muslim girls in a Canadian Islamic school. *Equity & Excellence in Education, 39*, 239–252.

Chapter 3

A Cultural Dialectics of Generational Change: The View From Contemporary Africa

JENNIFER COLE
University of Chicago

In recent years, the economic collapse that has plagued Africa has made the conventional markers of adulthood increasingly hard to attain. In many cases, civil conflict, sometimes paired with high rates of HIV/AIDS, exacerbates these difficult economic conditions. Given that young people compose more than 75% of the population (United Nations, 2008), these circumstances mean that vast numbers of people find themselves trapped in a state of extended dependence akin to social childhood. Most young people in Africa desperately want to become adult, but poverty, and the violence that sometimes accompanies it, prevents them from doing so according to existing institutional paths. Such straitened circumstances even force young people to grow up in ways that appear very far from any idealized norm.

Observing the predicaments of African youth, it often seems like the promises that accompanied African independence have been betrayed and that African nations have been ejected from what was once optimistically referred to as "the family of man" (Barthes, 1957; Ferguson, 1999, 2006; Malkki, 1995). After all, social and cultural reproduction is never a perfect process, but some transmission of existing social roles and cultural values is a central part of how any group reproduces itself over time, ensuring some kind of continuity between past and future. As the lynchpin between ascending and descending generations, young people on the cusp of assuming adulthood play a crucial role in this process. To have a society that cannot guarantee the conditions under which young people can achieve even the most basic markers of adulthood is to condemn a large part of the population to social limbo. Certainly African youth, frustrated with their lack of opportunities, feel this to be the case. In Zambia, for example, more and more young people say they are "stuck in the compound." Young people use this expression to evoke the way recent economic changes make it increasingly difficult for men, in particular, to accumulate the

Review of Research in Education
March 2011, Vol. 35, pp. 60–88
DOI: 10.3102/0091732X10391371
© 2011 AERA. http://rre.aera.net

capital that enables them to marry and found households (Hansen, 2005). Likewise, in Niger, one of the poorest countries in the world, economic hardship means that young men can no longer afford to buy the gifts that they are supposed to give to the bride's family in order to marry and form independent households (Masquelier, 2005). Since marriage and the establishment of a new household is the normative sine qua non of adulthood in these societies, the inability to marry according to existing social norms condemns these young men to social dependence. In Madagascar, as my own research has shown, the road to adulthood became so extended and so difficult to traverse over the course of the 1980s that during the political protests that brought down the socialist government in 1991, a major claim was "Our youth *want* to become adult" ("Crise," 1991). And in Guinea Bissau, many young men are terrified of becoming social castrati, stuck in the dependency of youth with no hope of gaining the power and authority that comes with adulthood (Vigh, 2006a). Some African youth even refer to themselves as a "lost generation" (Sharp, 2001).

Young people in Africa are not the only ones to describe their plight in terms of rupture, frustration, and loss. Some scholars similarly privilege ideas of rupture and "lost generations" in their analyses of the lives of young Africans (Cruise O'Brien, 1996; De Boeck & Honwana, 2005; Diouf, 2003; Sharp, 2001). According to this perspective, which echoes the views of African youth, not only have economic and political conditions made it more difficult for young people to achieve social adulthood, but they have also made existing ways of making meaning and organizing social life irrelevant for young Africans. For example, in their introduction to the volume *Makers and Breakers: Children and Youth in Postcolonial Africa*, Filipe De Boeck and Alcinda Honwana claim that for most African youth, neither the references provided by local traditions nor those provided by the modern state that emerged after independence offer youth a meaningful frame for interpreting their lives. Young people in Africa, De Boeck and Honwana (2005) argue,

move in worlds governed by rules, norms, ethics and moralities that seem to have broken quite radically with all kinds of pasts . . . older modes, frames, and aesthetic of living in, and giving order and meaning to, local and more global worlds seem to be replaced, to varying degrees, by alternative forms of sociality and being-in-the-world, opening up a space in which few of the former rules apply. (p. 11).

In his afterword to the volume, historian Mamadou Diouf (2005) further contends that African youth's participation in globalization generates "original creations [that] put forward alternative proposals for the future of the continent and go beyond not only mere physical emigration but also the mental disarticulation and the *erasure of the social imaginaries associated with Africa* [italics added]" (p. 231).

Whether one reads these scholarly analyses as emphasizing the way existing social and economic conditions marginalize youth or whether one sees them as foregrounding young people's role in rejecting existing social conditions, these ways of framing generational change in Africa imply that young people participate in a process of generational transformation characterized primarily by breaking with the past. Both marginalized from, and in turn rejecting of, modes of sociality and belonging associated with their elders, young people appear here as agents of radical cultural and historical discontinuity. They are emblematic of, and participate in, what some have called a crisis of social reproduction—that is to say, a crisis in the way African societies reproduce themselves over time (Comaroff & Comaroff, 2004).

In many respects, such concerns about crisis, lost generations, and failed social reproduction are part of an effort to make sense of and negotiate difficult social and economic conditions in Africa. African youth complain about being sacrificed or marginalized both to voice their frustrations and to claim their rights from political leaders or find the patrons who may give them practical aid. And Africanist scholars write about youth's predicaments out of a desire for social justice and a moral imperative to understand the causes of African hardship and suffering. Nevertheless, characterizing youth's efforts to achieve adulthood entirely in terms of rupture, crisis, and loss inadvertently echoes much older discourses about Africa as a so-called dark continent. Western popular, and sometimes scholarly, representations have all too often portrayed Africa as crisis ridden and in need of moral uplift and outside intervention (Mudimbe, 1988). During the centuries of the slave trade, for example, abolitionists often portrayed Africans as so depraved that they would sell even their own kin into slavery, a view they used to justify, and drum up public support for, Christian missionization in Africa (Comaroff & Comaroff, 1991). Throughout the colonial period, administrators regularly portrayed Africans as childlike, unable to govern themselves properly and therefore in need of European tutelage (Lugard, 1922). And today, popular discourse on HIV/AIDS in Africa further reinforces the idea that African "culture" is to blame for the disease ravaging the country (Dahl, 2009).

Yet if parts of this discourse about youth and crisis are specific to Africa, the concern that young people either cannot or will not grow up, or worries about rebellious or delinquent youth who behave in ways that threaten existing social arrangements or cultural values, is very widespread. Young people whose behavior threatens cherished social values have often been subject to moral panics (S. Cohen, 1972; Herdt, 2009; Rose, 1999). In London and New York, during the late 19th century, for example, moral panic spread about "street Arabs" or street urchins—young children who worked, begged, or stole in the streets. Today, scholars recognize that such panic among the middle classes was closely tied to their notions of child rearing and the increased visibility of working-class children in public space, itself a result of changing patterns of labor and urban housing. Likewise, during the 1980s in the United States, public commentators and experts evinced widespread concern about African American teenage mothers, whose early childbearing diverged from White, middle-class norms (Whiting, Burbank, & Ratner, 1986). These examples may differ in their particulars. Nevertheless, in each case, public concern emerged because of changes taking place in the fabric of everyday life that made certain groups highly visible. At the same time, such public concern often catalyzed social reforms.

In recent years, a discourse of "lost generations" and youth who have difficulty attaining adulthood has emerged in the United States and Europe that is not unlike what is taking place in Africa. In France, in August of 2010, a front-page story in *Le Monde* posed the question starkly: "Youth unemployment? A lost generation?" and ominously hinted at the possible negative social consequences (Barroux, 2010). Likewise, in June of 2010, *The New York Times* published an article announcing what appears to be an important shift in the way people experience their life course. Summarizing the findings of the MacArthur Foundation Research Network on Transitions to Adulthood, the article noted that whereas the baby boomers were once touted as the generation who "didn't want to grow up," it was their successors who were the "real Peter Pans": Americans between the ages of 20 and 34 were "taking longer to finish their educations, establish themselves in careers, marry, have children and become financially independent" (P. Cohen, 2010; see also Arnett, 2004; Jaminon, 1999; Molgat, 1999).

The similarity in the discourses about youth across these different contexts suggests that representations of generational change in terms of rupture and loss beg further scrutiny. After all, although there are similarities in what is taking place across Africa, Western Europe, and the United States, there are also important differences. Not only are these regions integrated into the global political economy differently, but local institutions and meanings also mediate the effects of global economic transformations in locally specific ways. In some African contexts, for example, youth continue to use older categories to interpret and act on their current dilemmas, despite economic and political difficulties (Cole, 2010; Gondola, 2007; Perry, 2009). Based on work in a provincial Ethiopian town, for example, Daniel Mains (2007) shows how local ideas about the social interactions associated with particular occupations powerfully shape young men's experience of unemployment. Young men who have attended school, but cannot find jobs suited to their level of education, refuse to accept lower status work because of the shame it incurs. Local conceptions of proper social relationships and shame are as important to understanding why these men are unemployed and what that means to them as are more general indicators of economic decline. In a related vein, James Straker (2007) argues that despite recent portrayals of African youth as inhabiting a world where "all that is solid melts into air," many young people in the forest region of Guinea continue to care deeply about older categories such as nation, state, development, and local custom.

The apparent persistence and significance of older categories emphasized in these examples suggests that the discourse of rupture and lost generations, so popular among young Africans and scholars alike, may obscure the complex ways in which generational change takes place. After all, if prior studies of moral panics have taught us anything, it is that there is an uneven relationship between how people talk about and understand change, and the way it happens. Although this point may be true for many domains of social life, it is especially true with respect to youth who often serve as a symbolic lightening rod for people's anxieties about the future (Cole & Durham, 2008).

This article considers recent work on youth in Africa, and particularly urban Africa, to argue for a view of generational change as characterized by a conjuncture between young people coming of age, on the one hand, and existing social, cultural, and economic arrangements on the other—what I am calling a dialects of generational change. My conception of generational change draws from, and elaborates on, both Karl Mannheim's (1927/1993) seminal ideas on the nature of generations and the practice theory of Pierre Bourdieu (1977, 1992). In his article "The Problem of Generations," Mannheim argued that each generation coming of age simultaneously adopts, rejects, or transforms the cultural material passed down by prior generations. Meanwhile, Bourdieu drew attention to the dialectical interplay between subjects, or agents, and existing social, economic, and cultural structures. According to Bourdieu's approach, which I take as emblematic of practice theory more generally, material and semiotic structures powerfully constrain individuals. Through their actions and appropriations, however, people also exert a measure of agency, transforming some social and cultural structures and reproducing others (see also Giddens, 1986; Ortner, 2006). These insights imply that generational change does not occur through a sudden rupture as young people come of age. Rather, as young people try to forge their position within the networks that signal adulthood, they draw from the cultural tools at hand. In applying those cultural tools to novel circumstances, however, they transform them in the process. There is a dialectical interplay between young people and the social and cultural structures that they encounter. Over time, this interplay may contribute to the emergence of new cultural forms.

Yet even as this approach foregrounds the uneven relationship between change and continuity that lies at the heart of generational transitions, the heterogeneity among both actors and among the existing social and cultural structures they encounter also plays an important role. Although certain dilemmas epitomize certain historical periods, not all young people who come of age in a given moment have the same resources, nor do they ever face exactly the same predicaments or react in exactly the same manner. Rather, as young people grow up, they move along different pathways, encounter different kinds of social and cultural practices, and have different experiences. The same point about variability applies to the category of "structure," which, as William Sewell (2005) has pointed out, corresponds not to an entire society or a single phenomenon but rather to "spheres or arenas of social practice of varying scope that intertwine, overlap and interpenetrate in space and time" (p. 206). This variation across both social structures and actors further contributes to the friction and social dis-coordination through which new social and cultural forms emerge. In the current moment of increasing global inequality, examining these different paths reveals that some young people may not achieve social adulthood at all.

YOUTH, ELDERS, AND ADULTHOOD IN AFRICA: A THUMBNAIL SKETCH

Neither age nor generation are natural categories: sociocultural processes and power dynamics shape who can claim to be, and accorded the right to be, called a child, youth, or adult (Cole & Durham, 2007, 2008). Studies from many different African societies make these complex cultural dynamics particularly clear by highlighting the disjuncture between chronological age and generational age. In Ghana, Meyer Fortes (1984) described how very young people can be senior to elderly people through the generational logic of lineal descent groups. In other words, one's social position within a kinship group—for example, being positioned as a mother or an aunt in relation to one's child or niece—rather than one's actual chronological age, endowed a person with seniority. In a context where a woman might bear children throughout her fertile years, her first-born son or daughter might begin bearing children before she had stopped. Nonetheless, any child born to the mother would still have generational seniority over a child born to the son or daughter, even though those children might be older in years.

Historically, most African societies have drawn on the social differentiation provided by age, generation, and gender to constitute social hierarchies, with older men usually holding positions of power (Alber, van der Geest, & Whyte, 2008; Carton, 2000; Cole & Durham, 2007; Evans-Pritchard, 1940; Fortes, 1987). Prior to colonization, land was plentiful. Men's ability to amass economic wealth and political authority usually relied on the control of labor (Goody, 1962, 1976; Guyer, 1993; Miers & Kopytoff, 1977). Children constituted wealth because of the labor they provided and the social connections they embodied and enabled. Having material resources and being able to support growing networks of dependents were—and still are—crucial to what it means to be an adult: It is to position oneself favorably within a thickly woven network of patterned social exchanges. To be an adult is to command the loyalty of networks of dependents who can labor on one's behalf; to be a child is to occupy a dependent position. In many languages the same word can be used for slaves as for children, making this association between childhood, dependency, and lack of power explicit.

Since land and people constituted political power, historically, African patriarchs sought to control young people's labor and to ensure the proper reproduction of gendered and generational hierarchies. They often did so by shaping young people's access to social adulthood. One way that older men managed youth's transition to adulthood was by giving or withholding their right to marry and have legitimate children. In many groups, sons could not marry unless their fathers provided them with the livestock needed to pay bridewealth to the girl's family (Comaroff, 1980; Hutchinson, 1996; Lindsay & Miescher, 2003). Fathers similarly controlled their daughter's sexuality, as well as their reproductive and laboring capacities, since these capacities were crucial to the creation and maintenance of local kinship networks (Meillassoux, 1981; Parikh, in press; Thomas, 2003). Women's sexual and reproductive potential was part of what they offered in a politics of alliance; marriage was central to the constitution of valued adulthood much as evidenced in the examples from Niger and Zambia with which I began.

The ties between the ability to marry and reproduce and the assumption of adult status are particularly visible in rituals of initiation, which helped produce proper social persons and reproduced gendered and generational hierarchies (see Kratz, 1994; Ngwane, 2004; Parikh, 2005; A. Richards, 1956/1982; Stambach, 2000; Thomas, 2003). Timed either just before or just after physical puberty, such rituals often involved physical trial such as circumcision, the seclusion of initiates, and the transmission of secret knowledge through songs, dance, and symbolically significant gestures. When she studied the Zambian female initiation ceremony called *chisungu*, for example, Audrey Richards (1956/1982) learned that elder women taught young women the proper ritual actions to take after sex, knowledge that was seen as necessary to make the dangerous potential of sex benign. Likewise, Lynn Thomas (2003) describes how in central Kenya during the 1950s, female initiation, including the practice of female excision, was so pivotal to the creation of proper reproductive women that British bans on the practice sparked local uprisings by the very young women whom the ban sought to protect. Male initiation ceremonies were equally important and more widespread. In South Africa, for example, the local chief appointed the men who were supposed to organize the ceremony. Only after the initiation could young men legitimately marry and have children. By associating the physical growth of young men with the continuation of the chiefship, the ritual made the reproduction of the polity seem like a natural event outside of human control (Ngwane, 2004).

Read together, these diverse examples illustrate how elders sought to control the labor of their juniors. Juniors could ascend toward social adulthood only by gaining access to productive resources controlled by their elders. Young people's reproductive, labor, and caring capacities were a crucial part of how they accrued social value, acquiring, if they were lucky, increasing social power and adult status as they positioned themselves as patrons rather than clients in patterned circuits of exchange. Given that many of these cultural assumptions continue to inform young people's lives today, it is no wonder that adult status is highly valued: In a sense, to be an adult means to be a full human being. As Chabal and Deloz (1999, p. 34) note, "Contrary to the Western view that youth is the most desirable station in life, adolescent Africans hunger after the age which will endow them with an authority currently denied."

THE ASCENT OF THE MODERN DREAM: THE GROWTH OF INSTITUTIONAL SCHOOLING ACROSS AFRICA

The growth of modern national economies, and with them mass education systems, changed intergenerational dynamics in urban areas, making adulthood more closely tied to wage labor and participation in national bureaucracies. But these forces never entirely erased local conceptions of adulthood as emerging from one's position within a hierarchical network of exchange. The arrival and spread of Western-style schooling over the course of the colonial period and until 1970—what most historians of Africa consider the early postindependence period—added a new set of institutions and practices through which youth sought adulthood.

Albeit for different reasons, both missionaries and colonial officials wanted Africans to read and write: missionaries so that people could read the Bible, and colonial administrators so that they could employ Africans in the lower ranks of the colonial administration. During the colonial period, many Africans obtained schooling from Christian missionaries, and later, with the growth of the colonial apparatus, in government-sponsored schools (Stambach, 2000). The basic assumption, shared by Africans and Europeans alike, was that schooling would act as a powerful agent of modernization. A remark made by a school teacher in Madagascar toward the end of the colonial period exemplifies this assumption:

The existence of even one modest school is a revolution, a radically new element in village life. The school introduces practices, rhythms, schedules and calendars hitherto unknown. It also introduces a new hierarchy where the prestige of a diploma replaces the hierarchy based on age. (Ledoux, 1951, p. 197, my translation)

According to this view, attending school lifts young people out of their social context, teaching them new skills and modern ways of being (see Levine, 1965, for a classic account of this process with respect to Ethiopia).

Although colonial regimes often discriminated against Africans, providing Africans less access to education and grooming them to become manual laborers and agriculturalists rather than businessmen and white-collar workers, the coming of independence brought new opportunities (Esoavelomandroso, 1976). During the period of decolonization, departing colonial regimes and newly emergent African states created universities across Africa (Ade Ajayi, Goma, & Johnson, 1996; Kitchen, 1962). The growth of African universities was part and parcel of the expansion of state infrastructure that occurred toward the end of the colonial period and during the early years of independence: Schooling and the expansion of the state were closely linked. The Malagasy saying "schooling makes you human" may be extreme. Nevertheless, the hope that schooling would ensure young adults' accession to modern jobs in state bureaucracies, and the value placed on book learning and the kind of jobs that it enabled, was widely shared.

In the 1960s, 1970s, and even early 1980s, many African states fostered the expansion of formal education as part of their modernizing projects. Statistics taken from three African capitals reveal the growth in levels of education that took place in the mid-20th century. In Senegal's capital city Dakar, the proportion of men who had never gone to school went from 30% for the generation born between 1930 and 1944 to only 15% of those people born between 1955 and 1964. The jump, however, is even more spectacular among women who previously had less access to education: In the span of 20 years, the number of women who had never gone to school dropped from 83% of the population to 32%. Meanwhile, in Yaoundé, the capital city of Cameroon, between 1962 and 1971, 66% of men attended either high school or college, compared with only 38% for the generation studying between 1942 and 1951. The situation was similar in Antananarivo, Madagascar, where more than half of young people going to school between 1964 and 1973 pursued their educations beyond high school (Antoine, Razafindrakoto, & Roubaud, 2001). This expansion of mass schooling during the mid- to late 20th century took place in many different countries across the continent.

Nevertheless, the new practices introduced by schooling, the creation of new economies, and the new kinds of work never entirely erased older notions of what it meant to be an adult or how one was supposed to establish authority through participating in networks of exchange. In Kenya, during the 1960s, many young urbanites had begun attending school, but fathers continued to sue their daughters' impregnators in court for monetary compensation. The fact that many fathers claimed that these young men had "ruined" their investment in school fees for their daughters reveals how older conceptions of intergenerational relations and wealth in children continued to inform more modern practices (Thomas, 2003). Nor did schooling as a route to adulthood entirely transform the meaning of adulthood as being a patron in a far-flung network of reciprocity and exchange. Men who achieved positions of wealth and power were still supposed to help less powerful kin and dependents, though the nature of that help might be paying for a child's school fees, whereas the labor commanded in return might be nothing more than running to the market to buy cigarettes.

Such continuities notwithstanding, the spread of schooling wrought subtle practical and symbolic transformations, producing new age groupings and transforming both the nature of youth as a life phase and what it meant to achieve a successful adulthood. The introduction of schooling took children and young adults out of their families, where they were expected to work and contribute to household production. For those who hoped to achieve success through the routes laid out by first the colonial and later national bureaucracies, youth came to be regarded as a period when young people and their families were supposed to invest in education to guarantee their futures. The completion of Western-style schooling, and with it the acquisition of a skilled job, perhaps even in the state bureaucracy, became the desired path to adulthood. If you asked any young African what it took to succeed in the contemporary world, at least until the 1990s, they were likely to tell you "school." In fact, just after independence, the dream of going to school and eventually getting a skilled job was realistic for many urbanites. As two Ivoirian youth told one anthropologist, "we Ivoirians like to work in an office, seated properly . . . they like to be seated somewhere, writing, and the money comes to them" (Newell, 2005, p. 168). This state of affairs in which formal schooling yielded an office job capable of supporting a family and providing a route to adulthood did not last long.

THE DISINTEGRATION OF THE MODERN DREAM: ECONOMIC STAGNATION, CIVIL STRIFE, AND CONSUMER CULTURE

In the mid-1980s and continuing through the 1990s, African economies entered into a severe and prolonged recession, making the dream of going to school and getting a desirable, "modern" job increasingly difficult to achieve. The practice of having business interests shape state policies and priorities—what many refer to as neoliberalism—has simultaneously exacerbated the disintegration of local infrastructure and brought an influx of global consumer culture and images of Western wealth on an unprecedented scale (Comaroff & Comaroff, 2005; Weiss, 2009). "Africans today," Brad Weiss (2004) notes,

[F]ind themselves seduced by the promise of compelling forms of identification and affiliation, which are facilitated by the presence of commodities and electronically disseminated images only recently available in a great many areas . . . At the same time, the means required to participate in these modes of interconnection seem to be available to an ever-narrowing range of people. (p. 8)

These diverse factors have transformed the conditions under which young people seek adulthood, creating the conjuncture in which contemporary generational change takes place.

Beginning in the 1980s, it became increasingly clear that African states' investment in large infrastructural projects that characterized the early years of independence could not be sustained. When, in the 1980s, the World Bank and the International Monetary Fund (IMF) imposed rigid structural adjustment policies to curb African debt, they forced many countries to enact severe austerity measures in order to qualify for loans. The various governments, many of them socialist, which came to power during the 1970s, began to wither. So too did the services that states had sought to provide as the new economic policy dramatically reduced the value of local currencies and forced states to withdraw from public projects, including housing and schooling (Hansen, 2005; Johnston, Taylor, & Watts, 2002). Although there were by this time many more people who were educated past secondary school than there had been at the time of independence, the disintegration of national economies made state employment difficult to find. Meanwhile, the devaluation of state currencies meant that those young people lucky enough to find jobs were increasingly poorly paid and unable to sustain the adult lifestyle to which they aspired. In Senegal, Cameroon, and Madagascar, household revenues dropped by almost 50% between 1961 and 1991, whereas the gross national product declined by about 38% during roughly the same period (Antoine et al., 2001). Again this pattern is widely shared across the continent.

These factors have prolonged the period between childhood and adulthood, transforming the normative life course. Ideally, in both precolonial contexts and according to the new regime established by formal schooling during the colonial period, adults should have jobs that enable them to support widening networks of dependents. With the long economic recession of the 1980s and 1990s, this position has become increasingly difficult to achieve. To return to the cities of Dakar, Yaoundé, and Antananarivo, statistics show that not only is the age of first entry into the labor market increasing but also that young people marry at an older age (Antoine et al., 2001). In many places, the institution of marriage also appears to be changing, a reflection less of new mores perhaps than of the inability to muster the material resources needed to engage in customary exchanges of bridewealth and pay for the formal ceremonies. In parts of South Africa, and Lesotho, for example, where the unemployment rate for young people is alarmingly high (an estimated 60% to 70% of young people are unemployed), marriage in any form appears to be out of most young people's reach (Boehm, 2006; Hunter, 2010).

Youth play a crucial role in many of the political struggles for scarce resources that are one of the many corrosive effects of sustained economic recession. Throughout the late 1960s and early 1970s, the Soviet Union provided many African socialist countries with financial backing and technical aid. Spurred by the fall of the Soviet Union in 1989, and the failure of governments to fulfill promises of change, youth have been ever more visible in mass political movements. Given the relative paucity of social organizations such as labor unions, political parties, or local nongovernmental organizations, Abbink and van Kessel (2005, p. 14) note, "the part played by youth is remarkable." African student movements are hardly new. In Madagascar, for example, young people participated in anticolonial movements prior to independence. They were also active in the revolution of 1972, which installed the socialist government (Covell, 1987; see also Burgess, 1999, and Donham, 1999, for similar examples from Ethiopia and Tanzania, respectively). However, the establishment of democracies in many African countries, which have popularized the idea that anyone old enough to vote has a voice regardless of age or social stature, has made youth political movements far more visible than in the past.

Even as young people try to improve their circumstances, adults continue to recruit youth into *their* projects: The labor and services that young people provide continue to be an important resource for adults. Many regimes, including those in Kenya, Cameroon, Malawi, Madagascar, and Zimbabwe, have created youth wings of the ruling party. In some cases, these groups recruit young people to intimidate opposition parties, for example, by tearing down their campaign posters after dark or physically threatening members of the opposition party (Konings, 2005). This type of political action has also devolved into criminal violence. In other cases, young people have been recruited as child soldiers in conflicts taking place across the continent (recall that according to the United Nation's definition, a child is someone younger than 18 years). Today, of an estimated 19 conflicts that took place in Africa in the past 10 years, 11 were known to have employed child soldiers (Coalition to Stop the Use of Child Soldiers, 2008). Over the course of the past 20 years, young people have fought in conflicts in Ethiopia, Angola, Mozambique, Uganda, Guinea Bissau, Somalia, The Democratic Republic of Congo, Zimbabwe, and, perhaps most notoriously, Liberia and Sierra Leone. In many cases, rebel soldiers abduct children from their families and forcibly incorporate them into armies. There, older soldiers break down their existing moral assumptions about how to behave in order to turn them into soldiers who are willing to kill. As one 13-year-old Ugandan recounted, "After four months of training they put me to the test. They put a person before me and ordered me to shoot him. I shot him. After the test they considered me good and they gave me a gun" (cited in Honwana, 2005, p. 38). Young people wield guns, man checkpoints, work in mines, and serve as spies. Their labor is crucial to the continuation of such wars.

Yet paradoxically, the poverty and civil strife that afflict many regions of Africa coexist with an influx of Western commodities and images of Western wealth, giving young people new aspirations and new ways to imagine themselves in relation to one another. The influx of youth cultural products into Africa is part and parcel of the growth of capitalist markets in Western Europe and the United States. Although in the United States the teenager as consumer/market segment has been a part of the American cultural landscape since the 1950s, today attention devoted to youth market segments is more visible still, with younger categories of people, such as "tweens," joining the ever-expanding youth market (Frank, 1997). Youth-centered cultural productions ranging from music and concerts to fashion and software games and electronic gadgets pervade contemporary Euro-American life. Social networking tools, such as Facebook, Twitter, and MySpace, further contribute to the creation of new ways of imagining oneself and connecting with others. Such practices have found an enthusiastic reception in many parts of Africa.

The dissemination of metropolitan popular culture in Africa is not particularly new. Numerous commentators have observed that urbanites in various parts of Africa have avidly consumed American movie Westerns and Hindi melodramas since at least the 1950s (Fair, 2009; Larkin, 1997; Powdermaker, 1962). It was in the context of colonial, and later neocolonial, schooling that a nascent consumer youth culture emerged, though on a restricted scale and with the characteristic colonial dynamic of drawing models from metropolitan centers such as England or France. So too, during the 1960s, ideas about youth fashion quickly spread across the continent, with African students taking their fashion cues from their Western peers. Cultural struggles and debates about the propriety of the miniskirt were common on African campuses, with male politicians, in particular, arguing that they represented a corrupting Western influence (Hansen, 2004; Raison-Jourde, 1997).

Nevertheless, the liberalization of African markets, and the proliferation of television networks and Internet access in African cities, has intensified Africans' awareness of global consumer products and images of the Western world. Elite, educated Africans may have long been aware of the standards of living that Europeans and Americans enjoyed, but they did not have images of Western wealth as easily accessible or as immediate as they are when reruns of *Friends* are viewed on TV. In the past 15 years, Africa has seen a striking rise in consumption of global consumer culture, marked by the media's expanded influence and commodities that come from many parts of the world. In Tanzania, as in many other parts of Africa, American rappers such as Tupac are wildly popular among young men (Stambach, 2000; Weiss, 2009). Top 40 performers as Celine Dion and the Backstreet Boys have large followings among young urban Malagasy, who also watch music videos to gain ideas about the latest fashions (Cole, 2004). In Niger and Kenya, American movies and Mexican soap operas have huge followings. Young people watch such shows, learning about romance and new ways to forge intimate relations along the way (Masquelier, 2009; Spronk, 2009). Meanwhile, young men watch Jean-Claude Van Damme and Sylvester Stallone action movies to learn how to fight (P. Richards, 1995). Cell phones are now considered so de rigueur in most African cities that the man who does not have one will be the butt of people's jokes, and certainly unworthy of any ambitious woman's attention. The African continent may be home to some of the poorest countries in the world, but even there consumerism is rampant.

NEGOTIATING THE CURRENT CONJUNCTURE: A CULTURAL DIALECTICS OF GENERATIONAL CHANGE

Faced with the failure of schooling and other institutional mechanisms to provide them with the resources and skills needed to achieve adulthood, many young Africans seek other ways to achieve these goals. To do so, they turn to some very old ideas about gender, personhood, and the value of young people's bodily capacities as well as the new communication technologies, commodities, and practices brought by recent economic liberalization. As they engage these tools to negotiate their predicaments and seek adulthood, they reconfigure both the meaning of the tools and the nature of adulthood at the same time. Examining the different ways that young people seek adulthood reveals the interplay of old and new practices, the shared conundrums, and the social heterogeneity that lie at the heart of generational change.

It is tempting to characterize the agency that young people exhibit as they carve new paths to adulthood in terms of an opposition between individuals and the social structures that constrain them. Such an interpretation appears especially fitting given that this conception of agency implicitly draws from much older, romantic Western ideas that cast youth as a phase in the life course, which is primarily about identity formation: the young person as hero of his or her own narrative (Durham, 2008). This oppositional model is, in fact, the conception of the relation between subjects and existing social structures that underpins both Bourdieu's (1977, 1992) and Mannheim's (1927/1993) theories that I sketched out above. It also lies behind much recent writing on youth and youth culture (Amit-Talai & Wulff, 1995; Bucholtz, 2002). But such a conception of agency does not map well onto the notion of people achieving adulthood through embedding themselves ever more deeply within networks of exchange that are prominent in many parts of Africa (Durham, 2008). When we start to look closely at how young people in Africa seek adulthood, we see how young people actively allow themselves to become recruited into particular kinds of subject positions that are either closely tied to the circulation of global commodities or to the reproduction of hierarchical patron–client networks. In neither case does resistance seem to apply. Rather, youth seek adulthood by subjecting themselves ever more intensively to the networks and social relations that provide economic and social opportunities. Theirs is not a story of standing outside existing structures of power: It is a story of trying to get inside them.

Converting Youth Cultural Products Into Social Capital:
Bengistes, Sapeurs, and *Jeunes*

Perhaps one of the most striking ways that young urbanites try to achieve adult status is by taking the commodities, practices, symbols, and technologies that in Euro-American contexts are usually seen as part of a present-oriented, ephemeral youth culture and converting them into the social capital that creates adult status. The drastic inequality between Western Europe, the United States, and Africa makes such a conversion possible because the commodities and styles associated with Western youth culture have a status in urban Africa that they do not at home: They signify a highly valued modernity. As a result, youth seize the material and semiotic aspects of youth culture as a valued social currency that they try to trade "upward" in order to establish themselves as patrons who can dispense goods within a larger social network. Whereas many studies of youth depict them in relation to their nation, their peers, or global youth culture (Maira & Soep, 2005), the examples I analyze here suggest that those units of analysis are both too large and too small. Young African urbanites seek to insert themselves into transnational networks of kin, on the one hand, bypassing failing states in the process. Or they try to insert themselves into patron–client relations, on the other. Global youth culture plays an important role insofar as it provides some of the tools that youth draw on in their quest for adulthood, but the idea of a "subculture" does not really capture the fluid, fragmentary, and sometimes transnational, kinship networks through which these young people circulate. Taken out of their original context, the ephemeral elements of Western youth culture become African tools for reaching longer-term, perhaps even "traditional," goals, creating a hybrid of old and new in the process.

The subtle ways in which young people use consumption practices to accrue the social power that confers adulthood is particularly visible in recent work on youth in Côte d' Ivoire. In his study of youth in Treichville, a poor neighborhood in Abidjan, Côte d'Ivoire, Sasha Newell (2005) describes the "bluff"—the performance of an image of success that implies that one has more resources than one actually does—and the "bengist" or person who has been to Europe. Newell further shows how young men make use of these practices to achieve adult status. Most young men in the neighborhood live off petty crime and the illegal buying and selling of goods referred to locally as *bizness*. Those men who command the commodities associated with Europe, or who have been to Europe, seen as the apex of valued modernity, enjoy enormous social status.

Limited opportunities in Côte d'Ivoire mean that all young men—educated and uneducated alike—dream of going to Europe: They want to come back and perform a new valued status for their friends (see also Jua, 2003). The trip is difficult, costly, and dangerous. Young men must rely on their kin and friends, as well as criminal networks that stretch between Côte d'Ivoire and France, to gain entry. When they get there, they often engage in work that is not that different from what they previously did at home: They work as dependents in the French informal economy, "working in underground African bars and restaurants, selling black-market goods smuggled from other European countries . . . hawking drugs, prostitution" (Newell, 2005, p. 180). Nevertheless, because the Euro is of more value than the Ivoirian CFA, *bengistes* can save enough money to travel home. When they do, they engage in a competitive potlatch, distributing the goods they have brought with them. They also reenter the informal neighborhood networks that they had only recently left behind.

The *bengiste*, however, returns to the local social world of Treichville on new— one might even say more adult—terms. Although the relative economic stability of Côte d'Ivoire during the 1970s and 1980s enabled members of the middle class to attain a European-inspired model of a nuclear family, including a salaried father as the head of a household, the model of the adult man as a patron who could dispense goods within a larger network of dependents nevertheless remained. Denot's (1990) observation that

He who is affluent is called grandfrère or tonton [big brother or uncle], even by people who are older. The latter pay allegiance to the individual with the most material wealth, delegating their power in exchange for his protection, which manifests itself concretely in gifts (Denot, 1990, p. 42, cited in Newell, 2005, p. 180)

exemplifies the way age status emerges from one's position in relations of exchange. Newell (2005) concludes that *bengistes* who return and occupy the position of patron ascend the social hierarchy; in the terms I am using here, they rise up the age hierarchy as well. They may not have that much more money than when they began, but they have more social status and influence. And in an economy where it is often who one knows that makes the difference between "starvation and success," such social influence, gained from mastering and trading on what might otherwise be seen as the ephemeral signs of youth culture, has tangible economic and social effects. It is one way to attain a position of dominance within the networks of exchange that signal adult social status.

Studies of *les sapeurs*, young, unmarried, and often underemployed young men from the Congo who invest vast sums of money in the competitive consumption of European-brand clothing, offer yet another example of the role played by elements of contemporary youth culture and commodities in young Africans' quest for adulthood. Taken from the French slang *se saper* or to dress oneself, *sapeurs* are young men who form social clubs that perform in the urban nightclubs of Brazzaville. It is a practice that draws on some enduring local ideas about the relationship between clothes and social status and that began long before the current phase of state retrenchment and economic liberalization, though it has intensified in the current context (Friedman, 1994; Gandoulou, 1989; Gondola, 1999). These groups form ranked hierarchies that compete with each for social status, based in part on what kind of European clothing the members wear. In Brazzaville, young men begin by accumulating "non-griffe" or ordinary ready-to-wear. Over time, however, young men increasingly seek to travel to Paris, the apex of the hierarchy. There, in a kind of liminal phase, they work desperately to collect the money that will let them buy clothes of the highest mark, or "haute gamme."

Eventually, the *sapeur*, much like the *bengiste*, returns to Brazzaville to display his newfound social status. Friedman (1994), drawing on Gandoulou (1989), depicts "the descent" (and note here how Europe is figured as "higher" so that one "descends" from Europe to Africa) when a sapeur returns from Paris:

[t]his process is the making of a great man or *un grand*, a true Parisian . . . it is accomplished by means of the ritual gala, an expensive affair . . . and the night of the trial is a veritable potlatch of elegance. (p. 179)

Similar to the bengists, the social prestige acquired through these competitive clothing practices can, on occasion, allow young *sapeurs* to acquire dependents, creating their social seniority in turn. "A great man attracts dependents, who are eager to work as his slaves in order to gain access, however temporary, to his prestige goods, the lower orders of which are quite sufficient to build up junior hierarchies" (Friedman, 1994, p. 180). When the accumulation of fashion labels creates patron/client networks, it may also generate still more income. In this respect, the practice of *le sape* offers one way that young men can move from the childlike position of client to the socially adult position of patron.

Young women similarly use aspects of metropolitan consumer culture, in tandem with their sexuality, to reposition themselves within the networks of exchange that confer adulthood. In urban Madagascar, for example, some young urbanites referred to by the French term for youth, *jeunes*, invest enormous amounts of time, effort, and money in acquiring the cultural competence and material trappings associated with Western youth culture (Cole, 2004, 2008, 2010). They pride themselves on owning the latest cell phone or all-terrain bicycle, knowing the latest European and American music and fashions, and being able to use the Internet. Although many young people do small jobs or get the money they need to participate in this consumer world from kin or wealthier friends, many more find that they get caught up in an ever-increasing spiral of consumer demand that they cannot meet. The fact that young people are keenly aware that schooling does not necessarily lead to adult status and social success makes this world of commodities and consumer pleasures all the more alluring. Moreover, since having the latest foreign commodities signals valued, modern social status, young people often feel that if they fail to acquire these things, others will regard them with disdain.

Although the category *jeunes* encompasses both young men and young women, it is young women's response to their predicament that has become iconic of how young people navigate the current conjuncture. Like the *bengistes* or the *sapeurs*, young women, too, try to accrue the social capital that comes from connections with Europe. Because family reunification, especially marriage, enables legal migration to Europe, women do not need to migrate illegally like young men. Rather they can try to find European, particularly French, men to marry. To do so, young women mobilize their networks of social relations, their knowledge of contemporary culture and technologies such as the Internet, and the self-presentational savoir faire that is essential to what it means to be *jeunes* (Cole, 2010). By seeking French men they can marry and with whom they can found families, contemporary Malagasy women engage in a practice that has deep roots on the east coast and has long been integral to the formation of local social hierarchies (Bois, 1997; Cole, 2010). But the new influx of consumer goods and practices, and new communication technologies that have accompanied economic liberalization, also play an important role.

When young women succeed in establishing long-term relationships with Europeans, the results are striking: The relationship literally catapults them into a valued adult status. One young woman, Franceline, who had only completed part of high school, gave a particularly vivid sense of the advantages in class terms:

When you marry a European, you give birth to the descendents of Europeans and the child's future will be much better, because they'll have access to foreign nationality and they can go to a good school in Europe and don't have to just stay here in Madagascar. They have much more of a chance to go far in life! Our children have gone to continue their studies in France. The younger one is still at the Lycee Français here in town. There are very few Malagasy who study at that school! That is already one huge advantage. And another advantage is that people respect you. (Cole, 2008, p. 115)

Still others described how they built houses, gave money to their parents, or were able to finance their younger siblings' education. Successful women manage to translate the short-term performance of a desired status through consumption, an important part of what it means to be a *jeune*, into long-term relationships that may provide opportunities to their children and their natal families: the ideal embodiment of a coveted female adulthood.

Congolese *sapeurs* and Ivoirian *bengists* both use consumer products of various kinds to perform an African version of imagined European success. They use migration as a strategy to fuel the continued production of that illusion. The illusion of success, in turn, creates the possibility of situating actors in a more advantageous, adult position within the networks through which resources flow. Female *jeunes* hope to achieve a similar kind of alchemy by successfully performing a modern, Westernized version of African youth and ensnaring European men. In each case, young people try to parlay their knowledge of Euro-American consumer culture combined with performative virtuosity and physical youth into the ability to command resources in a network of reciprocity and exchange.

Other Paths: Child Soldiers and Transactional Sex

In many ways, the *bengistes*, *sapeurs*, and *jeunes* are the lucky ones; they carve a precarious path, to be sure, but they do so through a skillful form of self-production as they manipulate aspects of contemporary popular consumer culture to create a niche for themselves. By contrast, young people who live amid political instability and without access to the same networks and resources often find their choices even more constrained. When young people seek adulthood amid dire poverty or civil unrest, they may find that their bodies become one of the primary tools they can use to achieve adulthood. Much as young men used to labor on their fathers' farms or tend their herds on the path toward adulthood, and women's sexual and reproductive potential was an important part of what they brought to kinship economies and systems of exchange, here too, we see the way young people's bodies become a part of how they accrue value. But again, their practices differ from some of the ways that young people's labor and reproductive capacities were recruited into their elders' projects in the past. These young people's practices also diverge from those of the *bengistes*, *jeunes*, and *sapeurs* that I discussed above. Not only do they have access to fewer resources than those young people who manage to forge connections with Europe, but also many fewer of them will obtain adulthood, revealing the social diversity within and the uneven nature of generational change.

In the context of political conflict that has divided many countries in Africa, working for a powerful political patron by participating in a war may offer one route to adulthood, albeit a very dangerous one (Honwana, 2005, 2006; McIntyre, 2005; P. Richards, 1995, 1996; Utas, 2003; Vigh, 2006a, 2006b). During the war in Sierra Leone in the early through mid-1990s, for example, rebel groups expanded their ranks by capturing young people from villages and forcing them to work as soldiers, even giving them crack-cocaine to make them fearless in battle. Drawing on long-term practices of conducting initiation rituals in the bush, rebel groups also saw their bush camps as an "alternative to the failed schooling found in the wider society." As one Revolutionary United Front (RUF) soldier put it, "a society has already collapsed when majority [sic] of its youth can wake up in the morning with nothing to look up for" (cited in P. Richards, 1996, p. 28). P. Richards (1995, p. 29) notes that for many young people who were seized in the diamond districts of Sierra Leone, functional schooling had broken down long before the RUF arrived. In seeking to recruit young people, the RUF drew from certain local practices associated with adolescent initiation and combined them with the symbolic elements of formal schooling.

Captives report being schooled in RUF camps, using fragments and scraps of revolutionary texts for books, and receiving a good basic training in the arts of bush warfare. Many captive children . . . exult in their new found skills, and the chance . . . to show what they can do. Stood down boy-soldiers in Liberia have spoken longingly of their guns not as weapons of destruction but as being the first piece of modern kit they have ever known how to handle. (P. Richards, 1995, p. 29)

Although formal schooling had disintegrated prior to the arrival of the RUF, it still had enormous symbolic importance. The RUF drew on aspects of what they knew about formal education—including revolutionary training—to bolster their legitimacy by offering an unconventional kind of "schooling." For many young people who did not have other options, participating in such schooling could lead toward adulthood if they managed successfully to use their skills to forge relations with patrons, eventually amassing the resources to establish networks of their own.

Writing about youth living in Guinea Bissau, Henrik Vigh (2006a) describes how the disintegration of state schooling and poverty means that most young people can no longer rely on their family networks to amass the resources that enable adulthood: Their bodies become the only tool they have left. Consequently, many young men try to become involved in patrimonial politics, seeking to establish themselves as the clients of more powerful patrons who may give them financial support in return. For the most part, a shortage of resources means that patrons profit from their clients, without much hope of reciprocity. However, in some cases, political factionalism offers these dependent youth the opportunity for social advancement. In times of conflict, the older patrons who usually exploit young men may start to provide opportunities for social advancement as "young men go from being secondary to their existence to being prime agents in defense of their access to resources and positions of redistribution" (Vigh, 2006b, p. 118).

Young men's efforts to deploy their bodily potential in war so as to move from the social death of extended youth to a coveted adulthood are evident in many young men's narratives. When asked why he joined an informal militia, one young man remarked,

Because I understood that the government forces would be able to send me my day of change . . . After the war, if all went well and we won, there was something . . . If you had a good level you would get money to put in your pocket, or they would find you work. (cited in Vigh, 2006a, p. 53)

Another young man made the association between fighting in the war and adulthood even more explicit when on hearing about the start of the war, he remarked, "we sat there and we thought like, we are clever, we can go and join the troops. We can quickly become someone big, quickly" (Vigh, 2006a). Note the use of "big" here, which signifies both a desirable social status and age. In these narratives, young people weigh the possibility of social death against the chance that they can gain adulthood through war. Only a very few will succeed. Many more will die in the process.

Not unlike young men's efforts to accrue social status by fighting in wars, young women with few resources often use their bodies to forge relationships with men who will give them the food, money, or other kinds of support that they need to live. Although in the past, the exchange of resources and labor would have taken place within the normative confines of marriage, today's economic circumstances, as we have seen, make marriage increasingly precarious and difficult to achieve. Lacking other opportunities, young women build relationships with more than one partner to make ends meet (Cornwall, 2002; Dugger, 2010; Hunter, 2010; Newell, 2009; Nyamnjoh, 2005; Poulin, 2007). In some cases, young women form relationships with older, wealthier African men to acquire consumer goods. Others who come from poorer neighborhoods use the goods and money they obtain from sex simply for survival (Hunter, 2002). In my own work, I found that while middle-class urban Malagasy focus on the young women who marry Europeans, many other women use their bodies to gain resources in a far more precarious manner. For example, one young woman I knew had a baby out of wedlock. Her family could not help her. And so to piece together enough money to survive, she began forging relationships with several men at the same time while also engaging in more short-term kinds of prostitution. In another case, a young woman had been married to a trucker and lived off his earnings. As a married woman, she had achieved local ideals of adult-hood. However, when her husband died, she went back to live with her in-laws for a year, as local custom dictated. Eventually, her in-laws tired of her dependence and told her to get a job. Unable to find one, she turned to prostitution, a job that offered little money and made it more likely that she would fall sick with a sexually transmit-ted disease or even HIV/AIDS. Although she had fleetingly acquired a precarious adulthood through her marriage to the trucker, she lost that status when he died. Young women who find themselves compelled to rely on their bodies in ways that do not help regenerate existing kinship networks may age physically, but socially they may remain forever young.

CONCLUSION

Young Africans born in the 1980s and early 1990s enjoy neither the same educa-tion nor the same employment opportunities as their fathers and mothers. In the past 20 years economic inequality between Africa and the rest of the world has increased. In the context of the new economic conditions created in part by eco-nomic liberalization, national education systems can no longer provide young people with the adult social status that they desire. Global consumer capitalism and new technologies spread their influences ever deeper into African daily life, while compe-tition for scarce resources and civil conflict fuels social disruption and war. These circumstances compel young people to forge new paths to the future and new ways to be adult.

When young urbanites relied on education as a path toward an adult future, that process was structured by state-sponsored institutions. In theory, getting a degree corresponded to a certain skill set that enabled a person to fulfill the requirements for a given job. Through remuneration for labor came financial independence and the ability to sustain a family. The skills that one acquired while young were not dependent on the physical qualities of youthfulness per se; reading and writing, or even working as a mechanic, are skills that can be carried into physical old age.

Today, young people's use of youth cultural products and practices or their bodies to achieve adulthood differs from this scenario in several respects. In particular, there is no institutional boundary between youth culture and the kinds of performative self-styling in which young people engage. Nor is there any institutional regulation of how young people can use their bodies. To be sure, participation in youth cultural practices such as those exhibited by the *bengistes* or the *jeunes* requires money or social connections—one must be able to consume and to have access to the technologies that provide actors with particular types of knowledge. And it is also true that not all bodies generate the same value: Everybody has a body, of course, but some bodies—the particularly strong child soldier, the beautiful young woman—are more likely to generate possibilities than others. But for the most part, the skills required to participate and to advance socially are not institutionally created or sanctioned; they emerge from the interactions of daily life.

Yet if these paths appear more widely accessible in the sense that state institutions do not determine who has access and who does not, they are also far more tied to fleeting qualities such as physical age *and* existing social networks. To put it another way, successful participation in these practices is time sensitive, differently so according to gender. Female *jeunes*, for example, have to be physically young to successfully perform that role and perhaps translate it into more long-term connections. The same is likely true for *bengistes* and *sapeurs*, though to a lesser degree. Arguably, there is a window of opportunity when one can use these techniques to socially advance, but as bodies age, that window passes. At the same time, these strategies illustrate the renewed importance of existing kin networks and social relations in providing access to resources in the absence of public institutions. Read together, they suggest that the way young people use their bodies—and the way those bodies get used and integrated into local social networks, the kind of wealth they can generate, and the possibility that their capacities will produce valued social adulthood—is not only more individualized and more risky, but also more socially stratified, than in the recent past. My observation that the ability to capitalize on individual bodily capacities and familial networks plays an increasingly important role in the attainment of adulthood resonates with recent depictions of neoliberalism as characterized by a shift in who bears responsibility for risk from governments and institutions to individuals.

Although the foregoing characterization is surely important, only by examining the Ivoirian *bengistes* or the Malagasy *jeunes*, the Guinean child soldiers, or the young women engaged in transactional sex, and drawing these disparate examples into a common frame, can we elucidate the uneven cultural dialectics through which these new patterns emerge. Young people respond to the dilemma of how to become adult by using the tools at hand. The way they do so defies any simple dichotomy between continuity and change: It is far more complicated and partial than a language of rupture and novelty allows. For the *jeunes*, *bengistes*, and *sapeurs*, the way they forge adulthood at first looks new, and in fact has become iconic of the current moment of neoliberal capitalism with its privileged use of commodities in the production of social value. Yet when we look more closely, we can see that the tools these young people use are no simple reflection of neoliberal capital. Instead, they are a complex, even curious, blend of old and new, such as when the Congolese *sapeurs* draw on the performative power of clothes, an idea that has long-standing resonance in the region, but now the clothes have to come from Paris and be from high status, designer brands. Or when the Malagasy *jeunes* use long-standing ideas about how women can deploy their sexual and reproductive capacities to build valued relationships, but inflect them with a sexy playfulness inspired by contemporary consumer youth culture. Similarly, by using their bodies to accrue value, child soldiers and women who engage in transactional sex also draw on very old ideas about young people's physical and reproductive capacities. But, again, the way young people use their productive and sexual labor differs considerably from how such labor was appropriated into kinship networks and local polities in the past.

Not only are the tools themselves an uneven blend of old and new, but the effects of using them also differ under contemporary historical conditions. To take the example of the Malagasy *jeunes,* which I know best, it was a very different matter for a young woman from the east coast of Madagascar to marry a European man during the 19th century, before colonization, than it is now. During that time, foreign men, rather than Malagasy women, were vulnerable because the local queen would not allow them to own land. By marrying local women, foreign men gained access to important capital, such as land and slaves. Today, however, rapid flows of information and goods embodying global inequalities between African and Europe, and restrictive immigration policies in Europe, mean that what a young woman brings to the marriage is very different. Rather than land and slaves, she offers herself. Although a woman may still use her relationship with a European man to gain access to resources and to place herself in the networks of exchange that signal adulthood, the nature of those relationships, and the balance of power within them, are very different in this new context.

The variations between the *bengistes*, the *sapeurs*, the *jeunes* on the one hand, and the child soldiers and women who engage in short-term transactional sex on the other, further reveal the heterogeneous, uneven nature of generational change. This heterogeneity and unevenness operates in a double sense. Although I have separated the *bengistes, sapeurs,* and *jeunes,* and the child soldiers and the women who engage in transactional sex for the purpose of analysis, in reality they exist simultaneously. The young men who tried to make it as *bengistes* prior to the civil conflict in Cote d'Ivoire may have had to seek work as soldiers after civil conflict irrupted. The young Malagasy women who find themselves forced into short-term transactional sex may, if they are very lucky, find opportunities to marry Europeans. When considered synchronically, the fact that these different paths and the people who trod them intermingle, and that there are conflicting ways to move forward, creates the contradictions and tensions that allow new practices to emerge.

When considered diachronically in terms of which paths are more likely to lead toward adulthood over time, however, we start to see that one of the major characteristics of generational change—at least as it is taking place in the current moment—is that not everyone who comes of age is going to achieve social adulthood. In this respect, generational change is central to the reproduction and transformation of social inequalities, here recast in the most basic terms of who counts as a social adult and who remains doomed to eternal childhood. Some young people successfully navigate the current conjuncture, creating new ways of being and new visions of adulthood. Others may not make the transition at all.

The practices I have sketched here may seem exotic, but there is evidence that the insights into generational change that emerge from contemporary Africa may be more relevant to life in the United States than one might at first think. Take for example, an article published in *The New York Times* titled "American Dream is Elusive for New Generation," in which the author reported that more young people are finding it difficult to attain the jobs to which they aspire (Uchitelle, 2010). As a result, the article noted, some are choosing to move back home, earning them the dubious moniker of the "boomerang" generation. The contrast between the young man featured in that article, who had just turned down a job that paid US$40,000 because it did not meet his aspirations, and the opportunities available to young people in much of Africa dramatically reemphasize the socioeconomic disparities between the two places. But the fact that an American youth was living at home, when for many years one of the key markers of adulthood was establishing an independent household, also hints at some important similarities with Africa. The recent socioeconomic downturn suggests that already young Americans negotiate a difficult economic conjuncture. As the casualization of labor increases and the social safety net further erodes, it seems likely that American young people too will be further forced to rely on their bodies and bear the risks associated with daily life in new ways.

To grasp the nitty-gritty of how these processes play out and how they come to be anchored in local contexts and contribute to emergent patterns of social change, it will be necessary to move beyond the rhetoric of crisis. The starkness of the African case dramatically foregrounds the conjuncture between young people coming of age and the social, economic, and cultural terrain they encounter. It reveals how young people pragmatically combine old and new practices and cultural meanings as they seek new paths to the future. And it foregrounds the important cleavages generated as some young people accede to social adulthood and others fail. Although there remain important differences between Africa and the United States, the concepts that emerge from examining the Africanist literature may prove useful to educators and scholars who want to think seriously about the relationship between young people, their precarious search for adulthood, and contemporary patterns of social change.

ACKNOWLEDGMENTS

This article benefited from the insightful comments of Judith Farquhar, Ritty Lukose, Daniel Mains, Shawn Smith, and Stanton Wortham.

REFERENCES

Abbink, J., & van Kessel, I. (Eds.). (2005). *Vanguards or vandals: Youth, politics and conflict in Africa.* Leiden, Netherlands: Brill

Ade Ajayi, J. F., Goma, L. K. H., & Johnson, G. A. (1996). *The African experience with higher education.* Oxford, England: James Currey.

Alber, E., van der Geest, S., & Whyte, S. R. (2008). *Generations in Africa.* Berlin, Germany: Lit Verlag Dr. W. Hopf.

Amit-Talai, V., & Wulff, H. (Eds.). (1995). *Youth culture: A cross-cultural perspective.* London, England: Routledge.

Antoine, P., Razafindrakoto, M., & Roubaud, F. (2001). Contraints de rester jeunes? Évolution de l'insertion dans les trois capitals africaines: Dakar, Yaoundé et Antananarivo [Constraints of staying young? The evolution of social integration within three African capital cities: Dakar, Yaoundé, Antananarivo]. *Autrepart, 18,* 17–36.

Arnett, G. (2004). *Emerging adulthood: The winding road from the late teens through the twenties.* Oxford, England: Oxford University Press.

Barroux, R. (2010, August 24). Contre Enquête: Chômage des jeunes: Une génération perdue? [Counter Investigation: Youth unemployment: A lost generation?] *Le Monde.*

Barthes, R. (1957). *Mythologies.* Paris, France: Editions du Seuil.

Boehm, C. (2006). Industrial labour, marital strategy and changing livelihood: Trajectories among young women in Lesotho. In C. Christiansen, M. Utas, & E. Henrik (Eds.), *Navigating youth, generating adulthood: Social becoming in an African context* (pp. 153–182). Uppsala, Sweden: Nordiska Afrikainstitutet.

Bois, D. (1997). Tamatave, la cité des femmes [Tamatave, city of women]. *CLIO, 6,* 61–86.

Bourdieu, P. (1977). *Outline of a theory of practice.* Cambridge, England: Cambridge University Press.

Bourdieu, P. (1992). *The logic of practice* (R. Nice, Trans.). Stanford, CA: Stanford University Press.

Bucholtz, M. (2002). Youth and cultural practice. *Annual Reviews in Anthropology, 31,* 525–552.

Burgess, T. (1999). Remembering youth: Generation in revolutionary Zanzibar. *Africa Today, 46,* 29–50.

Carton, B. (2000). *Blood from your children: The colonial origins of generational conflict in South Africa.* Charlottesville: University Press of Virginia.

Chabal, P., & Deloz, J. (1999). *Africa works: Disorder as political instrument.* Bloomington: Indiana University Press.

Coalition to Stop the Use of Child Soldiers. (2008). *Child soldiers Global report 2008.* Retrieved from http://www.childsoldiersglobalreport.org/regions/africa

Cohen, P. (2010, June 11). Long road to adulthood is growing even longer. *The New York Times.* Retrieved from http://www.nytimes.com/2010/06/13/us/13generations.html

Cohen, S. (1972). *Folk devils and moral panics: The creation of the mods and rockers.* London, England: MacGibbon & Kee.

Cole, J. (2004). Fresh contact in Tamatave, Madagascar: Sex, money and intergenerational transformation. *American Ethnologist, 31,* 571–586.

Cole, J. (2008). Fashioning distinction: Youth and consumerism in urban Madagascar. In J. Cole & D. Durham (Eds.), *Figuring the future: Youth and temporality in a global era* (pp. 99–124). Santa Fe, NM: School of American Research Press.

Cole, J. (2010). *Sex and salvation: Imagining the future in Madagascar.* Chicago, IL: University of Chicago Press.

Cole, J., & Durham, D. (Eds.). (2007). *Generations and globalization: Youth, age, and family in the new world economy.* Bloomington: Indiana University Press.

Cole, J., & Durham, D. (Eds.). (2008). *Figuring the future: Youth and temporality in a global era.* Santa Fe, NM: School of American Research Press.

Comaroff, J. L. (Ed.). (1980). *The meaning of marriage payments.* New York, NY: Academic Press.

Comaroff, J., & Comaroff, J. (1991). *Of revelation and revolution: Christianity, colonialism and consciousness in South Africa.* Chicago, IL: University of Chicago Press.

Comaroff, J., & Comaroff, J. (2004). Notes on Afromodernity and the neo world order: An afterword. In B. Weiss (Ed.), *Producing African futures: Ritual and reproduction in a neoliberal age* (pp. 529–548). Leiden, Netherlands: Brill.

Comaroff, J., & Comaroff, J. (2005). Reflections on youth: From the past to the postcolony. In A. Honwana & F. De Boeck (Eds.), *Makers and breakers: Children and youth in postcolonial Africa* (pp. 19–29). Oxford, England: James Currey.

Cornwall, A. (2002). Spending power: Love, money and the reconfiguration of gender relations in Ado-Obo, southwestern Nigeria. *American Ethnologist, 29,* 963–980.

Covell, M. (1987). *Madagascar: Politics, economics, society.* London, England: Francis Pinter.

Crise. (1991, January 7). *Tribune de Madagascar.*

Cruise O'Brien, D. B. (1996). A lost generation: Youth, identity and state decay in West Africa. In R. Werbner & T. Ranger (Eds.), *Postcolonial identities in Africa* (pp. 55–74). London, England: Zed Books.

Dahl, B. (2009). The failures of culture: Christianity, kinship, and moral discourses about orphans during Botswana's AIDS crisis. *Africa Today, 56,* 23–43.

De Boeck, F., & Honwana, A. (2005). Children and youth in Africa: Agency, identity and place. In A. Honwana & F. De Boeck (Eds.), *Makers and breakers: Children and youth in postcolonial Africa* (pp. 1–18). Oxford, England: James Currey.

Denot, C. (1990). *Petits metiers et jeunes descolarisés à Abidjan* [Small jobs and unschooled youth in Abidjan]. Sociologie, Université de Paris I, Panthéon-Sorbonne IEDES.

Diouf, M. (2003). Engaging postcolonial cultures: African youth and public space. *African Studies Review, 46,* 1–12.

Diouf, M. (2005). Afterword. In A. Honwana & F. De Boeck (Eds.), *Makers and breakers: Children and youth in postcolonial Africa* (pp. 229–234). Oxford, England: James Currey.

Donham, D. (1999). *Marxist modern: An ethnographic history of the Ethiopian revolution.* Berkeley: University of California Press.

Dugger, C. W. (2010, July 20). Studies offer 2 paths to cut H.I.V. rate for African women. *The New York Times,* p. A1.

Durham, D. (2008). Apathy and agency: The romance of agency and youth in Botswana. In J. Cole & D. Durham (Eds.), *Figuring the future: Globalization and the temporalities of children and youth* (pp. 151–178). Santa Fe, NM: School of American Research Press.

Esoavelomandroso, F. (1976). Langue, culture et colonisation à Madagascar: malgache et français dans l'enseignement officiel (1916-1940) [Language, culture and colonization in Madagascar: Malagasy and French in government schools (1916-1940)]. *Omaly sy anio, 3-4,* 105–165.

Evans-Pritchard. E. (1940). *The Nuer.* Oxford, England: Clarendon.

Fair, L. (2009). Making love in the Indian Ocean: Hindi films, Zanzibari audiences, and the construction of romance in the 1950s and 1960s. In J. Cole & L. M. Thomas (Eds.), *Love in Africa* (pp. 58–82). Chicago, IL: University of Chicago Press.

Ferguson, J. (1999). *Expectations of modernity: Myths and meanings of urban life on the Zambian copperbelt.* Berkeley: University of California Press.

Ferguson, J. (2006). *Global shadows: Africa in the neoliberal world order.* Durham, NC: Duke University Press.

Fortes, M. (1984). Age, generation and social structure. In D. I. Kertzer & J. Keith (Eds.), *Age and anthropological theory* (pp. 99–122). Ithaca, NY: Cornell University Press.

Fortes, M. (1987). *Religion, morality and the person: Essays on Tallensi religion.* Cambridge, England: Cambridge University Press

Frank, T. (1997). *The conquest of cool: Business culture, counterculture, and the rise of hip consumerism.* Chicago, IL: University of Chicago Press.

Friedman, J. (1994). The political economy of elegance: An African cult of beauty. In J. Friedman (Ed.), *Consumption and identity* (pp. 167–187). Chur, Switzerland: Harwood Academic.

Gandoulou, J. (1989). *Dandies à Bacongo: le culte de l'élégance congolaise contemporaine* [The dandies of Bacongo: The cult of elegance in the contemporary Congo]. Paris, France: L'Harmattan.

Giddens, A. (1986). *Constitution of society: Outline of the theory of structuration.* Berkeley: University of California Press.

Gondola, D. (1999). Dream and drama: The search for elegance among Congolese youth. *African Studies Review, 42,* 23–48.

Gondola, D. (2007). Review of Alcinda Honwana and Filip De Boeck (Eds.), Makers and breakers: Children and youth in postcolonial Africa. Trenton, N.J. Africa World Press. *African Studies Review, April,* 188–190.

Goody, J. R. (1962). *Death, property and the ancestors: A study of the mortuary customs of the LoDagaa of West Africa.* London, England: Tavistock.

Goody, J. R. (1976). *Production and reproduction: A comparative study of the domestic domain.* Cambridge, England: Cambridge University Press.

Guyer, J. (1993). Wealth in people and self realization in Equatorial Africa. *Man, 28,* 243–265.

Hansen, K. (2004). Dressing dangerously: Miniskirts, gender relations and sexuality in Zambia. In J. Allman (Ed.), *Fashioning Africa: Power and the politics of dress* (pp. 166–185). Bloomington: Indiana University Press.

Hansen, K. (2005). Getting stuck in the compound: Some odds against social adulthood in Lusaka, Zambia. *Africa Today 51,* 3–16.

Herdt, G. (Ed.). (2009). *Moral panics, sex panics: Fear and the fight over sexual rights.* New York, NY: New York University Press.

Honwana, A. (2005). Innocent and guilty: Child soldiers as interstitial and tactical agents. In A. Honwana & F. De Boeck (Eds.), *Makers and breakers: Children and youth in postcolonial Africa* (pp. 31–52). Oxford, England: James Currey.

Honwana, A. (2006). *Child soldiers in Africa.* Philadelphia, PA: University of Pennsylvania Press.

Hunter, M. (2002). The materiality of everyday sex: Thinking beyond prostitution. *African Studies, 61,* 99–120.

Hunter, M. (2010). *Love in the time of AIDS: Inequality, gender and rights in South Africa.* Bloomington: Indiana University Press.

Hutchinson, S. (1996). *Nuer dilemmas: Coping with money, war and the state.* Berkeley: University of California Press.

Jaminon, C. (1999). Dispositifs d'insertion professionelle et integration en Belgique, le paradoxe? [The arrangement of professional insertion and integration in Belgium: A paradox?]. In M. Gauthier, J.-F. Guillaume (Ed.), *Définir la jeunesse? D'un bout à l'autre du monde. Culture et Société* [Defining youth? From across the world. Series Culture & Society] (pp. 95–206). Montreal, Québec, Canada: Les éditions de l'IQRC.

Johnston, R. J., Taylor, P., & Watts, M. (Eds.). (2002). *Geographies of global change: Remapping the world in the late twentieth century* (2nd ed.). Oxford, England: Basil Blackwell.

Jua, N. (2003). Differential responses to disappearing transitional pathways: Redefining possibility among Cameroonian youths. *African Studies Review, 46,* 13–36.

Kitchen, H. (1962). *The educated African: A country-by-country survey of educational development in Africa.* New York, NY: Frederick A. Praeger.

Konings, P. (2005). Anglophone university students and Anglophone nationalist struggles in Cameroon. In J. Abbink & I. van Kessel (Eds.), *Vanguards or vandals: Youth, politics and conflict in Africa* (pp. 161–188). Leiden, Netherlands: Brill.

Kratz, C. A. (1994). *Affecting performance: Meaning, movement and experiences in Okiek women's initiation.* Washington, DC: Smithsonian Institution Press.

Larkin, B. (1997). Indian films and Nigerian lovers: The creation of parallel modernities. *Africa, 67,* 406–440.

Ledoux, M. A. (1951). *La jeunesse malgache* [Malagasy youth]. *Cahiers Charles de Foucauld* (Numéro spécial sur Madagascar, 1 trimestre).

Levine, D. (1965). *Wax and gold: Tradition and innovation in Ethiopian culture.* Chicago, IL: University of Chicago Press.

Lindsay, L., & Miescher, S. (Eds.). (2003). *Men and masculinities in modern Africa.* Portsmouth, NH: Heinemann.

Lugard, F. D. (1922). Methods of ruling native races. In F. D. Lugard (Ed.), *The dual mandate in British tropical Africa* (pp. 193–213). London, England: Blackwood.

Mains, D. (2007). Neoliberal times: Progress, boredom and shame among young men in urban Ethiopia. *American Ethnologist, 34,* 659–667.

Maira, S., & Soep, E. (2005). *Youthscapes: The popular, the national, the global.* Philadelphia: University of Pennsylvania Press.

Malkki, L. (1995). *Purity and exile: Violence, memory and national cosmology among Hutu refugees in Tanzania.* Chicago, IL: University of Chicago Press.

Mannheim, K. (1993). The problem of generations. In K. H. Wolff (Ed.), *From Karl Mannheim* (pp. 351–398). New Brunswick, NJ: Transaction. (Original work published 1927)

Masquelier, A. (2005). The scorpion's sting: Youth, marriage and the struggle for social maturity in Niger. *Journal of the Royal Anthropological Institute, 11,* 59–83.

Masquelier, A. (2009). Lessons from Rubi: Love, poverty and the educational value of televised drama in Niger. In J. Cole & L. Thomas (Eds.), *Love in Africa* (pp. 205–228). Chicago, IL: University of Chicago Press.

McIntyre, A. (2005). Children as conflict stakeholders: Toward a new discourse on young combatants. In J. Abbink & I. van Kessel (Eds.), *Vanguards and vandals: Youth, politics and conflict in Africa* (pp. 228–242). Leiden, Netherlands: Brill.

Meillassoux, C. (1981). *Maidens, meal and money: Capitalism and the domestic economy.* Cambridge, England: Cambridge University Press.

Miers, S., & Kopytoff, I. (1977). *Slavery in Africa: Historical and anthropological perspectives.* Madison: University of Wisconsin Press.

Molgat, M. (1999). De l'intégration à l'insertion . . . Quelle direction pour la sociologie de jeunesse au Québec? [From integration to insertion? Whither the sociology of youth in Quebec?] In M. Gauthier, & J. F. Guillaume (Eds.), *Définir la jeunesse? D'un bout à l'autre du monde. Culture et Société* [Defining youth? From across the world. Series Culture & Society] (pp. 77–93). Montreal, Québec, Canada: Les éditions de L'IQRC.

Mudimbe, V. (1988). *The invention of Africa.* Bloomington: Indiana University Press.

Newell, S. (2005). Migratory modernity and the cosmology of consumption in Côte d'Ivoire. In L. Trager (Ed.), *Migration and economy: Global and local dynamics* (pp. 163–190). Walnut Creek, CA: AltaMira Press.

Newell, S. (2009). Godrap girls, Draou boys, and the sexual economy of the bluff in Abidjan, Côte d'Ivoire. *Ethnos, 74,* 379–402.

Ngwane, Z. (2004). Real men reawaken their father's homesteads, the educated leave them in ruins: The politics of domestic reproduction in post-apartheid rural South Africa. In

B. Weiss (Ed.), *Producing African futures: Ritual and reproduction in a Neoliberal age* (pp. 167–192). Leiden, Netherlands: Brill.

Nyamnjoh, F. (2005). Fishing in troubled waters: Disquettes and Thiofs in Dakar. *Africa, 27*, 295–324.

Ortner, S. (2006). *Anthropology and social theory: Culture, power and the acting subject.* Durham, NC: Duke University Press.

Parikh, S. (2005). From auntie to disco: The bifurcation of risk and pleasure in sex education in Uganda. In S. L. Pigg & V. Adams (Eds.), *Sex in development: Science, sexuality and morality in global perspective* (pp. 122–158). Durham, NC: Duke University Press.

Parikh, S. (in press). *Regulating romance.* Nashville, TN: Vanderbilt University Press.

Perry, D. (2009). Fathers, sons and the state: Discipline and punishment in a Wolof Hinterland. *Cultural Anthropology, 24*, 33–67.

Poulin, M. J. (2007). Sex, money and premarital partnerships in southern Malawi. *Social Science & Medicine, 65*, 2383–2393.

Powdermaker, H. (1962). *Copper town: Changing Africa: The human situation on the Rhodesian Copperbelt.* New York, NY: Harper & Row.

Raison-Jourde, F. (1997). L'ici et l'ailleurs dans la construction identitaire: Le look des jeunes urbains à Madagascar [Here and there in the construction of identity: The look of young urbanites in Madagascar.] In J. Létourneau (Ed.), *Le lieu identitaire de la jeunesse d'aujourd'hui. Études de cas* [Spaces of identity among youth today: Case studies] (pp. 27–45). Paris, France: L'Harmattan.

Richards, A. (1982). *Chisungu: A girl's initiation ceremony among the Bemba.* London, England: Tavistock. (Original work published 1956)

Richards, P. (1995). Rebellion in Liberia and Sierra Leone: A crisis of youth? In O. Furley (Ed.), *Conflict in Africa* (pp. 134–170). London, England: I. B. Tauris.

Richards, P. (1996). *Fighting for the rain forest: War, youth and resources in Sierra Leone.* Oxford, England: James Currey.

Rose, S. O. (1999). Cultural analysis and moral discourses: Episodes, continuities and transformations. In V. E. Bonnell & L. Hunt (Eds.), *Beyond the cultural turn: New directions in the study of society and culture* (pp. 217–240). Berkeley: University of California Press.

Sewell, W. H., Jr. (2005). *Logics of history: Social theory and social transformation.* Chicago, IL: University of Chicago Press.

Sharp, L. (2001). *The sacrificed generation: Youth, history and the colonized mind.* Berkeley: University of California Press.

Spronk, R. (2009). Media and the therapeutic ethos of romantic love in middle-class Nairobi. In J. Cole & L. Thomas (Eds.), *Love in Africa* (pp. 181–203). Chicago, IL: University of Chicago Press.

Stambach, A. (2000). *Lessons from Mount Kilimanjaro: Schooling, community and gender in East Africa.* London, England: Routledge.

Straker, J. (2007). Youth, globalization, and millennial reflection in a Guinean forest town. *Journal of Modern African Studies, 42*, 299–319.

Thomas, L. M. (2003). *Politics of the womb: Women, reproduction and the state in Kenya.* Berkeley: University of California Press.

Uchitelle, L. (2010, July 6). American dream is elusive for new generation. *The New York Times.* Retrieved from http://www.nytimes.com/2010/07/07/business/economy/07generation.html?_r=1

United Nations. (2008). *World population prospects.* New York, NY: Author.

Utas, M. (2003). *Sweet battlefields: Youth and the Liberian civil war.* Unpublished doctoral dissertation, Uppsala University, Uppsala, Sweden.

Vigh, H. (2006a). Social death and violent life chances. In C. Christiansen, M. Utas, & H. E. Vigh (Eds.), *Navigating youth, generating adulthood: Social becoming in an African context* (pp. 31–60). Uppsala, Sweden: Nordiska Africainstitutet.

Vigh, H. (2006b). *Navigating terrains of war: Youth and soldiering in Guinea Bissau.* London, England: Berghan Books.

Weiss, B. (2004). Contentious futures past and present. In B. Weiss (Ed.), *Producing African futures: Ritual and reproduction in a neoliberal age* (pp. 1–20). Leiden, Netherlands: Brill.

Weiss, B. (2009). *Street dreams and hip hop barbershops: Global fantasy in urban Tanzania.* Bloomington: Indiana University Press.

Whiting, J. W. M., Burbank, V. K., & Ratner. M. S. (1986). The duration of maidenhood across cultures. In J. B. Lancaster & B. A. Hamburg (Eds.), *School age pregnancy and parenthood: Biosocial dimensions* (pp. 273–302). New York, NY: Aldine de Gruyer.

Chapter 4

Youth, Technology, and DIY: Developing Participatory Competencies in Creative Media Production

YASMIN B. KAFAI
University of Pennsylvania

KYLIE A. PEPPLER
Indiana University

Traditionally, educational researchers and practitioners have focused on the development of youths' critical understanding of new media as one key aspect of digital literacy (Buckingham, 2003; Gilster, 1997). Today, youth not only consume media when browsing the Internet and sharing information on social networking sites, but they also produce content when contributing to blogs, designing animations, graphics, and video productions (Ito et al., 2009). This new media landscape suggests an extension of what critical participation means in new media literacy, extending the metaphor of "reading the world to read the word" (Freire & Macedo, 1987) to include writing new media texts in a digital era. In an effort to map out the participatory competencies needed in this new media landscape, Jenkins, Clinton, Purushotma, Robinson, and Weigel (2006) included creative designs, ethical considerations, and technical skills to capture youths' expressive and intellectual engagement with new media. More recently, these efforts to produce your own media have also been associated with the growing do-it-yourself, or DIY, movement (Guzzetti, Elliott, & Welsch, 2010; Lankshear & Knobel, 2010), involving arts, crafts, and new technologies (Eisenberg & Buechley, 2008; Spencer, 2005). Educators should be especially interested in DIY communities given the amount of time youth voluntarily spend in intense learning as they tackle highly technical practices, including film editing, robotics, and writing novels among a host of other activities across various DIY networks.

Review of Research in Education
March 2011, Vol. 35, pp. 89–119
DOI: 10.3102/0091732X10383211
© 2011 AERA. http://rre.aera.net

One aspect of creative media production that has received little attention, if any, in these broad examinations of youths' DIY engagements with digital media concerns the use of programming as a production tool and the focus of a learning community (Peppler & Kafai, 2007). When youth program games, animations, interactive art, or digital stories, they not only create program code or texts in the traditional sense but also engage in creating, repurposing, and remixing multimodal representations (Jewitt, 2008). Although such activities may seem more pertinent to the more exclusive domain of the so-called computer geeks, they also engage designers in many of the same critical, creative, and ethical considerations that new media literacy researchers consider relevant practices in more common forms of creative media production. It can be no accident that researchers have attached the label of "geeking out" to these types of productions, noting that only a relatively small subset of youth participate in these more complex forms of engagement with media (Ito et al., 2009).

Until now, the discussions about the value of creative media production in education have taken place in two distinct communities—one in the community of new media literacies researchers and the other in the community of computer literacy educators—and these initially appear as incommensurate domains. However, research on recent developments in informal learning communities (Kafai, Peppler, & Chapman, 2009), the design of media-rich programming tools (Resnick et al., 2009), and social networks in DIY (Benkler, 2006) suggest that researchers studying new media literacies can connect with those studying computer literacy and vice versa. As we will argue, this connection is long overdue because understanding the participatory competencies of youth draws from both fields. The work highlighted in this review is a first effort to map out the overlapping territory and common issues that educators face as they attempt to bridge these domains in service of offering youth a more robust education. As they do so, opportunities arise to address the participation gap as well as issues of transparency and ethics while youth engage in creative media production (Jenkins et al., 2006). These issues encompass the need to ensure that every young person has access to the skills and experience needed to become a full participant in the 21st century, can articulate his or her understanding of how media shapes perception, and is knowledgeable of emerging ethical standards that shape his or her practices as a media maker and participant in online communities.

In this review chapter, we draw on findings from several recent studies, particularly the work on the new media-rich programming environment, Scratch, to demonstrate that contemporary youth communities move fluidly across these blurry boundaries to engage in both new media literacies and computer literacies in their DIY activities. We first provide a historical overview of the shifting perspectives of two distinct but related fields—new media literacies and computer literacy—before introducing how a focus on creative media production allows us to consider different participatory competencies in DIY under one umbrella. One goal with this chapter is to unravel some of the historical developments that might have promoted these distinct trajectories of new media literacies studies and computer education in and outside of schools. Special attention is given to digital practices of remixing, reworking, and repurposing popular media among disadvantaged youth. We conclude with considerations of equity, access, and participation in after-school settings and possible implications for K–12 education.

PERSPECTIVES ON CREATIVE MEDIA PRODUCTION

Before we examine creative media production in more detail, it helps to have a clear understanding of where we position our review in the midst of an, at times, confusing array of meanings around literacy studies and new literacy studies. Gee's (2010) recent essay is helpful in clarifying the distinctions and developments in the field. He points out that new literacies studies are about "studying new types of literacy beyond print literacy, especially digital literacies and literacy practices embedded in popular culture" (p. 31). The focus of our review on new media literacies emphasizes media literacy and how people give and get meaning to and from multimodal texts and become more reflective about it. In the following section, we explain how creative media production has come to play a growing role in new media literacies as an approach to engage people reflectively and critically with media.

In addition, we want to include a perspective on creative media production that traditionally has been left outside of the realm of media literacy, namely, efforts that focus on computer literacy and, more specifically, on programming. Although there is no clear academic home for computer literacy, which sometimes is also referred to as ICT curriculum, IT, or technology education (National Research Council, 1999), we refer to it in this review as computer education. Current efforts to define computer literacy or fluency see it as "the ability to reformulate knowledge, to express oneself creatively and appropriately, and to produce and generate information (rather than simply to comprehend it)" (National Research Council, 1999, p. viii). Others, like diSessa (2001), have connected these abilities to programming in disciplinary fields such as the sciences. Some might argue that programming is too technical and narrow a practice to be associated with new media literacies, and most certainly this sentiment has been prevalent among media researchers who clearly separate these efforts (see Hayes & Games, 2008). In our review, we contend that this exclusion is due more to old-standing academic boundaries between media studies and computer education rather than to a lack of conceptual convergence. Our review outlines how creative media production from either perspective converges as a venue to engage people reflectively and critically with media in the context of DIY productions.

Creative Media Production in New Media Education

Critical analysis of media texts has historically dominated the media education curriculum. From the early 1980s through the mid-1990s, theorists rarely explored the role that creative media production played in media literacy, and either held disdain for or purposefully condemned students' creative media production (e.g., Alvarado, Gutch, & Wollen, 1987; Ferguson, 1981; Masterman, 1980, 1985), despite trying to promote the scholarly nature of pop culture genres such as television. Buckingham (2003) states that this was due in part to the pervasive belief that student work lacked scholarly merit but was also attributed to the "'technicist' emphasis on production skills that was apparent in some of the new vocationally oriented media courses" (p. 124) emerging in the mid-1980s. Work produced in these media courses was seen by many as reproductions of dominant media ideologies, not end products of creative expression. A critical understanding of new media, therefore, became the central focus in this era, rigorously subordinating the "expressive" or "creative" potential of production.

This perspective has been overturned over the past two decades. For the most part, today's educators and researchers (e.g., Buckingham, 2003; Buckingham & Sefton-Green, 1994; Peppler & Kafai, 2007) are now arguing that production is a key component in new media education. However, media educators still seem to emphasize critical analyses over production (i.e., reading over writing practices). Initially, this could be explained by the lack of portability and dependability of older media (such as celluloid film, older cameras), but today's technologies have made more complex forms of production accessible to today's classroom environment.

Given this history, it should come as no surprise that there is only a small amount of academic research on youths' creative media production. Current studies have predominantly focused on youths' experiences producing media on one particular platform (i.e., television, radio, newspaper, etc.), and mostly within the classroom context (see, e.g., Booth, 1999; Loveless, 1999). We have referred to this as the "platform model to teaching and learning about production" (Peppler & Kafai, 2007). Although there are many merits to this approach, this perspective overlooks the importance of preparing youth for the new "Convergence Culture" (Jenkins, 2006). The convergence culture is the merger of previously distinct cultural forms and practices. In sum, this is a shift away from the previous platform model where students were taught explicitly about music, film, or television, and toward considering how these platforms are increasingly overlapping and enabling new functionality. As media converges, functionalities and tools previously only available to professionals have become accessible to the general public. TV, movies, and videos can now be produced cheaply with consumer tools and are distributed via the Internet, circumventing the limited broadcast medium. Perhaps most widely known is a type of fan art where DIY movie producers take advantage of the modifiable sets, characters, and three-dimensional (3D) rendering engines made available in commercial video games to create their own movies, called "machinima," and share these works with thousands of like-minded online fans via the Internet (Lowood, 2006). In this way, the DIY community conducts what is referred to as "transmedia navigation," crossing from one media type to another (i.e., games to film; Jenkins, 2006).

Today, the notion of a "participatory culture" expands our initial understanding of the older sender/receiver model predominantly emphasized in media literacy to include the "skills needed for participation and collaboration — speaking as well as listening, writing as well as reading, producing as well as consuming" (Jenkins, 2006, p. 2). Although the convergence culture has been widely acknowledged by media educators (see, e.g., Buckingham, 2003), there has been no formal realization of what this might mean for creative media production, more specifically on how we can talk in a coherent fashion about the various dimensions that are involved in creating new media artifacts. Although there are many types of new media artifacts that fall into this category—blogs, graphics, games, movies—we have chosen in this chapter to focus on a particular type of new media production—computer programs created in Scratch that allow the creation of various genres. We contend that our findings about media practices extend to other tools and genres as well.

Creative Media Production in Computer Education

In computer education, there has always been an emphasis on creative media production in the form of programming code. Although Logo programming was prominent in elementary schools in the 1980s, it literally disappeared from the school curriculum by the 1990s. (For a more detailed account of this rather contentious story of Logo in American schools and elsewhere, a chapter in Noss & Hoyles, 1996, provides the necessary background; see also Kafai, 2006.) It suffices to say that schools turned away from programming as the availability of multimedia packages and the Internet seemingly negated the need for learning programming, a turn that was further supported by the difficulty of finding teachers who were knowledgeable about computers and computer science.

On the tail end of this development, a new pedagogical approach to programming appeared, called instructional software design (Harel, 1991), in which students designed full-fledged multimedia software applications rather than just creating program code. This work was inspired by the idea of "design for learning" that had just gained traction in the larger education community (Perkins, 1986). This work drew particularly on Simon's *The Sciences of the Artificial* (1981) and Schön's *The Reflective Practitioner* (1983). Taken together, this work emphasized that professional practice in design disciplines are contexts that promote open-ended forms of problem solving and situate learners in the application of academic content in the design of meaningful, authentic applications. Harel's (1991) seminal study illustrated how students as designers of instructional mathematics software became invested in a long-term, meaningful, and integrated project for learning programming and academic content (Palumbo, 1990). Other work in that vein has employed students as designers of a media artifact—be it an instructional science simulation (Kafai & Ching, 2001), historical presentation (Erickson & Lehrer, 1998), mechanical device (Penner, Lehrer, & Schaeuble, 1998), or engineering design (Hmelo, Holton, & Kolodner, 2000).

One of the first studies that directly combined media education with computer education investigated game design in schools with a class of 16 fourth graders who created computer games that taught younger students in their school about fractions (Kafai, 1995). Over a period of 6 months, student designers set out to write and execute their own games using Logo programming and designed packaging and advertisements for their games. The designers met about once a month with their intended players—a group of younger students who provided them with feedback on various aspects of their games (see also Kafai, 1998). Most of the discussion about this work has focused on the observed gender differences in the game's narrative, components, aesthetics, and mechanics (Kafai, 1996a, 1998)—most likely because these findings aligned well with then-popular discourse about gender differences in interest and performance in technology and games (e.g., Cassell & Jenkins, 1998). Much less attention was given to the equally important aspects of design practices, such as collaborative planning, and public critiques, that contributed to students' understanding (Kafai, 1996b). These design practices resonate more closely with recent research on toolkits such as Gamestar Mechanic (Salen, 2007) or MissionMaker (Buckingham & Burn, 2007) that engage students in making or modifying games.

Convergence in Approaches to Creative Media Production

What we can learn from the overviews of research on new media literacies and computer literacy is that, at the outset, these two fields seem to have little in common, and indeed, their developments over time took very different trajectories. Our review of creative media production was framed by Sefton-Green's (2006) observation that the dialogue in media education and education research more broadly shifted in the 1990s from one that focused on effects of media on the audience to one that emphasized the empowerment of participants. This paradigm shift might explain why creative media production was rare in early media education in the 1980s and 1990s, when educators mostly focused on critical understandings of text or Internet searches. During the same time period, programming as a form of creative media production moved from near-universal presence to extinct practice as navigating multimedia applications, searching the Internet and preparing PowerPoint presentations became the hallmark of digital literacy in school settings (diSessa, 2001). In addition, other researchers have referred to the "geek mythology" associated with programming culture (Margolis & Fisher, 2002; Schofield, 1995), making it appear an exclusive "clubhouse" that is not accessible to girls and minorities. It could well be that this whiff of exclusivity and the relatively high status of computer programming also hampered media educators' interest in considering these tools accessible for youth. Others also noted that the accessibility and costs of production equipment kept these tools out of reach for most youth (Sefton-Green, 2006). In the case of programming, however, it was not finances but rather the lack of experience and cultural perceptions that limited access and participation in creative media production.

In today's participatory culture (Jenkins et al., 2006), media production and creative writing are far more commonplace. In Ito et al.'s (2009) view, the majority of youth are already contributors and producers of media when looking at social networking and blogging sites—an observation that is also bolstered by numerous other national surveys (Lenhart & Madden, 2007; Rideout, Foehr, & Roberts, 2010). These scholars distinguish between friendship-driven activities, such as sharing information on social networking sites, and interest-driven activities, such as contributing to blogs, designing animations, graphics, and video productions. Particularly, the interest-driven social activities characteristic of "messing around" and the interest-driven activities characteristic of "geeking out" (Ito et al., 2009) lead into a territory formerly occupied near exclusively by the techie crowd. These types of creative media production are now being attributed to a growing DIY movement (Guzzetti et al., 2010; Lankshear & Knobel, 2010; Spencer, 2005) that brings together the previously disparate communities of computer education and new media educators in unexpected ways. Although initially the term *DIY* referred to home improvement projects, it has now become part of the Internet space, most prominently on YouTube where more than 500,000 videos have been tagged as providing DIY information. One aspect that is of interest to us concerns self-made media artifacts by youth and how this relates to new media literacies. The ubiquity of webcams and the ease of doing simple, and even more complex, video production, plus the YouTube distribution model have evidently led to a lot of sustained video production ("channels") and, with time, these seem to grow more technically sophisticated, or at least more experimental. Our next section will review the different ways in which DIY is taken on in school and community spaces.

CREATIVE MEDIA PRODUCTION AS DIY

In conceptualizing creative media production as DIY, we are drawing on a small but growing body of work that has studied youth practices in schools, afterschool clubs, and community technology centers (Guzzetti et al., 2010; Lankshear & Knobel, 2010; Spencer, 2005). Although the term *DIY* has only recently become officially attached to these efforts, they all share the spirit of self-produced and originated projects. For instance, one of the few mentions of DIY in and around schools appeared in a recent ethnographic study of youth and new technologies (Ito et al., 2009) that focused on a high school lunchtime computer club as a breeding ground for DIY youth culture and DIY capitalism. In the former case, a young artist represented a DIY approach to creative media production in the creation of his own Manga. In the latter, another youth engaged in the economic aspect of DIY entrepreneurial activity by selling ramen and refurbished computers. It is especially prescient that these DIY efforts were supported within the context of an informal, lunchtime computer club, rather than traditional classrooms. Similarly, in a DIY approach to writing and publishing, Black's (2005, 2009) research on fan fiction sites and Guzzetti and Gamboa's (2004) research on youths' use of zines point to ways that youth are enjoying academic styles of writing, publishing, and critiquing in the out-of-school hours, positively developing their identities as writers in the process.

Within the classroom context, researchers have begun to bring in popular DIY forms of writing and publishing. For example, Lankshear and Knobel (2003) have explored youths' blogs as potent forms of "Do-It-Yourself Broadcasting," creating links to academic writing while making connections to potentially broad audiences, informing affinity groups among youth. Other researchers, including Congdon and Blandy (2003), have introduced zines into the classroom to engage youth in both the writing process as well as the participatory culture. In Kahn-Egan's (1998) view, writing can also become a form of DIY activism. In his work titled *Pedagogy of the Pissed*, he showcases the use of punk fanzines and a countercultural zeitgeist in his undergraduate writing courses. Furthermore, Guzzetti et al. (2010) expand these discussions and evangelize DIY media practices as both a type of classroom activity as well as literacy in their own right.

Other approaches have focused on game design activities in which youth use construction kits or programming languages to design their own games or modify existing games. For instance, in Gamestar Mechanic, a player is invited to play, design, and share top-down and side scrolling video games in a highly scaffolded environment. In contrast, in the programming language Scratch, players either modify existing games or design their own using visual programming. Designing video games in Scratch allows players to have greater control over the types of avatars and interactions they have in-game, but the environment is open-ended and thus provides no specific scaffolding to create games. Today, programming or designing games is by far one of the most popular DIY approaches inside and outside of schools (e.g., Hayes & Games, 2008; Peppler & Kafai, 2007) in a surprising alliance of promoting girls' interest and skills in technology (Denner & Campe, 2008; Heeter & Winn, 2008; Pelletier, 2008). A range of different tools such as Alice (Kelleher, 2008) and Scratch (Resnick et al., 2009) have been designed that facilitate the creation of media in 2D (Scratch) and 3D (Alice) for storytelling and game designs, which we will discuss later in more detail. Even media literacy researchers such as Buckingham and Burn (2007) and Salen (2007) are using game design now as an equally valid approach for promoting the new literacies in education. For them, game design combines cultural experiences that vary by age, gender, cross-media knowledge, and appreciation of particular features and genres. Game design encapsulates multiple professional practices, including expertise "in graphic design (visual design, interface design, information architecture), product design (input and output devices), programming, animation, interactive design (human computer interaction), writing, and audio design, as well as experts in content areas specific to a game" (Salen, 2007, p. 318).

Similarly, work in community technology centers such as the Computer Clubhouse (Kafai, Peppler, & Chapman, 2009) provides another context in which youth are engaged in making their own media artifacts. In particular, our work has focused on Scratch as a DIY software production tool because youth can make their own software for games, digital stories, simulations, interactive art, dance videos, or other genres of work. The Scratch community's DIY culture is unique because it uses programming as a means to engage youth in facets of creative media production. Since its introduction in 2008, the online Scratch community has quickly grown to more than a half-million registered users and more than a million uploaded projects (see http://scratch.mit.edu). Scratch differs from other visual programming environments (Guzdial, 2004) by using a familiar building-block command structure (Maloney, Burd, Kafai, Rusk, Silverman, & Resnick, 2004; Resnick, Kafai, & Maeda, 2003), eliminating thorny debugging processes and the risk of syntax errors (see Figure 1). Furthermore, programmed objects can be any imported 2D graphic image, hand-drawn, or downloaded from the Web, to further personalize each project. This makes it particularly amenable to an array of novice programmers wanting to build their own software and engage in the participatory culture.

In previous studies, youth likened Scratch to paper (Peppler, 2010), as the program's flexibility allowed them to create projects in whatever style or genre they wanted, even enabling them to imitate Flash-based media, TV, and video games. This is further evidenced by the vast multitude of project genres represented in the Scratch online community, ranging from digital stories and interactive art to music videos and simulations. For example, one youths' digital story, "CreationStory," alternates between text on colored background and animated sequences featuring moving characters and speech bubbles to depict theories of creation in different cultures (see Figure 2). In another example, a youth used Scratch to create a virtual calculator, one that responded to addition, subtraction, multiplication, and division. In yet another example, one youth programmed a music video, "DanceDressUp," to facilitate user interactivity, where four onscreen dancers in an urban cityscape respond to specific key commands on the keyboard (see Figure 3). Each of these projects has a distinctive visual aesthetic, determined by the programmers' choices of hand-drawn or imported graphical elements. Furthermore, the programmers varied their approaches to user interactivity and interface design to create very different experiences for the player, rendering the Scratch software "invisible" by making each project the unique representation of its creator, regardless of their level of programming ability.

These efforts inside and outside of school are bolstered by an even larger movement in many other DIY communities that use programming as a tool for their productions. There are now communities around sites such as makezine.com or instructables.com where members have posted hundreds of thousands of videos on virtually any topic (Torrey, McDonald, Schilit, & Bly, 2007). In some cases, these communities follow the open source movement and have networks develop around the use of a particular programming language, Processing (Reas, 2006a, 2006b; see also http://processing.org), which is used in the design and media arts community. In other cases, these communities have developed around the use and development of an open-source construction kit, called Arduino, that hobbyists around the world use to design projects, such as their own laser printers. For example, in the Lilypad

FIGURE 1
Screenshot of the Scratch User Interface

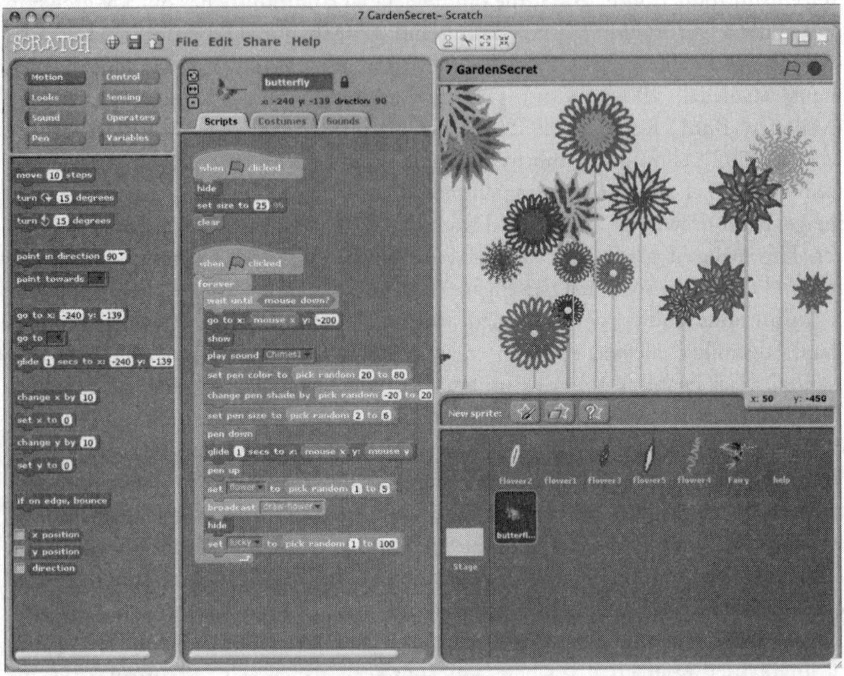

Arduino kit (Buechley & Eisenberg, 2008), textile productions now can include sensors and LED lights to be programmed for informative feedback and artistic purposes. Although these DIY communities have much of the flair of exclusive clubs found among earlier programmers, their growing presence also signals a larger trend.

As Ito et al. (2009) noted in their multisite ethnography, only a small subset of youth engage in these type of "geeking out" or DIY activities. This invariably brings to mind issues of the digital divide that have been described elsewhere in more detail (Warschauer & Matuchniak, 2010). And yet, although access still remains a considerable issue for particular demographic groups (in which minorities are overrepresented), new discussions of a "participation gap" uncover issues that might be more at the heart of the matter. Jenkins et al. (2006) argued that policymakers and educators face three issues as they attempt to bridge the gap between those that contribute and those that do not: the participation gap, the transparency problem, and the ethics challenge. These three issues encompass the need to ensure that every young person has access to the skills and experience needed to become a full participant, can articulate their understanding of how media shapes perception, and is

FIGURE 2
Screenshot From the Scratch Project, CreationStory

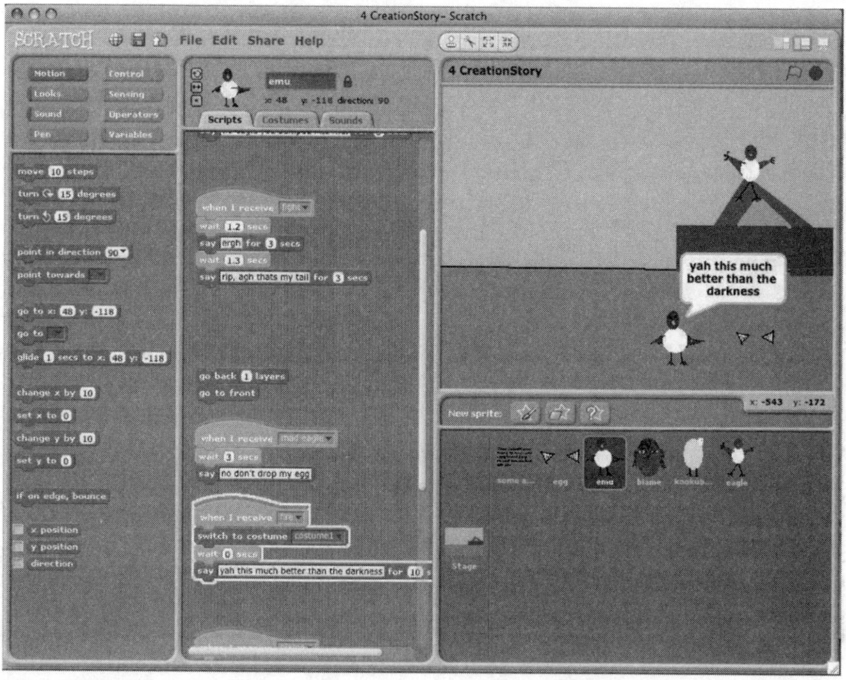

knowledgeable of emerging ethical standards that shape their practices as media makers and participants in online communities. Although Jenkins et al. (2006) view the participation gap as the unequal access to the opportunities, experiences, skills, and knowledge necessary to prepare youth for full participation in a digital culture, we expand on this notion and apply it specifically to DIY, which can be vehicles of change as both critical consumers and designers in an industry that has an increasing importance for schools and society at large.

PARTICIPATORY COMPETENCIES IN CREATIVE MEDIA PRODUCTION

As highlighted above, DIY youth are participating in diverse efforts to make and remix a variety of media. As youth engage in this work, they are not just participating in the DIY movement, but they are also engaged in multiple literacies and learning to authentically participate in a number of communities (Guzzetti et al., 2010; Lankshear & Knobel, 2010; New London Group, 1996). We introduce participatory competencies as a convergence of diverse literacies important to the DIY culture

FIGURE 3
Screenshot From the Scratch Project, DanceDressUp

and draw on our early work in this area (Peppler, 2010) and that of others (Gee, 2010; Jenkins, 2006). We see youths' creative media production as part of a larger DIY effort in which youth engage, and provide a model of observation that expands the palette of previously conceptualized literacies to include a broader spectrum of design activities that are important to youth culture. Particularly, we add the artistic and creative forms that DIY projects take, the critical practices that are often left out of the discussion of youths' DIY efforts, and the ethical considerations in which youth engage. Building on Jenkins et al.'s (2006) work, we argue that these technical, creative, critical, and ethical competencies are needed for full participation in the growing DIY culture (for an overview, see Table 1). In the coming sections, we review prior work in media education, computer education, and arts education with the goal to provide a common language that can help us articulate a set of participatory competencies found in DIY production.

Technical Practices

Analyses of these communities reveal that youths' technical DIY practices often include learning computer education concepts and skills (e.g., sustained reasoning,

TABLE 1
Overview of Technical, Critical, Creative, and Ethical
Practices of Do-It-Yourself Production

Participatory Competencies	Practices	Definitions
Technical practices of production	Coding	Practice of computer programming, particularly the use of loops, conditional statements, parallel execution, object-oriented programming, sequencing, synchronization, time triggering, real-time interaction, Boolean logic, variables, event handling, user-interface design, statements, and numerical representations (Malan, 2007; Maloney, Peppler, Kafai, Resnick, & Rusk, 2008)
	Debugging	Practice of persisting when confronted with technical problems either prior to or during production (National Research Council, 1999)
	Repurposing	Practice of reusing earlier ideas or chunks of materials to build on in a single work or in multiple works (National Research Council, 1999). This is also a common practice particularly in the professional computer programming community
Critical practices of production	Observing and deconstructing media	Careful observation by youth looking more closely than ordinarily at everyday objects (Hetland, Winner, Veenema, & Sheridan, 2007) and deconstructing both the parts of the text (at a literal level) and the meaning behind the text
	Evaluating and reflecting (i.e., critique)	Practice of peers negotiating what constitutes a "good" project (Peppler, Warschauer, & Diazgranados, 2010; Soep, 2005). Asking one another (even informally), given a particular artistic goal, how successfully has this goal been met?

(continued)

TABLE 1 (continued)

Participatory Competencies	Practices	Definitions
	Referencing, reworking, and remixing	Practice of creating original works that make knowing reference to previous works (such as games, cartoons, music, etc.). Wholly original work produced as art falls into the category of playable art and is excluded from this category (see Mitchell & Clarke, 2003). The modification of existing games, images, or sounds, often to create new interactive pieces or "machinima" or noninteractive movies. Also the act of creating new genres, combining genres, or taking something from one genre and making it into something else (see Erstad, Gilye, & de Lange, 2007)
Creative practices of production	Making artistic choices	Practice of learning about, appreciating, and applying artistic principles (similar to Gee, 2003), including choosing objects as well as their colors, size, movement, and on-screen positioning. This is further defined as working within a single modality to augment meaning
	Connecting multimodal sign systems	Practice of learning about, appreciating, and designing interrelations within and across multiple sign systems (images, word, and action; Gee, 2003; Jewitt & Kress, 2003; Kress & van Leeuwen, 2001). This is further defined as working across two or more modalities to augment meaning
Ethical practices of production	Crediting owner-ship	Practice of referencing intellectual origins of "text" in use of media production (Perkel, 2008)
	Providing inside information	Practice of judiciously sharing insider codes, shortcuts, and solutions according to the cultural values in the community (Fields & Kafai, 2010)

managing problems and finding solutions, and using graphics and/or artwork packages to express ideas creatively) as well as high-level skills such as algorithmic thinking and programming (Cunningham, 1998; diSessa, 2001; Maloney et al., 2008). Programming within the context of DIY is a particularly important technical practice because it allows the creator to manipulate the medium of the computer (Peppler, 2010; Reas, 2006a, 2006b). In an effort to introduce the essentials of programming and other technical skills to youth, we argue that learning to code is important but by no means the only building block for understanding how digital media is designed; it can provide an additional venue for originality and expression in digital media. We have identified in Table 1 three central technical practices that are important to youths' creative digital production: *coding* (which involves the use of loops, conditional statements, parallel execution, object-oriented programming, sequencing, synchronization, time triggering, real-time interaction, Boolean logic, variables, event handling, user-interface design, statements, and numerical representations; Malan, 2007; Maloney et al., 2008), *debugging* (practices of persisting when confronted with technical problems either prior to or during production; National Research Council, 1999), and *remixing* (the practice of reusing earlier ideas or chunks of materials to build on in a single work or in multiple works; National Research Council, 1999).

We have already noted that the new literacies studies community has studied forms of "geeking out" (Ito et al., 2009), but their efforts have primarily focused on particular kinds of activities such as video making, graphics, blogging, fanzines, and cosplay (i.e., engaging in costume play based on popular media characters), thus overlooking the role of programming as a form of creative media production. This largely ignores a number of DIY communities that use programming as a core tool for creative media production, including robotics communities, e-textile communities, and programming communities such as those that have evolved around Scratch, Arduino, and Processing languages. For instance, Processing is a programming language, development environment, and online community that has promoted software literacy within the visual arts, graphic arts, and design communities. Processing.org is a novice-friendly, open-source community where individuals can post projects, share code, learn more about programming, and take part in curated online exhibitions. Of course, these programming activities involve, to some degree, fairly technical knowledge of scripting and other aspects of visual programming, but this specialized skill set is not unique in the world of creative media production. In fact, it parallels the history of video and audio production in the media education curriculum, which originally involved fairly difficult technical skills. And, as the tools became cheaper and easier to use, they were more readily adopted by schools and particularly by media educators. Now, as programming tools become easier to use—even easy enough to allow preliterate youth to program before they are able to read and write (Peppler

& Warschauer, 2010)—we may see a similar trend to embrace such tools in the new media literacies community.

DIY communities themselves publish a great deal of work on tools, techniques, and instructions on how to do DIY programming and physical computing (see http://makezine.com and www.instructables.com for examples), so it is not surprising that technical practices have long-since guided these informal discussions. In newer iterations, large online communities have grown around more beginner-friendly tools such as Alice, Scratch, and Processing, sharing ideas and remixing one another's work. These new tools further reshape contemporary literacy practices in DIY communities, helping youth to meet the goals of becoming fluent with technologies. Computer programming, for example, is a central tool that has entered the new landscape. We use computer literacy synonymously with the term *technology fluency* to expand what it means to be literate with technology as we move beyond just basic functions, such as word processing and Web surfing, to higher-end skills and dispositions (diSessa, 2001; National Research Council, 1999). In our view, computer literacy includes higher-level skills and concepts such as algorithmic thinking, programming, debugging, and repurposing bits of information or code.

In the context of digital production, learning to write a computer program is often a central component of becoming "software literate" or having the ability to create novel user interfaces with the computer. This type of creativity with technology is at the core of what professionals are able to do with new media and it overlaps with what Smith (2006) would describe as "computational flexibility." Being computationally flexible builds on literate practices involving knowing how to use computationally rich software (e.g., word processors, spreadsheets, and presentation tools) as well as to develop fluency (i.e., knowing how and why existing tools do not meet current needs), but extends this to include the ability to create the tools that one can otherwise only imagine.

Critical Practices

More recently, several approaches have examined DIY cultures as a way to involve youth in critically viewing media and using this understanding when creating original work. As youth begin to take advantage of living in a digital world by capitalizing on the wealth of images, sounds, and videos accessible as "materials" to reuse in their own work, media educators grow particularly concerned about the ways in which youth are reinscribing or questioning existing dominant norms (Buckingham, 2003; Buckingham & Burn, 2007). Such critical practices include youth being able to reflect critically on and evaluate media texts, understand references made in popular texts, and deconstruct and interpret the meaning behind such texts (Peppler & Kafai, 2007). By observing the critical practices of DIY youth in this way, we gain an understanding of the extent to which young designers understand and question the popular texts that they incorporate in their work, apart from what they learn about software programming and new media. Additionally, as youth engage in DIY efforts, they are learning to read and write the world critically. Critical practices are those that enable youth to make meaningful statements about local conditions and even their larger societal contexts, and include practices such as observing, deconstructing, remixing, or critiquing media or larger sociopolitical structures.

More specifically, we identified three sets of practices: observing and deconstructing media; evaluating and reflecting; and referencing, reworking, and remixing. Observing and deconstructing media practices involve careful observation by youth looking more closely than ordinarily at everyday objects (Hetland, Winner, Veenema, & Sheridan, 2007) and deconstructing both the parts of the text (at a literal level) and the meaning behind the text. Evaluating and reflecting (i.e., the practice of critique) practices involve peers negotiating, for example, what constitutes a "good" project (Peppler, Warschauer, & Diazgranados, 2010; Soep, 2005), or by asking one another (even informally) how successfully a goal has been met given a particular artistic goal. Finally, referencing, reworking, and remixing practices include the creation of original works that make knowing reference to previous works (such as games, cartoons, music, etc.). Wholly original works produced as art fall into the category of playable art and are excluded from this category (see Mitchell & Clarke, 2003), whereas the modification of existing games, images, or sounds, often to create new interactive pieces or "machinima" (or noninteractive movies), are included. We include here also the act of creating new genres, combining genres, or taking something from one genre and making it into something else (see Mitchell & Clarke, 2003).

In education today, one must arguably deal with the pervasive contemporary visual culture familiar to youth. Learning how to remix appropriately (Erstad, Gilye, & de Lange, 2007; Manovich, 2001; Perkel, 2006) and rework popular media is a key skill needed for developing a sense of criticality. In our prior work, we have found that much of youths' creative media production in new media has entailed a great deal of reworking or remixing of popular media texts such as video games and music videos (Peppler & Kafai, 2007) and further that this "remixing" of popular texts led to sustained creative media production over the course of several days at the after-school center (Peppler, 2010). This work demonstrated that youth who made reference to popular culture texts in their work (i.e., Beyoncé, Bart Simpson, Chris Brown) were invariably likely to persist in creative media production for more than a day at the after-school center, as opposed to projects without such references that were half as likely to persist (Peppler, 2010). The act of remixing involves selecting and combining semiotic resources into new multimodal texts. Erstad et al. (2007) have focused on the remixing of such resources because it moves youth fluidly between analysis and production—between critically reading and writing semiotic texts. As such, a new media studies lens contributes to our understanding of youths' relationship to popular culture as they engage in creative media production by shifting our focus away from traditional conceptions of self-expression to the skills that prepare youth for engagement in a participatory culture. Jenkins et al. (2006) outline 11 such skills that, while building on a foundation of traditional literacy, research skills, technical skills, and critical analysis taught in the classroom, focus instead on communal skills that are developed through collaboration and networking, including youths' ability to remix media content meaningfully, evaluate the credibility of different information sources, and follow the flow of information across multiple modalities, among others.

And to what ends do youth use such literacies? Historically, efforts to articulate the goals of media education have emphasized critically consuming popular media as a core aim of any media education curriculum (Alvarado et al., 1987; Ferguson, 1981; Masterman, 1980, 1985). This is also a shared aim in the field of arts education, which has previously emphasized critically evaluating and reflecting on visual culture (Hetland et al., 2007; Soep, 2005). By observing the process through which youth transform from consumers to creators of new media, we can assert that it is not just in the consumption of media but also in its production that youth develop a critical lens of popular culture. We have argued in our previous work that it is possible to develop a critical lens through participation in creative media production, even in informal learning spaces (Peppler & Kafai, 2007). The extent to which these practices represent the larger community is unknown and is at the core of our rationale for investigating vast data sources that were amassed by multiple members of the community.

Creative Practices

Youth involved in DIY efforts expand beyond technical and critical considerations toward creative or artistic ends. Researchers have explored different media cultures, such as those found in punk, zines, and cosplay, that outline the aesthetic and symbolic language encoded in the dress and costumes in these popular subcultures (Guzzetti & Gamboa, 2004; Manifold, 2008). For instance, in punk culture, youth adhere to a specific style of dress in order to communicate membership, whereas in cosplay, youth use dress and costume to represent and reenact media figures such as those found in comics and movies. As youth encode and decode the dress and other iconic imagery that is worn by members of the group, they are honing skills in line with the new literacies studies and multimodal theories of literacy, such as the importance of being able to interpret and express original ideas in a variety of modalities (such as through music, dance, sculpture, or dramatization), and are frequently able to make meaningful connections between two or more of these modalities (Gee, 2003; Kress & van Leeuwen, 2001). In observing creative practices as they pertain to youths' DIY designs, we have observed that youth learn about and appreciate artistic principles by *making artistic choices* within a single modality (e.g., visual, audio, or kinesthetic), as well as by *connecting multimodal sign systems* across two or more modalities (e.g., visual and sound, visual and movement or gesture, and sound and movement) to convey an artistic idea (Peppler, 2010).

For instance, when making artistic choices, designers learn about, appreciate, and apply artistic principles, including choosing objects as well as their colors, size,

FIGURE 4
Partial Screenshot From the Scratch Project, RobotDance

movement, and positioning. For example, in the Scratch project "RobotDance," the designer worked with a variety of artistic principles to create a 3D perspective (see Figure 4). Heightening the visual realism of the image, the designer used lines on a disco dance floor that converge into a single vanishing point. To create an illusion of depth, dancing robots diminish in size as they approach the horizon line. In both of these instances, the realism of the piece is achieved through the designer's choices within a single, visual modality. To further augment the meaning of the piece, the designer introduced animation and audio to the project, with flashing lights on the robots that change colors in synchronization with the flashing of an overhead disco ball, accompanied by a robotic-sounding disco track. The aligning of visual, audio, and animated effects then becomes part of a unified message to the viewer. In the connecting of multimodal sign systems, designers learn about, appreciate, and design interrelations within and across multiple sign systems (images, word, and action), further defined as working across two or more modalities to augment meaning. Youths' use of these practices demonstrates a more in-depth understanding of the complexity of new media production.

Scholars have argued for a view of art as the creation of meaning (Dewey, 1934/1980; Eisner, 2002), which shares many of the underpinnings of the afore-mentioned theories in the study of literacy. As youth make artistic choices in traditional subject areas such as the visual arts, they are learning about the grammar of visual design, which posits that aesthetic choices are culturally understood and put together in meaningful combinations (Kress, 1996). Similarly, other related art fields have attempted to articulate semiotic theories of action (Martinec, 1998), sound (van Leeuwen, 1999), and theater (McInnes, 1998), among others. As youth use any of these modes in their work, they learn about cultivating various types of novice understandings about a range of design grammars, whether they be visual, aural, or theatrical. For example, a subcommunity of DIY producers in south Los Angeles began making Scratch projects based on Low Riders—highly personalized cars often characterized by having low suspensions and original paint and hubcap designs. Low Riders originated circa World War II in the Mexican American community as a form of DIY car customization and is now a prominent DIY practice within urban com-munities (Cowan, 2004). Scratch designers appropriated the Low Rider discourse while playing with grammatical conventions to convey aspects of Low Rider cars that would be unable to be represented through visuals alone (e.g., simulating the bounc-ing motion of hydraulic suspensions; Peppler & Kafai, 2007). In doing so, the small choices that they made in the composition became more meaningful. As youth make a series of choices, this ultimately leads to more fuller forms of literacy as they become more practiced in these decision-making processes. One might wonder whether expertise grows over time in these informal communities, and indeed it does. Pre- and posttest analyses revealed that youth learned about the big ideas of computer programming as well as visual/multimodal media arts production over the course of 2 years in absence of direct instruction (Maloney et al., 2008). These analyses were consistent for individual learning as well as community learning (i.e., new members were being apprenticed into the community to produce more sophisticated work over the course of the study).

Although prior work has focused on monomodal domains of the arts and articu-lated the associated grammars of each individual system of communication (i.e., visual, auditory, oral, etc.), researchers are now promoting a multimodal view of literacy and learning that is key to understanding newer digital art forms (Kress & van Leeuwen, 2001; Narey, 2008). These efforts broaden our conceptions of multi-modal literacy and what it might mean to "make meaning" across a range of modal-ities. By nature of media art being a meta-medium, there is plenty of opportunity to develop a multimodal literacy, which is the interaction and combination of multiple modes of communication (Jewitt & Kress, 2003; Kress & van Leeuwen, 2001). Multimodal literacy challenges dominant ideas around learning and representation, arguing that people work across a range of representational and communicational modes involved in learning through image, animated movement, writing, speech, or gesture in new media (Jewitt & Kress, 2003; Kress & van Leeuwen, 2001). Scholars like Kress and van Leeuwen have attempted to move the discussion beyond the different modes of communication (i.e., language, image, music, sound, gesture, etc.) as separate discourses, and have instead strived to outline a coherent grammar of new media. They point out that across semiotic modes, similar meanings can be established in different modes. To unify prior theories at devising grammars of any singular modality, Kress and van Leeuwen (2001) sought to articulate common principles across a variety of modalities in their outline of multimodal discourse.

However, literacy goes beyond reading such multimodal forms to creating them and, in doing so, learning to write these discourses. In the creation of new multimodal forms of media, Jewitt and Kress (2003) argue for two central practices in their theory of multimodal literacy, including "design thinking" as encapsulating the intentions of a designer in absentia of the materials and the "production thinking" that goes into the realizing of those ideas in the materials. DIY communities deeply engage in both forms of thinking as they imagine, create, and share their work with others. As youth design with Scratch, oftentimes they have project ideas that are inspired by popular media, including video games, MTV dance videos, and other types of media. They go through a series of steps in their design thinking, choosing their characters (e.g., the Incredible Hulk and Spider-Man) as well as how they will interact (e.g., in a battle to see who's the strongest). Oftentimes, in this stage of the design thinking, youth come up with fairly complicated ideas. As they settle into the process of Scratch production, this thinking takes a shift to operationalize the steps needed to accomplish the project (e.g., first finding the images on Google image search, then downloading to the desktop, then importing them in their Scratch project, etc.). This shift toward production thinking calls into question a number of the earlier decisions made in the design thinking process, which results oftentimes in a more streamlined, simplified product that deals with the constraints of the media as well as the technical expertise of the designer (e.g., hand-drawing images when one can't find what one would like on the Web). In sum, creation within a multimodal medium tasks users to make sense of individual modalities with the ultimate goal of making connections between several different types of modalities. Engagement in creative media production, therefore, is the act of developing literacies in uni- and cross-directional ways and gaining the ability to translate one type of literacy to another.

Ethical Practices

Popular DIY practices, such as remixing, bring up important issues of ethics in new media literacies. For example, the ease with which a MySpace user can access and appropriate content from others' pages can be problematic (Jenkins et al., 2006). In our prior work, this feature of new digital media spurred a lively debate in an after-school Scratch club (Kafai, Fields, & Burke, 2010). Similarly, Perkel (2008) describes his encounter with Sharon, a 15-year-old aspiring photographer who placed a number of her photographs online only to discover they had been subsequently copied and spread over multiple websites—MySpace pages included. When asked if she considered such copy-and-paste appropriation to be some form of a compliment, Sharon replied that she actually saw it as an intrusion of her privacy. "No, I don't feel complimented," she remarked incredulously. Sharon subsequently removed the remainder of her pictures posted online, unwilling to allow them to also become future fodder for remixing. "This kind of activity," writes Perkel in his blog, "deeply upset Sharon's sense of right and wrong." The ease with which her pictures could be accessed and appropriated directly led to wider ethical considerations.

Ethical practices then add a fourth dimension to the critical, technical, and creative DIY practices and deserve further examination, especially when individuals are reappropriating others' work for their own purposes. The fact that such activity is occurring in schools further complicates the issue. Schools, in general, have a precise notion of cheating, but this rather rigid conception of what constitutes cheating does not necessarily serve kids well when it comes to the ethics of creating video games and online content where the cut-and-paste feature is commonplace in sites such as MySpace. Although research (Consalvo, 2007; Salen & Zimmerman, 2004) recognizes the practice of cheating in video games to be complex and occurring for a whole assortment of reasons, schools too often treat cheating as a "black-and-white" issue that happens simply because of some ethical failure on the part of students.

In contrast, two other types of ethical practices that we have observed in youths' creative media production include *crediting ownership* and *providing inside information*. Crediting ownership consists of referencing the intellectual origins of "text" used in media productions. For instance, remixing Scratch projects (i.e., taking an existing project and modifying code or graphics) is a common practice in the larger Scratch community; in fact, more than 40% of all projects posted on the website are remixes of existing Scratch projects (Senivirate & Monroy-Hernández, 2010). In an after-school club, Scratch programmers aged 10 to 12 years were adamant that their fellow programmers credited the origins of programs that they had remixed and posted online. Although Scratch programmers initially were concerned about others taking their programs, they also came to understand the remixes as a form of recognition that represented the attention they received from others (Kafai et al., 2010). An example of providing inside information includes the practice of judiciously sharing insider codes, shortcuts, and solutions according to the cultural values in the community. We located more than 200 cheat sites on the Internet that players of the virtual world Whyville.net had designed for new visitors to provide them with solutions to science games and tips on how to style their online avatars. The online newspaper written by the Whyville players featured articles that debated the pros and cons of different forms of cheating and their impact of game play (Fields & Kafai, 2010). Notably, what consists of cheating—whether it is revealing a solution to a puzzle or whether it is copying code—differs across contexts and what might be a perfectly permissible way of sharing information within another community might not be acceptable in another.

Summing up, we see DIY participatory competencies consisted of four inter-related practices (i.e., the technical, critical, creative, and ethical practices) rather than having a single focus. Building on our prior work, we conceptualize the inter-section of these practices as four overlapping circles in a Venn diagram. Each of these sets of practices then aligns with the authentic and meaningful practices of experts. Any overlap of two or more circles creates an area that best describes the domain of youths' DIY practices—it is really at this intersection that youth work, crossing dis-ciplinary boundaries and moving fluidly between these four types of practices. This conceptualization is grounded in the findings from the current study, as well as our earlier work (Fields & Kafai, 2010; Peppler, 2010; Peppler & Kafai, 2007), but also builds on the extensive work done by researchers in the other fields.

Our descriptions of participatory competencies are not meant to be final; rather, they are intended to lay out a roadmap for further investigations. For instance, we see the development of tangible media that extend creative media production into the physical realm as a promising candidate—a more detailed description can be found in the next section. Such developments pose new, but also interesting, chal-lenges to interface designs that have focused predominantly on visual aspects, leaving out sensory qualities such as sound and texture that are equally informative. Other developments could focus on leveraging the large scale of social networks that youth navigate and contribute to with their creative media productions and would examine what it means to participate fully and actively in such large communities. These changes in the materials and social aspects of media also generate new input for the developments of design and media arts. As technologies change, new practices are developed and integrated, and so will the need for participatory competencies.

TOWARD A CONVERGENCE OF PARTICIPATORY COMPETENCIES

For our final considerations, we return to the beginning of our review, that is, the development of a common language to understand the multiple literacies involved in creative media production. We argued that given the changing nature of participa-tory culture, and what it takes to actively and fully participate in it, more emphasis is needed on students' acquiring of design and production skills. We see these devel-opments as part of the burgeoning DIY movement that has its roots in youth and media culture promoting alternative production. Our focus on DIY as a context for creative media production is not a radical departure from prior approaches in media and computer education; rather, we view it as complementary, expanding existing media literacy approaches that have previously focused on critical reflection and understanding to be more grounded in youths' creative practices. We have formu-lated a provisional list of advantages for DIY production with the intention of mov-ing toward a convergence of literacies.

First, a common set of DIY practices increases flexibility and fluency when mov-ing across platforms, as well as aids in research of these practices. Youth who may not otherwise be involved in computer programming or a formal media education curriculum are now being drawn into the participatory culture through creative media production. The main point we are trying to make in this review is that particular forms of creative media production (programming) have not been part of the discourse of new media literacies in youth media engagement. Ito et al. (2009) previously provided a more multifaceted account of the diverse forms of interest-driven participation in new media. When youth are "messing around" or "geeking out" in DIY, they invariably begin to use and master design languages—programming, interface design, animation, graphics, 3D design, and more. But in today's media culture, we lack a history of educating students about these features prominent in interface and software design, as most school activities are concerned with using rather than producing technologies. We argue that we should be as equally concerned with "opening the black box" of digital technologies as we are about media ownership and control issues. In our own work, we saw numerous examples of how youth engaged in DIY production dealt with a host of complex interface design issues that reveal the underpinnings of software interactions. Such understandings are crucial for today's citizenship, as more aspects of life have moved into the digital domain. Interfaces happen to be one of the most difficult artifacts to design, as many assumptions about human interaction are built in, assumptions that most people are not aware of unless faced with designing them. Ultimately, we hope that this has an impact on issues of access and participation at large, in particular who contributes to the design of new technologies and applications, some of which we discuss in more detail below.

Second, creative media production enables critical reflection on media culture, expressed through visual instead of oral or written discourse. What makes DIY a promising combination is not only its focus on creative media production but also how it highlights critical readings and equity issues. In DIY, some researchers see the construction and swapping of zines as a far more galvanizing activity—a decision to circumvent traditional modes of communication in order to establish particular affinity groups operating outside of mainstream culture. This pushback on the mainstream—and oft-labeled "consumerist"—culture is a central vein running the projects. Such motivations relate well to a perennial concern for media educators, that is, the relationship between creative media production and critical media analyses. In our view, creative media production pushes youth to question their current observations and understandings, make explicit their assumptions about new media, and discover the conventions of writing the language of new media by learning the visual, semiotic, aural, and technological literacies necessary to inscribe one's self into the larger participatory culture. What takes place during creative media production is a critical reflection on what constitutes new media, how it is constructed, and how one would question or use these same design conventions toward different ends. The traditional role of formal media education still remains in media consumption because it involves stimulating critical reflection on a greater variety of media texts and engendering youth to write and reformulate those ideas critically. In this context, creative media production operates on two levels to serve both an educational and a cultural/political function in media education. Primarily, the educational function of creative media production lies in learning to write these multimodal texts but also in understanding the complexity of the design process. The cultural and political function of production includes a better understanding of larger issues about power, representation, and access: Who is doing the writing? Whose voice is being heard? Who is being positioned in certain ways within a particular text and for what purposes? In addition, the emphasis on writing empowers individuals to insert themselves to redefine their position within these power structures.

Third, DIY production provides access to the digital equivalents of functional literacies of reading and writing. Previous discussions have cast this issue mostly in terms of access to digital equipment (the digital divide) instead of the participation gap, the transparency problem, and the ethics challenge (Jenkins et al., 2006). Here our work gathers particular relevance in light of the inequitable access and participation of minority youth in digital technologies. In the digital age, media education needs to foster both critical understanding and creative media production of new media to encourage urban youth to be consumers, designers, and inventors of new technologies. Based on prior research, we know that the technology industry is not a welcoming place for women and minorities, but creative media production has been shown as a key avenue for change in the industry as it moves the field away from narrowly technical computer science applications to a focus on arts and design (Margolis & Fisher, 2002). We see the approach of creative media production as an appropriate and healthy counterpoint to a culture of consumption. Although the boundaries between media consumers and producers are perhaps not as distinct as they used to be, there is still a large rift between those who own and control media and those who have the possibilities of creating them. To be a full member in today's participatory culture should mean much more than knowing how to play video games, for example; it should also mean knowing how to design video games.

So far, we have focused mostly on creative media production in DIY cultures. One could argue that we artificially imposed a separation of production from consumption (Lemke, personal communication) and, furthermore, that such separation assigns values to design/production as "work," whereas play/consumption is devalued as nonproductive, nonwork, and nonserious. Indeed, the transitions between play and production in today's participatory culture are less distinct as some of the discussions in this chapter might suggest. We have promoted this distinction simply because we found creative media production a neglected topic in current discussions on new digital media and learning that deserved a more extended treatment. Moreover, the role of computer programming or computer literacy seems to be undervalued in the current climate, with an emphasis instead on safer Web surfing, introducing Microsoft Office products, and other Flash-based video games as the core of computer education in schools. In fact, all production involves, even requires, some form of consumption or play as an entrance point into the larger technology culture.

Our final observations are intended to look to coming trends on the developments in digital media that will affect youths' activities beyond the screen: namely, those aspects of media construction and design that dovetail with hands-on crafts, physical construction and design, and material play. There is a range of DIY practices already underway, but one such example can be found in computational crafts, called electronic textiles (e-textiles). These include young people's design of programmable garments, accessories (such as jacket patches), and costumes. Such designs incorporate elements of embedded computing (for controlling the behavior of fabric artifacts), novel materials (e.g., conductive fibers or Velcro, etc.), sensors (e.g., for light and sound), and actuators (e.g., LEDs and speakers), in addition to traditional aspects of fabric crafts. Most notable here are developments of textile construction kits such as the Lilypad Arduino (Buechley & Eisenberg, 2008) that can be placed into garments and where LED lights and sensors can be connected via conductive thread and programmed via the computer to interact with the environment. Such examples where creative media production moves from the screen into the physical space are not new but, unlike the familiar robotics construction kits, they appeal to different audiences and also integrate decorative elements. New DIY communities are emerging around these materials, which will inevitably change the face of what we know about the larger DIY culture.

These extensions into the physical world suggest a vast expansion of the traditional notion of digital learning—one that can enrich youths' expressive and intellectual lives by combining the affordances of the virtual world with those of tangible media designs and creations. We argue that as today's notions of "media texts" are expanding beyond print to include dress, speech, drawing, and dance, we need to consider how engagement with digital media can include tangible media texts. We are reminded of early formulations of the New London Group that saw all kinds of media as part of the new literacies, not just those that adhere to the flat surface of computer, television, video, or phone screens:

Childhood cultures are made up of interwoven narratives and commodities that cross TV, toys, fast-food packaging, video games, T-shirts, shoes, bed linen, pencil cases, and lunch boxes . . . teachers find their cultural and linguistic messages losing power and relevance as they compete with these global narratives. Just how do we negotiate these invasive global texts? (New London Group, 1996, p. 70)

DIY production provides opportunities for personal expression, creativity, and critical reflection on media culture, expressed through visual instead of oral or written discourse, and allows youth to reflect on their knowledge of culturally meaningful texts and dominant discourses and formulated a response through their work.

CONCLUSION

In this chapter, we focused on creative media or DIY production drawing on work from new literacy studies and technology education and provided a framework that would allow us to understand the multiple practices of learning and creating with new digital media. We applied this framework to research in the context of media-rich computer programming to illustrate the range of participatory competencies in practice. The larger goal of our chapter, however, is beyond the particulars of programming and argues that creative media production should be considered an essential part of our discussions of learning with new digital media, inside and outside of school.

ACKNOWLEDGMENTS

This material is based on work supported by the National Science Foundation (CIS-0855868 and 0855886) to the authors, in addition to prior funding to the first author (ITR-0325828). We also thank our reviewers Jay Lemke, Mark Warschauer, Stanton Wortham, and William Burke for their insightful comments on earlier drafts of this manuscript.

REFERENCES

Alvarado, M., Gutch, R., & Wollen, T. (1987). *Learning the media.* London, England: Macmillan.

Benkler, Y. (2006). *The wealth of networks: How social production transforms markets and freedom.* New Haven, CT: Yale University Press.

Black, R. W. (2005). Online fanfiction: What technology and popular culture can teach us about writing and literacy instruction. *New Horizons for Learning Online Journal, XI*(2), Spring 2005.

Black, R. W. (2009). English-language learners, fan communities, and 21st-century skills. *Journal of Adolescent & Adult Literacy, 52,* 688–697.

Booth, J. (1999). PhotoWork: A case study in educational publishing for and by young people. In J. Sefton-Green (Ed.), *Young people, creativity and new technologies* (pp. 42–56). London, England: Routledge.

Buckingham, D. (2003). *Media education: Literacy, learning and contemporary culture.* Cambridge, England: Polity Press.

Buckingham, D., & Burn, A. (2007). Game literacy in theory and practice. *Journal of Educational Multimedia and Hypermedia, 16,* 323–349.

Buckingham, D., & Sefton-Green, J. (1994). *Cultural studies goes to school.* London, England: Taylor & Francis.

Buechley, L., & Eisenberg, M. (2008). The LilyPad Arduino: Toward wearable engineering for everyone. *Wearable Computing Column in IEEE Pervasive, 7*(2), 12–15.

Cassell, J., & Jenkins, H. (1998). *From Barbie to Mortal Kombat: Gender and computer games.* Cambridge, MA: MIT Press.

Congdon, K. G., & Blandy, D. (2003). Zinesters in the classroom: Using zines to teach about postmodernism and the communication of ideas. *Art Education, 56*(3), 44–52.

Consalvo, M. (2007). *Cheating.* Cambridge, MA: MIT Press.

Cowan, P. (2004). Devils or angels: Literacy and discourse in lowrider culture. In J. Mahiri (Ed.), *What they don't learn in school: Literacy in the lives of urban youth* (pp. 47–74). Oxford, England: Peter Lang.

Cunningham, H. (1998) Digital culture: The view from the dance floor. In J. Sefton-Green (Ed.), *Digital diversions: Youth culture in the age of multimedia* (pp. 128–148). London, England: UCL Press.

Denner, J., & Campe, S. (2008). What do girls want? What games made by girls can tell us. In Y. Kafai, C. Heeter, J. Denner, & J. Sun (Eds.), *Beyond Barbie and Mortal Kombat: New perspectives on gender and gaming* (pp. 129–145). Cambridge, MA: MIT Press.

Dewey, J. (1980). *Art as experience*. New York, NY: Berkley Publishing Group. (Original work published in 1934)

diSessa, A. (2001). *Changing minds: Computers, learning and literacy*. Cambridge, MA: MIT Press.

Eisenberg, M., & Buechley, L. (2008). Pervasive fabrication: Making construction ubiquitous in education. *Journal of Software, 3*(4), 62–68.

Eisner, E. W. (2002). *The arts and the creation of mind*. New Haven, CT: Yale University Press.

Erickson, J., & Lehrer, R. (1998). The evolution of critical standards as students design hyper-media documents. *Journal of the Learning Sciences, 7*, 351–386.

Erstad, O., Gilye, Ø., & de Lange, T. (2007). Re-mixing multimodal resources: Multiliteracies and digital production in Norwegian media education. *Learning, Media and Technology, 32*, 183–198.

Ferguson, B. (1981). Practical work and pedagogy. *Screen Education, 38*, 42–55.

Fields, D. A., & Kafai, Y. B. (2010). Stealing from grandma or generating cultural knowledge? Contestations and effects of cheating in Whyville. *Games and Culture, 5*, 64–87.

Freire, P., & Macedo, D. (1987). *Literacy: Reading the word and the world*. Westport, CT: Bergin & Garvey.

Gee, J. P. (2003). *What video games have to teach us about learning and literacy*. New York, NY: Palgrave Macmillan.

Gee, J. P. (2010). *New digital media and learning as an emerging area and "worked examples" as one way forward*. Cambridge, MA: MIT Press.

Gilster, P. (1997). *Digital literacy*. New York, NY: Wiley.

Guzdial, M. (2004). Programming environments for novices. In S. Fincher & M. Petre (Eds.), *Computer science education research* (pp. 127–154). London, England: Taylor & Francis.

Guzzetti, B., Elliott, K., & Welsch D. (2010). *DIY media in the classroom: New literacies across content areas*. New York, NY: Teachers College Press.

Guzzetti, B. J., & Gamboa, M. (2004). Zines for social justice: Adolescent girls writing on their own. *Reading Research Quarterly, 39*, 408–436.

Harel, I. (1991). *Children Designers: Interdisciplinary constructions for learning and knowing mathematics in a computer-rich school*. Norwood, NJ: Ablex.

Hayes, E. R., & Games, I. A. (2008). Making computer games and design thinking. *Games & Culture, 3*, 309–332.

Heeter, C., & Winn, B. (2008). Implications of gender, player type and learning strategies for the design of games for learning. In Y. Kafai, C. Heeter, J. Denner, & J. Sun (Eds.), *Beyond Barbie to Mortal Combat: New perspectives on gender and gaming* (pp. 165–177). Cambridge, MA: MIT Press.

Hetland, L., Winner, E., Veenema, S., & Sheridan, K. M. (2007). *Studio thinking: The real benefits of visual arts education*. New York, NY: Teachers College Press.

Hmelo, C. E., Holton, D. L., & Kolodner, J. (2000). Designing to Learn about Complex Systems. *Journal of the Learning Sciences, 9*, 247–298.

Ito, M., Baumer, S., Bittanti, M., Boyd, D., Cody, R., Herr, B., . . . Tripp, L. (2009). *Hanging out, messing around, geeking out: Living and learning with new media*. Cambridge, England: MIT Press.

Jenkins, H. (2006). *Convergence culture: Where old and new media collide*. New York: New York University Press.

Jenkins, H., Clinton, K., Purushotma, R., Robinson, A. J., & Weigel, M. (2006). *Confronting the challenges of participatory culture: Media education for the 21st century*. Chicago, IL: MacArthur.

Jewitt, C. (2008). Multimodality and literacy in school classrooms. *Review of Research in Education, 32*, 241–267.

Jewitt, C., & Kress, G. R. (2003). *Multimodal literacy*. New York, NY: Peter Lang.

Kafai, Y. B. (1995). *Minds in play: Computer game design as a context for children's learning.* Mahwah, NJ: Erlbaum.

Kafai, Y. B. (1996a). Gender differences in children's constructions of video games. In P. M. Greenfield & R. R. Cocking (Eds.), *Interacting with video* (pp. 39–66). Norwood, NJ: Ablex.

Kafai, Y. B. (1996b). Learning through making games: Children's development of design strategies in the creation of a computational artifact. In Y. Kafai & M. Resnick (Eds.), *Constructionism in practice* (pp. 71–96). Mahwah, NJ: Erlbaum.

Kafai, Y. B. (1998). Video game designs by children: Consistency and variability of gender differences. In J. Cassell & H. Jenkins (Eds.), *From Barbie to Mortal Kombat: Gender and computer games* (pp. 90–114). Cambridge, MA: MIT Press.

Kafai, Y. B. (2006). Constructionism. In K. Sawyer (Ed.), *Cambridge handbook of the learning sciences* (pp. 35–46). New York, NY: Cambridge University Press.

Kafai, Y. B., & Ching, C. C. (2001). Affordances of collaborative software design planning for elementary students' science talk. *Journal of the Learning Sciences, 10,* 323–363.

Kafai, Y. B., Fields, D. A., & Burke, W. Q. (2010). Entering the clubhouse: Case studies of young programmers joining the scratch community. *Journal of Organizational and End User Computing, 22*(2), 21–35.

Kafai, Y. B., Peppler, K., & Chapman, R. (Eds.). (2009). *The computer clubhouse: Constructionism and creativity in youth communities.* New York, NY: Teachers College Press.

Kahn-Egan, S. (1998). *Pedagogy of the pissed: Punk pedagogy in the first-year writing classroom.* Urbana, IL: National Council of Teachers of English.

Kelleher, C. (2008). Motivating middle school girls: Using computer programming as a means to the end of story telling via 3D animated movies. In Y. Kafai, C. Heeter, J. Denner, & J. Sun (Eds.), *Beyond Barbie to Mortal Combat: New perspectives on gender and gaming* (pp. 247–265). Cambridge, MA: MIT Press.

Kress, G. (1996). *Reading images: The grammar of visual design.* London, England: Routledge.

Kress, G., & van Leeuwen, T. (2001). *Multimodal discourse: The modes and media of contemporary communication.* New York, NY: Oxford University Press.

Lankshear, C., & Knobel, M. (2003). *New literacies: Changing knowledge and classroom learning.* Berkshire, England: Open University Press.

Lankshear, C., & Knobel, M. (2010). *DIY media: Creating, sharing and learning with new technologies* (New literacies and digital epistemologies). New York, NY: Peter Lang.

Lenhart, A., & Madden, M. (2007). *Social networking websites and teens: An overview.* Washington, DC: Pew Internet and American Life Project.

Loveless, A. (1999). A digital big breakfast: The Glebe School Project. In J. Sefton-Green (Ed.), *Young people, creativity and new technologies* (pp. 32–41). London, England: Routledge.

Lowood, H. (2006). High-performance play: The making of machinima. *Journal of Media Practice, 7,* 25–42.

Malan, D. (2007). *Scratch for budding computer scientists.* Retrieved from http://www.eecs .harvard.edu/~malan/scratch/printer.php

Maloney, J., Burd, L., Kafai, Y. B., Rusk, N., Silverman, B., & Resnick, M. (2004, January). *Scratch: A sneak preview.* Paper presented at the second international conference on Creating, Connecting, and Collaborating through Computing, Kyoto, Japan.

Maloney, J., Peppler, K., Kafai, Y., Resnick, M., & Rusk, N. (2008). *Programming by choice: Urban youth learning programming with Scratch.* Portland, OR: ACM Special Interest Group on Computer Science Education.

Manifold, M. C. (2008). Cosplay. In R. Reid, (Ed.), *Women in science fiction and fantasy* (Vol. 2, pp. 75–77). Westport, CT: Greenwood Press.

Manovich, L. (2001). *The language of new media.* Cambridge, MA: MIT Press.

Margolis, J., & Fisher, A. (2002). *Unlocking the clubhouse: Women in computing.* Cambridge, MA: MIT Press.

Martinec, R. (1998). Cohesion in action. *Semiotica, 120,* 161–180.

Masterman, L. (1980). *Teaching about television.* London, England: Macmillan.

Masterman, L. (1985). *Teaching the media.* London, England: Comedia.

McInnes, D. (1998). *Attending to the instance: Towards a systemic based dynamic and responsive analysis of composite performance text* (Unpublished doctoral thesis). University of Sydney.

Mitchell, G., & Clarke, A. (2003). *Videogame art: Remixing, reworking and other interventions.* Digital Games Research Association (DiGRA), Utrecht University. Retrieved from http://www.digra.org/

Narey, M. (2008). *Making meaning: Constructing multimodal perspectives of language, literacy, and learning through arts-based early childhood education.* New York, NY: Springer.

National Research Council. (1999). *Being fluent with information technology.* Washington, DC: National Academies Press.

New London Group. (1996). A pedagogy of multiliteracies: Designing social futures. *Harvard Educational Review, 66,* 60–92.

Noss, R., & Hoyles, C. (1996). *Windows on mathematical meanings: Learning cultures and computers.* Dordrecht, Netherlands: Kluwer Academic.

Palumbo, D. (1990). Programming language/problem-solving research: A review of relevant issues. *Review of Educational Research, 45,* 65–89.

Pelletier, C. (2008). Producing difference in studying and making computer games: How students construct games as gendered in order to construct themselves gendered. In Y. Kafai, C. Heeter, J. Denner, & J. Sun (Eds.), *Beyond Barbie to Mortal Combat: New perspectives on gender and gaming* (pp. 145–161). Cambridge, MA: MIT Press.

Penner, D. E., Lehrer, R., & Schaeuble, L. (1998). From physical models to biomechanical systems: A design-based modeling approach. *Journal of the Learning Sciences, 7,* 429–449.

Peppler, K. (2010). Media arts: Arts education for a digital age. *Teachers College Record, 112*(8). Retrieved from http://www.tcrecord.org

Peppler, K., & Warschauer, M. (2010). *Lessons from Brandy: Creative media production by a child with cognitive (dis)abilities.* Paper presented at the American Educational Research Association (AERA), Denver, CO.

Peppler, K., Warschauer, M., & Diazgranados, A. (2010). Developing a culture of critical game design in a second grade classroom [Special issue]. *E-Learning, 7,* 35–48.

Peppler, K. A., & Kafai, Y. B. (2007). From SuperGoo to Scratch: Exploring creative digital media production in informal learning. *Learning, Media, and Technology, 32,* 149–166.

Perkel, D. (2006, September). *Copy and paste literacy: Literacy practices in the production of a MySpace profile.* Paper presented at the DREAM-Conference: Informal Learning and Digital Media: Constructions, Context, Consequences, Odense, Denmark.

Perkel, D. (2008). No I don't feel complimented: A young artist's take on copyright. *Digital Youth Research.* Retrieved from http://digitalyouth.ischool.berkeley.edu/node/105

Perkins, D. N. (1986). *Knowledge as design.* Hillsdale, NJ: Erlbaum.

Reas, C. (2006a). Media literacy: Twenty-first century arts education. *AI & Society, 20,* 444–445.

Reas, C. (2006b). Processing: Programming for the media arts. *AI & Society, 20,* 526–538.

Resnick, M., Kafai, Y., & Maeda, J. (2003). *ITR: A networked, media-rich programming environment to enhance technological fluency at after-school centers in economically disadvantaged communities.* Proposal [funded] by the National Science Foundation.

Resnick, M., Maloney, J., Hernández, A. M., Rusk, N., Eastmond, E., Brennan, K., . . . Kafai, Y. B. (2009). Scratch: Programming for everyone. *Communications of the ACM, 52*(11), 60–67.

Rideout, V., Foehr, U., & Roberts, D. (2010). *Generation M2: Media in the lives of 8- to 18-year-olds.* Menlo Park, CA: Kaiser Family Foundation.

Salen, K. (2007). Gaming literacies: A game design study in action. *Journal of Educational Multimedia and Hypermedia, 16,* 301–322.

Salen, K., & Zimmerman, E. (2004). *The rules of play*. Cambridge, MA: MIT Press.

Schofield, J. (1995). *Computers and classroom culture*. New York, NY: Cambridge University Press.

Schön, D. A. (1983). *The reflective practitioner*. New York, NY: Basic Books.

Sefton-Green, J. (2006). Youth, technology, and media cultures. *Review of Research in Education, 30,* 279–306.

Senivirate, O., & Monroy-Hernández, A. (2010). Remix culture on the web: A survey of content reuse on different user-generated content websites. *Web Science 2010.* Retrieved from http://www.websci10.org/home.html

Simon, H. A. (1981). *The sciences of the artificial* (2nd ed.). Cambridge, MA: MIT Press.

Smith, B. K. (2006). Design and computational flexibility. *Digital Creativity, 17*(2), 65–72.

Soep, E. (2005). Critique: Where art meets assessment. *Phi Delta Kappan, 87,* 38–63.

Spencer, A. (2005). *DIY: The rise of lo-fi culture*. London, England: Marion Boyars.

Torrey, C., McDonald, D. W., Schilit, B. N., & Bly, S. (2007). How-to pages: Informal systems of expertise sharing. In D. Olsen, R. Arthur, K. Hinckley, M. R. Morris, S. Hudson, & S. Greenberg (Eds.), *Proceedings of the 10th European conference on computer supported cooperative work* (pp. 391–410). Boston, MA: Association for Computing Machinery.

van Leeuwen, T. (1999). *Speech, music, sound*. London, England: Macmillan.

Warschauer, M., & Matuchniak, T. (2010). New technology and digital worlds: Analyzing evidence of the equity in access, use and outcomes. *Review of Research in Education, 34,* 179–225.

Chapter 5

Global Ill-Literacies:
Hip Hop Cultures, Youth Identities, and
the Politics of Literacy

H. SAMY ALIM
Stanford University

This article focuses on the emergence of what I shall refer to as "global ill-literacies," that is, the hybrid, transcultural linguistic and literacy practices of Hip Hop[1] youth in local and global contexts (Alim, 2006; Alim, Ibrahim, & Pennycook, 2009; Androutsopoulos, 2003; Ibrahim, in press; Pennycook, 2007), as well as the pedagogical possibilities that scholars open up as they engage these forms (Desai, 2010; Fisher, 2007; Hill, 2009; Kinloch, 2009; Low, 2011; Morrell & Duncan-Andrade, 2004). By reviewing a broad but focused range of literature in education, literacy studies, Hip Hop studies, sociolinguistics, and linguistic anthropology, I focus my attention on research that examines the ways that engagement with Hip Hop cultural practices mediates a variety of social, cultural, linguistic, and educational processes that impact youth. In doing so, I work toward the development of a theoretical framework of ill-literacies by integrating, critiquing, and advancing the insights of this new body of work, which I refer to throughout as ill-literacy studies.

After a brief introduction of the concept of ill-literacies, I review several studies on the *poetics of global ill-literacies* to demonstrate how scholars have engaged the inventive linguistic and literacy practices of Hip Hop youth. Then I examine the *politics of global ill-literacies* to show how youth literacies have been studied in relation to local configurations of race, class, gender, and language in the United States and globally, as well as the challenges these pose for schools and for language and educational policymakers. Third, I survey the *pedagogies of global ill-literacies* and

Review of Research in Education
March 2011, Vol. 35, pp. 120–146
DOI: 10.3102/0091732X10383208
© 2011 AERA. http://rre.aera.net

focus on critical Hip Hop pedagogies that attempt to harness the potential of, and critique the tensions within, Hip Hop cultural practice. In the last section, I share some final observations about the *possibilities of global ill-literacies* by suggesting ways in which educational research can move forward by developing *critical literacy awareness* as a central component of ill-literacy studies. Ultimately, research is moving toward not only a reconceptualization of literacy within and beyond the classroom but also a re-imagining of the purposes and possibilities that ill-literacies hold for public education more generally.

INTRODUCING ILL-LITERACIES

Before reviewing the literature, I first define some terms. I choose the term *ill-literacies* to draw attention to a profound and persistent irony that either implicitly or explicitly frames the majority of the studies reviewed herein: While the vast majority of public discourses, including some academic ones (McWhorter, 2003), are quick to point to Hip Hop Culture's "illiteracy," Hip Hop youth are even quicker to point to Hip Hop's *ill* literacy ("Damn, that cat is *ill*!," meaning in this case, "That poet is incredibly skilled," and more generally used by Hip Hop practitioners to positively evaluate creative and/or counterhegemonic practices). Although most pedagogies of language and literacy spend an inordinate amount of time on "grammar," many Hip Hop youth question the value of an almost exclusive focus on prescriptive approaches. This Hip Hop–centered language and educational ideology is made explicit by Jubwa of Soul Plantation (a Hip Hop emcee and deejay from East Palo Alto, California), who refers to "standard English" as *limited* and Black Language as *limitless*. Jubwa signifies, in the Gatesian sense (1988), on Toni Morrison, who described the "cruel fallout of racism" in American schools because Black children's linguistic system allows them more present-tense forms than the school's language (cited in Rickford & Rickford, 2000, p. 82). In his statement below, he captures the irony of language and literacy learning for Black students by describing it as a process of learning a limited version of language:

> You have to teach them that in everything there's limits. You have to teach their mind limits. To grammar . . . [Teachers/Speakers of dominant varieties of English, here "limited English"] want the words to come in this order. If the words don't come in this order, these people that live by this language and thrive by this language, won't understand what you're talking about. So, you have to get the word order in the way *they* want it to be in cuz they're limited. (Alim, 2006, p. 14)

"Limited English," in Jubwa's terms—and we can add here language and literacy instruction more generally—is limited by its own prescriptivism. Critiquing limited notions of correctness, he adds, "You're only right when you do it the way that the rules prescribe" (p. 15).

Even in creative writing courses, as Fischer (2007) and Low (2011) point out, the focus can oftentimes be almost exclusively on grammar as opposed to creative, artistic production. Damu, a student in Sutton's (2004) exploration of performance poetry, complements Jubwa's perspective. He dropped out of high school, in part, because writing teachers negatively evaluated his grammar, and more generally, because schooling lacked a "connection to his life":

I took a creative writing course and I got judged a lot for my grammar, but my grammar was how I write . . . I was being judged on like a Shakespearean scale [norms], but I'm talking about things that's happening today, not in the sixteenth century . . . It was like my choice of words, my phrases, my sentences, sometimes even my topic. And they wanna change things and it's like, yeah, this is grammatically correct, but it would change the whole composition, so it's like, I ran into artistic differences. (p. 223)

As we will see throughout, Hip Hop youth practice, in general, reframes notions of correctness and creativity by linking them not to institutionally sanctioned norms but rather to Hip Hop cultural priorities and tastes, inverting Bourdieu's (1984) top-down model of distinction. Importantly, even as these activities are sometimes consciously about legitimizing particular cultural practices, they are also often about foregrounding the artistic creativity involved in the production of the ill-legitimate.

The concept of ill-literacies[2] will be explicated further throughout this article, but suffice it to say that the neologism itself relies on Hip Hop linguistic practices, or what Richardson (2006) refers to as "Hiphop literacies," in at least five important ways. These will provide the foundation of an understanding of ill-literacies. First, the term draws on the ubiquitous Hip Hop practice of *semantic inversion* (Holt, 1972), whereby "standard" negative meanings attached to words are inverted to produce positive ones, to highlight the irony of youth described by educational institutions as "semi-literate" (Morrell & Duncan-Andrade, 2004) or "illiterate" (Morrell, 2008). The *ill* in ill-literacies refers *not* to a "lack of literacy" but to the presence of skilled literacies. Second, the term draws attention to the multiple, textual interpretations made possible by Hip Hop's use of coded language, or "counterlanguage" (Morgan, 2001), which is often used as a means to critique dominant discourses. Ill-literacy studies, following Hip Hop youth like Jubwa and Damu, call into question the very concept of "illiteracy," pointing to it as a sociopolitically constructed notion defined with respect to only certain, dominant forms of literacy. So, in this case, both the irony and the injustice of dominant discourses of (il)literacy are highlighted to provide a counterhegemonic reading of American educational institutions themselves as illiterate, that is, unable to read and meet the needs of marginalized youth. Here, illiteracy refers to schools' "misreading" of the cultural gap as an achievement gap (Ladson-Billings, 2009) and their inability to "decode" students' lived experiences and identities in an era of culturally and linguistically complex classrooms (Ball, 2009).

Third, this term privileges not just the politics but also the poetics of Hip Hop linguistic practice, and reminds us that "textuality and orality bear a strained relationship" (Perry, 2004, p. 2). Although represented orthographically as "ill-literacy" for the sake of clarity, it is indeed intended to be a case of "organized konfusion," where the wordplay quite deliberately creates multilayered, subtextual understandings for participants while at the same time producing potential confusion for non-participants. Fourth, while neologisms are always created in Hip Hop, in part, for the pure pleasure involved in their verbal production, they also index youth's attempts to negotiate their ever-changing, unstable, and fluid realities. At their best, they can provide the beginnings of a new theory of social processes, in this case, the emergence of local and global ill-literacies and what I refer to later as ill-literacy studies. Last, in true Hip Hop fashion, these new studies can be represented by the pervasive practice of assigning an acronym to highlight the aspects of the new theory (e.g., Tupac Shakur's encoded acronym for "Thug Life," The Hate U Gave Little Infants Fucked Everybody, which has embedded within it a theory of systemic social inequality, Spady, Alim, & Lee, 1999, p. 566). In this case, I present *ILL*, not just as meaning "skilled" or "talented," but as referring to the three major components of literacy put forth within ill-literacy studies: Literacy must be Intimate, Lived, and Liberatory. Throughout the remainder of this article, I develop this point by first exploring the poetics and identity politics of Hip Hop practices, demonstrating how they are linked to broader politics of race, class, and language. Youth employ ill-literacies to challenge not only dominant constructions of static, one-dimensional relationships between languages and cultures, but they also creatively express intimate, lived experiences as a means to work toward a collective social transformation.

THE POETICS OF GLOBAL ILL-LITERACIES

To illustrate the concept of global ill-literacies, and the inventiveness that youth around the world display through their ill-literacy practices, I will begin with a number of examples from Asia, in which youth engage a range of local and global identifications. In these examples, youth negotiate local arrangements of politics, language, and culture through the global form of Hip Hop, simultaneously redefining Hip Hop (creating Hip Hop*s*) and local cultural and linguistic practice. Through their manipulation of a diverse range of languages, ideologies, and cultural practices, these youth create what Chang (2007) refers to as "the sounds of the future." Chang describes a scene where two rappers "face off, microphones in hand," trading improvisational rhymes in a competitive verbal duel. On first glance, he notes, the verbal artists appear like "typical" Hip Hop emcees, dressed in "baggy pants" and "baseball caps," but a closer listen reveals that they are performing in multiple language varieties. "One rapper spits out words in a distinctive Beijing accent, scolding the other for not speaking proper Mandarin," whereas "his opponent from Hong Kong snaps back to the beat in a trilingual torrent of Cantonese, English, and Mandarin, dissing the Beijing rapper for not representing his people" (p. 58). The crowd—not in Los Angeles, not in New York, but in Shanghai—"goes wild!"

This example of a specific Hip Hop discourse genre, the freestyle rap battle, demonstrates that, as Blommaert (2003, p. 608) pointed out more generally for the globalization of linguistic practice, "What is globalized is not an abstract Language, but specific speech forms, genres, styles, and forms of literacy practice." The literacy practice of Hip Hop poetics (Bradley, 2009) can be extremely complex, as Lin (2009) demonstrates in her exploration of the local and global practices of the Cantonese verbal art of Hip Hop youth. Inspired by numerous Black American artists, from

Public Enemy to Tupac Shakur, to spit that *fo* (Cantonese for "fire")—that is, to speak in the voice of the *siu shih-mahn* ("grassroots people"), to disrupt hegemonic, middle-class norms with their use of *chou-hau* ("vulgar mouth"), and to compose complex *multirhyme matrices* (Alim, 2006)—youth like MC Yan offer rhymed social critiques by manipulating "the special tonal and syllabic features of the Cantonese language" (Lin, 2009, p. 170). MC Yan refers to these complex literacy practices as "double-rhyming" or "3-dimensional rhyme," meaning that, as Lin explains, "several levels of phonetic parallelism can be drawn upon to create a multilevel rhyming aesthetic" where youth can "use words with same vowels (rhyming), same consonants (alliteration), same sounds (homonyms), same number of syllables, and same or similar syllable pitch (tone) patterns for multisyllabic words" (p. 171).

The literacy practice of Hip Hop rhyming has reconfigured poetic genres in Japan as well, where Hip Hop youth restructure Japanese to create rhymes in relation to time ("flow") (Condry, 2006; Fischer, 2007; Tsujimura & Davis, 2009). Along with Chinese (Lin, 2009) and Korean youth (Pennycook, 2007), Japanese youth have produced similar poetic structures such as the *bridge rhymes* and *back-to-back chain rhymes* found in Black American Hip Hop (Alim, 2006). What makes the Japanese case particularly intriguing is that, according to Tsujimura and Davis (2009), rhyme had not previously existed in traditional Japanese verse. Although this innovation may be readily viewed as merely a reflection of global Hip Hop rhyming practice, the way in which youth adapt rhyme into Japanese Hip Hop undergoes a specific linguistic process of localization, whereby the "context and resources of the Japanese language" require that rhymes "faithfully conform to the notion of *mora*, a crucial linguistic concept of the language, but not necessarily relevant in many others" (p. 183). For example, where the rhyming domain in English consists of everything after the stressed syllable in a word (*promotion-lotion*), the rhyme domain of Japanese consists of at least two moraic elements, which are vowels and consonants at the end of the syllable.

Not only are youth localizing Hip Hop literacy practices in accordance with the varying local configurations of languages, ideologies, and politics, but these complex literacy practices are pushing scholars to critique and expand even our very notions of language. Pennycook's (2003, 2007) analyses of "linguistic remixing" in Japan and Malaysia have been critical here. Table 1, for example, is drawn from Pennycook's discussion of three texts by Japanese Hip Hop youth Rip Slyme.

In his analysis of the song "Bring Your Style" (Example 1), Pennycook (2003, pp. 515–517) discusses the co-occurrence of Black American Hip Hop Nation Language Varieties (Alim, 2009b), such as the globally omnipresent indexical *Yo!*, with the Japanese *jinrui saigo no furiikiisaido* "the last freaky side of the human race," in what these youth call "freaky mixed Japanese." The Japanese lyric, however, is already "mixed," with the first part of the phrase written in Japanese *kanji* and the second part written in both *katakana* (used generally for the transcription of non-Japanese words) and *hiragana* (used mainly for Japanese morphemes and grammatical items) (p. 516). Furthermore, as Pennycook explains, "in *furiikiisaido* we have a created, English-based word (*saido* [side] is commonly used, *furriikii* [freaky] less

TABLE 1
Examples of Lyrics From Rap Songs by Japanese Youth Rip Slyme

Lyrics	Transliteration and translation
(1) Yo Bringing That, Yo Bring Your Style 人類最後のフリーキーサイド (from *Bring Your Style*)	*Yo bringing that, Yo bring your style* *Jinrui saigo no furikiisaido* "Yo bringing that, Yo bring your style The last freaky side of the human race"
(2) By the Way Five Guy's Name (x3) Five Guy's Name is Rip Slyme 5' (from *By the Way*)	By the Way Five Guy's Name (x3) Five Guy's Name is Rip Slyme 5'
(3) 錦糸町出 Freaky ダブルの Japanese (from *Tokyo Classic*)	Kinshichoo de freaky daburu no Japanese "Freaky mixed Japanese from Kinshichoo"

Note. Adapted from Pennycook (2003, pp. 515–526).

so)." Pennycook's work on linguistic remixing raises fundamental questions about the supposed one-to-one relationship between language and identity, between "English for global purposes and Japanese for local purposes," and between "a language" and "a structure." Again, we see ill-literacies working to undermine narrow, dominant constructions of the relationship between language, culture, and identity with practices that prioritize the multiple and hybrid identifications that characterize their lived experiences.

What might be extremely perplexing to Japanese educators who confront such diverse literacy practices is that Hip Hop youth in Japan are strongly influenced by Black American Hip Hop Nation Language Varieties. The naming practice itself engages the tradition of creative wordplay in that it exploits the sometimes globally mocked *r/l* distinction (Chun, 2004) in Japanese English to produce "Lips Rhyme" (Pennycook, 2003, p. 530). But despite this global influence, the linguistic practices of these youth are indexical of multiple cultural affiliations and identifications. As Pennycook (2003) concludes, Rip Slyme's use of multiple Japanese varieties and multiple forms of local and global Englishes avoids designations of local or global and appears to "flow itself across the boundaries of identity" (p. 527).

These brief examples illustrate that the ideologies of language in youth productions of ill-literacies move far beyond the mania over standard languages and correctness in educational institutions, which youth (and ill-literacy studies) view as *limited* approaches to language and literacy. Ill-literacies demand a reconceptualization of school-based approaches to language and literacy and a redefinition of language that prioritizes youth conceptions of language as an "ever free-forming and flowing" system that is "not defined at any state in time, and it's not a permanent state. It's sorta like . . . limitless . . . because [rules] can be broken and changed at any time. And it will always change" (Jubwa in Alim, 2006, p. 15).

The multiple indexicalities brought to the fore by such complex, multilayered, creative literacy practices underscores the need to develop pedagogies that give a more central role to linguistic agency on the part of youth (Alim, 2009b), as these heteroglot language and literacy processes become more widespread and ever more central to youth identities. These creative hybrid ill-literacies can implicitly and explicitly draw attention to the politics of language and identity, which, as we will see below, presents difficult challenges for schools as well as crucial opportunities for learning.

THE POLITICS OF GLOBAL ILL-LITERACIES

In this section, I begin with studies that focus on the politics of identity, particularly the intersection of language and race, and then move toward studies that explore how global ill-literacies present challenges for local language policies and educational institutions. First, it is well documented in the Hip Hop studies literature more generally (Chang, 2005; Decker, 1993; Perry, 2004; Rose, 1994; Spady & Eure, 1991) that Hip Hop Culture in the United States during the 1980s and 1990s held an ideological commitment to black nationalism, various forms of Islam and Afrocentrism (Alim, 2006; Swedenburg, 2002), and a race-consciousness that centered on Blackness and pushed Whiteness to the periphery. In fact, recent scholarship (Osumare, 2007; Pennycook, 2007) suggests that, through the global spread of Hip Hop, resistance to White supremacist ideologies has itself become a globalized popular cultural form. The studies reviewed in this section begin with U.S. racial politics and move toward the global politics of race.

In the United States, studies have concentrated largely on the construction and status of Blackness and masculinity within Hip Hop, and how both constructions maintain their dominance despite serious challenges from within (Pough, 2004; Richardson, 2006). The dominance of Blackness within Hip Hop Culture in the United States (Perry, 2004; Rivera, 2003; Rose, 1994) led Cutler (1999) to examine the ways in which Mike, a "white upper middle class New York City teenager" employed "African American Vernacular English" toward various (and I would say, opposing) ends: the attempted production of himself as an "authentic" member of the Hip Hop Nation and the reproduction of White male privilege and racism.

Building on Boyd (2002) and Alim (2006), Cutler (2009) continued to develop a notion of Hip Hop Culture in the United States as a cultural sphere where Blackness is seen as normative. In this case, we see another White Hip Hop youth, Eyedea, who uses multiple linguistic strategies to defeat his predominantly Black opponents. Linguistically, Eyedea maintains "racial boundaries" through strategies of "avoidance" (e.g., never using the term *nigga*) as well as his use of "hyper-rhotic/r/" as a means to mark himself racially as White and as middle class. Importantly, in this case, both Eyedea and his Black competitors work together to co-construct Whiteness through the above strategies, as well as through the converging practices of stance and style (Bucholtz, 2009; Goodwin & Alim, 2010; Jaffe, 2009).

Building on Cutler's analysis of "Whiteness" in Hip Hop, Alim, Lee, and Carris (2010) show how Asian, Black, and Latino youth in freestyle rap battles in Los Angeles draw from and perform a broader range of racial and ethnic identities. The study also demonstrates that the dominance of Blackness in this particular scene does not always go unchallenged, nor does it unproblematically produce alternative racial hierarchies. First, Black youth's practices of "styling the Other" (Rampton, 1999) and "performing the Other" (Pennycook, 2003) are "loaded with the cultural and linguistic erasure that dominance engenders" (Alim et al., 2010, p. 125). As such, although artists may be producing new meanings of Blackness and Whiteness by reversing their status in this local scene (as seen in Cutler, 2009), this "reversal" comes along with the reinscription of dominant, hegemonic discourses of race, ethnicity, and citizenship at the expense of Asians and Latinos. Furthermore, Alim et al. (2010) show that non-Black emcees simultaneously uphold and challenge their marginalization (e.g., by avoiding making explicitly racial insults while at the same time protesting their racialization through embodied signs of disaffiliation). Moreover, a nuanced examination reveals that not only do emcees sometimes draw on hegemonic ideologies of race and language to defeat their opponents, but through a particular construction of Blackness—one that is masculine, working-class, heterosexual, and street-affiliated—they privilege their more broadly marginalized class status while reinscribing dominant ideologies of gender and sexuality.

These issues play out differently in Rivera's (2003) study of "New York Ricans in the Hip Hop zone," which focuses on how, because of the dominant status of Blackness in Hip Hop, Nuyorican youth must negotiate their racial and Hip Hop authenticities by representing Latinos, but not beyond an unwritten threshold where *Latinidad* becomes viewed as a device to garner attention (p. 154). Rivera moves beyond Anglo/Latino and master/subaltern dichotomies by insisting that the linguistic and literacy practices of Nuyorican youth must be read within an Afrodiasporic context. By speaking and writing in a variety of English more closely aligned with Black American varieties of Hip Hop Nation Language in New York, she argues, these youth's ill-literacies demonstrate both their resistance to an imposed "Latinization" (by being positioned as Spanish speakers) and charges of "Anglocentrism" (that equate the use of English with Anglo practices).

While these practices are not wholly unproblematic, they do highlight creative ways that Black and Nuyorican youth use linguistic and literacy practice to create spaces that counter their continued marginalization in broader society. Although not permanently transforming racial hierarchies, some scholars have suggested that Afrodiasporic youth, through their performances, have imposed a DuBoisian double-consciousness on White and other non-Black youth (Cutler, 2009) and youth around the world (see Dyson cited in Jones, 2006). Through their engagement with Hip Hop, these youth have begun, at least partly or temporarily, to see themselves through the eyes of the Other. Through creative practices, Hip Hop youth use language in ways that center their cultural priorities and their commitments to the specific, multiple identifications within their social worlds.

Globally, several studies have focused on the racialized, gendered process of "becoming Black" (Ibrahim, 1999) or the social and linguistic processes by which youth produce and interact with Hip Hop texts as a primary means of racial identification. The normative status of Blackness in U.S. Hip Hop has crossed geopolitical borders and interacted with local configurations of race in Cuba (Fernandes, 2003; Wunderlich, 2006), France (Helenon, 2006; Meghelli, 2007), South Africa (Magubane, 2006), Morocco (Asen & Needleman, 2007), Ghana (Jacobs-Fantauzzi, 2009), and other African and Afrodiasporic communities (see Basu & Lemelle, 2006; Osumare, 2007; Spady, Alim, & Meghelli, 2006). Studies of Brazil (Pardue, 2004a, 2004b; Roth-Gordon, 2009) and Australia (Pennycook & Mitchell, 2009), in particular, show how youth negotiate local ideologies of indigeneity and colonialism with Hip Hop's race-consciousness through language and literacy practice.

In Roth-Gordon's (2002, 2009) explorations of Brazilian youth's ill-literacies, she explores how youth become Black through their engagement with American ideologies of race imported into Brazil via U.S. Hip Hop texts. She outlines the concept of "conversational sampling," where youth recycle and recontextualize Hip Hop texts in their daily discourse, drawing on global youth culture to align themselves with Blackness and the prestige associated with U.S. First World modernity (Roth-Gordon, 2009, p. 67). Roth-Gordon's studies in Brazil demonstrate that along with the transcultural flow of languages comes the flow of ideologies, as in Appadurai's (1996) "ideoscapes." Through what she refers to as "race trafficking"—"the controversial and underground importation of U.S. racial and political ideology"— Brazilian youth identify as Black despite the embodied stigma of Blackness in Brazil and the efforts of the Brazilian nation-state to endorse "race mixture . . . under the racist assumption that Whiteness would bleach both African and Indigenous racial impurities" (p. 70). The public performance of *negritude* ("Black consciousness") by these artists, along with the linguistic revival of terms such as *mano* (Black brother) and *playboy* (White, wealthy male youth), points to the complex interaction of U.S. racial ideologies with local ideologies and regimes of racism. Hip Hop youth create new, relevant social meanings by employing global processes and ideologies to navigate their local experiences of marginality.

Another perspective on the normative status of Blackness can be seen in studies of Australian youth ill-literacies as well. White youth in Maxwell's (2003) study, much like the White American youth described in Kitwana (2005), centered ideologies of Hip Hop as racially inclusive and distanced the equally available set of cultural practices from a Blackness that they could never embody (despite their expressed desire "to be Black," p. 66). At the same time, Aboriginal youth in Pennycook and Mitchell (2009) chose to foreground ideologies that essentialized Hip Hop as "Black" or "African" in order to construct linkages between Black American and local traditions. The situation in Australia becomes more complicated as the politics of race intersect with the politics of language. This tension is revealed in Pennycook and Mitchell (2009), where some White Australians' attempts to encourage Black youth to "sound more Aussie" in their Hip Hop performances by adopting White varieties of Australian English are read as efforts to "co-opt" Hip Hop Culture. These efforts are met with exasperation by some Black youth ("I don't talk ocker [stereotypical white Australian male]. I talk how I'm talkin' . . . Are you trying to colonize me again dude?!," p. 37). In their attempts to highlight racial inclusivity, White youth are clearly identifying more as Australians, a national identity, while some Black youth construct Australian as including the possibility of being both Australian and aligning oneself with a transnational Black identity. Rather than solely an importation of U.S. ideologies of Blackness, this "doubling of racial identity" (Pennycook & Mitchell, 2009) is equally concerned with the broader global politics of being Black as well as the local, specific politics of Indigenous histories. These multivalent racial identities can be witnessed in the global ill-literacies of African youth in Nigeria (Omoniyi, 2006, 2009), Tanzania (Higgins, 2009), and Canada (Forman, 2005; Ibrahim, 2003) as well.

The following studies further demonstrate ways that Hip Hop youth from diverse locales participate in global ill-literacies to empower themselves as transnational subjects as well as to rearticulate their race, gender, and class positions. Given the diverse histories of colonialism, slavery, and immigration involved in these transnational sites of global ill-literacy practice, I highlight studies that explore how youth challenge the sociopolitical arrangement of the relations between languages, identities, and power through their engagement with Hip Hop. Consistent with Hip Hop youth's ill-legitimizing practices, these studies demonstrate the dual focus of language as both a source of creative pleasure and counterhegemonic politics, both of which routinely escape the attention of educators.

Sarkar and Allen's (2007) and Sarkar's (2009) work on "the transformative power of Hip Hop language mixing" provides one example of these sociopolitical struggles in Montréal, Quebec, which has experienced sweeping demographic changes in the past two to three decades. The increasing racial, religious, and linguistic diversity since the 1970s has been followed by the concomitant influx of Hip Hop cultural practices, which youth have employed to help describe and transform their realities. Afrodiasporic youth, dealing with often tumultuous immigration experiences and their subsequent subjugation because of skin color, draw on their knowledge of Black American ideologies of race and nationalism (partly through the role of Malcolm X as a Hip Hop icon, Sarkar & Allen, 2007) to introduce local narratives of racism in order to critique a global system of racialized oppression. Symbolically, many of them have engaged in the process of semantic inversion by reclaiming *nègs* in the same way that many Black American Hip Hop youth have reclaimed *nigga*, that is, as a term of camaraderie or endearment, or as a neutral term for "a Black person" (as we see in J. Kyll's lyrics below).

Within this broad context, young women like the Haitian-origin J. Kyll also critique the sexism they experience at dance clubs and parties, where young men feel entitled not just to gaze at women's bodies but to put their hands on them. In this example, Standard Quebec French is unmarked; **European French** is bold and underlined; Standard North American English is underlined; African American Vernacular English is *italicized*; *Hip Hop keywords* are italicized and underlined; and

Haitian Creole is bold and italicized. J. Kyll writes (incidentally using the inverted "ill" in the first line):

Show me respect, j'suis la true *ill* **nana**
Pourquoi t'es venu, si tu *front **sou kote**?*
Fais pas ton **mean**, j'vois ton ***bounda*** sauter
Si tu sais pas danser, qu'est-ce que t'as à te moquer?
Dis-le, t'aimes mes **moves**, pas vrai, t'es choqué?
Hey! Mais qu'est-ce ta main fait là? Go away!
Neg pa lave, pafume . . . No way!
You tha man, toutes les femmes te veulent . . . oh! ouais!
You wanna get down, you go down! O.K.

The following is the English gloss:

[Show me respect, I'm a woman to reckon with
Why did you come, if you're going to sneak around?
Don't be nasty, I saw your ass jumpin'
If you can't dance, quit making fun of me
C'mon, you like my moves, admit you're pissed off
Hey! What's your hand doing there? Go away!
Black who'd rather wear perfume than wash . . . No way!
You tha man, all the girls are after you . . . yeah, right!
You wanna get down, you go down! O.K.] (J. Kyll of Muzion, 1999, "Lounge with us,"
    Mentalité moune morne)

   As they work to make sense of shifting terrains of race and gender, the global ill-literacies of Montreal youth like J. Kyll are marked by mixing and shifting between nine different language varieties and styles, including several varieties of French, English, Black Language from the United States, Haitian and Jamaican Creole, and Spanish. Through interviews and analyses of their linguistic practice, Sarkar (2009) demonstrates how these youth consciously contribute to the creation of the cultural and linguistic diversity around them, rather than merely reflecting it. Their active efforts to model for other youth how to expand and mix their linguistic repertoires stand in direct opposition to Quebec's historically inflexible language-against-language divide and propose a progressive model for community where difference and hybridity are celebrated as strengths. For these youth, global ill-literacies operate as a positive, unifying social force, even as they disregard staunch efforts by the state and educational institutions to maintain a "rigidly normative, prescriptive French-language dominance" (p. 154).
   Related social, political, and linguistic processes occur throughout Africa, as documented in the work of Perullo and Fenn (2003), Omoniyi (2006, 2009), and Higgins (2009). Higgins situates her study of Tanzanian youth's ill-literacies within the context of Tanzania's complex history of colonialism, the struggle for independence from Britain in 1961, and the subsequent shift from socialism to capitalism.

Linguistically, the country moved from an explicit anti-English language policy to one of Swahili–English bilingualism. These language policy shifts were never seen as on-the-ground realities, and today, Tanzanian youth are redefining themselves and their local environments through ill-literacy practices that rely on a combination of "African American English," specifically Hip Hop Nation Language in the United States, a local street code known as *Kihuni*, and kiSwahili. In doing so, they are performing new, local forms of indigeneity that recast their marginalization as an empowered transnational form of identification (p. 109).

Similarly, Omoniyi (2009) posits Hip Hop literacy practice in Nigeria as a new site for the articulation and contestation of multiple identities during an age of glo-balization where neocolonial subjects are "exploring strategies of reinvention in order to break completely either from the colonial yoke or neocolonial elite domination" (p. 121). These identities are articulated, in large part, through the use of multiple language varieties, including a complicated mix of local languages (some being vari-eties other than their mother tongues). Youth often codeswitch, for example, between Yoruba, Igbo, and (African) American English, while using Nigerian Pidgin as a new sort of lingua franca. These ill-literacy practices not only put Nigeria on the Hip Hop map, that is, help these youth formulate a particular local identification within the global, but they also create what may be a pan-Nigerian identity that acts as "an ideological departure from the kind of establishment identity [one] associates with Nigeria's 'English-as-official language' policy." This raises serious educational, political, and policy concerns since these youth are constructing multilingual texts based on a widely accessible Nigerian Pidgin, a practice that undermines official language and educational policies that are based on the dominant view of English as the *lingua franca* of Nigeria (p. 125).

In all these studies, global ill-literacies are seen as agentive, progressive, linguistic acts of identification and social transformation in that youth's spoken, rhymed, and written texts challenge prescriptive, restrictive, and antidemocratic notions of cul-ture, citizenship, language, literacy, and education. With few exceptions, as we shall see in the next section as well, studies rarely look critically at the ways in which youth might reify existing hegemonic discourses regarding these same social processes. In other words, studies of global ill-literacies have tended to be largely celebratory and have ignored the contradictory forces found within all popular cultural forms (Giroux, 1996). The simultaneously progressive and oppressive currents in these innovative ill-literacies must be interrogated and critiqued, as has been done consis-tently for U.S. forms by scholars such as Rose (1994), Perry (2004), Neal (2006), and Alim et al. (2010). From the work reviewed thus far, it would appear that global ill-literacies present us with no internal inconsistencies, or "contradictory articula-tions" (Koza, 1999), where resistance is partial, where some hegemonic discourses are countered whereas others are bolstered, or where new hegemonic discourses are pro-duced. Ill-literacies challenge dominant discourses of language and identity, but critically, scholars must pay attention to both the liberatory and non-liberatory cur-rents within these forms. In the next section, we see how educators—perhaps because of the fact that their work takes place in dominant, mainstream institutions such as schools—work to tackle these complex contradictions in the classroom.

THE PEDAGOGIES OF GLOBAL ILL-LITERACIES

In the previous two sections, I reviewed research on the poetics and the politics of youth ill-literacies to demonstrate that official school-based language and literacy pedagogies fall woefully short of the creativity of contemporary Hip Hop youth. Not only do they ignore the wealth of cultural and linguistic resources that diverse youth bring to the classroom, but they are also not aligned with, and sometimes are even opposed to, youth ideologies of language and literacy. As such, they are based on closing down rather than opening up multiple possibilities for true learning to occur. In the remainder of this article, I review the pedagogical possibilities that scholars open up as they engage youth ill-literacies, offer some caveats, and point to a number of directions for future research.

Much of the research reviewed here will cover the specific ill-literacy practices of Hip Hop and Spoken Word, two Black American verbal artistic forms that have gained and been shaped by the participation of a broad, ethnically diverse group of youth. These studies build on a tradition of research in education, literacy studies, sociolinguistics, and pedagogies of popular culture that views literacies as social practices that are multiple, varied, and exist within diverse sociocultural contexts (Gee, 1996; Heath, 1982, 1983; Scribner & Cole, 1981; Street, 1984). Literacy scholars worked alongside sociolinguists and linguistic anthropologists who used the framework of the ethnography of communication (Hymes, 1972) to drive home the message that students on the margins of school success were often socialized (Ochs & Schieffelin, 1984; Philips, 1970) into different, not deficient, language and literacy practices in their communities.

Two notable examples are Heath's (1983) classic, decade-long study in Appalachia, which demonstrated how families from Black and White working-class communities socialized their children into varying language and literacy practices, and Zentella's (1997) pioneering, 14-year ethnography of the rich and complex linguistic repertoires of Puerto Rican children in New York, who displayed skills in five different varieties of Spanish and English. Heath and Zentella, among others, noted that the literacy practices of some communities were closer to practices valued by schools and that in the case of Black and Puerto Rican working-class children, their practices were not sufficiently understood or rewarded (Zentella, 1997, p. 1). The glaring irony, of course, is that these very children were busy spending their out-of-school lives building what has now become a multilingual and multiethnic Global Hip Hop Nation fueled by a love affair with language.

From there, scholars began viewing the term *cultural mismatch*, the oft-heard reason given for children's failure to learn the discourses of school, as problematically neutral, and began exploring the "stigmatization of difference" (Zentella, 1997, p. 276) as a more politicized source of schools' failure to read cultural and linguistic diversity. The "New Literacy Studies" (Hull & Schultz, 2002; Street, 1993)—or what Ball and Freedman (2004) termed *new literacies for new times*—worked along-side these scholars to interrogate dominant discourses of language and literacy and to frame literacies as ideological, political, and situated within the social and cultural practices that are constitutive of everyday life (Hull & Schultz, 2002). As Gee described (personal communication, cited in Mahiri, 2004), the New Literacy Studies

integrate a variety of disciplines (e.g., linguistics, social theory, anthropology, critical theory, cognitive science, and education) in order to take a view of cognition, language, and literacy as not just "mental" phenomena, accessible to cognitive psychology, but as socially, culturally, historically, and politically situated practices through which people's identities are formed and transformed (pp. 1–2)

and "through which institutions are produced and reproduced."

This focus on individual and institutional identities, ideologies, and sociopolitical processes redirected literacy studies into the more critical arena of ill-literacy studies. Ill-literacy studies eschew notions of neutrality and make the politics of literacy explicit by framing literacy as a contested site of unequal power relations. In line with critical theorists, they foreground issues of race, class, gender, and sexuality and focus on how literacy operates vis-à-vis difference, oppression, and marginalization, often drawing from youth ill-literacies themselves to build their frameworks. Morrell and Duncan-Andrade (2004), Hill (2009), and Desai (2010) draw inspiration from the work of critical theorists (Freire, 1970; Freire & Macedo, 1987), for example, to define "being literate" as being "present and active in the struggle for reclaiming one's voice, history, and future" (Morelle & Duncan-Andrade, 2004, p. 249). The goal of literacy, then, is to enable students to "critique the hegemonic practices that have shaped their experiences and perceptions in order to free themselves from dominant ideologies, structures, and practices" (p. 250).

Focusing specifically on language, Alim (2004, 2005) integrates the insights of the New Literacy Studies, critical literacy, and the British tradition of Critical Language Awareness and argues for a pedagogy that "interrogates dominating discourses on language and literacy and centralizes the examination of the interconnectedness of identities, ideologies, and the hierarchical nature of power relations between groups in a given society" (Alim, 2004, p. xxiii). This research later developed into "Critical Hip Hop Language Pedagogies (CHHLPs)" (Alim, 2007a, 2009a), which work to make the invisible visible and examine the ways in which well-meaning educators attempt to silence "languages of color" in White public space by inculcating speakers of heterogenous language varieties into what are, at their core, White ways of speaking and seeing the word/world—that is, the norms of White, middle-class, heterosexual males. As noted in Morrell and Duncan-Andrade (2004), to be literate is about more than reading the word, it is about developing an ability to "read the world" or, as Alim (2004) states, to engage in the process of consciousness-raising, that is, "the process of actively becoming aware of one's own position in the world and, importantly, what to do about it" (p. xxiv).

These works and those that follow draw significant inspiration from Lee's (1993, 2007) evolving cultural modeling framework, as well as Ladson-Billings's (1995,

1998) work in culturally relevant pedagogy and critical race theory in education; Gutierrez's (2008) development of sociocritical literacy; Smitherman's (1977, 2000) insights into the relations between language, literacy, and liberation; as well as Giroux and Simon's (1989; Giroux, 1996) and Dimitriadis's (2001) work on popular cultural texts in (in)formal learning environments. The following works overlap on two significant points. First, as Alim (1997) concluded in relation to Hip Hop Culture's firm grasp on urban students in Philadelphia schools, it is unreasonable for American educational institutions to demand dominant varieties of language and literacy practices from their students "while most teachers ignore and remain wholly, even happily, ignorant of their students' capabilities" (p. 73). Ill-literacy scholars share a belief that this ignorance, or the schools' illiteracy, cannot continue in contemporary times without serious detriment to marginalized youth, particularly as ill-literacies become embedded within the rapidly evolving technologies that are the primary means by which youth engage popular culture more generally. As Dimitriadis (2001) pointed out a decade ago, school culture today "has been overtaken by media culture," which has "provided models for self-fashioning that are . . . now more compelling than the ones offered in traditional schools and through traditional curricula" (p. xi). By completely ignoring youth identifications and self-fashioning, schools quickly fall behind popular culture in their ability to speak to, or articulate with, youth desires.

Second, ill-literacy studies, when taken as a whole, move beyond gimmicky approaches to using Hip Hop Culture in the classroom (as critiqued in Akom, 2009; Petchauer, 2009; Stovall, 2006) and even more serious culturally relevant approaches by framing as incomplete studies that exploit students' local cultures, knowledges, and languages only to "take them somewhere else," or teach them some curricular standard or canon, without teaching the intrinsic value of students' ill-literacies (Alim, 2007b; Kirkland, 2008; Morrell & Duncan-Andrade, 2004; Williams, 2009). Ultimately, ill-literacy studies work toward replacing broad strokes of "students' cultures" with the more intimately defined strokes of "student's lives." Recall that *ILL* refers to the notion that literacy instruction must be Intimate, Lived, and Liberatory if schools are to be effective in teaching marginalized populations. Ill-literacy studies begin with the linguistic, literacy, and liberatory potential evident in youth forms of ill-literacies. They also move beyond specific ill-literacy forms (e.g., Hip Hop, Spoken Word, or other creative literacies) by centralizing students' *lives* in an effort to reconceptualize the purposes and possibilities of public education.

I will devote the rest of this article to an in-depth review of several recent book-length studies (Desai, 2010; Fisher, 2007; Hill, 2009; Low, 2011) that provide models of how we might begin to reconceptualize the purpose of public education and develop ill-literacy pedagogies with a more critical, liberatory lens. Fisher's (2007) ethnography of an elective spoken word poetry class for a diverse group of Latino and African American 9th and 12th graders in Bronx, New York, taught by an extremely talented and caring teacher (Joe), met 2 to 3 days per week and collectively "(re)defined literacy and what it meant to be literate using the medium of spoken word poetry" (p. 4). Through using an "open mic" tradition characterized by acts of reciprocity, Fisher described the processes by which teacher and students together built a *literocracy* as an "intersection of literacy and democracy" that engages multiple literacies "while emphasizing that language processes exist in partnership with action in order to guide young people to develop a passion for words and language" (Fisher, 2005, p. 92). For Fisher, literacy is a critical, social practice to mobilize students toward social transformation.

Desai's (2010) ethnographic, teacher–researcher case study of spoken word poetry in a weekly after school elective class with a diverse group of (immigrant) Latino and African American students in Los Angeles, California, built on the work of Fisher (2003, 2007), Morrell and Duncan-Andrade (2004), and Jocson (2006) and framed spoken word as "a site/sight of resistance, reflection and rediscovery" (p. 1). Desai investigated spoken word as "a student-centered practice," which provides youth with a safe educational space to examine the world more critically by interrogating issues of race, class, gender, and sexuality. He frames spoken word as an anticolonial/decolonizing literacy practice that privileges "alternative forms of knowledge" by engaging students in "self-reflexive processes" (p. viii). Ultimately, literacy for Desai draws on critical race theoretical concepts of "voice" and "storytelling" to foster "critical consciousness, dialogue, and action" (p. 330).

Like Desai, Hill (2009) and Low (2011) also celebrate the potential of using Hip Hop texts in the classroom. Hill designed and taught "Hip Hop Lit," a Hip Hop–centered English literature class in the evening education program of an alternative high school in South Philadelphia with predominantly Black students (and a few Asian and White students). Low co-taught and observed a White high school teacher, Tim, teach a Hip Hop and spoken word course for predominantly Black (and a few White and Latino) high schoolers in a mid-sized city in the northeastern United States. Importantly, both scholars push the envelope of Hip Hop pedagogies, along with Newman's (2005, 2009) work in New York City, by not glossing over the tensions inherent between Hip Hop practices and schools. In Hill's (2009) terms, these pedagogies "inevitably create spaces of both voice and silence, centering and marginalization, empowerment and domination" (p. 10). While students in "Hip Hop Lit" were able to engage in "critical conversations and transgressive moments," within the very same context, they sometimes also "revealed highly problematic ideologies that were in direct conversation with, and sometimes buttressed by, prominent themes within mainstream hip-hop culture" (p. 10). Both Hill and Low recognize Hip Hop as a complex, contradictory, and problematic space, but like Ibrahim (1999), McLaren (1995), Alim (2007b), and Newman (2009), Low (2011) posits that the very real and difficult tensions around the politics of race, gender, generation, class, and violence, for example, simultaneously inhibit and demand Hip Hop's use in schools.

In all these studies, authors advocate an "intimate" engagement with Hip Hop Culture, which itself demands a high level of intimacy based on notions of sincerity, loyalty, and making oneself vulnerable by revealing personal narratives (Perry, 2004).

Ill-literacies require particular levels of self-sharing, which requires careful negotiation as shown in these studies. Fisher (2007) writes in several places about how Joe describes his spoken word poetry students as a "family," and the class as a "home," where students "feed" each other through critical feedback and the care that is shown through the reciprocal sharing of one's fears, desires, dreams, and nightmares. Because his philosophy of learning connected literacy to developing one's full humanity, students often described Joe as a "healer." Similarly, Hill (2009) describes the process of "wounded healing," and Desai's (2010) students describe the safe space created as a "catharsis" and a space for "healing." The latter two studies discuss the ways that their classrooms transformed when they reciprocated personal narratives of anxiety about becoming fathers, wrestling with poverty, the possibility of abortion, and so forth. For Low (2011), she highlights one particular moment in Tim's class, his genuine, reflexive narration of his internal battle with the racism that he had been socialized into as a child, as the reason that the dynamics of Tim's classroom changed for the better.

Given the impersonal nature of many of America's large urban high schools (Noguera, 2003), the focus on intimacy is revolutionary in that it demands that learning occur in safe spaces of reciprocity, mutual respect, and the development of meaningful relationships with youth. All these studies emphasize that students' out-of-school lives are filled with struggle, but it is the building of reciprocal, caring relationships that allows students to be vulnerable, sometimes writing about the anxieties of being pregnant, undocumented, stereotyped, devastated by deception, losing loved ones, experiencing violence or abuse from family members or lovers, and other tragedies. Desai, building on Valenzuela's (1999) concept of *educación*—which has a broader semantic field than "education" and includes not only schooling but also the development of moral and social responsibility (see also Valdés, 1996)—concludes that we should not fear intimacy, but rather we should run toward it as it allows us to view youth not just as students, but as human beings with whom we share the world. In addition to intimacy, all these studies highlight the need to use the "lived curriculum" of Hip Hop (Dimitriadis, 2001) to access the "lived experiences" of our students. In this way, I argue that ill-literacy studies move beyond previous literacy studies by viewing students not merely as members of marginalized social groups but as individuals with hopes, fears, anxieties, and complicated lives outside the classroom. They also redefine literacy to "include mastering one's life story and providing rich details about everyday life" (Fisher, 2007, p. 68).

Finally, as we have seen, ill-literacy studies view literacy as liberatory, not merely celebratory. For Joe, in Fisher (2007), mastering one's life story is about rewriting the master narrative about urban youth of color (their "ascribed lives," p. 67, or the way public discourses continually constructed them as lazy, unintelligent, and destined for low-wage labor) and escaping the "higher mathematics of America" (p. 99; or the statistics on youth educational failure, imprisonment, etc., as documented in Winn, this volume). She was not always sure, however, if students understood Joe's decolonizing methodology, and some of their interview responses regarding "Bronxonics" (Joe's term for the mixed language variety he and his students spoke) betrayed a limited critical language awareness, although certainly far greater than traditional approaches (p. 44).

Hill (2009), citing Ortner's (2006, p. 47) critique of social scientists' tendency to "sanitize the internal politics of the dominated," chose to highlight moments of both resistance and oppression in the Hip Hop classroom, for example, where some White students felt marginalized by Black students' (and all students') construction of Hip Hop as a "Black [only] sphere." Both Black and White students felt that the racialized nature of Hip Hop, and hence, the class, prohibited constructive race talk. For example, some White students remained "colormute" (Pollack, 2004) throughout the course, feeling awkward mentioning race:

Maggie: I'm not gonna talk about racial people in the same way that I do when I'm in a regular class.
Researcher: When you say "racial people," you mean . . .
Maggie: [laughing] You know what I mean. Like [pauses for a moment then resumes in a lower voice], Black people. Like in a regular class I could just talk. In here I can't.
Kristina: . . . it's gonna be like, "Who is this White chick getting all racial?"
Maggie: Yeah, exactly . . . I don't want any drama because we start talking about Black people.

Interestingly, some Black students remained colormute as well, as in the case of Keisha and Dorene, but for different reasons:

Keisha: Sometimes, it's hard to talk about race because it can start trouble. When I talk about hip-hop and hip-hop people, it makes it easier.
Researcher: Even if everybody knows what you're talking about?
Keisha: Yeah, because "hip-hop" doesn't make people mad like the way they would if I say "Black people do this or Black people do that . . ."
Dorene: . . . if I talk about colored people in class, White people might not feel right. But if I say "hip-hop," now everybody could talk about it. (pp. 52–53)

Terms like "racial people" and "hip-hop people" (see also Bucholtz, 2011) highlight the widespread tension of American race talk dilemmas and underscore the challenge of using overtly race-conscious forms such as Hip Hop in diverse classrooms. Ironically, in this case, White students felt silenced because of their view that Hip Hop was essentially Black property (they relinquished the authority to speak to their Black classmates), whereas Black students, recognizing the normative status of Blackness within Hip Hop, avoided reproducing the marginalizing practices of conventional classrooms by silencing themselves on issues directly related to race. This double-silencing demonstrates that the racial politics of Hip Hop discussed earlier in the article (whether between White and Black Australians or Americans), that is, the politics that youth struggle with as they engage Hip Hop outside schools, can make their way inside schools and present challenges for students and teachers.

Therefore, as Low (2011) notes, future scholarship must be willing to engage conflict, which is central to learning processes. We can use tense moments such as these to perhaps engage complex issues such as marginalization, privilege, or more specifically, the phenomenon of colormuteness in America. As Low notes, Hip Hop culture might open up various possibilities for many students of color, "as it validates the experiences of social marginalization and oppression," but it might also close down opportunities for others (p. 11). Engaging these tensions helps create a literacy that is liberatory in the sense that it incorporates and moves far beyond the mechanics of literacy and into its deeper meanings and relations to students' lives. This also demands that we focus on ways to help students resist and challenge the sociostructural forces and discourses that can not only silence them but also negatively affect learning and limit their future possibilities.

THE POSSIBILITIES OF GLOBAL ILL-LITERACIES

In this final section, I briefly point to some caveats and then to directions for future studies. I address two main caveats, both of which might prevent ill-literacy studies from falling victim to their own critiques of previous literacy studies. First, there is a widespread tendency for Hip Hop pedagogies to sanitize Hip Hop for inclusion in schools. Many scholars, as pointed out in Low (2011), self-select Hip Hop texts, or only allow students to bring in texts that are morally in line with progressive, middle class, or even bourgeois politics and sensibilities. This is widely different from an approach that begins with texts that youth, their peers, families, and community members are listening to and creating themselves and runs the risk of being outright rejected as boring, ancient, or confusing, as occurred in some of these studies. Perhaps instead, Hip Hop pedagogies could develop a broader, more nuanced understanding of Hip Hop that moves from sociological and political interpretations that privilege socially and politically "conscious music," and consider Perry's (2004) theorizing of Hip Hop as a rare, democratic space where the sacred sits right alongside the profane, allowing for "open discourse" and prioritizing expression over "the monitoring of the acceptable" (pp. 5–6). This ideological democracy, Perry argues, resists interpretations of Hip Hop as a unified political framework and narrow characterizations of the form as "liberation music" (p. 7). In other words, rather than selecting Hip Hop texts that align with our politics and sensibilities and run the risk of marginalizing students' interpretations and uses of Hip Hop texts (which Dimitriadis, 2001, and Hill, 2009, have both shown to be impossible to prefigure), or worse, developing an elitist canon within the developing "anthology of rap" (Bradley & DuBois, 2010), we might begin with explorations of the Hip Hop texts that our students make use of in their "lived experiences." By doing this, ill-literacy studies will avoid the pitfall of reproducing dominant ideologies in marginalized clothing, that is, reproducing narrow notions of what it means to be "progressive" or "socially or politically conscious" by spending a great deal of effort monitoring the acceptable. Studies might benefit from assuming a posture that is as egalitarian and democratic as the ill-literacy forms themselves, allowing for internal inconsistencies and celebrating open, discursive spaces.

Second, while all these studies are highly receptive and even laudatory of Hip Hop texts, there is an apparent unease in some of the studies vis-à-vis the relations between Hip Hop texts and spoken word texts. Building on the first caveat, there is some acknowledgment that spoken word poetry is an easier sell than Hip Hop for schools, but we have to recognize the ways that our compliance with this ideology makes us complicit in the uncritical popular discourses that elevate "spoken word *poetry*" over "Hip Hop *music*," upholding the false binary of spoken word as "intellectual" and "conscious" and Hip Hop as "bling-bling" and "about nothing." This bifurcating ideology emerges when teachers positively evaluate youth as "poets" when their rhymes align with institutionally sanctioned behavior and negatively evaluate them as "rappers" when they do not. The danger in viewing Hip Hop texts in this monolithic fashion is that we undermine the "critical" mission of ill-literacies by demonstrating our own inability to read popular culture's contradictory currents, the political economy of the Hip Hop culture industry, and the reductive representations of Black popular culture that have historically accompanied its commodification.

Future ill-literacy studies, my own included, must bear these possible contradictions in mind as we engage this very difficult, tense terrain of popular culture in the classroom. All these book-length studies, with the exception of Low (2011), occurred in nontraditional spaces, in elective courses, or in after-school and evening programs. And even Low's teacher, Tim, had to warn his students that he could "lose his job" over these unconventional approaches to literacy. I recognize the potential irony of my concern over classrooms, given that pedagogies of ill-literacy often "look outward into the larger world of which classrooms are a part" (Pennycook, 2007, p. 148). However, I contend that we look outward with the dual intention of redefining literacy in our private sphere as well as reconceptualizing education in the public sphere. Second, there is a need for future studies to show not only product (student affirmation of their curricula through interviews) but also process (the difficult negotiation of teaching and learning). Several of these studies have done that well, but there is a need for more analysis of classroom interaction through discourse analytic techniques that uncover, for example, not simply the fact that safe, critical spaces were achieved, but how and when we either were or were not successful in creating them (Hill's, 2009, reflexive analysis of what he described as his "unwitting invocation of male privilege," p. 95, is a powerful example of an unsuccessful attempt that resulted in an "act of silencing").

Third, while many of these studies draw on critical literacies and critical pedagogies, few, if any, take up the challenge of introducing critical literacy theory or critical race theoretical understandings of literacy, for example, to youth themselves. These theories inform the studies, but they do not enter the classroom in any organized, disciplined way. There is still a need to recognize that the full body of available research on literacy (from sociocultural and critical approaches), including both its historical and modern implications in slavery, colonization, and the disenfranchisement of particular groups, and so forth, as well as its role in slave revolts, decolonization (as political and mental processes, a la wa Thiong'o, 1986; Desai, 2010), independence, and social transformation, is not produced solely for the consumption of academics. This kind of *critical literacy awareness*—by promoting explicit attention to the contentious histories and uses of literacy, as well as how literacy is invested with power relations and (un)conscious ideological processes (as in Fairclough's, 1992, case for "critical language awareness")—can help develop a *metaliteracy* in students for the purposes of raising their social consciousness.

Last, we need more examinations of the possibilities of global ill-literacies in schools. Much of the work has been done in Canada, where Ibrahim's (1999, 2003, in press) critical ethnographic research shows how Francophone, African immigrant youth's identifications with a Hip Hop stylized "Black English" not only represented their identification with a Global Hip Hop Nation but also influenced how and what they learned. The research delineated these youth's desire for and identification with particular forms of Blackness through their learning of "Black English as a Second Language (BESL)," which they accessed through their participation in U.S. Hip Hop Culture. In becoming Black, these youth, like those mentioned in other global contexts earlier in this article, displayed a facility with multiple language varieties, which was largely ignored by teachers. However, they also performed sometimes regressive notions of Blackness through Hip Hop, as seen in the case of some Moroccan youth (Asen & Needleman, 2007), which predictably, was not overlooked by teachers.

In conclusion, I have shown throughout this article that young people, both locally and globally, are producing creative, hybrid texts that speak about their realities. These creative practices are often employed to challenge dominant ideologies of language, culture, and identity. In the process, youth prioritize what is important to them by drawing strength from and reenvisioning their lived experiences of marginality. The possibilities of global ill-literacies lie both in the politics and poetics of youth texts created largely outside of schools and our ability to create pedagogies that center on the texts that our youth use, create, and manipulate in their daily lives. The possibilities of ill-literacies will depend on our ability to discover new ways to center these practices without foregoing traditional skills. All these works have demonstrated not only that this tension can be overcome, but also that educational policymakers' fixation with it can actually slow the much-needed work of creating *ILL* pedagogies that frame literacies as *intimate*, *lived*, and *liberatory*. In other words, the true potential of ill-literacies lies in the new possibilities that they create for theorizing literacy and other social processes and, importantly, for how we teach literacy in public schools. Ill-literacies present us with the possibility of developing our collective critical literacy awareness to work toward social transformation through not only engaging students' cultures but also centralizing their lives.

ACKNOWLEDGMENTS

I would like to acknowledge Stanton Wortham, Vivian Gadsden, and Mary Bucholtz for their support and extremely close reading of this manuscript. Thank you for making invaluable comments and suggestions throughout this process. I would also like to thank Awad Ibrahim, Alastair Pennycook, and the rest of the Global Linguistic Flows intellectual cipha for shaping my thinking on these issues and Ernest Morrell, Maisha Winn, Shiv Desai, Brownen Low, Marc Lamont Hill, and Arnetha Ball for their work and feedback. Of course, all shortcomings are theirs, not my own. Just playin.

NOTES

[1]Many in the Hip Hop community avoid the traditional spelling *hip-hop*, choosing either *Hip Hop* or *Hiphop*. Because of this, I have chosen to use *Hip Hop* throughout this chapter.

[2]While the term *ill-literacies* represents my reading of creative youth linguistic and literacy practice, it is also important to note that the term itself has been used by other Hip Hop youth locally, globally, and throughout the blogosphere. For example, emcee Ill-literate from Maine/Pittsburgh defines his name through this equation: Ill = sick, either good or bad. Literate = can read, literary. Ill-literate = sick with the writs. Writs, of course, being short for "writtens," which refer to rhymes that are written down as opposed to improvised. Then there's the relatively new Hip Hop collective representing Cape Town, South Africa, Ill-Literate-Skill, or Ill Skillz, for short. In the social networking age, we also have the Internet-based iLL-Literacy collective, who pushes the ill semantic inversion to the extreme with members of their "famILLy" displaying their "iLL-twitteracy" (a la Twitter) skills in the "digitILL age" (http://www.ill-literacy.com).

REFERENCES

Akom, A. (2009). Critical hip hop pedagogy as a form of liberatory praxis. *Equity and Excellence in Education, 42*, 52–66.

Alim, H. S. (1997). *Teaching standard English in the inner city: A hip hop approach* (Unpublished thesis). University of Pennsylvania, Philadelphia.

Alim, H. S. (2004). *You know my steez: An ethnographic and sociolinguistic study of styleshifting in a Black American speech community*. Durham, NC: Duke Press.

Alim, H. S. (2005). Critical language awareness in the United States: Revisiting issues and revising pedagogies in resegregated society. *Educational Researcher, 34*(7), 24–31.

Alim, H. S. (2006). *Roc the mic right: The language of hip hop culture*. New York, NY: Routledge.

Alim, H. S. (2007a). Critical hip hop language pedagogies: Combat, consciousness, and the cultural politics of communication. *Journal of Language, Identity, and Education, 6*, 161–176.

Alim, H. S. (2007b). "The Whig party don't exist in my hood": Knowledge, reality, and education in the Hip Hop Nation. In H. S. Alim & J. Baugh (Eds.), *Talkin Black talk: Language, education, and social change* (pp. 15–29). New York, NY: Teachers College Press.

Alim, H. S. (2009a). Creating "an empire within an empire": Critical hip hop language pedagogies and the role of sociolinguistics. In H. S. Alim, A. Ibrahim, & A. Pennycook (Eds.), *Global linguistic flows: Hip hop cultures, youth identities, and the politics of language* (pp. 213–230). New York, NY: Routledge.

Alim, H. S. (2009b). Translocal style communities: Hip Hop youth as cultural theorists of style, language, and globalization. *Pragmatics, 19*, 103–127.

Alim, H. S., Ibrahim, A., & Pennycook, A. (Eds.). (2009). *Global linguistic flows: Hip hop cultures, youth identities, and the politics of language*. New York, NY: Routledge.

Alim, H. S., Lee, J., & Carris, L. M. (2010). "Short fried-rice-eating Chinese MCs" and "good-hair-havin Uncle Tom niggas": Performing race and ethnicity in freestyle rap battles. *Journal of Linguistic Anthropology, 20*, 116–133.

Androutsopoulos, J. (2003). *Hip hop: Globale kultur, lokale praktiken*. Bielefeld, Germany: Transcript.

Appadurai, A. (1996). *Modernity at large: Cultural dimensions of modernity*. Minneapolis, MN: University of Minnesota Press.

Asen, J., & Needleman, J. (Directors). (2007). *I love hip hop in Morocco* [Documentary film]. United States: Rizz Productions.

Ball, A. F. (2009). Toward a theory of generative change in culturally and linguistically complex classrooms. *American Educational Research Journal, 46*(1), 45–72.

Ball, A. F., & Freedman, S. (Eds.). (2004). *Bakhtinian perspectives on language, literacy, and learning.* Cambridge, England: Cambridge University Press.

Basu, D., & Lemelle, S. (Eds.). (2006). *The vinyl ain't final: Hip hop and the globalization of Black popular culture.* Ann Arbor, MI: Pluto Press.

Blommaert, J. (2003). Commentary: A sociolinguistics of globalization. *Journal of Sociolinguistics, 7,* 607–623.

Bourdieu, P. (1984). *Distinction: A social critique of the judgment of taste.* Cambridge, MA: Harvard University Press.

Boyd, T. (2002). *The new H.N.I.C.: The death of civil rights and the reign of hip hop.* New York, NY: New York University Press.

Bradley, A. (2009). *Book of rhymes: The poetics of hip hop.* New York, NY: Basic Civitas Books.

Bradley, A., & DuBois, A. (Eds.). (2010). *The anthology of rap.* New Haven, CT: Yale University Press.

Bucholtz, M. (2009). From stance to style: Gender, interaction, and indexicality in Mexican immigrant youth slang. In A. Jaffe (Ed.), *Stance: Sociolinguistic perspectives* (pp. 203–223). New York, NY: Oxford University Press.

Bucholtz, M. (2011, June). "It's Different for Guys": Gendered narratives of racial conflict among White California youth. *Discourse & Society, 22*(4).

Chang, J. (2005). *Can't stop won't stop: A history of the hip hop generation.* New York, NY: St. Martin's Press.

Chang, J. (2007, November/December). It's a hip hop world. *Foreign Policy, 163*(4), 58–65.

Chun, E. (2004). Ideologies of legitimate mockery: Margaret Cho's revoicings of Mock Asian. *Pragmatics, 14,* 263–289.

Condry, I. (2006). *Hip-hop Japan: Rap and the paths of cultural globalization.* Durham, NC: Duke University Press.

Cutler, C. (1999). Yorkville crossing: White teens, hip hop, and African American English. *Journal of Sociolinguistics, 3,* 428–442.

Cutler, C. (2009). "You shouldn't be rappin', you should be skateboardin' the X-games": The coconstruction of Whiteness in an MC battle. In H. S. Alim, A. Ibrahim, & A. Pennycook (Eds.), *Global linguistic flows: Hip hop cultures, youth identities, and the politics of language* (pp. 79–94). New York, NY: Routledge.

Decker, J. L. (1993). The state of rap: Time and place in Hip Hop nationalism. *Social Text, 34,* 53–84.

Desai, S. R. (2010). *Emancipate yourself from mental slavery/None but ourselves can free our minds: Spoken word as a site/sight of resistance, reflection and rediscovery* (Unpublished doctoral dissertation). University of California, Los Angeles.

Dimitriadis, G. (2001). *Performing identity/performing culture: Hip-Hop as text, pedagogy, and lived practice.* New York, NY: Peter Lang.

Fairclough, N. (Ed.). (1992). *Critical language awareness.* London, England: Longman.

Fernandes, S. (2003). Fear of a Black nation: Local rappers, transnational crossings, and state power in contemporary Cuba. *Anthropological Quarterly, 76,* 575–608.

Fischer, D. (2007). *"Kubudhi agero! (pump ya fist!)": Blackness, "race" and politics in Japanese Hip Hop* (Unpublished doctoral dissertation). University of Florida, Gainesville.

Fisher, M. T. (2003). Open mics and open minds: Spoken word poetry in African diaspora participatory literacy communities. *Harvard Education Review, 73,* 362–389.

Fisher, M. T. (2005). Literocracy: Liberating language and creating possibilities. *English Education, 37,* 92–95.

Fisher, M. T. (2007). *Writing in rhythm: Spoken word poetry in urban classrooms.* New York, NY: Teachers College Press.

Forman, M. (2005). "Straight outta Mogadishu": Prescribed identities and performative practices among Somali youth in North American high school. In S. Maira & E. Soep (Eds.), *Youthscapes: The popular, the national, and the global* (pp. 3–22). Philadelphia, PA: University of Pennsylvania Press.

Freire, P. (1970). *Pedagogy of the oppressed*. New York, NY: Continuum.

Freire, P., & Macedo, D. (1987). *Reading the word and the world*. Westport, CT: Bergin & Garvey.

Gates, H. L. (1988). *The signifying monkey: A theory of Afro-American literary criticism*. New York, NY: Oxford University Press.

Gee, J. (1996). *Social linguistics and literacies: Ideology in discourses*. Bristol, PA: Taylor & Francis.

Giroux, H. (1996). *Fugitive cultures: Race, violence, and youth*. New York, NY: Routledge.

Giroux, H., & Simon, R. (1989). *Popular culture, schooling, and everyday life*. New York, NY: Bergin & Garvey.

Goodwin, M., & Alim, H. S. (2010). "Whatever (neck roll, eye roll, teeth suck)": The situated coproduction of social categories and identities through stancetaking and transmodal stylization. *Journal of Linguistic Anthropology, 20,* 179–194.

Gutierrez, K. (2008). Developing sociocritical literacy in the third space. *Reading Research Quarterly, 43,* 148–164.

Heath, S. B. (1982). Protean shapes in literacy events: Ever-shifting oral and literate traditions. In D. Tannen (Ed.), *Spoken and written language: Exploring orality and literacy* (pp. 91–117). Norwood, NJ: Ablex.

Heath, S. B. (1983). *Ways with words: Language, life, and work in communities and classrooms*. Cambridge, England: Cambridge University Press.

Helenon, V. (2006). African on their mind: Rap, blackness, and citizenship in France. In D. Basu & S. Lemelle (Eds.), *The vinyl ain't final: Hip hop and the globalization of black popular culture* (pp. 151–166). Ann Arbor, MI: Pluto Press.

Higgins, C. (2009). From da bomb to *bomba*: Global Hip hop Nation Language in Tanzania. In H. S. Alim, A. Ibrahim, & A. Pennycook (Eds.), *Global linguistic flows: Hip hop cultures, youth identities, and the politics of language* (pp. 95–112). New York, NY: Routledge.

Hill, M. L. (2009). *Beats, rhymes and classroom life: Hip-hop pedagogy and the politics of identity*. New York, NY: Teachers College Press.

Holt, G. S. (1972). "Inversion" in Black communication. In T. Kochman (Ed.), *Rappin' and stylin' out: Communication in urban Black America* (pp. 152–159). Urbana: University of Illinois Press.

Hull, G., & K. Schultz (Eds.). (2002). *School's out! Bridging out-of-school literacies with classroom practice*. New York, NY: Teachers College Press.

Hymes, D. (1972). On communicative competence. In J. B. Pride & J. Holmes (Eds.), *Sociolinguistics* (pp. 269–293). Harmondsworth, England: Penguin.

Ibrahim, A. (1999). Becoming Black: Rap and hip-hop, race, gender, and identity and the politics of ESL learning. *TESOL Quarterly, 33*(3), 349–369.

Ibrahim, A. (2003). "Whassup, homeboy?" Joining the African diaspora: Black English as a symbolic site of identification and language learning. In S. Makoni, G. Smitherman, A. F. Ball, & A. Spears (Eds.), *Black linguistics: Language, society, and politics in Africa and the Americas* (pp. 169–185). London, England: Routledge.

Ibrahim, A. (in press). *"Hey, whassup, homeboy?" Becoming Black: Hip-hop language and culture, race, performativity, and the politics of identity in high school*. Toronto, Ontario, Canada: University of Toronto Press.

Jacobs-Fantauzzi, E. (Director). (2009). *Homegrown: Hiplife in Ghana* [Documentary film]. Ghana: Clenched Fist Productions.

Jaffe, A. (Ed.). (2009). *Stance: Sociolinguistic perspectives*. New York, NY: Oxford University Press.

Jocson, K. M. (2006). Bob Dylan and hip hop: Intersecting literacy practices in youth poetry communities. *Written Communication, 23,* 231–259.

Jones, M. D. W. (2006). An interview with Michael Eric Dyson. *Callaloo, 29,* 786–802.

Kinloch, V. F. (2009). *Harlem on our minds: Place, race, and the literacies of urban youth.* New York, NY: Teachers College Press.

Kirkland, D. E. (2008). The rose that grew from concrete: Postmodern Blackness and the new English education. *English Journal, 97*(5), 69–75.

Kitwana, B. (2005). *Why white kids love hip hop: Wankstas, wiggers, wannabes and the new reality of race in America.* New York, NY: Basic Civitas Books.

Koza, J. (1999). *Rap music: The cultural politics of official representation.* In C. McCarthy, G. Hudak, S. Miklaucic, & P. Saukko (Eds.), *Sound identities: Popular music and the cultural politics of education* (pp. 65–96). New York, NY: Peter Lang.

Ladson-Billings, G. (1995). Toward a theory of culturally relevant pedagogy. *American Educational Research Journal, 32,* 465–491.

Ladson-Billings, G. (1998). Just what is critical race theory and what's it doing in a nice field like education? *Qualitative Studies in Education, 11,* 7–24.

Ladson-Billings, G. (2009). Foreword. In M. L. Hill (Eds.), *Beats, rhymes and classroom life* (pp. vii–x). New York, NY: Teachers College Press.

Lee, C. D. (1993). *Signifying as a scaffold to literary interpretation.* Urbana, IL: National Council of Teachers of English.

Lee, C. D. (2007). *Culture, literacy, and learning: Taking bloom in the midst of the whirlwind.* New York, NY: Teachers College Press.

Lin, A. (2009). Respect for da chopstick hip hop: The politics, poetics and pedagogy of Cantonese verbal art in Hong Kong. In H. S. Alim, A. Ibrahim, & A. Pennycook (Eds.), *Global linguistic flows: Hip hop cultures, youth identities, and the politics of language* (pp. 159–178). New York, NY: Routledge.

Low, B. E. (2011). *Slam school: Learning through conflict in the hip-hop and spoken word classroom.* Palo Alto, CA: Stanford University Press.

Magubane, Z. (2006). Globalization and gangster rap: Hip hop in the post-Apartheid city. In D. Basu & S. Lemelle (Eds.), *The vinyl ain't final: Hip hop and the globalization of black popular culture* (pp. 208–229). Ann Arbor, MI: Pluto Press.

Mahiri, J. (2004). *What they don't learn in school: Literacy in the lives of urban youth.* New York, NY: Peter Lang.

Maxwell, I. (2003). *Phat beats, dope rhymes: Hip hop down under comin' upper.* Middletown, CT: Wesleyan University Press.

McLaren, P. (1995). Gangsta pedagogy and ghettoethnicity: The hip hop nation as a counterpublic sphere. *Socialist Review, 25*(2), 9–55.

McWhorter, J. (2003). How hip-hop holds Blacks back. *City Journal, Summer.* Retrieved from http://www.city-journal.org/html/13_3_how_hip_hop.html

Meghelli, S. (2007). The making of a global hip hop nation, from the Bronx to the *Banlieues*: An oral history with Sidney Duteil. *Black Arts Quarterly, 12,* 21–26.

Morgan, M. (2001). "Nuthin' but a G thang": Grammar and language ideology in Hip Hop identity. In S. Lanehart (Ed.), *Sociocultural and historical contexts of African American Vernacular English* (pp. 187–210). Athens: University of Georgia Press.

Morrell, E. (2008). *Critical literacy and urban youth: Pedagogies of access, dissent, and liberation.* New York, NY: Routledge.

Morrell, E., & Duncan-Andrade, J. M. (2004). What they do learn in school: Hip-hop as a bridge to canonical poetry. In J. Mahiri (Ed.), *What they don't learn in school: Literacy in the lives of urban youth* (pp. 247–268). New York, NY: Peter Lang.

Neal, M. A. (2006). *New Black man.* New York, NY: Routledge.

Newman, M. (2005). Rap as literacy: A genre analysis of hip-hop ciphers. *Text, 25,* 399–436.

Newman, M. (2009). "That's all concept; it's nothing real": Reality and lyrical meaning in rap. In H. S. Alim, A. Ibrahim, & A. Pennycook (Eds.), *Global linguistic flows: Hip hop Cultures, youth identities, and the politics of language* (pp. 195–212). New York, NY: Routledge.

Noguera, P. A. (2003). *City schools and the American dream: Reclaiming the promise of public education.* New York, NY: Teachers College Press.

Ochs, E., & Schieffelin, B. B. (1984). Language acquisition and socialization: Three developmental stories and their implications. In R. A. Shweder & R. A. LeVine (Eds.), *Culture theory: Essays on mind, self, and emotion* (pp. 276–320). Cambridge, England: Cambridge University Press.

Omoniyi, T. (2006). Hip-hop through the World Englishes lens: A response to globalization. In J. S. Lee & Y. Kachru (Eds.), *World Englishes: Symposium on world Englishes in popular culture, 25,* 195–208.

Omoniyi, T. (2009). "So I choose to do am Naija style": Hip hop, language, and postcolonial identities. In H. S. Alim, A. Ibrahim, & A. Pennycook (Eds.), *Global linguistic flows: Hip hop cultures, youth identities, and the politics of language* (pp. 113–135). New York, NY: Routledge.

Ortner, S. (2006). *Anthropology and social theory: Culture, power, and the acting subject.* Durham, NC: Duke University Press.

Osumare, H. (2007). *The Africanist aesthetic in global hip-hop: Power moves.* New York, NY: Palgrave Macmillan.

Pardue, D. (2004a). Putting *mano* to music: The mediation of race in Brazilian rap. *Ethnomusicology Forum, 13,* 253–286.

Pardue, D. (2004b). Writing in the margins: Brazilian hip-hop as an educational project. *Anthropology and Education Quarterly, 35,* 411–432.

Pennycook, A. (2003). Global Englishes, Rip Slime and performativity. *Journal of Sociolinguistics, 7,* 513–533.

Pennycook, A. (2007). *Global Englishes and transcultural flows.* London, England: Routledge.

Pennycook, A., & Mitchell, T. (2009). Hip hop as dusty foot philosophy: Engaging locality. In H. S. Alim, A. Ibrahim, & A. Pennycook (Eds.), *Global linguistic flows: Hip hop cultures, youth identities, and the politics of language* (pp. 25–42). New York, NY: Routledge.

Perry, I. (2004). *Prophets of the hood: Politics and poetics in hip hop.* Durham, NC: Duke University Press.

Perullo, A., & Fenn, J. (2003). Language ideologies, choices, and practices in Eastern African hip hop. In H. Berger & M. Carroll (Eds.), *Global pop, local language* (pp. 19–52). Jackson, MS: University Press of Mississippi.

Petchauer, E. (2009). Framing and reviewing hip hop educational research. *Review of Educational Research, 79,* 946–979.

Philips, S. U. (1970). Participant structures and communicative competence: Warm Springs children in community and classroom. In J. E. Alatis (Ed.), *Bilingualism and language contact: Anthropological, linguistic, psychological and social aspects* (pp. 370–394). Washington, DC: Georgetown University Press.

Pollack, M. (2004). *Colormute: Race talk dilemmas in an American school.* Princeton, NJ: Princeton University Press.

Pough, G. (2004). *Check it while I wreck it: Black womanhood, hip hop culture, and the public sphere.* Boston, MA: Northeastern University Press.

Rampton, B. (Ed.). (1999, November). Styling the other [Special issue]. *Journal of Sociolinguistics, 3*(4).

Richardson, E. (2006). *Hiphop literacies.* New York, NY: Routledge.

Rickford, J., & Rickford, R. J. (2000). *Spoken soul: The story of Black English.* New York, NY: Wiley.

Rivera, R. (2003). *New York Ricans from the hip hop zone.* New York, NY: Palgrave Macmillan.

Rose, T. (1994). *Black noise: Rap music and Black culture in contemporary America.* Middletown, CT: Wesleyan University Press.

Roth-Gordon, J. (2002). Hip Hop *Brasileiro*: Brazilian youth and alternative Black consciousness movements. *Black Arts Quarterly, 7,* 9–19.

Roth-Gordon, J. (2009). Conversational sampling, race trafficking, and the invocation of the *gueto* in Brazilian hip hop. In H. S. Alim, A. Ibrahim, & A. Pennycook (Eds.), *Global* linguistic flows: Hip hop cultures, youth identities, and the politics of language (pp. 63–78). New York, NY: Routledge.

Sarkar, M. (2009). "Still reppin *por mi gente*": The transformative power of language mixing in Quebec hip hop. In H. S. Alim, A. Ibrahim, & A. Pennycook (Eds.), *Global linguistic flows: Hip hop cultures, youth identities, and the politics of language* (pp. 139–158). New York, NY: Routledge.

Sarkar, M., & Allen, D. (2007). Hybrid identities in Quebec hip-hop: Language, territory, and ethnicity in the mix. *Journal of Language, Identity & Education, 6*, 117–130.

Scribner, S., & Cole, M. (1981). *The psychology of literacy*. Cambridge, MA: Harvard University Press.

Smitherman, G. (1977). *Talkin and testifyin: The language of Black America*. Detroit, MI: Wayne State University Press.

Smitherman, G. (2000). *Talkin that talk: Language, culture, and education in African America*. New York, NY: Routledge.

Spady, J. G., Alim, H. S., & Lee, C. G. (1999). *Street conscious rap*. Philadelphia, PA: Black History Museum Press.

Spady, J. G., Alim, H. S., & Meghelli, S. (2006). *Tha global cipha: Hip Hop culture and consciousness*. Philadelphia, PA: Black History Museum Press.

Spady, J. G., & Eure, J. (1991). *Nation conscious rap: The hip hop vision*. Philadelphia, PA: Black History Museum Press.

Stovall, D. (2006). We can relate: Hip hop culture, critical pedagogy, and the secondary classroom. *Urban Education, 41*, 585–602.

Street, B. (1984). *Literacy in theory and practice*. Cambridge, England: Cambridge University Press.

Street, B. (Ed.). (1993). *Cross-cultural approaches to literacy*. Cambridge, England: Cambridge University Press.

Sutton, S. S. (2004). Spoken Word: Performance poetry in the Black community. In J. Mahiri, (Ed.), *What they don't learn in school: Literacy in the lives of urban youth* (pp. 213–242). New York, NY: Peter Lang.

Swedenburg, T. (2002). Hip hop music in the transglobal Islamic underground. *Black culture's global impact. Black Arts Quarterly, 6*(3), 12–21.

Tsujimura, N., & Davis, S. (2009). Dragon Ash and the reinterpretation of hip hop: On the notion of rhyme in Japanese hip hop. In H. S. Alim, A. Ibrahim, & A. Pennycook (Eds.), *Global linguistic flows: Hip hop cultures, youth identities, and the politics of language* (pp. 179–194). New York, NY: Routledge.

Valdés, G. (1996). Con respeto: *Bridging the distances between culturally diverse families and schools*. New York, NY: Teachers College Press.

Valenzuela, A. (1999). *Subtractive schooling: U.S.-Mexican youth and the politics of caring*. New York, NY: State University of New York Press.

wa Thiong'o, N. (1986). *Decolonising the mind: The politics of language in African literature*. New Hampshire, England: Heinemann Educational.

Williams, A. D. (2009). The critical cultural cipher: Remaking Paulo Freire's cultural circles using Hip Hop Culture. *International Journal of Critical Pedagogy, 2*, 1–29.

Wunderlich, A. (2006). Cuban hip hop: Making space for new voices of dissent. In D. Basu & S. Lemelle (Eds.), *The vinyl ain't final: Hip hop and the globalization of black popular culture* (pp. 167–179). Ann Arbor, MI: Pluto Press.

Zentella, A. C. (1997). *Growing up bilingual: Puerto Rican children in New York*. Oxford, England: Blackwell.

Chapter 6

The Right to Be Literate: Literacy, Education, and the School-to-Prison Pipeline

MAISHA T. WINN
NADIA BEHIZADEH
Emory University

In 1988, the Modern Language Association hosted "The Right to Literacy" conference at the Ohio State University. Arguing that literacy was a "right" as opposed to a "privilege," participants in this conference grappled with the relationship between literacy, freedom, democracy, and citizenry (Lunsford, Moglen, & Slevin, 1990, p. 2). Twenty years later, scholars contributed to an edited volume titled *Literacy as a Civil Right: Reclaiming Social Justice in Literacy Teaching and Learning* (S. Greene, 2008). In this volume, S. Greene and his colleagues, who initially presented their work at the 2006 National Council of Teachers of English Assembly for Research, challenge and reclaim "the notions of civil rights and social justice," which they posit "have been appropriated by conservatives to explain the goal of increased accountability and testing" (p. 3). Scholars in Greene's edited volume confront the culture of accountability and testing as well as practices that put African American and Latino youth in American public schools under the watchful and critical gaze of the rest of the country. While Greene builds on Nieto's components of social justice, and more specifically her assertion that "social justice is about understanding education and access to literacy as *civil rights*" (Nieto cited in S. Greene, 2008, p. 4), Greene and others question and critique power and privilege through the lens of critical race theory making race and class central to the relationship between schooling, literacy, citizenship, and civil rights. Classroom practitioners and education nonprofits have joined this growing body of research. In *The Right to Literacy in Secondary Schools: Creating a Culture of Thinking*, Plaut (2009) and her colleagues seek to show what schools that adhere to teaching literacy as a "right" may look like in order "to spark a social movement to ensure our education system empowers every student to become fully literate" (p. 1). As scholarship increasingly explores literacy

Review of Research in Education
March 2011, Vol. 35, pp. 147–173
DOI: 10.3102/0091732X10387395
© 2011AERA. http://rre.aera.net

as a "right" for youth, incarcerated and formerly incarcerated youth are often missing from this discussion. Childhood poverty, the lack of early childhood education, and the denial of a college-preparatory K–12 education promoting critical literacies have contributed to producing what has been referred to as the school-to-prison pipeline (Children's Defense Fund, 2007; Duncan, 2000; Fisher, 2008; Meiners, 2007; Polakow, 2000). Youth in underserved and underperforming schools that focus more on discipline policies as opposed to academic rigor would benefit the most if educational institutions adopted the view of literacy as a right. "Unequal life chances" among America's children (Polakow, 2000, p. 10) and the denial of literacy as a civil right are two ways African American and Latino youth are ushered into this pipeline (Lipman, 2008). This review of the research seeks to address how and why particular youth have become potential victims of the school-to-prison pipeline and why scholarship seeking to examine the relationship between literacy and civil rights must make these young lives central to the discussion.

Racial disparities in the U.S. juvenile justice system are widespread (Duncan, 2000; McGrew, 2008; Meiners, 2007; Poe-Yamagata & Jones, 2000; Polakow, 2000). Arguing that the "racial and ethnic disparity in discipline sanctions has not received the attention it deserves," Gregory, Skiba, and Noguera (2010) posit that more studies examining the relationship between the achievement gap and "discipline gap" are needed (p. 65). The purpose of this chapter is to examine the literature on the school-to-prison pipeline—that is, the ushering of African American and Latino youth from schools to jails and prisons through suspensions, expulsions, miseducation, and "diploma denial" (Fine & Ruglis, 2009). We interrogate this literature to examine and complicate the relationship between this so-called pipeline and the denial of literacy as a civil right. Ultimately, we argue that youth-centered scholarship focusing on cultivating critical literacy skills for urban youth can generate possibilities for disrupting and dismantling this pipeline. Educational research needs to raise critical questions about children in urban public schools who routinely encounter surveillance and policing more than a rigorous curriculum and safety net of caring adults. For example, scholarship examining the school-to-prison pipeline has asked, "Whose children do we see when we construct the meaning of childhood at the dawn of the new century in the United States? Which young lives matter and which young lives do not?" (Polakow, 2000, p. 2). Some questions are even more straightforward: "Are the children our future or are they not?" (Gallagher, 2007). These questions challenge education research and the role of teacher education and policymakers in disrupting and dismantling this pipeline.

In this chapter, we provide a selective review of both research and policy represented in part by two concepts that have been discussed in educational research—the "right to learn" (Darling-Hammond, 1997, 2006) and the notion of "literacy as a civil right" (S. Greene, 2008; Plaut, 2009) and how these issues of access and equity are undermined by the school-to-prison pipeline. First, we outline how scholarship, and literacy research in particular, has embraced the ideology of looking at critical literacy and learning as civil rights in an effort to convey the urgency of creating young learners who are equipped for 21st-century ways of knowing. Critical literacy, according to Morrell (2008), "is necessary not only for the critical navigation of hegemonic discourses; it is also essential to the redefining of the self and the transformation of oppressive social structures and relations of production" (p. 5). We argue that the lack of opportunities for youth to engage in literate practices such as reading, writing, and speaking feeds the school–prison nexus.

Next, we provide a narrative of the history of the "educational debt" that has contributed to and in some cases propelled inequities by ushering youth from schools to jails and prisons (Ladson-Billings, 2006). We contextualize salient issues facing urban youth in a larger discourse of the "educational debt" as opposed to focusing on the language of the "achievement gap" because of the legacy of denying education and thus literacy as a "civil right" (S. Greene, 2008). The historical framing is followed by an examination of school-to-prison pipeline literature, both scholarly works as well as policy reports, in order to examine the factors that create this so-called pipeline and how it affects urban youth. We offer a discussion of emerging scholarship that challenges the school-to-prison pipeline by focusing on critical literacy development and how critical literacy can be used as a tool for urban youth. Finally, we offer researchable and practice-focused issues to consider. Throughout this chapter, we use a sociocritical lens to understand literacy (Gutiérrez, 2008)— that is, a lens that underscores "historicizing literacy." We aim to show the relationship between the school-to-prison pipeline and a legacy of leaving particular students behind.

LITERACY AS A CIVIL RIGHT

Civil rights are composed of skills and actions necessary for political and civil involvement. Voting and protesting are commonly viewed as civil rights, but reading and writing are also activities crucial for civic involvement, specifically the ability to read and write *critically*. Because of the destructive consequences of denying both basic and critical literacies to students (e.g., due to incarceration), literacy has become a new civil rights frontier (S. Greene, 2008) alongside a similar movement connecting civil rights to mathematical literacy (Moses & Cobb, 2001). "Education," argues Gomez, "is the one realm in which constitutional guarantee of equal opportunity has not been adequate to promote and protect the social equity embedded in the promise of U. S. democracy" (Gomez cited in S. Greene, 2008, p. 3). Although we disagree that education is the sole realm, Gomez is correct in illuminating the neglected nature and potential power of education in the role of civic engagement. Education is a civil right, especially learning to read and write critically, for students to both interrogate written texts and disseminate their own writings. Critical reading and writing skills are tools students need to navigate and transform the world around them (Freire & Macedo, 1987). Reading and writing critically are essential tools for survival in a current educational system in which students of color are disproportionately in special education, suspended, and expelled, which all contribute to a higher likelihood of incarceration (Meiners, 2007).

A key link between inequitable school policies and prisons is low-quality education or a lack of education. Official policies such as zero-tolerance discipline and unofficial policies such as overrepresentation of students of color in special education affect the quality and quantity of education students receive, which affects students' academic achievement and opportunities (Meiners, 2007). Time spent in out-of-school and in-school suspensions or misplaced in self-contained special education classrooms contributes to the gap in standardized test scores between White and Black students. As data from the National Center for Education Statistics (NCES) demonstrate, Black students are significantly trailing behind their White counterparts in terms of standardized test scores. Across all subject areas, White students on average score 26 points above Black students on a 500-point scale (Vanneman, Hamilton, Baldwin Anderson, & Rahman, 2009). Gaps in test scores are misleading and are not the real problems. The real problems are a focus on basic skills, remediation, and overzealous test preparation that occurs more often in classrooms serving students of color (Apple, 2001; Gillborn & Youdell, 2000).

Low-quality literacy education is a key component of the school-to-prison pipeline. In this section, we review research on how literacy education, which values student backgrounds and develops critical reading and writing skills, is all too often missing in classrooms serving students of color. The causes for violations of the right to literacy are explored, including narrow constructions of literacy, the impact of federal accountability policies, false beliefs in color blindness, a discourse of deficiency regarding students of color, and deficit views of languages other than mainstream American English. Even one of these issues can limit a student's access to critical literacy; unfortunately, many of these issues appear together.

AN EVOLVING CONSTRUCT OF LITERACY

An essential question for literacy researchers and educators is, "If literacy is a civil right, how is literacy defined?" To understand the relationship between the denial of literacy and prisons, we first examine how literacy has been defined over time and how narrow constructions of what it means to be literate contribute to the school-to-prison pipeline. Historically, literacy in the United States has been commonly defined as "the bare ability to read and write" (Good & Merkel, 1973). The content, context, and purpose of reading were unimportant; literacy was conceptualized as a neutral, decontextualized skill (Goody & Watt, 1963; Olson, 1977; Ong, 1982). It was not until the 1980s and 1990s when sociocultural research became more prominent (Barton & Hamilton, 1998; Dyson, 1993; Heath, 1983; Scribner & Cole, 2001; Szwed, 1981) that how literacy was defined, taught, and tested was significantly called into question, although there was (and still is) "little agreement among educators on the meaning of 'literacy'" (Barrow & Milburn, 1990).

One useful model that emerged was Street's (1984) ideological model of literacy, which includes the social context and political nature of literacy, as well as allows for multiple versions of literacy (literacies) versus one monolithic literacy. Street cautions that being defined as literate or illiterate depends on who creates the definition.

Cross-culturally, literate practices are not the same. By the first decade of the 21st century, UNESCO reported that early literacy campaigns internationally "revealed that literacy cannot be sustained by short-term operations or by top-down and uni-sectoral actions primarily directed toward the acquisition of technical skills that do not give due consideration to the contexts and motivations of learners" (UNESCO Education Sector, 2004). In other words, the social context of learning cannot be ignored. Teaching basic literate skills that are not equally valued or even valid across countries needs to be replaced with literacy education that connects to the specific social realities and literate practices of culturally diverse communities.

We use Street's (1984) conception of literacy when we speak of literacy as a civil right, including critical reading skills, learning to analyze and synthesize materials, making meaning in multiple texts, and engaging in literary reasoning (Lee, 2001). Denying this right can put young learners at a disadvantage when competing for jobs or college admissions. Even more alarming, denial of literacy contributes to the possibility of dropping out or going to prison (Lipman, 2008). It is important to note that by being offered only one version of literacy, students are in effect denied literacy because isolated and irrelevant instruction often fails to result in the development of rich literate practices that are necessary for social and political involvement (Bakhtin, 1981; Cope & Kalantzis, 2000). Literacy as a civil right really translates into "literacies" as a civil right, including children's right to their own creative and cultural literate practices, academic literacy, which is on the test, and critical literacy, which transcends what can be tested, for example, epistemic writing in which writing becomes "a personal search for meaning" (Bereiter, 1980, p. 88).

If literacy acquisition is viewed through the lens of civil rights, then administrators, teachers, and researchers must provide students access to hybrid literate practices, which then allow students to be successful on tests and challenge narrow definitions of literacy that perpetuate the discourse of deficiency. Both school and student literacies are needed, with the student literacies providing a bridge to school literacies (Lee, 2001; Mahiri, 2000/2001). Schooling is political, and teaching students from diverse backgrounds the language of power while valuing students' cultures (Delpit, 1995) is an important part of dismantling the school-to-prison pipeline because this form of instruction increases students' abilities to question, criticize, and create. At the same time, students have the right to their own language(s) and the language of power (Kinloch, 2010; Smitherman, 1999). To reduce these apparent tensions, students need classrooms that value multiple literacies.

NO CHILD LEFT BEHIND AND DECLINING ACADEMIC RIGOR

The decline of academic rigor in schools has contributed to the culture of the school-to-prison pipeline. Academic rigor is characterized by complex intellectual problems that expand and develop higher cognitive thinking skills such as synthesizing and evaluating (Bloom, 1956). To achieve academic rigor in literacy, students need a literacy education that is social, contextualized, and values multiple literacies. Yet No Child Left Behind (NCLB) and the testing culture induced by this policy of education assume homogeneous students and one literacy (Au, 2007; S. Greene, 2008; Lipman, 2008). Current reform assumes that literacy can be reduced to a set of skills separate from any cultural ideology or practices (S. Greene, 2008). Although sociocultural perspectives on literacy learning have become widespread (Engëstrom, 1987; Gutiérrez, Baquedano-Lopez, & Tejada, 1999; Gutiérrez, Rymes, & Larson, 1995; Lee, 2001, 2006; Nasir & Hand, 2006; Roth & Lee, 2007), the dominant paradigm employed by NCLB is that literacy is neutral. When policymakers employ a neutral conception of literacy, a result has been to increase the amount of time struggling students spend with irrelevant and basic curriculum that does not connect to their personal and cultural literate practices, resulting in low academic rigor (Au, 2007). By centering on acquisition of basic and standardized skills, federal policies such as NCLB, which intend to close the Black–White achievement gap, actually widen it (Mintrop & Sunderman, 2009). In addition, the idea of neutral literacy represented in standardized tests may encourage administrators and teachers to develop a color-blind ideology and discourse of deficiency regarding students who have different literate practices (S. Greene, 2008; Ladson-Billings, 2009a; Lipman, 2008).

Lipman (2008) argues that "rather than enrich teaching and learning and promote the sorts of literacies and academic dispositions prized in the new economy, accountability policies promoted a narrow focus on skills to pass high-stakes tests" (p. 53). Scholars like Lipman demonstrate how declining academic rigor (specifically, an emphasis on basic skills rather than higher level skills) because of a focus on high-stakes testing occurs most often in schools with students of color who have been historically underserved (S. Greene & Abt-Perkins, 2003; Lipman, 2008). Students who are already behind because of the "education debt" owed to them (Ladson-Billings, 2006) are then presented with a watered-down curriculum that reinscribes the subordination of knowledge and identity historically experienced by marginalized groups (Lipman, 2008). Of course, the irony is that this is the very curriculum intended to reduce the achievement gap.

As Fecho and Skinner (2008) argue, "If literacy is a civil right, we need a literacy that gets beyond the rote skill and drill of phonics, decoding, and comprehension" (p. 105). Without higher-level skills such as writing persuasively and reading critically, low-achieving students are not given access to the tools necessary to succeed both in and out of school. Mintrop and Sunderman (2009) through their work with the Civil Rights Project have detailed how the federal accountability system encourages states to adopt low standards of achievement so that struggling schools can meet their goals. Teachers are then pushed "to run a tight ship around test-driven basic skills remediation . . . This is particularly destructive for poor students and students of color who, more so than White students, are concentrated in the schools that NCLB identifies as failing" (Mintrop & Sunderman, 2009, p. 360). Furthermore, Au (2007) established that high-stakes testing contracted curriculum, fractured knowledge, and led to teacher-centered pedagogy. In fact, in his meta-synthesis of 49 studies, this dominant "theme triplet" was evident in 75% of the studies that generated themes in all three aspects of curriculum (p. 263). When students of color are denied access to a rigorous and challenging education, their job options become limited, supporting a "barbell economy" with students of color channeled into low-paying jobs or prisons (Lipman, 2008).

THE MYTH OF COLOR BLINDNESS AND DISCOURSE OF DEFICIENCY

In addition to federal policies, another factor contributing to the denial of critical literacy education is institutional illiteracy within schools as demonstrated by two related concepts: the myth of color blindness and the discourse of deficiency. Although seemingly contradictory beliefs, the combination of claiming not to see skin color and then expecting students of color to be inferior prevents schools from providing the culturally responsive teaching that students need. The practices of teachers who unknowingly (or knowingly) participate in the discourse of deficiency also contribute to students of color being denied access to literacy (Ballenger, 1999; Paley, 1979). Lewis (2008) reflected on her first-year teaching when a fellow teacher and the principal listed all the students with discipline problems in her class. She recalled being dumbfounded when she realized that "they had named every single Black male from our class" (p. 70). When Lewis decided to study other classrooms to see how race factored into how teachers treated students, she found that although many teachers claimed to treat students of color the same as their White counter-parts, claiming to be "color-blind," in reality, the teachers were more likely to disci-pline students of color more severely than White students. When students are sent out of class, they are denied the education that is their right. African American stu-dents "are disciplined and suspended more frequently than White students for sub-jective behaviors like disrespect, excessive noise, threats, and loitering" (Meiners, 2007, p. 33). Teachers and administrators have come to expect this disparity, produc-ing a culture of normality with regard to the school–prison nexus (Dixson, 2008; Lewis, 2008; Meiners, 2007).

Another component in the discourse of deficiency is the media portrayals that contribute to perceptions of youth as violent, dangerous, and in need of manage-ment (Meiners, 2007; Rapping, 2003). Specifically, Meiners (2007) suggests that television and media portray youth as the "superpredator," while "disproportionately using images of street crime that highlight African-Americans or Latinos as perpetra-tors" (p. 83). Dorfman and Schiraldi (2001) corroborate this claim with their meta-synthesis of social science research highlighting how the media portrayal is "off bal-ance" in the overemphasis on youth committing crime, youth of color in particular. This means that teachers who watch the news and see young people of color con-stantly represented as violent, lawless criminals may internalize this image and have lower expectations for their students of color in terms of their behavior. A vicious cycle can develop where teachers expect students of color to misbehave, focus on order in the classroom rather than academic rigor, discipline students of color more severely, and, in short, deny students the academic tools they need to be successful.

Along with inequitable discipline practices, color-blind ideology is the antithesis of culturally relevant pedagogy (Ladson-Billings, 2009b; Lewis, 2008). When students' identities, ways of knowing, and linguistic diversity are ignored or coopted, color-blind ideology encourages irrelevant curriculum for students of color. "Misperspectives" or incorrect versions of Latino contributions to literacy (J. C. Greene, 1994), as well as the lack of acknowledgement of literacies in Native American (McCarty, 2005) and Southeast Asian (Li, 2008) communities, affect children in K–12 schooling. These omissions can make it difficult for students from nondominant communities to view themselves among the "literate and literary" (McHenry & Heath, 1994). In Dixson's (2008) study, she analyzed two classrooms, documenting the beliefs and actions of both the teachers and students as related to race and curriculum. She detailed one White teacher, Ms. Green, whose color-blind ideology caused the teacher's failure to acknowledge the negative impact the one-sided curriculum had on her African American students. Dixson (2008) asserted,

Denzel, Makayla, and other students in the study stated that they explicitly wanted a curriculum that focused on what they described as Black history . . . These students would have welcomed explicit overtures by Green to hand them books and materials that focused on Black people. Green's unwillingness to acknowledge and notice race and distribute materials to students that reflected their cultural backgrounds demonstrates the ways in which she is oblivious to her students' desire for a culturally relevant curriculum. (p. 141)

Ms. Green most likely thought teaching all her students from one standardized text was equitable, yet the text she saw as neutral was only presenting a particular literacy "associated with the transmission and mastery of a unitary Western tradition" (Giroux, 1987, p. 3). For students with different cultural backgrounds who do not see themselves in the text, school can be alienating.

Today, students of color are dropping out and being pushed out of high school, which limits job options and contributes to the school–prison nexus. According to a report from the Center for Research on Students Placed At Risk (CRESPAR), "A majority minority high school is five times more likely to have weak promoting power (promote 50% or fewer freshmen to senior status on time) than a majority white school" (Balfanz & Legters, 2004, p. v). Another study found that more than half of high school dropouts are minority students of color: Hispanic, African American, or Native American (Harada, Kirio, & Yamamoto, 2008). One theory for why students of color are dropping out of high school is that the curriculum is irrelevant, in part because schools fail to acknowledge that different students have different needs based on their cultural heritage. Native American students struggle to be successful in mainstream English-only schools and to balance their heritage with the values of popular culture introduced through the media (Nicholas, 2005). "Students who drop out claim that the curriculum is disconnected from real life and that their schools are impersonal systems where no one really cares about them" (Harada et al., 2008, p. 14). When the curriculum celebrates European history and ignores African history, Latin American history, Asian history, and the history of indigenous peoples, these omissions can insult and alienate students who are not of European heritage.

A RIGHT TO LANGUAGE: COUNTERING DEFICIT VIEWS OF LANGUAGE

Related to the failure to represent diverse cultures in the curriculum, another major component of the discourse of deficiency is the devaluation of different dialects of languages. In Larson's (2003) qualitative study of a Language Arts textbook pilot program, she discovered that

Teachers in the textbook study described their students as being without language, as not having appropriate background experiences to prepare them for school, and as being so far behind as to need extensive remediation to catch up to grade level. (p. 93)

Because these teachers failed to recognize the linguistic diversity of their students, the teachers reduced the curriculum to the minimum they thought the students could handle, mostly relying on worksheets that focused on isolated skills. Also, when African American students used African American Vernacular English (AAVE), they were told they were wrong. If classrooms redefined curriculum by creating a mosaic of the varied texts and literate practices of the students, using what Gutiérrez et al. (1995) call "social heteroglossia," students would have some agency in what counts as school-appropriate curriculum. Social heteroglossia increases academic rigor by aiding in the development of a variety of linguistic tools with which to problem solve, communicate, and access materials.

Students who do not speak what is often referred to as standard English, or the language of tests and textbooks, often encounter curricula and teachers that devalue their primary language. In a Navajo community, McCarty, Romero-Little, and Zepeda (2006) found that although some students were proud of their ability to speak Navajo and saw many positive cultural benefits from speaking their traditional language, other students were ashamed of being able to speak Navajo and scoffed at those who did so in school. These students had internalized the message taught in the boarding schools of their parents; speaking Navajo is backward and shameful. Students associated English with progress and opportunity and felt that they needed to make a choice between the two languages. Based on her research in schools that serve Hopi children, Nicholas (2005) forcefully states, "Essentially, schools have silenced the Hopi people" (p. 33). Similarly, in her work *Talkin' and Testifyin'*, Smitherman (1986) refers to the "linguistic tyranny of American education and its negative effects on Black students" (p. 243). AAVE or Black English is repeatedly devalued in academic settings, notwithstanding scholarship demonstrating its linguistic complexity and its benefits for Black children in terms of their cultural identity (Jordan, 1989; Rickford & Rickford, 2000; Smitherman, 1999). In a diverse classroom, Kinloch (2005) describes a day in her college composition class when a student laments how the way she talks results in other people not understanding her, giving her disapproving looks, and not respecting her opinion. In the words of the student, "the more proper or standard or the more you sound like the teacher, the more respect" (p. 92).

For all groups that have been historically oppressed, one element in their oppression was to devalue their language and categorize it as deficient. McCarty et al. (2006) posit, "The psychosocial and linguistic consequences of genocide, colonization, and language repression have been documented for speech communities around the world" (p. 671). As the previously detailed research has shown, the devaluing of language is still a functioning practice in American schools. Those who will not conform, who will not accept that their history and language is deficient, all too often end up dropping out of school, or more accurately, being pushed out. Clearly, the right to literacy has been and is being violated for students of color. When schools subscribe to an autonomous or neutral view of literacy (Street, 1984), students who have literate practices outside of this narrowly defined realm are ostracized. The bulk of this opening section on literacy as a civil right has focused on research at the school level, touching on how policies at the district or federal level are creating a culture that does not value multiple literacies. Next, we turn to a deeper analysis of the zero-tolerance policies that create a deleterious atmosphere for learning and explicitly prepare particular groups of students for prison rather than professional and academic success.

PUBLIC ENEMIES, EDUCATION'S PRISONERS, AND THE CREATION OF A SCHOOL-TO-PRISON PIPELINE

Youth have been increasingly portrayed as dangerous, undisciplined, and in need of surveillance in the news and other forms of media, thus constructing them as public enemies (Meiners, 2007). This notion of youth as public enemies has prompted some schools—especially those serving youth of color—to hire more security, install metal detectors and surveillance cameras, and even employ police officers in schools. We challenge and question the ways in which youth identities get created; the more youth are constructed as dangerous and in need of management, the fewer opportunities they will have to develop self-discipline and learn how to make responsible decisions for themselves. For example, McGrew (2008) has argued that youth in poor urban districts are actually "education's prisoners." In other words, overpolicing and zero-tolerance policies are enabling school security and campus police to punish students for the smallest infractions (Advancement Project, 2000). Zero-tolerance policies create a police state in urban public schools and detract from focused work on education and literacy. Duncan (2000) refers to such policies as "urban pedagogies." According to Duncan, urban pedagogies "work through and upon adolescents of color" by focusing on "discipline and control" as opposed to "intellectual rigor and the development of meaningful skills" (p. 30). Although discipline is important, the word has been misused. Recent scholarship argues that students need to develop self-discipline rather than be disciplined, which will be reviewed later in this article (Yang, 2009). Indeed, the relationship between the increased policing, zero tolerance, and a "public assault" (Polakow, 2000) on American children can be linked to an ideology that Black and Brown bodies are in need of surveillance and control in underserved urban public schools.

Scholars have argued that the police presence and ushering of particular youth from schools to jails "illustrates that a failure to control oneself, to keep that anger in check, to act and learn appropriately, in particular for those in any way marginalized, might mean school expulsion, criminalization, or pathologization" (Meiners, 2007, p. 30). Zero-tolerance policies and practices in schools have become one of the greatest contributing builders of this pipeline (see Civil Rights Project, 2000; National Association of the Advancement of Colored People Legal Defense and Educational Fund [NAACP Legal Defense and Educational Fund], 2005). Although schools have always encountered students fighting, skipping class, and breaking school rules, many of these infractions are now being handled by law enforcement rather than on-site conflict management or intervention strategies. As school administrators are increasingly pressured to raise test scores, students who are deemed as distractions and "throwaways" (Bell, 2000) are being removed from class rosters and attendance sheets. Youth are aware of this "throwaway" status; once they become disinvested in their education process they become targets for policies and practices that push them out of schools and into detention centers and jails (Fisher, 2008; Winn, 2010). Fine and Ruglis (2009) refer such ideologies and practices as "circuits of dispossession"—that is, a systematic funneling of public education funding to private enterprises. "With moves toward privatization," argue Fine and Ruglis, "state responsibility for the provision of adequate education falls off the hook, testing companies', private vendors', and publishers' profits swell; police-in-school and military recruitment budgets grow and youth of color slowly disappear" (p. 21). Building and sustaining relationships among students and their peers, students and teachers as well as students and school staff become secondary to using budget line items for the management of Black and Brown bodies.

The "zero-tolerance revolution" (Parenti, 2008, p. 70) has resulted in students being pushed out and an "overrepresentation" of African Americans in school suspension rates is well documented (Gilliam, 2005; Gilliam & Shahar, 2006; NAACP Legal Defense and Educational Fund, 2005; Noguera, 2003b). Expulsions and suspensions from school increase the likelihood for incarceration, thus making African American students prime candidates for the movement from schools to jails. In a multisited ethnography following incarcerated girls' trajectory in a theater program to their involvement after being released from detention centers, Fisher found that peer conflicts in school, as well as searches by school security (including male security officers searching girls), feed the pipeline (Fisher, 2008; Winn, in press). Furthermore, girls who have infractions that initially took place off campus receive probation violations for any school suspensions.

Many children and youth are scanned, wanded, and greeted by security guards or polices officers who have been hired as security long before they are greeted by teachers, counselors, and administrators. This culture of surveillance and policing diminishes opportunities for children to view schools as a potential safety net and teachers as well as other school personnel as their advocates. Teachers are under increasing pressure to raise test scores and to meet accountability measures with fewer resources, making them less patient to take care of classroom conflict "in house." When students have been criminalized through such policies, their "developmental needs" have been compromised "by not allowing students to form strong and trusting relationships with key adults and by creating negative attitudes toward fairness and justice" (Advancement Project, 2000, p. 33). Zero-tolerance hides behind a "race-neutral vocabulary." However, the reality is that Black and Latino students are entering the school-to-prison pipeline more than their White and Asian peers. Although the normalizing of expectations for incarceration has profound consequences for poor youth of color (Meiners, 2007), it also has implications for teachers and administrators looking for alternatives to harsh punishments (Yang, 2009). When detention centers and jails are considered a viable option, school administration and staff often cease to think critically about strategies, solutions, and alternative ways to address problems that arise with students and depend on the culture of incarceration.

FROM "EDUCATION DEBT" TO "ACHIEVEMENT GAP": HISTORICIZING THE SCHOOL-TO-PRISON PIPELINE

The overrepresentation of poor youth of color in detention centers, jails, and prisons is part of a larger landscape in which communities of color have been denied access to educational institutions and the tools needed to navigate the American workforce. In an effort to contextualize the achievement gap in American public schools, Ladson-Billings (2006) signaled a call to critically examine the "education debt" the United States owes its children. Ladson-Billings posits that pervasive historical, economic, political, and moral debts must frame any discussion of an achievement gap. Families of color, according to Ladson-Billings, "have regularly been excluded from the decision-making mechanisms that should ensure their children receive quality education" (p. 7). Literacy scholars have demonstrated the ways in which this debt looms over children and youth in Native American (McCarty, 2005), African American (Ball & Lardner, 2005; Fisher, 2009; Ladson-Billings, 2005; Lee, 2006, 2007; Smitherman, 1999), Latino/a (Gutiérrez, Ali, & Henríquez, 2010), and South East Asian (Li, 2008) communities.

The notion of an educational debt is inextricably linked to the building as well as to the potential dismantling of the school-to-prison pipeline. For example, Duncan (2009) argues that the historical significance of "race-making" in America—beginning with the enslavement of Africans in America—cannot be undermined when examining the 21st-century crisis of America's fixation with incarceration. "By stigmatizing black populations with the institutional brands of 'slave' or 'felon,'" Duncan posits, "race-making institutions, such as plantations and prisons, have provided a public rationale for why certain groups are systematically denied the full rights of citizenship" (p. 5). Tracing the trajectory of the "Negro job"—that is, menial and sometimes degrading work without adequate compensation—Duncan asserts the new "Negro job" is being a prisoner. James Anderson's (1988) pivotal study of education in the South traces the Black struggle for public education after the enslavement of Africans in America and elsewhere; scholars have argued that a period of "re-enslavement" took place between the Civil War and World War II (Blackmon, 2008). Blackmon asserts that in the late 19th century when public education was emerging, Black and White per-pupil spending was the same. According to Blackmon, White people found it "infuriating" to know that part of their "white taxes" helped educate Black children "rather than solely their own" (p. 105). Immigrant families and children of migrant farm workers have also experienced discrimination and marginalization in educational institutions (Gutiérrez, 2008; Gutiérrez et al., 2010; Gutiérrez & Vossoughi, 2010).

Similarly, Ladson-Billing's (2006) concept of an education debt is evidenced in the discrepancies among per-pupil spending in urban school districts versus districts in affluent suburbs. For example, Ladson-Billings posits that New York City per-pupil spending is $11,627 with 72% Black and Latina/o students, while the 91% White Manhasset schools spend $22, 311 per pupil. Chicago public schools are 87% Black and Latina/o and spend $8,482 per pupil, while the Highland Park suburb spends $17,291 per pupil in a district that is 90% White (Kozol cited in Ladson-Billings, 2006). These figures raise questions about the impact of desegregation in American public schools. Siddle Walker's (1996) groundbreaking study of education in a segregated African American school found that the teachers and students developed relationships with students that encouraged students to reach "their highest potential." Although Siddle Walker's work is not typically considered in a discussion of the school-to-prison pipeline, it is essential to question the ways in which the ethic of care became lost during desegregation. Siddle Walker's scholarship also forces the education community to interrogate how integration and the forced separation of teachers from students who shared ways of being, knowing, as well as core values were disrupted. Schools focused on appearing to be equitable and just while focusing on roles as opposed to relationships. Black youth moved from spaces where they were surrounded by a safety net of loving, caring teachers who knew and understood them, their families, and their values to hostile environment, where their intellect and humanity were consistently questioned and challenged. More specifically, scholars are challenging the education research community to consider the *Brown v. Board of Education* ruling and what must happen in literacy instruction in order to ensure that another 50 years does not pass in vain (Ball, 2006).

Issues of inequity are not relegated to the American educational system or to the juvenile justice system. In fact, countries are replicating America's juvenile policies without empirical evidence that these policies work. Next, we explore the ways in which American juvenile justice practices have far-reaching implications abroad.

EXPLORING (IN)JUSTICE: THE GLOBALIZATION OF THE SCHOOL-TO-PRISON PIPELINE

Although schools are not the sole factor in cultivating these values, they form part of America's potential to foster democratic engagement in all its citizens (Noguera, 2003a). A focus on personal responsibility, which is undoubtedly important yet not paramount, has discouraged juvenile courts from contextualizing young peoples' lives against the backdrop of poor and underserved schools and communities in the United States and abroad. In fact, the notion of youth justice in the context of the United States has been replaced with, "Look out kid, it's something you did" (Dohrn, 2000).

Asserting that "public policies make and unmake young lives," Polakow (2000, p. 2) and others have uncovered the ways in which the school-to-prison pipeline is inextricably linked to eradicating social programs and emphasizing the privatization of public failures (Meiners, 2007; Muncie, 2005). Eradicating social problems was part and parcel of focusing on personal responsibility and scholars have argued that neoliberal agendas, defined later in this section, undermine public education for youth in urban schools (Fine & Ruglis, 2009; Lipman, 2008). As the United States earned its reputation as the "most avid incarcerator" or the "incarceration nation," it may not be surprising that it is the only developed country that did not sign the 1989 U.N. Convention on the Rights of the Child. This document underscores in its preamble that ". . . the child should be fully prepared to live an individual life in society . . . and in particular in the spirit of peace, dignity, tolerance, freedom, equality, and solidarity." Dignity, tolerance, freedom, equality, and solidarity are often nonexistent as urban schools struggle with fewer resources, including trained and credentialed teachers, books, and physical space (Darling-Hammond, 2006; Kozol, 1991, 2005).

The disappearance of youth justice has also demonstrated "transatlantic replicability" (Muncie, 2005, p. 39). In a study examining the globalization of neoliberal policies in the shaping of youth and juvenile justice, Muncie asserts that young people all over the globe are being governed "through" crime and disorder (p. 40). Muncie defines neoliberal policies as "the privatizing of the state sector" and in the context of youth justice the "commodifying of crime control." Lipman (2008) asserts that neoliberalism is

an ensemble of economic and social policies that promote the primacy of the market and individual self-interest, unrestricted flows of capital, deep reductions in the cost of labor, sharp retrenchment of the public sphere, and withdrawal of government from providing social welfare. (p. 45)

For example, youth and juvenile justice systems in the United Kingdom and Canada have become increasingly Americanized by focusing on youth who are "at risk" for committing crime. In the context of the United States, there has been a strategic shift in the ways youth/juvenile justice has been viewed in the 1970s, where it experienced a more social focus. However, in the aforementioned 1980s, there was a shift from examining contexts of crime to the crime itself. This purposeful movement to focus on "deeds rather than needs," according to Muncie (2005), creates a "double jeopardy" for young people who he argues are "sentenced for their background as well as their offence" (p. 38).

For example, Spain adopted the "model of responsibility" in 1992 as part of its Juvenile Court Reform Act of 1992 (and ratified it in 2000). Although this model was supposed to create a "balance between education and punishment," Alberola and

Molina (2008) argue that the act favors the English *No more excuses* more than the U.N. Rights of the Child. Other European countries' discourse of youth culture mirror the United States' characterization of youth as becoming increasingly more dangerous and delinquent. Although France has many options available to magistrates and prosecutors (Wyvekens, 2008), questions have been raised about the number of immigrant and minority youth who are considered "suspects" in French cities (Terrio, 2009). Following the October 2005 riots that ensued after Paris police shot and killed two French youth of North African ancestry, Terrio conducted an ethnography and archival study of the Paris juvenile courts. Terrio interrogates the "delinquency of exclusion" (p. 13). This term, coined by former juvenile judge Denis Salas "was a category conflated with disadvantaged Muslim youth, both French citizens and immigrants, spatially rooted in stigmatized urban and suburban places" (p. 13).

Even in studies examining the globalization of American incarceration policies and practices, there is not much focus on the experiences of girls in the juvenile justice system. In the following section, we look at the gendering of the school-to-prison pipeline and the ways in which scholars are framing issues with girls and incarceration.

GENDERING AND RACE-ING THE SCHOOL-TO-PRISON PIPELINE

Girls and woman are the fasting growing population in detention centers, jails, and prisons (Dohrn, 2000; Gadsden, Jacobs, Bickerstaff, Park, & Kane, 2008). In fact, the juvenile justice system includes "young people who are disproportionately minority, under-educated, and female" (Fine & McClelland, 2006, p. 303). Although remaining largely invisible from the discussion of juvenile justice, girls represent one in four youth arrests in the United States (Dohrn, 2000). Girls and women of color, in particular, are experiencing a "global lockdown" (Sudbury, 2005) as they are overrepresented in jails and prisons in countries such as Italy (Angel-Ajani, 2005) and even Australia (Kina, 2005). In 2008, the Pew Center on the States released its report "1 in 100: America behind bars," which asserted that America incarcerates more of its citizens than any other country; not only are 1 in 100 Americans in jails, in prisons, on probation, or on parole, but Black women's incarceration rate has reached the 1 in 100 mark as well.

Black girls in particular are being "celled" more than their White counterparts (Fisher, 2008; Winn, in press) in spite of the fact there is "no new crime wave" among this group (Richie, 2005). Girls are often charged for less serious crimes than boys or what are sometimes referred to as "contempt citations," including running away (Dohrn, 2000; Simkins, Hirsch, Horvat, & Moss, 2004). Additionally, girls are subject to "double standard paternalism/harshness" as well as "loss of freedom" (Dohrn, 2000, p. 173). In other words, girls are not supposed to commit crimes or get in trouble; therefore, once they enter the system they are punished for their gender as well as their offense. This punishment is sometimes cloaked under the title of being neutral or unbiased when it comes to gender. "Gender-neutral" policies and practices in detention centers, jails, and prisons have translated into harsh handling of women and girls as a form of punishment for women's desire to be seen as equal to men. A lack of programs designed specifically for girls means girls often do not have opportunities to engage in any positive or meaningful experiences while incarcerated that will prepare them for lives beyond bars (Chesney-Lind, 1997; Dohrn, 2000; Fisher, 2008; Fisher, Purcell, & May, 2009; Simkins et al., 2004). Simkins et al. argue, "Unlike boys, the formation of a girl's mature identity must also include meaningful and stable relationships with adults" (p. 58).

Because many of the new arrests of girls are taking place in schools (Simkins et al., 2004), it is imperative to consider the ways in which the school-to-prison pipeline has been gendered. According to Simkins et al., the incarcerated girls interviewed in their study had already "experienced a lifetime's worth of abuse" by the time they entered middle and high school (p. 60). Simkins and her colleagues also found that girls who struggled with suspensions, expulsions, truancy, and being held back a grade were contenders for the school-to-prison pipeline. High school proved to be the most difficult transition, thus making ninth grade a pivotal year. Additionally, for girls who have already become entangled in the juvenile justice system, life outside of school consumed them, making coursework and the possibility of participating in a school community an afterthought. Girls often worried about safe and adequate housing, family, and meeting basic needs (food, toiletries, and transportation). Studies that have included interviews of adjudicated girls have demonstrated how girls can point to changes occurring in their lives around their middle school years where school became increasingly difficult (Fisher, 2008; Richie, 2005, Simkins et al., 2004). These "changes" occurred during adolescence as girls became prey for sexual abusers. Some scholars argue that the omission of sexuality education from the school curriculum (Fine & McClelland, 2006) and forums to discuss these issues can make girls more vulnerable to unhealthy relationships that contribute to poor decision making.

A factor that has largely been ignored when considering the burgeoning numbers of girls in the juvenile justice system is that most incarcerated girls and women report having been physically and sexually abused at different points in their lives (Fine & McClelland, 2006). Abstinence only until marriage (AOUM) curriculum or the omission of any sex and sexuality education further marginalizes girls who were abused by silencing their histories of abuse and forcing them to internalize anger, rage, and profound guilt. "As a form of social control on girls, and disproportionately Black and Latino girls," according to Fine and McClelland, "juvenile detention fails to remedy the original problems and serves instead to criminalize and diminish the education, economic, and health outcomes of the young women" (p. 304). Many girls and women have found themselves "compelled to crime" (Richie, 1996) following a history of being physically and sexually abused. More recently, scholarship has examined the assault on queer Black youth and Black girls in particular in the juvenile justice system (Richie, 2005). As these girls refuse to embrace heteronormative values found in their schools, they are often targets of zero-tolerance and gender-neutral policies enacted on urban youth. Once they are incarcerated, girls are typically detained in facilities that house boys as well. Few programs and opportunities, if any, address their needs.

One common thread in studies of incarcerated women and girls is that throughout the process of arrest and detainment they are seldom, if ever, asked to tell their stories. In fact, scholars who interview the incarcerated and the formerly incarcerated are often the first to record their perspectives. Perhaps even more compelling is the fact that when these narratives are finally shared, the incarcerated or formerly incarcerated often lack the tools and critical literacy skills needed to question their experiences (Meiners, 2007; Winn, 2010). This inability to name and challenge the school-to-prison pipeline often means that "potentially revolutionary evidence" gets omitted (Meiners, 2007, p. 140).

TOWARD A PEDAGOGY OF POSSIBILITY: CHANGING THE POWER DYNAMIC

Disrupting and dismantling the school-to-prison pipeline requires research and action challenging the connections between schools and prisons and illuminating the school practices that halt the movement of students to prisons. Emerging scholarship seeking to challenge the school/prison nexus and offer teachers and teacher educators a way to understand their roles in creating a safety net for urban youth, and adjudicated youth in particular, is promising (Fisher, 2008; Fisher et al., 2009; Kinloch, 2009; Winn, in press; Yang, 2009). Some of the central features of such practices include providing students with opportunities to exercise agency in their learning, engage in research with adult allies, write for a variety of purposes, and perform original writing as they prepare for lives beyond high school. In this final section, we review emerging scholarship that has the potential to restore the right to be literate and that repositions marginalized youth as deserving and worthy of a robust education.

Yang (2009) argues the achievement gap is indeed a "mirror image" to the punishment gap; in other words, students who receive the most punishment in schools are often those who are not excelling in their academic work. Yang is careful not to use the word "discipline" as a substitute for "punishment." In his work with teachers, administrators, and school communities seeking to revisit policies and practices that contribute to the school-to-prison pipeline, Yang (2009) posits,

I am not ideologically opposed to suspensions; rather, I ask educators to prove that their discipline system is inclusionary. Crudely speaking, more discipline should result in more achievement. (p. 51)

Yang (2009) recommends programs that support students in developing self-discipline—or a set of practices a young person will undoubtedly need throughout his or her K–12 experience and beyond. Two pathways leading to this notion of self-discipline, argues Yang, include "a framework for differences in discipline across classrooms" and a model of practitioner inquiry "through which we might develop discipline in the particulars of our different learning spaces" (p. 53). Yang's work has implications for small learning communities and schools that underscore the power of relationships as opposed to roles and titles. Young people need self-discipline; however, this discipline must be developed through habits of the mind and personal goal setting as opposed to law enforcement and school security.

Fisher (2008) examines the school-to-prison pipeline through the narratives of formerly incarcerated girls who use playwriting and performance to challenge and acquiesce to the schools that left them behind, institutions that detained them, and the communities as well as families who at times misunderstood them (Fisher, 2008; Fisher et al., 2009; Winn, in press). These narratives were collected over the course of 3 years (2006–2009) from formerly incarcerated girls in the Girl Time playwriting and performance summer program. As a participant observer in the Girl Time program, Fisher co-taught playwriting workshops to incarcerated girls with a team of women-teaching artists in regional youth detention centers (RYDCs). RYDCs, in theory, are transitional facilities in which youth who have been arrested are detained as they await juvenile court dates, placements (e.g., to group homes or foster care), or release to their families. However, many young people get stuck in the RYDC maze until their fate is decided, creating a tenuous environment where children and youth are dealing with many unknowns. In the urban southeast where this study took place, these facilities may hold 200 youth with most space reserved for boys. Although youth attend school in these facilities, there are few opportunities for other kinds of learning enrichment beyond Bible study classes. Girl Time is one of the only teaching and learning experiences focused on girls and providing literacy-centered activities such as reading, writing, and public speaking. Fisher (2008) found from her study, including three cohorts of formerly incarcerated girls in Girl Time's intensive summer theater program, that they used playwriting and performance as tools to reintroduce themselves to their peers, families, social service workers, and the public. Writing and performing in plays also became tools for these girls, who are primarily African American and aged 14 to 17 years, to redefine lives that have been "betwixt and between" incarcerated and liberated lives (Winn, in press). Furthermore, the process of writing and building an ensemble—as opposed to the product or polished performance—is an opportunity for girls to experience dialogue through the characters they play and can serve as a rehearsal for dialogue that they often hope will ensue as a result of their newly acquired understanding of particular relationships (Fisher, 2008; Fisher et al., 2009). Producing youth writing—especially the writings of incarcerated youth—is, of course, not new. Student Press Initiative (SPI) has published the poetry and prose of incarcerated youth on Rikers Island (Horizon Academy Students, 2006). Similar to Fisher's (2008) study, Gordon and Stovall (2009) argue that the writing process invites incarcerated youth to define and redefine themselves through their work. However, most of the youth writing in SPI anthologies has been collected from incarcerated boys. Girl Time's work not only provides a potential pathway toward disrupting the pipeline but also focuses on the needs of girls. Participants cited playwriting and the ability to demonstrate that they were more than their incarceration records as having a profound impact on their self-image, healing relationships with family; and building bridges with teachers, probation officers, and community members who attend their public performance. Additionally, public performances provide a forum where formerly incarcerated girls get to "talk back to their audiences (educators, Department of Juvenile Justice personnel, and families) about what they learned throughout the process.

Increasingly, scholarship is illuminating the ways in which urban youth are redefining themselves and using critical literacy skills to interrogate their environment. For example, Kinloch's (2009) study with two Harlem youth, Phillip and Khaleeq, re-centers the young lives of African American males. Kinloch, Phillip, and Khaleeq examine their lived experiences during the political gentrification in their Harlem neighborhood through critical readings of race and space. Critical readings of race and notions of space in the context of Kinloch's study challenge stereotypes about Harlem and the people, primarily Black and Latino, who have called Harlem home prior to the most recent wave of gentrification. From their blocks in Harlem to the walls of a major university, Phillip and Khaleeq learned to "take a stand" by questioning and challenging their disappearing rights in their own neighborhood (Kinloch, 2009, p. 178). This participatory action research group began as a writing workshop covering a range of topics but ultimately focusing on the Harlem community. Kinloch and her students made the city and specifically Harlem their classroom. Much like Fisher's (2005a, 2005b, 2007; Winn & Ubiles, in press) study of youth poets and their teachers in the Power Writing community in the Bronx, Kinloch wanted these young people to know that they had access to their city, neighborhood, and the cultural institutions they housed. Phillip and Khaleeq attended tenants' association meetings with Kinloch to learn and eventually interrogate the language of gentrification in Harlem. Kinloch's mentoring followed these boys—now young men—to college, and their reflections on this participatory action research experiences were also published with Kinloch's study. Kinloch's strategy, an important way to think about disrupting the pipeline through helping young people cultivate critical literacy skills, was listening to young people:

One specific way I sought to better understand the issues Phillip and Khaleeq were confronting was by listening to *their* perspectives. For instance, I listened to them discuss how the mass media portray Black males as dangerous, the increasing incarceration of youth, and adult activism and youth political rights. (p. 179)

Morrell's (2008) ethnographic work with urban high school students documents the multiple literacy practices of his students, such as reading varied texts on sports and fashion, watching movies or listening to music and then critically evaluating lyrics, writing notes and e-mails, and constructing poems and songs to share with others. Morrell (2008) asserted,

Their non-school lives were saturated with sophisticated literacy practices; and this was true for even the most underperforming students. To label these pupils as illiterate bordered on irresponsible; to say that their literacies were not valued placed the onus squarely on the dominant institution responsible for the devaluing as it also pointed toward a viable plan of action for my curriculum and pedagogy. (p. 92)

Part of the pedagogy of possibility is creating learning environments that are "hybrid" and include multiple literate forms necessary for students and teachers to achieve critical literacies. Students have a right to their own literate practices and the mainstream academic literate practices needed for college and job success; to deny either is to impede students from developing the rich literate identities that are rightfully theirs.

For six consecutive summers, Morrell (2008) cofacilitated a critical research seminar for youth attending underresourced and underperforming schools. Collaborating with K–12 teachers, this group of 25 to 30 students "designed and carried out their own projects, usually investigating issues related to educational equity and youth empowerment . . ." (p. 117). Again, writing in this context focused on agency and change, including "writing for personal understanding and writing for social change" (p. 118). Morrell's project was more than the learning experiences that prepared them for life after high school graduation. Through public speaking at forums and conferences and publishing scholarly papers, students were able to influence state legislation and "most importantly acquire much needed skills for academic advancement, professional membership, and civic engagement" (p. 122).

Similarly, Gutiérrez (2008) has conducted empirical research on a long-term project serving students from migrant-farmworker backgrounds. Housed on the University of California, Los Angeles campus, the Migrant Student Leadership Institute (MSLI) provides a space "in which students begin to conceive who they are and what they might be able to accomplish academically and beyond" (p. 148). Writing is also central to the MSLI and specifically the concept of "testimonio" or rendering of people's understanding of themselves and their social worlds. Gutiérrez's analysis of one testimonio in particular revealed "how poverty, discrimination, exploitation, anti-immigrant sentiment, language ideologies, and education and social practices gone awry complicate current understanding in the learning sciences about learning and development" (p. 149).

Also based in California, Ginwright's (2010) study of radical healing demonstrates the ways in which youth, and African American youth in particular, can develop ways of knowing and being that give them power and agency over their lives. Arguing that youth who grow up in "urban conditions" such as joblessness, a drug economy (and specifically a "crack cocaine economy"), lack of historical connection, and racism need to experience radical healing (e.g., agency, awareness—both political and social, resistance, hope and optimism, personal transformation, and the ability to struggle against racism, sexism, homophobia, and classism). As a scholar and youth advocate with 15 years of experience working with urban youth in Oakland, California, Ginwright (2010) examined the "educational and organizational processes and practices that promote youth healing and agency" (p. 27). One of these practices was the creation of a youth camp, Camp Akili, which worked with cohorts of 100 youth referred by county probation offices, local high schools, churches, and other community-based organizations. Camp Akili had three goals: "to provide structured activities that develop and enhance political awareness, to provide participants with opportunities that encourage and promote psychological and physical wellness, and to provide hands on experiences that are intended to stimulate learning about activism and leadership" (Ginwright, 2010, p. 81). This 5-year study found that experiences such as Camp Akili—like many of the aforementioned studies, "recalibrates what is possible for [young people's] lives and their communities."

CONCLUDING THOUGHTS

Throughout this chapter, we examine the policies, such as miseducation, diploma denial, and the discipline or punishment gap, that contribute to what has been referred to as the school-to-prison pipeline. In this pipeline, particular youth learn that their lives are disposable and that detention centers, jails, and prisons have somehow become an expected part of their life cycle. We assert that specific practices that focus on collaborating with youth to foster critical literacy, such as students performing their writing, students conducting research with adult allies, and students having forums where their voices, ideas, and lived experiences can be heard, will disrupt and potentially dismantle such a pipeline.

Agency is the common thread in the case studies presented throughout this review. Inviting youth to sit at a metaphorical table where they can be engaged in their education, and learn how to read, write, speak, and thus act for themselves, while providing opportunities for youth to view themselves as worthy and deserving participants in community and civic engagement is critical. We argue that the right to be literate, and the right to be critically literate in particular, must be the right of all children and youth.

Educational research should consider focusing on youth-centered research much like those studies discussed in the final section of this chapter. Youth Participatory Action Research (YPAR) projects as well as studies that include the voices of youth could illuminate how youth are experiencing literacy, education, and school-to-prison pipeline issues in their school communities. More studies grounded in sociocultural learning theories examining classrooms using multiple and critical literacies should also be a focused line of inquiry in forthcoming scholarship. Finally, studies of classrooms and schools that promote academic rigor and create a culture of college readiness as opposed to focusing on punishment and surveillance can offer a vision for schools hoping to dismantle the school-to-prison pipeline.

REFERENCES

Advancement Project. (2000, June). *Opportunities suspended*. Retrieved from http://www
.advancementproject.org/sites/default/files/publications/opsusp.pdf
Alberola, C. R., & Molina, E. F. (2008). Continuity and change in the Spanish juvenile justice system. In J. Junger-Tas & S. H. Decker (Eds.), *International handbook of juvenile justice* (pp. 325–348). New York, NY: Springer.

Anderson, J. (1988). *The education of Blacks in the South, 1860–1935.* Chapel Hill: University of North Carolina Press.

Angel-Ajani, A. (2005). Domestic enemies and carceral circles: African women and criminalization in Italy. In J. Sudburys (Ed.), *Global lockdown: Race, gender, and the prison-industrial complex* (pp. 3–18). New York, NY: Routledge.

Apple, M. W. (2001). *Educating the "right" way: Markets, standards, god, and inequity.* New York, NY: RoutledgeFalmer.

Au, W. (2007). High-stakes testing and curricular control: A qualitative metasynthesis. *Educational Researcher, 36,* 258–267.

Bakhtin, M. M. (1981). *The dialogic imagination: Four essays by M. M. Bakhtin.* Austin: University of Texas Press.

Balfanz, R., & Legters, N. (2004). *Which high schools produce the nations dropouts? Where are they located? Who attends them?* Baltimore, MD: Center for Research on the Education of Students Placed At Risk. Retrieved from http://www.csos.jhu.edu/crespar/techReports/Report70.pdf

Ball, A. (Ed.). (2006). *With more deliberate speed: Achieving equity and excellence in education—realizing the full potential of Brown v. Board of Education.* Malden, MA: Blackwell.

Ball, A., & Lardner, T. (2005). *African American literacies unleashed: Vernacular English and the composition classroom.* Carbondale: Southern Illinois University Press.

Ballenger, C. (1999). *Teaching other people's children: Literacy and learning in a bilingual classroom.* New York, NY: Teachers College Press.

Barrow, R., & Milburn, G. (Eds.) (1990). *A critical dictionary of educational concepts: An appraisal of selected ideas and issues in educational theory and practice* (2nd ed.). New York: Harvester Wheatsheaf.

Barton, D., & Hamilton, M. (1998). *Local literacies: Reading and writing in one community.* London, England: Routledge.

Bell, J. (2000). Throwaway children: Conditions of confinement and incarceration. In V. Polokow (Ed.), *The public assault on American's children: Poverty, violence and juvenile injustice* (pp. 157–187). New York, NY: Teachers College Press.

Bereiter, C. (1980). Development in writing. In L. W. Gregg & E. R. Steinberg (Eds.), *Cognitive processes in writing* (pp. 73–93). Hillsdale, NJ: Erlbaum.

Blackmon, D. A. (2008). *Slavery by another name: The re-enslavement of Black-Americans from the Civil War to World War II.* New York, NY: Double Day.

Bloom, B. S. (Ed.). (1956). *Taxonomy of educational objectives, the classification of educational goals—Handbook I: Cognitive domain.* New York, NY: McKay.

Chesney-Lind, M. (1997). *The female offender: Girls, women, and crime.* Thousand Oaks, CA: Sage.

Children's Defense Fund. (2007). *America's cradle to prison pipeline.* Washington, DC: Author. Retrieved from http://www.childrensdefense.org/site/PageServer?pagename=c2pp_report2007

Civil Rights Project. (2000). *Opportunities suspended: The devastating consequences of zero tolerance and school discipline policies.* Retrieved from http://civilrightsproject.ucla.edu/research/k-12-education/school-discipline/opportunities-suspended-the-devastating-consequences-of-zero-tolerance-and-school-discipline-policies

Cope, B., & Kalantzis, M. (2000). *Multiliteracies: Literacy learning and the design of social futures.* London, England: Routledge.

Darling-Hammond, L. (1997). *The right to learn: A blueprint for creating schools that work.* San Francisco, CA: Jossey-Bass.

Darling-Hammond, L. (2006). Securing the right to learn: Policy and practice for powerful teaching and learning. *Educational Researcher, 35*(7), 13–24.

Delpit, L. (1995). *Other people's children: Cultural conflict in the classroom.* New York, NY: The New Press.

Dixson, A. (2008). "Taming the beast": Race, discourse, and identity in a middle school classroom. In S. Greene (Ed.), *Literacy as a civil right: Reclaiming social justice in literacy teaching and learning* (pp. 125–147). New York, NY: Peter Lang.

Dohrn, B. (2000). Look out kid, it's something you did: The criminalization of children. In V. Polakow's (Ed.), *The public assault on American's children: Poverty, violence and juvenile injustice* (pp. 157–187). New York, NY: Teachers College Press.

Dorfman, L., & Schiraldi, V. (2001). *Off balance: Youth, race & crime in the news.* Retrieved from http://www.buildingblocksforyouth.org/media/media.html

Duncan, G. A. (2000). Urban pedagogies and the celling of adolescents of color. *Social Justice, 27*, 29–42.

Duncan, G. A. (2009, April). *Toward the abolition of the school-to-prison pipeline.* Paper presented at the American Educational Research Association annual meeting, San Diego.

Dyson, A. H. (1993). *Social worlds of children learning to write in an urban primary school.* New York, NY: Teachers College Press.

Engëstrom, Y. (1987). *Learning by expanding: An activity theoretical approach to developmental research.* Helsinki, Finland: Orienta-Konsultit Oy.

Fecho, B., & Skinner, S. (2008). For what it's worth: Civil rights and the price of literacy. In S. Greene (Ed.), *Literacy as a civil right: Reclaiming social justice in literacy teaching and learning* (pp. 87–106). New York, NY: Peter Lang.

Fine, M., & McClelland, S. I. (2006). Sexuality and desire: Still missing after all these years. *Harvard Educational Review, 76*, 297–338.

Fine, M., & Ruglis, J. (2009). Circuits and consequences of dispossession: The racialized realignment of the public sphere for U.S. youth. *Transforming Anthropology, 17*, 20–33.

Fisher, M. T. (2005a). Literocracy: Liberating language and creating possibilities. *English Education, 37*, 92–95.

Fisher, M. T. (2005b). From the coffee house to the school house: The promise and potential of spoken word poetry in school contexts. *English Education, 37*, 115–131.

Fisher, M. T. (2007). *Writing in rhythm: Spoken word poetry in urban classrooms.* New York, NY: Teachers College Press.

Fisher, M. T. (2008). Catching butterflies. *English Education, 40*, 94–100.

Fisher, M. T. (2009). *Black literate lives: Historical and contemporary perspectives.* New York, NY: Routledge.

Fisher, M. T., Purcell, S. S., & May, R. (2009). Process, product, and playmaking. *English Education, 41*, 337-355.

Freire, P., & Macedo, D. (1987). *Literacy: Reading the word and the world.* Westport, CT: Bergin & Garvey.

Gadsden, V., Jacobs, C., Bickerstaff, S., Park, J., & Kane, S. (2008, March). *Health and education: Addressing risk and community health disparities through interdisciplinarity.* Paper presented at the American Educational Researchers Association Annual Meeting, New York, NY.

Gallagher, K. (2007). *The theatre of urban: Youth and schooling in dangerous times.* Toronto, Ontario, Canada: University of Toronto Press.

Gillborn, D., & Youdell, D. (2000). *Rationing education: Policy, practice, reform, and equity.* Philadelphia, PA: Open University Press.

Gilliam, W. S. (2005). *Prekindergarteners left behind: Expulsion rates in state prekindergarten systems.* New Haven, CT: Yale University Child Study Center.

Gilliam, W. S., & Shahar, G. (2006). Preschool and child care expulsion and suspension: Rates and predictors in one state. *Infants & Young Children, 19*, 228–245.

Ginwright, S. (2010). *Black youth rising: Activism and radical healing in urban America*. New York, NY: Teachers College Press.

Giroux, H. A. (1987). Introduction: Literacy and the pedagogy of political empowerment. In P. Freire & D. Macedo (Eds.), *Literacy: Reading the word and the world* (pp. 1–29). Westport, CT: Bergin & Garvey.

Good, C. V., & Merkel, W. R. (Eds.). (1973). Literacy. *Dictionary of education*. New York, NY: McGraw-Hill.

Goody, J., & Watt, I. (1963). The consequences of literacy. *Comparative Studies in Society and History, 5*, 304–345.

Gordon, E., & Stovall, D. (2009, November). *Curriculum-based publication projects. Why? How? What?* Paper presented at the National Council of Teachers of English Annual Convention, Philadelphia, PA.

Greene, J. C. (1994) Misperspectives on literacy: A critique of an anglocentric bias in histories of American literacy. *Written Communication, 11*, 251–269.

Greene, S. (2008). Introduction. In S. Greene (Ed.), *Literacy as a civil right: Reclaiming social justice in literacy teaching and learning* (pp. 1–25). New York, NY: Peter Lang.

Greene, S., & Abt-Perkins, D. (2003). How can literacy research contribute to racial understanding? In S. Greene & D. Abt-Perkins (Eds.), *Making race visible: Literacy research for cultural understanding* (pp. 1–31). New York, NY: Teachers College Press.

Gregory, A., Skiba, R. J., & Noguera, P. A. (2010). The achievement gap and discipline gap: Two sides of the same coin. *Educational Researcher, 39*, 59–68.

Gutiérrez, K. D. (2008). Developing a sociocritical literacy in the third space. *Reading Research Quarterly, 43*, 148–164.

Gutiérrez, K. D., Ali, A., & Henríquez, C. (2010). Syncretism and hybridity: Schooling, language, and race and students from non-dominant communities. In M. W. Apple, S. J. Ball, & L. A. Gandins (Eds.), *The Routledge international Handbook of the sociology of education* (pp. 358–369). New York, NY: Routledge.

Gutiérrez, K. D., Baquedano-Lopez, P., & Tejada, C. (1999). Rethinking diversity: Hybridity and hybrid language practices in the third space. *Mind, Culture, and Activity, 6*, 286-303.

Gutiérrez, K. D., Rymes, B., & Larson, J. (1995). Script, counterscript, and underlife in the classroom: *James Brown versus Brown v. Board of Education. Harvard Educational Review, 65*, 445–471.

Gutiérrez, K. D., & Vossoughi, S. (2010). Lifting off the ground to return anew: Mediated praxis, transformative learning, and social design experiments. *Journal of Teacher Education, 61*, 100–117.

Harada, V. H., Kirio, C., & Yamamoto, S. (2008). Project-based learning: rigor and relevance in high schools. *Library Media Connection, 26*, 14–18.

Heath, S. B. (1983). *Ways with words: Language, life, and work in communities and classrooms.* Cambridge, England: Cambridge University Press.

Horizon Academy Students (2006). *Killing the sky: Oral histories from Horizon Academy, Rikers Island* (Vol. 2). New York, NY: Student Press Initiative at Teachers College.

Jordan, J. (1989). *Moving towards home: Political essays*. London, England: Virago.

Kina, R. (2005). Through the eyes of a strong black woman survivor of domestic violence: An Australian story. In J. Sudbury (Ed.), *Global lockdown: Race, gender, and the prison-industrial complex* (pp. 67–72). New York, NY: Routledge.

Kinloch, V. F. (2005). Revisiting the promise of students' rights to their own language: Pedagogical strategies. *College Composition and Communication, 57*, 83–113.

Kinloch, V. F. (2009). *Harlem on our minds: Place, race, and the literacies of urban youth*. New York, NY: Teachers College Press.

Kinloch, V. F. (2010). To not be a traitor of Black English: Youth perceptions of language rights in an urban context. *Teachers College Record, 112*, 103–141.

Kozol, J. (1991). *Savage inequalities.* New York, NY: Crown.

Kozol, J. (2005). *The shame of a nation.* New York, NY: Crown.

Ladson-Billings, G. (2005). Literacy practices in diverse classroom contexts. In T. L. McCarthy (Ed.), *Language, literacy, and power in schooling* (pp. 127–133). Mahwah, NJ: Erlbaum.

Ladson-Billings, G. (2006). 2006 Presidential address: From the achievement gap to the education debt: Understanding achievement in U.S. schools. *Educational Researcher, 35*(7), 3-12.

Ladson-Billings, G. (2009a). Just what is critical race theory and what's it doing in a nice field like education? In E. Taylor, D. Gillborn, & G. Ladson-Billings (Eds.), *Foundations of critical race theory in education* (pp. 17–37). New York, NY: Routledge.

Ladson-Billings, G. (2009b). *The dreamkeepers: Successful teachers of African American children* (2nd ed.). San Francisco, CA: Jossey-Bass.

Larson, J. (2003). Negotiating race in classroom research: Tensions and possibilities. In S. Greene & D. Abt-Perkins (Eds.), *Making race visible: Literacy research for cultural understanding* (pp. 89–106). New York, NY: Teachers College Press.

Lee, C. D. (2001). Is October Brown Chinese? A cultural modeling activity system for underachieving students. *American Educational Research Journal, 38,* 97–141.

Lee, C. D. (2006). Every good-bye ain't gone: Analyzing the cultural underpinnings of classroom talk. *International Journal of Qualitative Studies in Education, 19,* 305–327.

Lee, C. D. (2007). *Culture, literacy, and learning: Taking bloom in the midst of the whirlwind.* New York, NY: Teachers College Press.

Lewis, A. (2008). Even sweet, gentle Larry? The continuing significance of race in education. In S. Green (Ed.), *Literacy as a civil right: Reclaiming social justice in literacy in literacy teaching and learning* (pp. 69–86). New York: Peter Lang.

Li, G. (2008). *Culturally contested literacies: America's "rainbow underclass" and urban schools.* New York, NY: Routledge.

Lipman, P. (2008). Education policy, race, and neoliberal urbanism. In S. Greene (Ed.), *Literacy as a civil right: Reclaiming social justice in literacy teaching and learning* (pp. 125–147). New York, NY: Peter Lang.

Lunsford, A., Moglen, H., & Slevin, J. (Eds.). (1990). *The right to literacy.* New York, NY: Modern Language Association of America.

Mahiri, J. (2000/2001). Pop culture pedagogy in the end(s) of school. *Journal of Adolescent & Adult Literacy, 44,* 382–386.

McCarty, T. L. (Ed.). (2005). *Language, literacy, and power in schooling.* Mahwah, NJ: Erlbaum.

McCarty, T. L., Romero-Little, M. E., & Zepeda, O. (2006). Native American youth discourses on language shift and retention: Ideological cross-currents and their implications for language planning. *International Journal of Bilingual Education and Bilingualism, 9,* 659–677.

McGrew, K. (2008). *Education's prisoners: Schooling, the political economy, and the prison industrial complex.* New York, NY: Peter Lang.

McHenry, E., & Heath, S. B. (1994). The literate and the literary: African Americans as writers and readers—1830-1940. *Written Communication, 11,* 419–444.

Meiners, E. R. (2007). *Right to be hostile: Schools, prisons, and the making of public enemies.* New York, NY: Routledge.

Mintrop, H., & Sunderman, G. L. (2009). Predictable failure of federal sanctions-driven accountability for school improvement—and why we may retain it anyway. *Educational Researcher, 38,* 353–364.

Morrell, E. (2008). *Critical literacy and urban youth: Pedagogies of access, dissent, and liberation.* New York, NY: Routledge.

Moses, R. P., & Cobb, C. E. (2001). *Radical equations: Civil rights from Mississippi to the Algebra Project.* Boston, MA: Beacon Press.

Muncie, J. (2005). The globalization of crime control—the case of juvenile justice: Neoliberalism, policy convergence and international conventions. *Theoretical Criminology, 9,* 35–64.

Nasir, N. S., & Hand, V. M. (2006). Exploring sociocultural perspectives on race, culture, and learning. *Review of Educational Research, 76,* 449–475.

National Association of the Advancement of Colored People Legal Defense and Educational Fund. (2005). *Dismantling the school-to-prison pipeline.* Retrieved from http://naacpldf .org/files/publications/Dismantling_the_School_to_Prison_Pipeline.pdf

Nicholas, S. (2005). Negotiating for the Hopi way of life through literacy and schooling. In T. L. McCarty, (Ed.), *Language, literacy, and power in schooling* (pp. 29–46). Mahwah, NJ: Erlbaum.

Noguera, P. A. (2003a). *City schools and the American dream: Reclaiming the promise of public education.* New York, NY: Teachers College Press.

Noguera, P. A. (2003b). Schools, prisons, and social implications of punishment: Rethinking discipline practices. *Theory Into Practice, 42,* 341–350.

Olson, D. (1977). From utterance to text: The bias of language in speech and writing. *Harvard Education Review, 47,* 257–281.

Ong, W. J. (1982). *Orality and literacy: The technologizing of the word.* London, England: Routledge.

Paley, V. (1979). *White teacher.* Cambridge, MA: Harvard University Press.

Parenti, C. (2008). *Lockdown America: Police and prisons in the age of crisis.* London, England: Verso.

Pew Center on the States. (2008). *One in 100 behind bars in America 2008.* Washington, DC: Pew Charitable Trusts.

Plaut, S. (Ed.). (2009). *The right to literacy in secondary schools: Creating a culture of thinking.* New York, NY: Teachers College Press.

Poe-Yamagata, E., & Jones, M. A. (2000). *And justice for some: Differential treatment of minority youth in the justice system.* Washington, DC: Building Blocks for Youth.

Polakow, V. (Ed.). (2000). *The public assault on American's children: Poverty, violence and juvenile injustice.* New York, NY: Teachers College Press.

Rapping, E. (2003). *Law and justice as seen on TV.* New York, NY: New York University Press.

Richie, B. (1996). *Compelled to crime: The gender entrapment of battered black women.* New York, NY: Routledge.

Richie, B. (2005). Queering antiprison work: African American lesbians in the juvenile justice system. In J. Sudbury (Ed.), *Global lockdown: Race, gender, and the prison-industrial complex* (pp. 73–85). New York, NY: Routledge.

Rickford, J. R., & Rickford, R. J. (2000). *Spoken soul: The story of Black English.* New York, NY: John Wiley.

Roth, W., & Lee, Y. (2007). Vygotsky's neglected legacy: Cultural-historical activity theory. *Review of Educational Research, 77,* 186–232.

Scribner, S., & Cole, M. (2001). Unpackaging literacy. In E. Cushman, E. R. Kintgen, B. M. Kroll, & M. Rose (Eds.), *Literacy: A critical sourcebook* (pp. 123–137). Boston, MA: Bedford/St. Martin's.

Siddle Walker, V. (1996). *Their highest potential: An African American school community in the segregated south.* Chapel Hill: University of North Carolina Press.

Simkins, S. B., Hirsch, A. E., Horvat, E. M., & Moss, M. B. (2004, Winter). The school to prison pipeline for girls: The role of physical and sexual abuse. *Children's Legal Rights Journal, 24,* 56–72.

Smitherman, G. (1986). *Talkin' and testifyin': The language of Black America*. Boston, MA: Houghton Mifflin.

Smitherman, G. (1999). Language and culture. In G. Smitherman (Ed.), *Talkin that talk: Language, culture, and education in African America* (pp. 11–15). London, England: Routledge.

Street, B. V. (1984). *Literacy in theory and practice*. Cambridge, England: Cambridge University Press.

Sudbury, J. (2005). Introduction: Feminist critiques, transnational landscapes, abolitionist visions. In J. Sudbury (Ed.), *Global lockdown: Race, gender, and the prison-industrial complex* (pp. xi–xxviii). New York, NY: Routledge.

Szwed, J. F. (1981). The ethnography of literacy. In M. F. Whiteman (Ed.), *Writing: The nature, development, and teaching of written communication* (pp. 13–23). Mahwah, NJ: Erlbaum.

Terrio, S. (2009). *Judging Mohammed: Juvenile delinquency, immigration, and exclusion at the Paris Palace of Justice*. Palo Alto, CA: Stanford University Press.

UNESCO Education Sector. (2004). *The plurality of literacy and its implications for policy and programmes*. Paris, France: Author.

Vanneman, A., Hamilton, L., Baldwin Anderson, J., & Rahman, T. (2009). *Achievement gaps: How Black and White students in public schools perform in mathematics and reading on the National Assessment of Educational Progress* (NCES 2009-455). Washington, DC: National Center for Education Statistics, Institute of Education Sciences, U.S. Department of Education.

Winn, M. T. (2010). Our side of the story: Moving incarcerated youth voices from margins to center. *Race, Ethnicity, and Education, 13*, 313–325.

Winn, M. T. (in press). Betwixt and between: Literacy, liminality, and the celling of Black girls. *Race, Ethnicity, and Education*.

Winn, M. T., & Ubiles, J. R. (in press). Worthy witnessing: Collaborative research in urban classrooms. In A. Ball & C. Tyson (Eds.), *Studying diversity in teacher education*. Washington, DC: American Educational Research Association.

Wyvekens, A. (2008). The French juvenile justice system. In J. Junger-Tas & S. H. Decker (Eds.), *International handbook of juvenile justice* (pp. 173–186). New York, NY: Springer.

Yang, W. K. (2009, September). Discipline or punish? Some suggestions for school policy and teacher practice. *Language Arts, 87*, 49–61.

Chapter 7

Adolescent Literacies in Latin America and the Caribbean

LESLEY BARTLETT
DINA LÓPEZ
Columbia University, New York

ERIKA MEIN
University of Texas at El Paso

LAURA A. VALDIVIEZO
University of Massachusetts Amherst

INTRODUCTION

In 2000, approximately 36 million youth and adults living in Latin America and the Caribbean were reported to be unable to read or write basic texts. Of these, 20 million were women. According to official statistics, some countries in Central America (Guatemala, Nicaragua, El Salvador, and Honduras) have a youth and adult literacy rate of 80% or lower. The Caribbean countries currently have literacy rates between 80% and 90%, except for Haiti, which has an estimated rate of 50% (UNESCO-OREALC, 2004a, p. 39, as reported in Umayahara, 2005, p. 42). Yet what do these official statistics mean? To what language do they refer? What social inequalities are reflected but not illuminated by such statistics? And how are youth, specifically, using reading and writing in creative ways not captured by these official measures? In this chapter, we review official statistics and examine literacy policy and programming for youth across Latin America and the Caribbean. We contrast these official discourses on youth and literacy and programs or policies for youth literacy with empirical studies of adolescent literacy practices—noting a discrepancy that

Review of Research in Education
March 2011, Vol. 35, pp. 174–207
DOI: 10.3102/0091732X10383210
© 2011 AERA. http://rre.aera.net

goes beyond being a discursive problem, one that reveals persisting forms of social exclusion and marginalization.

This chapter is informed by the anthropology of literacy, specifically studies of adolescent literacy. Anthropologists of literacy have demonstrated that literacy is not a neutral or autonomous set of skills; instead, what is considered to be literacy and the ways in which people take up and use reading and writing are shaped by social inequalities and cultural systems of significance (Street, 1984). Contrary to dominant conceptions of literacy, which emphasize the ability to decode and write in a country's dominant language, anthropologists examine the ways in which literacy practices mediate and are shaped by social structures and cultural meanings (see, e.g., Barton & Hamilton, 2000; Street, 1993). In the United States and the United Kingdom over the past 20 years, scholars of "adolescent literacy" have investigated the reading and writing practices of youth, including their digital literacies, emphasizing the disconnect between fossilized, school-based literacy instruction and the reading and writing routinely engaged in by youth.[1] An anthropological notion of literacy has infiltrated academic work on literacy practices throughout Latin America and the Caribbean, leading scholars to focus on *cultura escrita* (written culture) in the late 1980s in Mexico (Kalman, 2008), *literacidad* in many parts of South America in the contemporary period (e.g., De la Piedra, 2004; Zavala, 2004), and *letramento* in Brazil (Kleiman, 1995; V. M. Ribeiro, 2003). This literature informs our approach to the topic of youth literacies, which highlights the stark contrast between official discourses, policies, and programs and the actual literacy practices of youth documented by various scholars.

To prepare this chapter, we did a thorough search of the existing literature on literacy, youth literacy, and youth cultures in Latin America and the Caribbean. We reviewed available statistical information on youth and literacy in the region. Finally, we interviewed 15 policymakers, academics, and leaders of nongovernmental organizations working in the area of youth education and, specifically, youth literacy programs in Mexico, Guatemala, Peru, Ecuador, and the Dominican Republic. Those interviews gave us insights into policy challenges in the region.

Based on these sources, this chapter discusses youth literacies in areas across Latin America and the Caribbean. We examine how conceptions and representations of youth and literacy have changed over time in the region as a result of important social, political, and economic shifts. The body of the chapter then juxtaposes policies for youth literacy with studies of youth literacy practices in a range of contexts. We first present official data regarding levels of youth literacy, including national and international reports on literacy rates and key educational statistics. Next, we examine two key orientations guiding youth literacy policies and programs—workforce development and political socialization—in light of literacy policies and programs stimulated by international development organizations that adhere to these orientations. We then review the available literature on adolescent literacies in Latin America and the Caribbean, demonstrating the gap between policies and programs to stimulate youth literacy and what scholars have shown about youth literacy practices in the region. We conclude that an increase in anthropologically informed approaches to literacy in the region could help to combat technorational approaches that inadvertently "blame the victim"; such anthropological studies of literacy instead highlight both the creative appropriation and adaptation of literacy by youth and the ways in which economic and political structures have constrained greater access to literacy.

EDUCATIONAL AND LITERACY RATES FOR YOUTH ACROSS THE REGION: HISTORICAL PERSPECTIVES AND OFFICIAL STATISTICS

Given the multiethnic and multilingual landscape of Latin America, questions about youth literacies necessarily involve issues of language and struggles for meaning and power. Ideologies about language and literacy are deeply rooted in a history of colonization—a legacy that continues to bear on the social, cultural, political, and economic realities of youth and adults in the region. From the time of Hernán Cortez's arrival in 1519, the Spanish Empire sought to establish authority over its territories, and it did so in part through the use of Spanish alphabetic literacy (Mignolo, 1992, 2000). Before the arrival of the Spanish, the Amerindian groups living in Latin America had developed and maintained their own complex systems of communication that were primarily orally based but that also drew on written pictorial forms. The arrival of the Spanish, however, coincided with the arrival of a dominant ideology about language and literacy that stemmed from Renaissance notions about the superiority of the written over the spoken and that served as a primary mechanism for distinguishing the "civilized" from the "barbarians" (Jiménez & Smith, 2008; Mignolo, 1992; Rockwell, 2006). Spanish missionaries and *letrados* ("men of letters") perpetuated this ideology and colonized indigenous language and literacy by two primary means: by writing grammars of Amerindian languages using the Roman alphabet as the basis and by writing the histories of Amerindian peoples using Spanish discursive genres rather than those that were indigenous to Amerindian communication and storytelling (Mignolo, 1992). The imposition of the Roman alphabetic system on the indigenous communicative structures already in place thus became an instrument of domination, inasmuch as alphabetic literacy became linked to the "economic, political, pedagogical, and religious management of the New World" (Mignolo, 1992, p. 310).

In *Literacy and Literacies: Texts, Power, and Identity*, Collins and Blot (2003) argue that although literacy was used as an instrument of domination, it also became a means of resistance in colonial Latin America. Although they agree that colonizers subjected indigenous people to European ways of knowing, being, reading, and writing that were considered "literate" and "civilized" while rejecting the local ways of being and knowing, they argue that some indigenous people adopted and adapted the colonizer languages for their own purposes, and in so doing, forged the creation of "counter-subject" identities (Collins & Blot, 2003, p. 122). In other words, like the youth we discuss later in this chapter, people creatively adopted and adapted resources (such as literate genres) for their own ends.

Throughout the 20th century, formal schooling was the primary means for promoting universal literacy in Latin America. Efforts to increase literacy rates embraced human capital theories that linked literacy in the country's dominant or official language with national economic development. However, Seda Santana (2000) notes that nonformal literacy programs beginning in the 1960s used popular education approaches, based largely on the work of Paulo Freire, in an effort to raise critical consciousness and promote the transformation of social relations. This period also witnessed a proliferation of youth and adult literacy programs designed and funded by international organizations such as the United Nations Educational, Scientific, and Cultural Organization (UNESCO) and the World Bank. Thus, governments and nongovernmental organizations alike were on a quest to eradicate illiteracy, and as a consequence they found it necessary to gather data in order to monitor trends, assess the impact of efforts, and guide new policy interventions. National and international reports, which provided quantitative findings on literacy rates, became commonplace tools for assessing progress on national goals and promoting cross-country and regional conversations about youth and literacy.

Before discussing recent literacy statistics, it is important that we call attention to the fact that literacy is notoriously hard to measure. First, official rates are based on highly variable data, including self-report, other report, and the completion of a short literacy task.[2] The language of testing frequently excludes literacy abilities in non-dominant languages—a particularly relevant issue in a region with millions of speakers of indigenous languages, who in some cases are monolingual. From an anthropological perspective, problems emerge when imposing an etic, externally defined and normed measure, rather than examining how literacy is locally defined and used. Nevertheless, standardized measures of literacy do reveal interesting trends and help locate youth literacy practices within a broader social and political context.

The data in Table 1 suggest several important insights. First, illiteracy as defined by UNESCO was reduced significantly across the region from 1980 to 2000, thanks largely to the expansion of access to basic and secondary education. Second, literacy inequalities persist within the region. Haiti, Guatemala, Nicaragua, Honduras, El Salvador, and the Dominican Republic maintain unusually high percentages of people deemed illiterate. Although Brazil's rate has gradually declined, its massive population means that a substantial proportion of the people deemed illiterate in the region are Brazilian.

Statistical data confirm that indigenous youth, in particular, are affected by illiteracy, poverty, and social exclusion. In Bolivia, indigenous peoples constitute 91.6% of the total of the illiterate population (López & Hanemann, 2009; UNESCO, 2003). While the national rate of illiteracy in Ecuador is 9%, indigenous illiteracy is 28.2% (population aged 15 years old or older); poverty in Ecuador affects 56% of the national population but 73% of indigenous populations there (UNESCO, 2003). Similar trends hold throughout Central America. For example, in 2002, the

TABLE 1
Illiteracy Rates in Latin America, Aged 15 Years and Older
(as Percentage of Population)

Country	1980	1990	2000
Argentina	6.0	4.2	3.1
Bahamas	6.6	5.0	3.9
Bolivia	30.9	21.6	14.4
Brazil	24.5	18.3	14.7
Chile	8.5	6.0	4.3
Colombia	15.6	11.3	8.2
Costa Rica	8.3	6.1	4.4
Cuba	7.9	5.2	3.6
Dominican Republic	26.2	20.5	16.2
Ecuador	18.1	11.6	8.1
El Salvador	33.8	27.4	21.3
Guatemala	46.2	38.5	31.3
Guyana	5.4	2.8	1.5
Haiti	69.1	60.7	51.4
Honduras	39.0	33.0	27.8
Jamaica	22.5	17.3	13.3
Mexico	17.0	12.3	9.0
Nicaragua	41.8	38.7	35.7
Panama	14.3	11.2	8.1
Paraguay	14.1	9.7	6.7
Peru	20.2	14.3	10.1
Surinam	12.4	8.2	5.8
Trinidad and Tobago	5.0	3.2	1.8
Uruguay	5.3	3.4	2.2
Venezuela	15.1	9.9	7.0

Source. CEPAL ([Comisión Económica para América Latina y el Caribe] 2003), as cited in Umayahara (2005).

literacy rate for Guatemalan Ladinos older than 15 years was 79.6%, whereas indigenous populations had a significantly lower literacy rate of 52.3% (Verdugo & Raymundo, 2009). Illiteracy rates among Nicaraguan youth and adults (6 years and older) living in the autonomous regions—predominantly indigenous communities—can be as high as 55%, compared with a 26.8% illiteracy rate found in the rest of the country (Cunningham Kain, 2009, p. 304).

The expansion of basic and secondary education in the region has important implications for adolescent literacy and literacy practices. Net enrollment rates have improved, though they vary widely and remain particularly low in Guatemala, Nicaragua, the Dominican Republic, and Ecuador (see Table 2). Educational outcomes vary substantially within the region of Central America (Alvarez, Dassin, Rosenberg, & Bloom, 1999). Primary completion rates are on the lower end for Guatemala (77%) and Nicaragua (75%) whereas 91% of children in Costa Rica complete a full course of primary education (UNESCO Institute for Statistics,

TABLE 2
Net Enrollment Rates in Primary Education in Pre-Dakar (ca. 1998) and Post-Dakar (ca. 2001)

	Net Enrollment Rate (Both Genders)	
	ca. 1998	ca. 2001
Argentina	100.0	99.8
Bolivia	96.0	94.2
Brazil	94.1	96.5
Chile	87.9	88.8
Colombia	86.7	86.7
Costa Rica	—	90.6
Cuba	98.9	95.7
Dominican Republic	88.3	97.1
Ecuador	97.0	99.5
El Salvador	81.0	88.9
Guatemala	76.5	85.0
Honduras	—	87.4
Mexico	99.5	99.4
Nicaragua	77.9	81.9
Panama	96.5	99.0
Paraguay	91.7	91.5
Peru	99.8	99.9
Uruguay	92.4	89.5
Venezuela	85.9	92.4

Source. UNESCO Institute for Statistics database as cited in Umayahara (2005, p. 22).

2009). These figures are unsurprising when we consider that Guatemala and Nicaragua have larger indigenous populations than Costa Rica, and it is youth of Mayan, Miskitu, and Garífuna descent who have historically been excluded from systems of education and are less likely to have access to literacy and formal schooling (López & Hanemann, 2009).

Three critically important educational challenges persist in the region: high repetition rates, high dropout rates, and low quality of schooling (Umayahara, 2005; Wolff, Schiefelbein, & Schiefelbein, 2002). These are systemic issues that plague Latin American schools and limit the choices and opportunities for many youth, for the most part those who already live in poverty in urban and predominantly rural sectors. The region has long struggled with high repetition rates, which cause significant inefficiencies in the system. Despite improved net enrollment rates, dropout rates remain high in the region; in Bolivia, Brazil, El Salvador, Honduras, Guatemala, Nicaragua, and Venezuela, 20% or more of students drop out before completing basic education, with the majority of those located in rural areas and/or living in poverty (Umayahara, 2005, p. 23). Notably, while the number of years of completed education doubled in Latin America and the Caribbean between the 1960s and 2000, increases in other regions of the world were higher (Umayahara, 2005, p. 8). Unequal opportunities are clearly shaped by ethnicity throughout the region. For example, in Guatemala, while nonindigenous 18-year-olds have an average of 7 years of schooling, their indigenous peers only have 4.4 years of schooling (Verdugo & Raymundo, 2009, p. 186). Similarly, in Ecuador, indigenous and Afro-Ecuadorians in rural sectors have half the average length of schooling in comparison to the population nationally (Torres, 2005). Access to education and persistence in school has expanded, to be sure, but only along the old lines of class, ethnic, gendered, and rural/urban social inequalities.

Furthermore, the consensus on education in Latin America and the Caribbean holds that although more students are studying longer, the quality of that education is insufficient. The results from the Program for International Student Assessment (PISA) 2000 sent tremors through the region, revealing that countries performed well below expected, given their gross domestic products (Umayahara, 2005, pp. 36–37); even in countries such as Chile and Argentina, whose education levels are considered advanced, almost half of the 15-year-old students had only the most rudimentary level of reading skills or even lower (UNESCO-OREALC, 2004a, pp. 48–51). The skills of the actual population are much more limited than what the PISA reveals, since PISA does not assess 15-year-olds who have not completed primary education and/or are not enrolled in secondary school (UNESCO-OREALC, 2004b, p. 38). While some question the validity of relying on a single test to measure quality, various critics have decried the reduced quality of the secondary education, the irrelevant and uninteresting curricula that predominate, the gap between the lives and interests of youth and what they are taught, the devaluation of the diploma, and the precarious transition from school to work; some argue that inequality of educational opportunity and quality of education are further excluding the already marginalized (Braslavsky, 2001; Tedesco, 2001).

Measures such as literacy rates and PISA scores, however, tell only part of the story. In the remainder of this chapter, we consider how international economic, political, and educational trends and international and national organizations have shaped literacy programming for youth, and we contrast official understandings of youth and their literacy needs to actual youth literacy practices. We argue that official discourses present very fixed notions of youth as potential workers or political subjects who must be cultivated to fit neatly within a development agenda, while ethnographically informed studies of literacy demonstrate how youth engage with literacy in creative and unpredictable ways and how literacy practices are inextricably tied to issues of language and identity.

SHIFTING REPRESENTATIONS OF YOUTH AND LITERACY IN LATIN AMERICA AND THE CARIBBEAN

To speak of youth in Latin America and the Caribbean is to speak of an extremely multilingual, multiethnic, and pluricultural group of young people with varying positions of vulnerability, inclusion, and exclusion. Differential access to resources such as schooling, technology, and culturally and linguistically responsive services means that it is impossible to discuss the literacy and language practices of a "typical"

Latin American young person: The educational experiences and literacy practices of a middle-class high school student in Mexico City differ vastly from a teenage street worker in Guatemala or an indigenous youth in a remote and rural area of Bolivia. What follows is an exploration of the historical and discursive processes that have shaped categories of "youth" and, in turn, youth literacy policies and programs.

The category "youth" is a modern construction that emerged in the 18th century among families of means and spread, slowly, in the mid-20th century to societies and individuals that could afford the luxury of separating childhood from adult responsibilities. The distinct social phase was made possible (and perhaps even necessary) by a number of social changes, including changes in the organization of work and expectations for specialized training in many areas, the expansion of basic and secondary education systems, the massification of effective birth control, and the prolonged life expectancies around the world (Jacinto, 2002, p. 67). Obviously, various factors such as socioeconomic status of the family and community, rural/urban location, and cultural norms, influence contemporary conceptions of "youth," leading some scholars to call for a study not of adolescence but of adolescences (Jacinto, 2002). Although governments and sectors in Latin America and the Caribbean employ slightly different age ranges to bound the category of "youth," the category corresponds generally to young people between the ages of 10 and 20 years (Krauskopf, 2003).

The term *youth* carries varying meanings and underlying assumptions that play out in the development of national policies and programs. Two distinct approaches inform policymaking and programming: youth as strategic actors in economic development (workforce formation) and youth as citizens (political formation). In the following sections, we show how these concerns have shaped representations of youth in the region, and we demonstrate how international actors such as the World Bank, United Nations organizations, United States Agency for International Development (USAID), and Comisión Económica para América Latina y el Caribe/ Economic Commission of Latin America and the Caribbean (CEPAL) have taken up these concerns to inform literacy policy and programming for youth. We then discuss how linguistic diversity in the region has shaped literacy programming and policies. Finally, we review studies on local literacy and language practices that reveal the contradictions and limitations of official rhetoric in the conceptualizations of youth and literacy.

Youth, Literacy, and Economic Development

Throughout Latin America and the Caribbean, conceptions of youth and opportunities for youth have been shaped by profound economic changes in the region. The region experienced a sharp increase in poverty in the late 1980s, and by 1996, 36.7% of the population across Latin America and the Caribbean was poor (a higher incidence than in the mid-1980s). Inequality across the region rose markedly in the late 1980s (Wodon, 2000, pp. 1–2). On average, the region experienced modest per capita growth of between 1% and 2% in the 1990s, though inequality stubbornly persisted (Perry, Arias, López, Maloney, & Servén, 2006, p. 24; Wodon, 2000). On

TABLE 3
Aggregate Poverty Ratios, 1981–2004, World Bank Data
(Percentage of Population)

	1981	1990	1996	2002	2004
Extreme poverty					
Latin America	10.2	9.6	8.1	8.4	8.0
Latin America without Brazil and Mexico	8.5	7.4	9.3	11.7	11.1
Medium four countries	4.0	1.7	6.9	10.9	10.1
Poorest six countries	24.0	26.8	27.4	27.0	25.7
Small countries with signs of progress	15.6	13.0	7.5	7.0	7.0
Moderate poverty					
Latin America	27.9	25.6	24.4	24.0	21.4
Latin America without Brazil and Mexico	21.8	20.5	25.5	27.5	26.7
Medium four countries	13.1	11.0	21.9	26.7	25.3
Poorest six countries	46.3	49.2	49.0	49.4	48.0
Small countries with signs of progress	34.5	29.9	21.5	18.7	19.1

Source. Helwege and Birch (2007, p. 19).

Note. "Latin America" includes Argentina, Bolivia, Brazil, Chile, Colombia, Costa Rica, Dominican Republic, Ecuador, El Salvador, Guatemala, Haiti, Honduras, Mexico, Nicaragua, Panama, Paraguay, Peru, Uruguay, and Venezuela. The "small countries with signs of progress" are Chile, Costa Rica, Dominican Republic, El Salvador, Guatemala, and Panama. The "medium four countries" are Argentina, Colombia, Peru, and Venezuela. The "poorest six countries" are Bolivia, Ecuador, Haiti, Honduras, Nicaragua, and Paraguay.

average, moderate poverty and extreme poverty declined from 1990 to 2004. However, much of this change can be attributed to improvement in the highly populous countries of Mexico and Brazil; other countries entered the new millennium with large percentages of their population living in moderate and extreme poverty (see Table 3).

The region has experienced significant economic shifts. The enactment of free trade agreements such as NAFTA (North American Free Trade Agreement) and CAFTA (Central America Free Trade Agreement) and modifications of trade policies reduced tariffs on trade, undermined agricultural exports, expanded free trade zones, and further exposed vulnerable working-class labor to global shifts in capital. In the contemporary period, available jobs are increasingly informal in nature; even when formal, jobs are unstable and discontinuous, with low salaries and little to no labor protection (Jacinto, 2002, p. 78). The expanded reliance on tourism, especially in the Caribbean and Mexico, means that youth are seen as an important source of labor (including, it must be acknowledged, as sex workers), even as unemployed youth are considered threats to the images countries wish to portray.

Economic shifts have directly affected economic opportunities for youth in the region. With polarized economic and educational opportunities, those most fortunate began experiencing longer periods of better access to education and select, stable jobs in the expanding knowledge economy. Marketers targeted these middle-class and upper-class youth as critical consumers (Podalsky, 2008, p. 146). In contrast, these economic shifts have significantly curtailed the job prospects of poor and working-class youth in the region. Youth unemployment rates are, on average, double those of adults in the region, and the "unemployment rate for the 20% poorest urban population is six times as high as that for the 20% richest" (OIT, 2004, pp. 26–27). When one includes not only those who are unemployed but also those who are inactive, "one in four young people in LAC are jobless" (Cunningham, McGinnis, García Verdú, & Dorte, 2008, p. 8). Ironically, this expanded joblessness for poor youth coincides with a period of unprecedented access to secondary education (Hopenhayn, 2006, p. 4). In short, the region has witnessed a bifurcation of economic opportunities, with a small proportion of youth emerging as highly educated knowledge workers with considerable expendable income, and a large proportion of working-class and poor youth relegated to low-paying, informal work or joblessness.

In response to such situations, regional institutions such as the Organization for Economic Cooperation and Development (OECD) (through tests like the Programme for International Student Assessment and Trends in International Mathematics and Science Study) and global institutions such as the World Bank have exported and legitimized conceptions of "youth at risk," especially in relation to a perceived absence of skills and preparedness to compete for jobs in globally oriented markets (see, e.g., Cunningham et al., 2008). A study by CEPAL indicates that a person requires a minimum of secondary school completion and 12 years of schooling to improve the probability of earning sufficient income to live above the poverty line (CEPAL, 1997, as cited in Umayahara, 2005). Although well intentioned, such discussions often lead to public discourses that blame youth and their families for low test scores or the lack of human capital that, presumably, jeopardizes their own economic opportunities and national competitiveness (Hull, Zacher, & Hibbert, 2009, p. 123). In reality, in the face of shrinking formal employment and the expanding informal economy, educated youth find that they use higher levels of education to gain a comparative advantage for jobs that increasingly do not demand high levels of schooling or technical qualification (Jacinto, 2002, p. 93). Policies and programs for youth are built around an image of youth as "at risk" and underskilled, rather than around a critique of contemporary economic processes that routinely exacerbate inequality and, in some instances, poverty.

This concern with workforce preparation has led to vocationally oriented literacy programs that define literacy as a neutral, definable set of hierarchically arranged skills whose acquisition leads to increased levels of human capital and therefore of employability: in short, they rely on what Street (1984) identified as a misinformed "autonomous" model of literacy. During the 1980s, as the world's and the region's focus shifted to basic education for children, the education of youth and adults fell off the development agenda; basic literacy programs were largely left to universities, civil society, and volunteer efforts (UNESCO-OREALC, 2001). The small amount of funding left over for youth was dedicated to vocational training, continuing an emphasis on instrumentalist approaches to schooling that have endured since the emergence of human capital theory in the 1960s (see, e.g., World Bank, 2008). That approach expanded in the 1990s, when projects run through the Ministries of Labor and financed by the InterAmerican Bank and the World Bank included capacity-building for work in the formal market linked with internships in businesses; in contrast, programs run by nongovernmental organizations tended to be oriented to the informal sector and self-employment, with some emphasizing microenterprises.

Examples of vocationally oriented literacy programs abound throughout the region. In the Dominican Republic, according to Luis E. Holguín (interview, April 14, 2010), the Ministry of Education promotes Literacy for Youth and Adults programs that see youth literacy as a means to "continue the educational process," "stimulate labor formation, developing productive competencies," and "achieve entrepreneurial strategies," while expanding the "articulation" between literacy classes and employment opportunities. A related project, the Literacy and Work Habilitation of Youth and Adults Project supported by the Organization of Iberoamerican States, works in the Enriquillo region to "amplify access of youth and adults to literacy with an emphasis on their entrepreneurial and labor preparation" (Organización de Estados Iberoamericanos [OEI], n.d.).

In Mexico in the early 1980s, the federal government created the Instituto Nacional de la Educación de los Adultos/National Institute of Adult Education (INEA) to address the issue of educational access for adults and youth over the age of 15 years. At present, INEA sponsors certification-based youth and adult education programs at the basic literacy, primary, and secondary (middle school) levels. Based on the guidelines established through various international policies, including Education for All and CONFINTEA V, as well as national educational policies in Mexico, in 1997 INEA developed an educational framework known as the Educational Model for Life and Work (MEVyT; Galicia López, 2003). The intent of the MEVyT curriculum, which was developed at three levels (basic literacy, primary, and middle school), was to provide youth and adults with "educational options tied to the needs, interests, and expectations oriented towards the development of competencies in order to progress . . . in their personal, family, work, and community lives" (Galicia López, 2003, p. 203). In terms of participation, INEA has impressive numbers, with more than 1 million youth and adults enrolled at all three levels throughout the country, and with yearly graduation rates ranging between 600,000 and 700,000 (INEA, 2010). In spite of its success in numbers, INEA has continually struggled with limited resources and with a volunteer base of teachers who have limited training and little formal schooling (see Arnove & Torres, 1995; see also Kalman, 2001). The relevance of the MEVyT curriculum for youth has been questioned and needs further study.

Likewise, in Peru, official policy has emphasized vocational approaches to literacy. The Peruvian Ministry of Education assumed an important 10-year literacy project called the Plan Maestro de Alfabetización del Perú (Master Plan of Literacy Development of Peru; 2002–2012), with an emphasis on the preparation of literacy specialists (UNESCO, 2003). Still, most government resources are allocated for childhood or early childhood programs. As part of a National Education Project (Proyecto Educativo Nacional) to eradicate absolute and functional illiteracy, official policy and literacy programs primarily focus on early childhood populations of 4 and 5 years of age, while paying significantly less attention to youth and adult populations who have been excluded from regular basic education. Programs focusing on youth education, such as the National Council of Education (Consejo Nacional de Educación, CNE), aim at inserting members of the youth and adult populations beginning at 15 years of age in the job market through the development of literacy and fundamental technology skills (CNE, 2007). CNE's policy has clear vocational purposes and prioritizes women and individuals in rural areas who have children in school. As mentioned, resources to implement youth programs have been minimal in comparison with the resources that government programs for children's literacy receive.

Conventional programs targeting vocational skills that fail to take account of contemporary labor market availability and students' social and political lives and interests have been roundly critiqued as ineffective, and scholars have noted the disarticulation between education of youth, youth training programs, and the existing labor market (Gallart, 2000; Jacinto, 1999, 2002; Pieck, 2001). Referring to education programs for youth in Ecuador, Patricio Cajas, who is a regional coordinator for Ecuador's Contrato Social por la Educación (Social Contract for Education), argues that government policies are more responsive to urban than rural youth: They ignore vernacular languages, and they do not sufficiently weave in vocational skills that are relevant for youth in rural settings (interview, November 30, 2009).

Only a few literacy programs have more successfully linked literacy and vocational skills; those tend to be run by nongovernmental organizations. Examples include Escola Zé Peão and Saberes da Terra in Brazil, Municipio Emprendedor in El Salvador and Guatemala, and the Jamaican Foundation for Lifelong Learning (UNESCO, 2008). Other experimental and significantly smaller governmental and private programs, such as Colegio Integrado Siglo 21 in the rural region of Cauca, Colombia; Educación Práctica-Productiva y Transformadora, in Cuzco, Peru; and the Instituto de Educación Especial, in the city of Puya, Ecuador, are considered innovative for their linkage between literacy and social and economic inclusion (OEI, 2003).

Economic shifts across Latin America have had a significant impact in terms of both educational and economic opportunities for youth. In efforts to facilitate national and economic development, international funding agencies and nongovernmental organizations have responded by providing monies for vocational programming and functional literacy initiatives. This, in turn, has resulted in national policymaking that focuses on workforce formation—one that prioritizes equipping youth with the knowledge and skills needed to be (economically) productive members of Latin American societies. As we will see in the following section, conceptions of youth as citizens and political subjects lead to literacy policies and programming that focus on their political socialization.

Youth, Literacy, and Political Development

Political shifts likewise are reshaping public representations of youth in the region. Significant political changes across the region since the late 1980s greatly influenced the social realities of youth and their relationship to states. For example, the democratic "reopening" experienced in Brazil in the latter half of the 1980s made political affiliation and activism possible once again. In Mexico, major political changes culminated in the watershed election of conservative candidate Vicente Fox in 2000, after more than 70 years of ruling-party dominance in the Mexican political system. The Central American Peace Accords, which called for cease-fires in guerilla wars and signaled a transition to more democratic political processes, heralded important changes for Central American youth—particularly for youth in Nicaragua, El Salvador, and Guatemala. However, the political turmoil experienced during the conflict-ridden years was to have a lasting effect on the educational opportunities and economic possibilities for Central American youth. In Peru, the cessation of the Shining Path, which recruited mainly rural youth, brought a sense of social stability but also left a conflict-affected and disenfranchised generation with no education, work, or strong sense of community, already fragile spaces severely affected—if not vanished—after two decades of political violence.

The period was also marked by increasing visibility for the category "youth." In 1985, U.N. Secretary General Javier Pérez de Cuéllar proclaimed International Youth Year to focus attention on youth-related issues all over the world. This moment in history marked a turning point in international and governmental efforts—including research, policymaking, and program development—that addressed the needs and concerns of youth (Krauskopf, 2005). The Iberoamerican Convention on the Rights of Youth, ratified in 2005 by Ministers of Youth from Bolivia, Costa Rica, Cuba, Ecuador, El Salvador, Guatemala, Honduras, México, Nicaragua, Panamá, Paraguay, Perú, the Dominican Republic, Uruguay, and Venezuela, punctuated a period of proliferation of bureaucracies and policies dedicated to youth issues, such as health, education, and the transition to work.[3]

In the contemporary period, youth are often portrayed as politically apathetic. This impression results from significant shifts in political engagement. Surveys of youth in Chile, Colombia, Mexico, and Spain conducted in 2000 revealed a tendency among adolescents to discredit political institutions, the importance of voting, and the democratic system (CEPAL, 2007). Unlike prior generations, these youth reported low engagement with student movements, unions, political parties, and community organizations (CEPAL, 2007, p. 270). Surveys showed a strong belief in the value of participation paired with idiosyncratic and short-term commitment to political issues or parties and modest expectations of social change (as cited in Hopenhayn, 2006, pp. 14–17; CEPAL, 2007). However, the surveys suggested that youth value short-term volunteerism. Indeed, youth have become active volunteers in national projects. For example, the National Literacy Campaign in Guatemala—a collaboration between government and civil society sectors—mobilized 50,000 youth from high schools to teach 200,000 people across the country (Rodríguez, 2003).

Although perhaps not as conventionally participatory as previous generations, youth constitute new and important political actors. In Mexico, the youth vote contributed to the overthrow of ruling-party politics-as-usual, and since that time politicians have heavily courted the 60% of the population younger than 30 years (Campbell, 2006). In other parts of the region, the leftward political trend was both supported by youth activists and has further stimulated youth-fueled social movements. In Honduras, youth constituted an important component of the opposition to the coup to replace President Zelaya (Frank, 2010), while in Guatemala, commentators suggested that Twitter networking by youth contributed to the 2009 political crisis (LeBrón, 2009). Even as schools continue to be portrayed as key agents of political socialization, it is clear that political action mainly—although not exclusively—among urban youth is informed largely by social movements and online networking and information sharing. For example, an interesting study of Aymara rappers in El Alto, Bolivia, reveals politically active, indigenous youth who employ hip-hop music to question racism and exclusion in a democratic society, but who, at the same time, do not affiliate with a specific political party or trend (Mollericona, 2007).

Contemporary youth in Latin America and the Caribbean are experiencing a radical expansion in access to online networking and information, especially compared with other age groups. Indeed, contemporary youth in Latin America exercise citizenship through virtual networks, such as the World Social Forum (CEPAL, 2007, p. 271). (However, poor and/or indigenous youth in rural areas experience almost complete exclusion from such political outlets.) This trend leads to a paradox: Youth across Latin America and the Caribbean are simultaneously experiencing increased symbolic integration, especially through cultural consumption of video, radio, and Internet-delivered communications, and decreased material integration (Hopenhayn, 2006, p. 7). Cultural and social media give youth higher expectations of autonomy, even as economic conditions give them less hope of achieving it (p. 10).

At the same time, over the past 30 years, youth in the region have increasingly been portrayed as deviant and dangerous. In Mexico, discourses of deviancy have targeted groups such as *chavos banda*, which emerged in the 1980s and comprised urban working-class youth who were united by a shared interest in rock music and who resisted middle- and upper-class *fresa* norms (Feixa, 1998); other targeted groups include *punks*, *góticos*, and *emos*, whose identities are also connected, albeit in different ways, to music and resistance (Marcial, 2008).[4] In Central America, the formal conclusion of protracted civil wars led to the election of various governments determined to take a hard line on rising crime. Evidence suggests that, in the wake of these deadly civil wars, organized crime and drug traffickers took advantage of the ready availability of weapons and the desperation of conflict-affected, jobless youth (among others) to build their enduring underground empires. In the Andes, where lack of education, poverty, and unemployment are commonly deemed as the main reasons behind youth delinquency and violence in urban sectors, the involvement of college-educated rural youth in political violence—particularly in Peru during the 1980s and 1990s—complicated this picture and briefly turned attention to the severity of socioeconomic and political marginalization, although not to the opportunity and quality of education offered especially to rural youth. Increasingly, a focus on urban youth delinquency and the proliferation of gang activity, particularly in Peruvian cities, has become predominant in the media, where the narrative attributes as main factors for the involvement of youth in violence the lack of education, unemployment, and the unruly nature of marginalized urban youth.

As various scholars have argued, "youth" is an unstable category in the region, and young people themselves are often caught between the simultaneous allure of conformity, yearning to resist traditional structures, and the threat of repression (Marcial, 2008; Podalsky, 2008; Reguillo Cruz, 2000). In Mexico in the past three decades, according to media studies scholar Laura Podalsky (2008), youth have been assigned contradictory status:

[They] have become "newly" visible as important social, political, and economic agents (as members of urban gangs; as swing voters in the landmark presidential election in 2000; and as a new niche market) and, equally crucially, youth have served as a symbolic repository for ambivalent feelings about the fall of past Mexican social models in the face of new cultural globalization. (p. 146)

These contradictory discourses about youth in Mexico and elsewhere have led to a simplistic categorization of youth as mainstream or "properly socialized," versus deviant or "troublesomely marginal" (Podalsky, 2008, p. 146; Reguillo Cruz, 2000).

At the same time, gross social and economic inequalities have contributed to the emergence of gangs in the region (Jones & Rodgers, 2009; Krauskopf & Mora, 2000). The epidemic is arguably worst in the countries with the highest rates of poverty and income inequality and the lowest rates of human development (e.g., Guatemala, El Salvador, Honduras, and Nicaragua). Urban gangs such as the Mara Salvatrucha and M-18 have expanded rapidly; one source estimates that there are between 25,000 and 125,000 active gang members in El Salvador, Guatemala, and Honduras alone (Cunningham et al., 2008, p. 10; on gangs in Latin America, see also Pinheiro, 2007; Ribando, 2005). According to one source, "Youth gang members are responsible for three to five times the amount of violence and crime as non-gang, at-risk youth" (Cunningham et al., 2008, p. 109).

In part as a result of these trends, homicide rates in the region have skyrocketed: "LAC has the highest homicide rate of men between the ages of 15 and 29 (69 per 100,000) in the world" (Cunningham et al., 2008, p. 10). Colombia, Venezuela, and Brazil experience markedly high rates of violence among youth. In Peru and Bolivia, levels of delinquency (theft, drug dealing, and homicide) are seemingly higher among young men. The steady pace of drug trafficking and the expansion of gangs in the region have consumed youth not only as victims but also as perpetrators of violent crime; "perpetrators of violent crimes are mostly young men between the ages of 16 and 25" (Cunningham et al., 2008). Mexico similarly has seen an increase in violence in recent years as a result of a variety of factors, the most notable of which have been turf wars among drug cartels. The latest trend in these turf wars is the recruitment of youth via the Internet and other media to serve as *sicarios* (assassins) on the front lines of the violence (*El Universal*, 2010; Meza, 2010). The most vulnerable youth, according to popular media accounts, are those who are not enrolled in school and who are not employed (Meza, 2010).

In response, many governments have adopted a hard-line approach to youth, portraying young men as a threat to national security; this resulted in a reduction in the age at which youth could be sentenced as adults and police persecution of youth (CEPAL/OIJ [Organización Iberoamericana de Juventud], 2008, p. 105).[5] An ethnographic study in Nicaragua by Maclure and Sotelo (2004) suggests that the nature of gang membership is little understood, resulting in reactionary and ineffectual government responses, which adopt "zero tolerance" approaches but do little to address the structural inequalities and marginalization of youth. According to Winton (2005), research and official discourse around gang violence often criminalize youth, while failing to "consider the effects of violence on young people, and the extent to which they themselves are victimized" (p. 167). Winton's study found that gang violence in Guatemalan cities limited the social and spatial mobility of both gang members and non–gang members alike, as they coped with the everyday risk of violence in their communities.[6]

It is our contention that the ways in which youth are positioned in the broader context of Latin American society—as politically apathetic, socially deviant, or potentially dangerous—have much to do with how Latin American governments and non-governmental organizations approach their literacy policymaking and program development. Widespread concern over the political socialization of youth has led to two general types of literacy programs: projects that simply aim to "recuperate" youth and reduce their marginalization, and more ambitious projects, based on a human-rights framework, that encourage youth to become more politically active and engaged and to push for social change.

During the 1990s, important changes took place in the conceptualization of literacy work. The traditional realm of adult education was expanded to include youth explicitly, and the concept of education for youth and adults (EPJA) emerged in the region, with a critique of instrumentalist approaches to education (such as vocational education), an emphasis on life-long learning (based on basic and secondary education, but stretching across the life span), and an effort to promote human rights. EPJA was strengthened and solidified over a series of meetings, including the Fifth International Conference on Adult Education (CONFINTEA V) in Hamburg, the Sixth International Conference on Adult Education (CONFINTEA VI) in Belém, Brazil (in December 2009), and regional meetings over the 1990s and 2000s. At the same time, the United Nations Children's Fund (UNICEF) expanded its child-centered work to include youth (Torres, 2000). These changes were consolidated by the Education for All global policy initiative. Specifically, Goal 3 (Promote learning and life skills for young people and adults) and Goal 4 (Increase [youth and] adult literacy by 50%) stimulated a reconsideration of youth as worthy educational subjects.

In 2000, the Regional Framework of Action for Education of Young People and Adults in Latin America and the Caribbean (2000–2010) was adopted, outlining the following objectives: "to improve the unequal distribution of educational offer for young people and adults, to contribute to the creation of mechanisms that allow the silenced demands to be expressed, and to meet effectively such demands" (Umayahara, 2005, p. 46). The Framework established seven priority areas: "literacy; education and work; education, citizenship and human rights; education with peasants and indigenous populations; education and youths; education and gender; and education for sustainable local development" (Umayahara, 2005, p. 46). During this period, the Regional Office of Education for Latin America and the Caribbean (OREALC) in Santiago, Chile, helped to professionalize EPJA by promoting innovations in training youth/adult educators, improving curricula for EPJA programs, strengthening information networks, funding research on and systematization of relevant practices in the field, and developing monitoring and evaluation mechanisms.

Over the course of these regional and international meetings, practitioners rejected the reduction of EPJA to basic literacy skills and what they perceived as the false dichotomies between being illiterate and being literate and between "pure illiteracy" and "functional illiteracy"; instead, they argued that we are all in the process of expanding literacy abilities and acquiring new literacy practices over a lifetime. Following the Belém meeting, advocates decried

the persistence of a simplistic notion of literacy, seen as a process that can be completed in a short time period, in precarious conditions, with un- or poorly qualified educators, with single methods, scarce reading and writing materials, poor use of modern technology, without taking into account the linguistic and cultural diversity of students [and the absence of evaluation of lessons learned]. (GLEACE, 2009)

Several other international projects further stimulated attention to youth literacy. The Regional Project for Education in Latin America and the Caribbean (PRELAC) has supported progress toward the achievement of EFA goals throughout the region, and publicity from the U.N. Literacy Decade (2003–2012) has drawn attention to the importance of literacy programming for youth and adults. UNESCO's Literacy Initiative for Empowerment (LIFE) Program, which aims to accelerate literacy in the 35 countries with the greatest number of illiterates or with literacy rates under 50%, invested funds and support in Brazil and Haiti, where they helped develop materials and administer programs (Hanemann, 2009). The Plan Iberoamericano de Alfabetización y Educación Básica de Personas Jóvenes y Adultos (PAEBA) developed by the Organization of Iberoamerican States has offered financial and technical support to existing literacy programs. The Spanish government has offered literacy support for a number of countries, particularly in Central America, through PAEBA. According to Cortina and Sánchez (2007), the priorities of these projects include the "completion of basic education of young adults and adults (15 years or older) who are illiterate and live in rural or urban-marginal areas, giving special attention to reducing the illiteracy rates amongst women" (p. 271). Cuba's Yo Sí Puedo campaign rather famously offered technical expertise and a basic, adaptable curriculum to countries throughout the region, most notably Haiti, Venezuela, and Bolivia (Steele, 2008). In terms of literacy initiatives offering a rights-based framework in the Andes, Central America, and Mexico, while (indigenous) language and cultural rights—including language revitalization—underlie the conception of national bilingual education policy and programs, existing official literacy programs for indigenous youth and adults do not necessarily focus on a rights-based framework. It is important to mention, however, that in some instances indigenous and grassroots movements have resulted in adult literacy education based in a rights-based framework. Typically, this type of local initiative has been supported by nongovernmental organizations not affiliated with government policy or programs (Carnoy & Torres, 1990; García, 2003, 2005; La Belle, 2000).

Youth and Multilingual Literacy Programs in the Region

One important consideration in regard to the political inclusion of youth is the provision of literacy instruction in home languages. Latin America and the Caribbean boast incredible linguistic diversity. Mexico has an indigenous population comprising nearly 7.2 million, representing 62 different languages (Hamel, 2008a). Central America is also incredibly linguistically diverse with more than 50 living languages in Guatemala alone (Lewis, 2009). In the Andes, Quechua and Aymara are the major indigenous languages, but others are spoken in the region. However, despite timid efforts to move toward multilingual education in the region, literacy programs are offered almost exclusively in Spanish, and few programs have tackled the challenge of teaching literacy in home languages. Moreover, official bilingual programs are usually offered at the primary level, but not at the secondary level or in higher education programs, where instruction takes place in Spanish.

In 1978, the Mexican government formed the General Department of Indigenous Education (DGEI) with the goal of consolidating indigenous education programs at the primary level; at this point, schools continued to follow the federal curriculum, with indigenous languages used on an as-needed basis for instructional purposes (Hamel, 2008a). In the 1980s, the indigenous education program in Mexico took on the label of "bilingual/bicultural," and in the 1990s, the program became known as "bilingual and intercultural" education, with an emphasis on dialogue across different cultures (Hamel, 2008a; Schmelkes, 2000). Both programs aspired to increase the participation of indigenous communities in the educational system; to allow for greater flexibility in the national curriculum to account for indigenous languages, knowledge, and values; and to provide for increased autonomy of the schools (Schmelkes, 2000). In reality, however, the implementation of bilingual and intercultural education in indigenous communities has been uneven at best. Acculturation has prevailed over language maintenance, for Spanish continues to be the primary language of instruction in many bilingual education programs; at the same time, federal control over the national curriculum has remained steady, limiting local participation and control over curriculum content (Hamel, 2008b; King, 1994; Reinke, 2004).

Official policies in Guatemala have evolved from emphasizing "castillianization" and assimilation to promoting bilingualism and biliteracy in Spanish and Mayan languages (Richards & Richards, 1996; Verdugo & Raymundo, 2009). Early literacy efforts in Guatemala were developed to address the "Indian problem," or the need to assimilate Mayan communities through the teaching of Spanish (Najarro Arriola, 1995). In the 1960s, a national Castellanización Bilingüe program was launched to integrate indigenous children into the national culture. This program failed miserably, as the cultural and linguistic barriers between teachers and students prevented Mayan students from being fully engaged in the classes (Verdugo & Raymundo, 2009). With the support of international agencies and private universities, the Programa Nacional de Educación Bilingüe (PRONEBI) was created in 1985 to develop bilingual education programs, methods, and materials to teach indigenous children how to read and write in their mother tongue and to learn Spanish as a second language. In 1995, this was to become the Dirección de Educación Bilingüe Intercultural (DIGEBI). According to Verdugo and Raymundo (2009), DIGEBI still lacks programmatic efficiency and a genuinely responsive approach that takes into account Mayan identity and culture. Finally, the Comité Nacional de Alfabetización (CONALFA) was founded in 1987 and launched several literacy campaigns in various Mayan languages across the country. A partnership with CEPAL resulted in the first national biliteracy campaign "Bialfabetización" (BI-ALFA), which teaches children how to read and write in two languages simultaneously. This experimental program has been limited to the Q'anjob'al linguistic community in Santa Cruz Barillas (Verdugo & Raymundo, 2009).

In Nicaragua, literacy policies and programming were linked to national development strategies aimed at improving access to and quality of primary education. This approach dominated literacy programs from the 1950s to 1970s, reproducing social and economic inequalities rather than alleviating them (Arrien, 2006). The 1980s witnessed the emergence of the Sandinista Revolution, and with this, a shift in the discourse of literacy from human capital theory and development to human rights and radical social transformation. The Nicaraguan Literacy Crusade of the 1980s drew on the work of Paulo Freire as well as lessons learned from the Cuban literacy campaigns (Arnove & Torres, 1995; Arrien, 2006). However, despite the rhetoric around participatory pedagogical principles, literacy education was primarily a way for the Sandinistas to promote their political project (Street, 1984). The complex interethnic divisions and relationships on the Atlantic Coast of Nicaragua proved to be a challenge for the Literacy Crusade. Freeland (1995) suggests that it failed to acknowledge the sociolinguistic history of that region, the predominance of bilingualism, or the cultural constructs of the indigenous peoples around literacy, language, and education. In 1980, an organization of indigenous communities called MISURASATA organized a successful boycott of Literacy Crusade programs in Spanish, forcing the government to begin developing materials in Miskitu as well as other languages such as Sumu and English (Freeland, 1995). That same year, the government decreed the Law on Education in Languages of the Atlantic Coast (Decree Law 571), which encouraged teaching in native languages from preschool to fourth grade. The Nicaraguan Caribbean Coast regions were eventually given autonomous status in 1987 and developed the Regional Autonomous Education System (SEAR), which has since promoted and implemented intercultural and bilingual educational initiatives (Arrien, 2006; Cunningham Kain, 2009).

The constitutions of Bolivia (2008), Ecuador (2008), and Peru (1993) and their education laws were modified accordingly and included (at least rhetorically) intercultural education for indigenous and nonindigenous alike. However, much of what has been accomplished at the policy level in the past decades has not crystallized through implementation and practice (López & Hanemann, 2009; Valdiviezo, 2009), even less so in the case of youth and adult literacy, which also has received limited policy consideration (Kalman, 2008; López & Hanemann, 2009; Umayahara, 2005).

Indigenous organizations and civil society have promoted bilingual intercultural literacy programs in the Andes, not without controversy (see García, 2003, for an analysis of tensions between advocates for bilingual education and indigenous communities' expectations of formal education). In Bolivia, while President Evo Morales's attention to youth and adult education has been positively received, government provision of basic literacy services continues in Spanish only, with nongovernmental organizations—which, prior to the Morales government, had been implementing bilingual adult literacy projects in indigenous communities—now dedicated to implementing "postliteracy" bilingual programs with already Spanish-literate indigenous people (López & Hanemann, 2009; UNESCO, 2003). López and Hanemann (2009) warn against a problematic tendency to homogenize the extremely diverse needs emerging from approximately 36 different linguistic groups under one tidy proposal (López & Hanemann, 2009). In Ecuador, the national literacy campaign El Programa Nacional de Educación Básica para Jóvenes y Adultos (EBJA, National Program of Basic Education for Youth and Adults) aims to assist youth and adults. One of EBJA's five subprojects teaches literacy in Quichua to indigenous populations (UNESCO, 2009); other subprojects target populations with special needs and individuals who are institutionalized, such as those in correctional institutions.

The critiques of policy initiatives in the region point at their mainly rhetorical character; actual practice continues to perpetuate grave social inequalities and exclusion of historically underserved populations. During an interview (July 28, 2009), literacy researcher M. T. De la Piedra mentioned that, in the Andes, although at the policy level there is interest in using texts in indigenous languages for youth and adult literacy, there is no existing pedagogy to implement it. In practice, literacy is still understood in its relation to the development of Spanish as a dominant language and not of literacy in the indigenous language, while bilingual education generally is implemented as a remedial program. Mayra Daniel, who has done extensive literacy research with teachers in Guatemala, spoke of several challenges that limit the effectiveness of many of Guatemala's bilingual education programs. In addition to a lack of resources, such as bilingual texts or books of any kind, many teachers in these programs are simply not adequately trained in bilingual instruction methods (interview, May 4, 2010). This suggests that although government literacy campaigns may be promoting bilingualism and biliteracy at the level of policy and public discourse, the reality of program implementation and pedagogical practices is rather discouraging. Literacy policies and programs group youth with adults without sufficiently conceptualizing the specific social, economic, and political needs of youth. Finally, there is evidence that government actors and indigenous groups are differentially conceptualizing programs and policies (García, 2003, 2005). In their ethnographic study of indigenous teachers in Bolivia, Howard-Malverde and Canessa (1995) warn about how the changing relationship between indigenous communities and state has not redefined education for both in the same way. For the state, there is a continuation of the civilizing, "Bolivianizing" (referring to the creation of a national Bolivian identity), and colonizing goal of education, while for indigenous people, intercultural education promises access and possibilities of social and political empowerment. The tensions between these contradictory goals of education become clear in the context of the local education practice taking place in the indigenous school and the indigenous community (Hornberger, 1988, 2000; Howard-Malverde & Canessa, 1995; Valdiviezo, 2009). These tensions are also clearly highlighted in ethnographic studies of literacy practices in indigenous communities in Peru, where rigidly imposed literacy practices from formal schooling tend to be valued above cultural practices or literacies taken place outside school, in the indigenous setting (De la Piedra, 2004; Zavala, 2004).

Bilingual and biliteracy programs for youth also fail to acknowledge what ethnographic studies of language have found to be a complex relationship between language and identity for indigenous youth. In Guatemala, Bitar, Pimentel, and Juarez (2008) examine the emerging hybrid language practices—which they call "K'iche'tellano"—of a Mayan community in Nueva Santa Catarina Ixtahuacán. Their analysis suggests how competing economic and social structures manifest themselves in the language practices of these bilingual Maya, who work to preserve K'iche while recognizing the need to learn Spanish to access social, political, and economic resources. Although some data suggested a rigid division between the use of K'iche in home/community environments and the use of Spanish in official and public contexts, "a deeper analysis of the data suggest that participants produce hybrid language practices that reflect ongoing racial projects and linguistic transformations that Maya peoples undergo" (p. 30). Among the Maya in Momostenango, Choi (2002) suggests that the K'iche language serves as an icon that portrays and indexes Mayan identities. Momostenango is one of a few places in Guatemala where Mayan socioeconomic conditions are better than those of poor Ladinos. According to Choi, Mayans here take up contradictory language ideologies, since they associate K'iche with that of lower-class rural Maya while also embracing it as a marker of an "authentic" Mayan identity in the larger sociopolitical context.

The struggle for multilingual literacy in the region continues. The emergence of international policies and agendas such as the Universal Declaration of Linguistic Rights (1996), and, recently, the United Nations Declaration on the Rights of Indigenous People (2007), have fueled calls for the expansion of educational access, the right of education in the mother tongue, and the attention to language and cultural diversity (Valdiviezo, 2009). It remains to be seen whether such global declarations will translate into well-designed, sustainable multilingual literacy programs for youth.

YOUTH LITERACY PRACTICES

Finally, our review of research in the region reveals a sharp distinction between school-based literacy practices for youth, which are informed by a deficit perspective, and out-of-school literacy practices.

Research in Mexico on the meaning and uses of literacy within classroom settings, particularly at the primary level, has shown that writing tends to be emphasized over reading (Jiménez, Smith, & Martinez-Leon, 2003). Writing in primary classrooms tends to be highly controlled, with a great deal of emphasis on correct spelling, punctuation, and handwriting (that is, emphasis on "form") and with few opportunities on writing for self-expression or meaning-making (Jiménez et al., 2003; Smith, Jiménez, & Martinez-Leon, 2003). This focus on form is also present in oral reading, while fewer restrictions tend to be placed on spoken language in the classroom (Smith et al., 2003). Teachers often require students to copy texts from blackboards into their notebooks, with little dialogue about content and much attention to form (Smith, Murillo, & Jiménez, 2009).

These school-based expressions of literacy contrast with the wide range of texts and literacy practices in which youth engage outside of school. Although research is still needed in this area, it has been found that youth have been involved in graffiti production (Hernández Flores, 2009), musical production (Urteaga Castro-Pozo, 1998), and multiple digital forms of communication (Davenport & Gunn, 2009; Smith et al., 2009). In one study of youth literacy practices within and outside an adult learning center, Hernández Flores (2003) found that whereas educators tended to represent youth in terms of their deficiencies and their absence of reading and writing habits, the youth themselves demonstrated a wide array of literacy practices that surpassed the demands of academic instruction found in the learning center. A study by Jiménez et al. (2003) contrasts the in-school emphasis on correctness in writing with unconventional, but equally rule-driven, approaches to spelling found in the community, especially through help-wanted ads and other public displays of writing. The schism between in-school and out-of-school approaches to language became particularly apparent in their description of a language-arts exam where a first-grade student answered "*von vero*" to a question asking who puts out fires; the grader of the exam, who was a government representative, marked the answer incorrect, since the student did not use the correct spelling of "*bombero*" ("firefighter"), in spite of the fact the student had clearly made sense of the question. In such instances, the out-of-school literacies enacted by young people are rarely recognized or affirmed by schools. More research is needed in this area to better understand youth's literacy practices and to allow school-based literacy efforts to build on youth literacy practices and capacities.

The gap between school-based approaches to literacy and the out-of-school literacy practices has grown in recent decades as a result of the rapid changes associated with globalization, which in turn have spurred a rapid growth in technology and new forms of literacy. Youth, in particular, have been affected. As reported by Winocur (2009), Mexico's 2005 Encuesta Nacional de Jóvenes (National Youth Survey) found that while only 28% of young people between the ages of 15 and 29 had a computer in the home, 69.55% were familiar with its use; moreover, although only 20% of youth had an Internet connection in the home, 60.75% reported knowing how to use the Internet. In other words, states Winocur, youth's socialization into the use of information technologies in Mexico "does not depend solely and fundamentally on the possession of a device or on training in school, but on other social spaces outside of home and school, such as cybercafés and networks of friends" (p. 179). Young people's engagement with digital forms of communication in Mexico represents a symbolic space of meaning-making and identity construction. For Winocur (2009), young people's engagement in technology, generally, and social networking, particularly, represents "an individual and collective strategy of cohesion, visibility, and social inclusion" (p. 185). More studies of youth digital literacy practices are needed to understand the connections between literacy and technology as youth go about shaping new social spaces and identities.

While globalization has led to increased connectivity through technology within Mexico, it has also led to increased connectivity across geographic spaces. Many youth in Mexico have family members living in the United States; in some cases, they themselves have lived in the United States. The term *transnational literacies* has emerged to describe this movement and the reading, writing, and language practices that people engage in across geographic spaces (Jiménez, Smith, & Teague, 2009; Warriner, 2007). Through their engagement with digital forms of communication, immigrant youth create and enact particular identities and relationships that reflect their transnational situation, a situation that involves being both "there" in the home country as well as "here" in the adopted country (Lam & Rosario-Ramos, 2009; McGinnis, Goodstein-Stolzenberg, & Saliani, 2007). In their study of 35 immigrant high school students from different backgrounds, for example, Lam and Rosario-Ramos (2009) found that the youth engaged in an array of digital practices, including social networking and informational media, in multiple languages, which in turn served as a means of increasing communication and contact across national boundaries. Lam and Rosario-Ramos argue that these forms of communication "allowed students to diversify their access to linguistic resources" (p. 183), which in turn helped them both to maintain their primary language while also acquiring English.

Likewise, scholars examining the literacy practices of children and youth in Central America have frequently found "discontinuity" between the texts and practices of the home and the texts and practices in school classrooms (Cordero Cordero,

2002). The social, cultural, and linguistic resources that children and youth bring to their academic environments often go unacknowledged and underappreciated by their teachers and school systems. For example, Purcell-Gates (2008) found that in first- and second-grade Costa Rican classrooms, instructional activities had students copying from the board, cutting and trimming worksheets, and gluing them into content area notebooks—bearing little resemblance to text and literacy practices in the home environment.

Ethnographic studies of literacy suggest that indigenous and immigrant youth often have to contend with various forms of xenophobia and racism in their schools. The Cultural Practices of Literacy Study (CPLS) conducted by the University of British Columbia in San Jose, Costa Rica, explored the marginalization and educational achievement of Nicaraguan immigrant children in Costa Rican primary schools. Scholars found that despite the predominant negative stereotyping and deficit perspectives with Nicaraguan children, these immigrant students actually were performing at levels of literacy development and academic achievement on par or higher than their Costa Rican classmates (Purcell-Gates, 2008). Stocker's (2005) ethnography of a Costa Rican high school examines placed-based racism among students and teachers who discriminate against students from an indigenous reservation. She found that students rejected an Indian identity as a way to overcome social stigmas and be successful in school. These studies highlight the relationship between youth identities and youth literacy practices situated in asymmetrical relations of power.

Research in the Andes reports surprising findings about school-based and out-of-school literacy practices. For example, De la Piedra's (2006) research focuses on the appropriation by indigenous youth of formal reading and writing practices, where outside texts of, for example, romantic poetry, although unrelated to formal school texts, were used and produced by students as a meaningful social practice outside the school setting in the rural locality (see also De la Piedra, 2010). Zavala (2004) investigated how school literacy practices—characteristically prescriptive and decontextualized—were alternately rejected and taken up in the nonschool practices of a Quechua rural community in the Peruvian Andes. Yapu's (2008) research on Aymara youth in Bolivia challenged common assumptions that youth lack political presence by revealing instead that indigenous youth actively engage in political participation within their rural communities and urban contexts, in part through using virtual communities and social networks such as Facebook, which disseminates information ranging from calls to meetings through links to blogs where political, linguistic, and ethnic issues are debated. However, the literacy practices of urban Andean youth remain an underexplored area in research. In our interview with her, De la Piedra pointed out the importance of researching multimodal and digital literacy practices by Peruvian youth in urban and rural settings (July 28, 2009).

Overall, we found that official literacy programs tended to center on arbitrarily selected, tightly delimited types of literacy skills, ignoring the broad range of what people actually do with literacy. This finding was captured very well in the critiques put forward by Rosa Maria Torres in her reports on literacy in Ecuador. Torres, an international scholar and literacy specialist, has argued that Ecuadorian officials "continue to use understandings of literacy and illiteracy coined by the UNESCO in the last century" (Torres, 2005, p. 6) and that the government's traditional notions of literacy and illiteracy are limited to formal settings rather than daily literacy practices, which continue to be ignored (Torres, 2009).

Knowledge of actual youth literacy practices in the multilingual and multiethnic Latin American landscape is fairly recent and the review of the literature included in this section shows important gaps between existing youth literacy programs and youth literacy practices in contexts other than school. The literacy and cultural practices that youth engage with in their daily lives remain ignored in educational institutions. As a result, in general, schools maintain delimited and too often irrelevant definitions of literacy, and view their students from a deficit stance.

Furthermore, the studies reviewed in this section suggested that globalization and the rapid diffusion of technology communication have widened the gap between school-based approaches to literacy and out-of-school literacy practices. Youth have become engaged with transnational literacies and new forms of reading, writing, and language use. They have also appropriated prescriptive and decontextualized school literacies and used them for meaningful new purposes in real contexts. Our review showed that youth literacy practices in the Latin American region are as diverse as the youth themselves, and that more research is necessary to gain the understanding of youth and literacy that can help transform present policy and literacy programs.

CONCLUSION

Our review of the available literature highlights a tension between official policies and pedagogies and adolescent literacies. Official policies are often guided by deficit perspectives, inadvertently blaming youth and their families for a lack of literacy skills while resolutely failing to acknowledge the ways in which social structures, racial projects, and the existing economy and labor market shape access to and use of literacy. We have discussed how national and international reports—providing largely quantitative findings on literacy rates—have become commonplace tools for assessing progress on national goals and having cross-country and regional conversations about youth and literacy. These standardized measures of literacy, which have largely informed policies and programs for youth, offer a panoramic view of important trends in the region, but they need to be analyzed within a broader macro social and political context. As we surveyed the region's national literacy rates and other key social indicators, we found differential levels of youth access to literacy that were directly related to entrenched forms of social, economic, and political disparities. The statistical data confirm that across the region indigenous youth, in particular, are affected by illiteracy, poverty, and social exclusion. We argue that, though useful, these quantitative measures and reports do not capture the sociocultural complexities of youth literacy practices or the discursive and political nature of youth literacy policymaking and programming.

In this chapter, we have also discussed the varying meanings and underlying assumptions surrounding the term *youth* and their role in the development of national policies and programs. Definitions of youth in this context have tended to portray them as deviant, dangerous, and politically apathetic, while policies and programs have attempted to define youth in their function in two roles: as strategic actors in economic development (workforce formation) and as citizens (political formation). These conceptualizations have been taken up by the World Bank, United Nations organizations, USAID, and CEPAL for the design of literacy policy and programming for youth. These global institutions have also exported and legitimized conceptions of "youth at risk," especially in relation to a perceived absence of skills and preparedness to compete for jobs in globally oriented markets.

Although Latin American scholars have adopted sociocultural understandings of literacy that examine the ways in which literacy practices are influenced by and help to perpetuate inequality, Latin American policy discourses under the influence of human capital theory have framed literacy as a key cause of underdevelopment, suggesting that providing adolescents and adults with access to literacy will enhance their economic and political incorporation into existing, and unproblematized, economic and political systems.

Given the multiethnic, multilingual, and pluricultural reality of Latin America and the Caribbean, the question of language figures prominently in literacy debates, though it has not been sufficiently integrated into formal policy and programming. Because language is inextricably tied to issues of culture and identity, efforts to promote literacy in indigenous languages have been a part of movements for indigenous rights and local struggles for power and self-determination. The literature suggests that bilingual and biliteracy educational initiatives challenge prevailing monolingual language ideologies but have yet to be funded or developed as fully as they deserve.

To understand how youth literacy policies, programs, and discourses are taken up, resisted, and reconstituted by Latin American youth at the local level, we turned our gaze toward more ethnographically informed research that examines the situated nature of youth literacy and language practices. The available literature suggests that young people have creatively adopted and adapted resources (like literate genres) for their own ends. The literature also suggests a significant gap between the literacy practices required at school and those practiced beyond school, and another gap between the deficit discourse employed by educators and the evidence regarding actual literacy practices among youth. Furthermore, even as schools continue to be portrayed as key agents of political socialization, it is clear that political action among urban youth is mainly—although not exclusively—informed by social movements and online networking and information. Studies suggest that indigenous youth have adopted and adapted globalizing trends for their own purposes. There is a clear need for more research in this area.

Overall, our chapter calls attention to anthropologically informed research that can combat technorational approaches that blame the victim and instead highlight both the creative appropriation and adaptation of literacy by youth and the ways in which economic and political structures have constrained greater access to literacy. What these studies provide is a close look at *how* youth are engaging with texts and using the cultural and linguistic resources available to them to assert their agency and negotiate their identities. This review of the literature of youth literacy has revealed the limitations of policies and programs surrounding youth literacy education, but it also has shown local youth practices as evidence of politically involved, unpredictable, and creative contemporary youth who continue to respond to the challenges of marginalization.

NOTES

[1]For studies of adolescent literacy, see Alvermann et al. (1996); Alvermann, Hinchman, Moore, Phelps, and Waff (1998); Alvermann (2002); Brozo, Shiel, and Topping (2007); Cassidy, Garrett, and Barrera (2008); Hopper (2005); Jetton and Dole (2004); Moje (2002); Moje, Overby, Tysvaer, and Morris (2008); Morrell (2004); Patel Stevens (2002); and Vacca (1998).

[2]UNESCO's (United Nations Educational, Scientific, and Educational Organization) Literacy Assessment and Monitoring Program (LAMP) initiative has endeavored to improve statistical measures of literacy.

[3]However, a survey of Iberoamerican governments in 2004 showed that only a few countries have, in their constitutions, laws specific to youth. In Bolivia, the only explicit reference to youth is the decree regarding rights and responsibilities of youth; in the Dominican Republic, a law created a state organization directed to youth, which initiated the Day of the Student; in Cuba, programs directed to youth began with the Revolution; in Chile, the National Institute of Youth was created (ECLAC, 2008). The other countries surveyed consider youth under the category of "minors" (Brazil, Ecuador, El Salvador, Guatemala, Uruguay, Venezuela and others; CEPAL, 2007, p. 283).

[4]For more information on youth cultures in Mexico, see Arce Cortés (2008), Feixa (1998), Levinson (1999), Reguillo Cruz (2000), and Urteaga Castro-Pozo (1998).

[5]See, for example, the "anti-tattoo" law in Honduras or "mano dura" measures in El Salvador (Washington Office on Latin America, 2006).

[6]In the face of political and economic instability, the continued outmigration of youth and their families, especially from Mexico, Central America, and the Caribbean, has in some ways made youth even more vulnerable, as they leave behind critical familial and social supports to face the difficulties of linguistic, social, and political incorporation in their new schools and societies. In uncertain times, increases in crime, combined with the U.S. Immigration and Customs Enforcement agency's aggressive efforts to deport foreign-born youth and adults with criminal convictions, have led to intensified feelings of insecurity and scapegoating of youth as a threat throughout Latin America and the Caribbean (Johnson & Muhlhausen, 2005).

REFERENCES

Alvarez, B., Dassin, J., Rosenberg, L., & Bloom, D. (1999). *Education in Latin America* (Development Discussion Paper No. 711). Cambridge, MA: Harvard Institute for International Development.

Alvermann, D. (Ed.). (2002). *Adolescents and literacies in a digital world.* New York, NY: Lang.

Alvermann, D. E., Hinchman, K. A., Moore, D. W., Phelps, S. F., & Waff, D. R. (Eds.). (1998). *Reconceptualizing the literacies in adolescents' lives.* Mahwah, NJ: Erlbaum.

Alvermann, D. E., Young, J. P., Weaver, D., Hinchman, K. A., Moore, D. W., Phelps, S. F., Thrash, E. C., & Zalewski, P. (1996). Middle and high school students' perceptions of how they experience text-based discussions: A multicase study. *Reading Research Quarterly, 31*, 244–267.

Arce Cortés, T. (2008). Subcultura, contracultura, tribus urbanas y culturas juveniles: ¿Homogenización o diferenciación? [Subculture, counterculture, urban tribes, and youth cultures: Homogenization or differentiation?]. *Revista Argentina de Sociologia, 6*(11), 257–271.

Arnove, R. F., & Torres, C. A. (1995). Adult education and state policy in Latin America: The contrasting cases of Mexico and Nicaragua. *Comparative Education, 31*(3), 311–325.

Arrien, J. (2006). *Literacy in Nicaragua*. Paris, France: UNESCO.

Barton, D., & Hamilton, M. (2000). Literacy practices. In D. Barton, M. Hamilton, & R. Ivanic (Eds.), *Situated literacies* (pp. 7–14). New York, NY: Routledge.

Bitar, M., Pimentel, C., & Juarez, A. (2008). Language gain, language loss: The production of K'iche'tellano in Highland Guatemala. *International Journal of Language, Society and Culture, 26*, 25–33.

Braslavsky, C. (Ed.). (2001). *La educación secundaria "Cambio o inmutabilidad" Análisis y debate de procesos europeos y latinoamericanos contemporáneos* [Secondary education "Change or immutability" Analysis and debates of contemporary European and Latin American processes]. Buenos Aires, Argentina: Editora Santillana.

Brozo, W., Shiel, G., & Topping, K. (2007). Engagement in reading: Lessons learned from three PISA countries. *Journal of Adolescent & Adult Literacy, 51*(4), 304–315.

Campbell, M. (2006, June 14). Rocking Mexico's voters. *Newsweek*. Retrieved from http://www.newsweek.com/id/52531

Carnoy, M., & Torres, C. A. (1990). *The politics of nonformal education in Latin America*. New York, NY: Praeger.

Cassidy, J., Garrett, S., & Barrera, E. (2008). What's hot in adolescent literacy 1997–2006. *Journal of Adolescent & Adult Literacy, 50*(1), 30–36.

Choi, C. (2002, April). *The role of language in ideological construction of Mayan identities in Guatemala*. Paper presented at the Tenth Annual Symposium about Language and Society. Austin, TX. Retrieved from http://studentorgs.utexas.edu/salsa/proceedings/2002/papers/choi.pdf

Collins, J., & Blot, R. K. (2003). *Literacy and literacies: Texts, power, and identity*. New York, NY: Cambridge University Press.

Comisión Económica para América Latina y el Caribe. (2007). *La juventud en Iberoamérica: Tendencias y urgencias* [Youth in Ibero-America: Trends and priorities]. Buenos Aires, Argentina: Author.

Comisión Económica para América Latina y el Caribe/Organización Iberoamericana de Juventud. (2008). *Juventud y cohesión social en Iberoamérica: Un modelo para armar* [Youth and social cohesion in Ibero-America: A model to build]. Santiago de Chile, Chile: Author.

Consejo Nacional de Educación. (2007). *Proyecto Educativo Nacional al 2021: La educación que queremos para el Perú* [National Educational Project to 2012: The education we want for Peru]. Lima, Peru: Author.

Cordero Cordero, T. (2002). Desencuentros entre prácticas escolares y vivencias familiares [Mismatches between school practices and family experiences]. *Actualidades Investigativas en Educación, 2*(2), 1–17.

Cortina, R., & Sánchez, M. T. (2007). Spanish bilateral initiatives for education in Latin America. *Prospects, 37*(2), 267–281.

Cunningham Kain, M. (2009). La experiencia de Nicaragua [The experience of Nicaragua]. In L. E. López & U. Hanemann (Eds.), *Alfabetización y multiculturalidad: Miradas desde*

América Latina (pp. 181–236). Guatemala City, Guatemala: UNESCO-UIL/GTZ-PACE.

Cunningham, W., McGinnis, L., García Verdú, C. T., & Dorte, V. (2008). *Youth at risk in Latin America and the Caribbean: Understanding the causes, realizing the potential.* Washington, DC: World Bank.

Davenport, M. G., & Gunn, K. (2009). Collaboration in animation: Working together to empower indigenous youth. *Art Education, 62*(5), 6–12.

De la Piedra, M. T. (2004). Oralidad y escritura: El rol de los intermediarios de literacidad en una comunidad Quechua-hablante de los Andes peruanos [Orality and writing: The role of literacy intermediaries in a Quechua-speaking community in the Peruvian Andes]. In V. Zavala, M. Niño-Murcia, & P. Ames (Eds.), *Escritura y sociedad: Nuevas perspectivas teóricas y etnográficas* (pp. 367–388). Lima: Red para el desarrollo de las ciencias sociales en el Perú.

De la Piedra, M. T. (2006). Literacies and Quechua oral language: Connecting sociocultural worlds and linguistic resources for biliteracy development. *Journal of Early Childhood Literacy, 6*(3), 383–406.

De la Piedra, M. T. (2010). Religious and self-generated Quechua literacy practices in the Peruvian Andes. *International Journal of Bilingual Education and Bilingualism, 13*(1), 99–113.

ECLAC. (2008). *Social Panorama of Latin America.* Santiago, Chile: ECLAC.

El Universal. (2010, January 14). *Reclutan a jóvenes y menores para instruirlos como sicarios* [They recruit youth and minors to train them as hit men]. Retrieved from http://www.informador.com.mx/mexico/2009/71469/6/reclutan-a-jovenes-y-menores-para-instruirlos-como-sicarios.htm

Feixa, C. (1998). *El reloj de arena: Culturas juveniles en México* [The hourglass: Youth cultures in Mexico]. Mexico City, Mexico: Causa Joven.

Frank, D. (2010). *Out of the past, a new Honduras culture of resistance* (NACLA Report on the Americas). Retrieved from https://nacla.org/node/6541

Freeland, J. (1995). Why go to school to learn Miskitu? Changing constructs of bilingualism, education, and literacy among the Miskitu of Nicaragua's Atlantic coast. *International Journal of Educational Development, 15*(3), 245–261.

Galicia López, A. (2003). EPJA en México. *La educación de jóvenes y adultos en América Latina y el Caribe hacia un estado del arte: Informe regional de América Latina y el Caribe para la Conferencia de Seguimiento a CONFINTEA V, Bangkok, Septiembre de 2003* [Youth and adult education in Latin America and the Caribbean toward a state of the art: Regional report of Latin America and the Caribbean for the follow-up conference CONFINTEA V]. Hamburg, Germany: UNESCO.

Gallart, M. A. (2000). *Formación, pobreza y exclusión: Los programas para jóvenes en América Latina* [Training, poverty and exclusion: Youth programs in Latin America]. Montevideo, Uruguay: RET-CINTERFOR/OIT.

García, M. E. (2003). The politics of community: Education, indigenous rights, and ethnic mobilization in Peru. *Latin American Perspectives, 30*(1), 70–95.

García, M. (2005). *Making indigenous citizens: Identity development and multicultural activism in Peru.* Palo Alto, CA: Stanford University Press.

GLEACE. (2009, October 22). *Sobre alfabetismo y alfabetización: Declaración de miembros del Grupo Latinoamericano de Especialistas en Alfabetización y Cultura Escrita* [On literacy and literacy development: A declaration by members of the Latin American group of experts in literacy and written culture] (*GLEACE*).

Hamel, R. E. (2008a). Indigenous language policy and education in Mexico. In S. May & N. H. Hornberger (Eds.), *Encyclopedia of language and education* (2nd ed., pp. 1:301–313). New York, NY: Springer.

Hamel, R. E. (2008b). Bilingual education for indigenous communities in Mexico. In J. Cummins & N. H. Hornberger (Eds.), *Encyclopedia of language and education* (2nd ed., pp. 5:311–322). New York, NY: Springer.

Hanemann, U. (2009). *Advancing literacy: A review of LIFE 2006–2009*. Paris, France: UNESCO Institute for Lifelong Learning.

Helwege, A., & Birch, M. (2007). *Declining poverty in Latin America? A critical analysis of new estimates by international institutions* (Global Development and Environment Working Paper No. 07-02). Medford, MA: Tufts University.

Hernández Flores, G. E. (2003). Juventud y cultura escrita: Prácticas juveniles de escritura [Youth and written culture: Youth literacy practices]. *Decisio, 6*. Retrieved from http://tariacuri.crefal.edu.mx/decisio/d6

Hernández Flores, G. E. (2009). Identidades juveniles y cultura escrita [Youth identities and written culture]. In J. Kalman & B. Street (Eds.), *Lectura, escritura, y matemáticas como prácticas sociales: Diálogos con América Latina* (pp. 186–201). Mexico City, Mexico: Siglo XXI.

Hopenhayn, N. (2006). La juventud Latinoamericana en sus tensiones y sus violencias [Latin American youth in tension and violence]. In Moro, J. (Ed.), *Juventudes, violencia y exclusión: Desafíos para las políticas públicas* [Youth, violence, and exclusion: Challenges for public policy] (pp. 29-54). Guatemala: Magnaterra Editores.

Hopper, R. (2005). What are teenagers reading? Adolescent fiction reading habits and reading choices. *Literacy, 39*(3), 113–120.

Hornberger, N. H. (1988). *Bilingual education and language maintenance: A southern Peruvian Quechua case*. Dordrecht, Netherlands: Foris.

Hornberger, N. H. (2000). Bilingual education policy and practice in the Andes: Ideological paradox and intercultural possibility. *Anthropology & Education Quarterly, 31*(2), 173–201.

Howard-Malverde, R., & Canessa, A. (1995). The school in the Quechua and Aymara communities in highland Bolivia. *International Journal of Educational Development, 15*(3), 231–243.

Hull, G., Zacher, J., & Hibbert, L. (2009). Youth, risk, and equity in a global world. *Review of Research in Education, 33*(1), 117–159.

Instituto Nacional de la Educación de los Adultos. (2010). INEA en números [INEA in numbers]. Retrieved from: http://www.inea.gob.mx/ineanum/

Jacinto, C. (1999) *Programas de educación para jóvenes desfavorecidos: Enfoques y tendencias en América Latina* [Education programs for disadvantaged youth: Approaches and trends in Latin America]. Paris, France: IIPE-UNESCO.

Jacinto, C. (2002). Los jóvenes, la educación y el trabajo en América Latina. Nuevos temas, debates y dilemas. In M. Ibarrola (Ed.), *Desarrollo local y formación. Hacia una mirada integral de la formación de los jóvenes para el trabajo* [Youth, education, and work in Latin America. New themes, debates and dilemmas] (pp. 67–102). Montevideo, Uruguay: Cinterfor.

Jetton, T. L., & Dole, J. A. (2004). *Adolescent literacy research and practice*. New York, NY: Guilford.

Jiménez, R. T., & Smith, P. H. (2008). Mesoamerican literacies: Indigenous writing systems and contemporary possibilities. *Reading Research Quarterly, 43*(1), 28–46.

Jiménez, R. T., Smith, P. H., & Martinez-Leon, N. (2003). Freedom and form: The language and literacy practices of two Mexican schools. *Reading Research Quarterly, 38*, 488–508.

Jiménez, R. T., Smith, P. H., & Teague, B. L. (2009). Transnational and community literacies for teachers. *Journal of Adolescent & Adult Literacy, 53*(1), 16–26.

Johnson, S., & Muhlhausen, D. B. (2005). *North American transnational youth gangs: Breaking the chain of violence*. Washington, DC: Heritage Foundation. Retrieved from http://www.heritage.org/Research/UrbanIssues/bg1834.cfm

Jones, G., & Rodgers, D. (2009). *Youth violence in Latin America: Gangs and juvenile justice in perspective*. New York, NY: Palgrave Macmillan.

Kalman, J. (2001). Everyday paperwork: Literacy practices in the daily life of unschooled and underschooled women in a semiurban community in Mexico City. *Linguistics and Education, 12*(4), 367-391.

Kalman, J. (2008). Literacies in Latin America. In B. V. Street & N. Hornberger (Eds.), *Encyclopedia of Language and Education* (pp. 321–334). New York, NY: Springer.

King, L. (1994). *Roots of identity: Language and literacy in Mexico*. Palo Alto, CA: Stanford University Press.

Kleiman, A. B. (Ed.). (1995). *Os significados do letramento: Uma nova perspectiva sobre a prática social da escrita* [The meanings of literacy: A new perspective on the social practice of writing]. Campinas, Brazil: Mercado das Letras.

Krauskopf, D. (2003). La construcción de políticas de juventud en Centroamérica [The construction of youth policies in Central America]. In O. Davila (Ed.), *Políticas públicas de juventud en América Latina* (pp. 1–46). Viña del Mar, Chile: CIDPA.

Krauskopf, D. (2005, November–December). Desafíos en la construcción y implementación de las políticas de juventud en América Latina [Challenges in the construction and implementation of youth policies in Latin America]. *Nueva Sociedad, Noviembre-Diciembre,* 141–153.

Krauskopf, D., & Mora, M. (2000). *Condiciones de vida de la juventud centroamericana y el desarrollo de políticas sociales: El reto del 2000* [The living conditions of Central American youth and the development social policies: The challenge in 2000]. San José, Costa Rica: Organización Iberoamericana de la Juventud.

La Belle, T. J. (2000). The changing nature of non-formal education in Latin America. *Comparative Education, 36,* 21–36.

Lam, W. S. E., & Rosario-Ramos, E. (2009). Multilingual literacies in transnationally digitally mediated contexts: An exploratory study of immigrant teens in the United States. *Language and Education, 23,* 171–190.

LeBrón, M. (2009). *Guatemala's 'Twitter revolution'* (NACLA Report on the Americas). Retrieved from https://nacla.org/node/5874

Levinson, B. (1999). 'Una etapa siempre difícil': Concepts of adolescence and secondary education in Mexico. *Comparative Education Review, 43*(2), 129–161.

Lewis, M. P. (Ed.). (2009). *Ethnologue: Languages of the world* (16th ed.). Dallas, TX: SIL International.

López, L., & Hanemann, U. (Eds.). (2009). *Alfabetización y multiculturidad: Miradas desde América Latina* [Literacy and multiculturalism: Views from Latin America]. Guatemala City, Guatemala: UNESCO-UIL/GTZ-PACE.

Maclure, R., & Sotelo, M. (2004). Youth gangs in Nicaragua: Gang membership as structured individualisation. *Journal of Youth Studies, 7*(4), 417–432.

Marcial, R. (2008, July). Jóvenes en diversidad: Culturas juveniles en Guadalajara [Youth in diversity: Youth cultures in Guadalajara]. *Comunicação, Mídia e Consumo, 5*(13), 71–92.

McGinnis, T., Goodstein-Stolzenberg, A., & Saliani, E. (2007). Indnpride: Online spaces of transnational youth as sites of creative and sophisticated literacy and identity work. *Linguistics and Education, 18,* 283–304.

Meza, S. (2010, January 14). Recluta narcos a jóvenes 'ninis' [Narcos recruit out of school and unemployed youth]. *Noreste Grupo Editorial.* Retrieved from http://www.noroeste.com.mx/publicaciones.php?id=547674

Mignolo, W. (1992). On the colonization of Amerindian languages and memories: Renaissance theories of writing and the discontinuity of the classical tradition. *Comparative Studies in Society and History, 34*(2), 301–330.

Mignolo, W. (2000). *Local histories/global designs: Coloniality, subaltern knowledges, and border thinking.* Princeton, NJ: Princeton University Press.

Moje, E. B. (2002). Re-framing adolescent literacy research for new times: Studying youth as a resource. *Reading Research & Instruction, 41*, 211-228.

Moje, E. B., Overby, M., Tysvaer, N., & Morris, K. (2008). The complex world of adolescent literacy: Myths, motivations, and mysteries. *Harvard Educational Review, 78*(1), 107–154.

Mollericona, J. (2007). *Jóvenes hiphoppers aymaras en la ciudad de El Alto y sus luchas por una ciudadanía intercultural* [Aymara youth hip hoppers and their struggles for intercultural citizenship in the city of El Alto]. La Paz, Bolivia: PIEB.

Morrell, E. (2004). *Becoming critical researchers: Literacy and empowerment for urban youth.* New York, NY: Lang.

Najarro Arriola, A. (1995). La pertinencia cultural en los programas de alfabetización y post-alfabetización en Guatemala [Cultural relevance in literacy and post-literacy programs in Guatemala]. *Boletín de Lingüística Instituto de Lingüística de la Universidad Rafael Landívar, 9*(53), 6–8.

Organización de Estados Iberoamericanos. (2003). *Escuelas que hacen escuela: Formando para el trabajo en los países andinos* [Schools that make school: Workforce training in Andean countries]. Bogotá, Columbia: Organización de Estados Interamericanos Para la Educación, la Ciencia y la Cultura.

Organización de Estados Iberoamericanos. (n.d.). *Programa de alfabetización y de habilitación laboral para jóvenes y adultos vinculada con el desarrollo local, en la región de Enriquillo de República Dominicana, Octubre 2007–Septiembre 2010* [Literacy and job training program for youth and adults connected to the local development of the Enriquillo region in the Dominican Republic]. Retrieved from http://www.idiedominicana.org/documentos/PROGRAMAALFA2007-2010.pdf

OIT. (2004). *Panorama laboral 2004* [2004 job outlook]. Lima, Perú: OIT Oficina Regional para América Latina y el Caribe.

Patel Stevens, L. (2002). Making the road by walking: The transition from content area literacy to adolescent literacy. *Reading Research and Instruction, 41*(3), 267–278.

Perry, G., Arias, O. S., López, J. H., Maloney, W. F., & Servén, L. (2006). *Poverty reduction and growth: Virtuous and vicious circles.* Washington, DC: World Bank.

Pieck, E. (2001). *Los jóvenes y el trabajo: La educación frente a la exclusión social* [Youth and work: Education in the face of social exclusion]. Mexico City, Mexico: Universidad Iberoamericana.

Pinheiro, P. S. (2007). Youth, violence, and democracy. *Current History, 106*(697), 64–69.

Podalsky, L. (2008). The young, the damned, and the restless in contemporary Mexican cinema. *Framework, 49*(1), 144–160.

Purcell-Gates, V. (2008). *Constructions of deficit: Family and children on the margins.* Paper presented at the annual meeting of the American Educational Research Association, New York, NY.

Reguillo Cruz, R. (2000). *Emergencia de culturas juveniles: Estrategias de desencanto* [Emerging youth cultures: Strategies of disillusionment]. Buenos Aires, Argentina: Grupo Editorial Norma. Retrieved from http://www.oei.org.ar/edumedia/pdfs/T03_Docu7_Emergenciade culturasjuveniles_Cruz.pdf

Reinke, K. (2004). Globalisation and local indigenous education in Mexico. *International Review of Education, 50*(5–6), 483–496.

Ribando, C. (2005). Gangs in Central America [Electronic Version]. CRS Report for Congress, 1–6. Retrieved from http://fpc.state.gov/documents/organization/47140.pdf

Ribeiro, V. M. (Ed.). (2003). *Letramento no Brasil.* São Paulo, Brazil: Global.

Richards, J. B., & Richards, M. (1996). Mayan language literacy in Guatemala: A sociohistorical overview. In N. Hornberger (Ed.), *Indigenous literacies in the Americas: Language planning from the bottom up* (pp.189–212). Berlin, Germany: Mouton de Gruyter.

Rockwell, E. (2006). Apropriaciones indígenas de la escritura en tres dominios: Religión, gobierno y escuela [Indigenous appropriations of literacy in three domains: Religion, government and school]. *Cultura Escrita y Sociedad, 3*, 161–236.

Rodríguez, E. (2003). Políticas públicas de juventud en América Latina: La construcción de espacios específicos, al desarrollo de una perspectiva generacional [Youth public policies in Latin America: The construction of specific spaces in the development of a generational perspective]. *Revista Latinoamericana de Ciencias Sociales, Niñez y Juventud, 1*(2), 1–23.

Schmelkes, S. (2000). Education and Indian peoples of Mexico: An example of policy failure. In F. Reimers (Ed.), *Unequal schools, unequal chances: The challenges to equal opportunity in the Americas* (pp. 318–333). Cambridge, MA: Harvard University Press.

Seda Santana, I. (2000). Literacy research in Latin America. In M. Kamil, P. Mosenthal, P. Pearson, & R. Barr (Eds.), *Handbook of research in reading* (pp. 41–52). Mahwah, NJ: Erlbaum.

Smith, P. H., Jiménez, R. T., & Martinez-Leon, N. (2003). Other countries' literacies: What U.S. educators can learn from Mexican schools. *The Reading Teacher, 56*, 772–781.

Smith, P. H., Murillo, L. A., & Jiménez, R. T. (2009). The social construction of literacy in a Mexican community: Coming soon to your school? In J. Cobb Scott, D. Y. Straker, & L. Katz (Eds.), *Affirming students' right to their own language: Bridging language policies and pedagogical practices* (pp. 303–318). New York, NY: Routledge.

Steele, J. (2008). Yo, sí puedo: South-south educational collaboration in practice. *Society for International Education Journal, 5*(1), 29–43.

Stocker, K. (2005). *I won't stay Indian, I'll keep studying: Race, place, and discrimination in a Costa Rican high school.* Boulder: University Press of Colorado.

Street, B. (1984). *Literacy in theory and practice.* New York, NY: Cambridge University Press.

Street, B. (Ed.). (1993). *Cross-cultural approaches to literacy.* New York, NY: Cambridge University Press.

Tedesco, J. C. (2001). Desafíos políticos de las reformas de la educación [Political challenges of education reforms]. In S. Martinic & M. Pardo (Eds.), *Economía política de las reformas educativas en América Latina* (pp. 7–18). Santiago, Chile: CIDEPREAL.

Torres, R. M. (2000). *One decade of education for all: The challenge ahead.* Buenos Aires, Argentina: IIPE/UNESCO.

Torres, R. M. (2005). *Analfabetismo y alfabetización en el Ecuador: Opciones para la política y la práctica.* Estudios de caso encargado por UNESCO para su inclusión en el Informe 2006 de Seguimiento Global de la Educación para Todos [Illiteracy and literacy in Ecuador: Options for policy and practice. Case study commissioned by UNESCO for inclusion in the 2006 Global Monitoring Report of Education for All].

Torres, R. M. (2009). *Ecuador: "Patria alfabetizada." Carta abierta a Raúl Vallejo, Ministro de Educación* [Ecuador: "Literate country." An open letter to Raul Vallejo, Minister of Education]. Quito, Ecuador: Fronesis.

Umayahara, M. (2005). *Regional overview of progress toward EFA since Dakar: Latin America.* Paris, France: UNESCO.

United Nations Educational, Scientific, and Cultural Organization. (2003). *La educación de jóvenes y adultos en América Latina y el Caribe: Hacia un estado del arte* (Informe Regional de América Latina y el Caribe para la Conferencia de Seguimiento a CONFINTEA V. OREALC/UNESCO). Santiago, Chile: UNESCO.

United Nations Educational, Scientific, and Cultural Organization. (2008, September). *Regional Literacy and CONFINTEA VI Preparatory Conference for Latin America and the Caribbean, "From literacy to lifelong learning: Towards the challenges of the 21st century."* UNESCO regional conferences in support of Global Literacy, Mexico City, Mexico. Retrieved from http://unesdoc.unesco.org/images/0018/001835/183527e.pdf

UNESCO. (2009). *La alfabetización en el Ecuador: Evolución histórica, información actualizada, y mapa nacional del analfabetismo.* [Literacy in Ecuador: Historical evolution, updated information, and national map of illiteracy]. Quito: UNESCO Ecuador.

UNESCO Institute for Statistics. (2009). *UIS statistics in brief* (Country Profile Information). Paris, France: UNESCO.

UNESCO-OREALC. (2001). *Balance de los 20 años del Proyecto Principal de Educación en Latin America y el Caribe* [Results of the 20 years of the Major Project of Education in Latin America and the Caribbean]. Santiago, Chile: UNESCO.

UNESCO-OREALC. (2004a). *Education for all in Latin America: A goal within our reach* (Regional EFA Monitoring Report 2003). Santiago, Chile: Author.

UNESCO-OREALC. (2004b). *Universal primary completion in Latin America: Are we really so near the goal?* (Regional report on education-related Millennium Development Goals). Santiago, Chile: Author.

Urteaga Castro-Pozo, M. (1998). *Por los territorios de rock: Identidades juveniles y rock Mexicano* [By rock territories: Youth identities and Mexican rock]. Mexico City, Mexico: Causa Joven.

Vacca, R. T. (1998). Let's not marginalize adolescent literacy (literacy issues in focus). *Journal of Adolescent & Adult Literacy, 41*(8), 604–609.

Valdiviezo, L. A. (2009). Don't you want your child to be better than you? Enacting ideologies and contesting intercultural policy in Peru. In F. Vavrus & L. Bartlett (Eds.), *Critical approaches to comparative education: Vertical case studies from Africa, Europe, the Middle East, and the Americas* (pp. 147–162). New York, NY: Palgrave Macmillan.

Verdugo, L., & Raymundo, J. (2009). Alfabetización de jóvenes y adultos indígenas en Guatemala [Literacy development among indigenous youth and adults in Guatemala]. In L. E. Lopez & U. Hanemann (Eds.), *Alfabetización y muliculturalidad: Miradas desde América Latina* (pp. 181–236). Guatemala City, Guatemala: UNESCO-UIL/GTZ-PACE.

Warriner, D. S. (2007). Transnational literacies: Immigration, language learning, and identity. *Linguistics and Education, 18*, 201–214.

Washington Office on Latin America. (2006). Youth gangs in Central America: Issues in human rights, effective policing, and prevention. Washington, DC: Author.

Winocur, R. (2009). Digital convergence as the symbolic medium of new practices and meanings in young people's lives. *Popular Communication, 7*, 179–187.

Winton, A. (2005). Youth, gangs and violence: Analysing the social and spatial mobility of young people in Guatemala City. *Children's Geographies, 3*, 167–184.

Wodon, Q. T. (2000). *Poverty and policy in Latin America and the Caribbean* (World Bank Tech. Paper No. 467). Washington, DC: World Bank.

Wolff, L., Schiefelbein, E., & Schiefelbein, P. (2002). *La educación primaria en América Latina: La agenda inconclusa* [Primary education in Latin America: The inconclusive agenda] (PREAL Working Paper 24). Santiago, Chile: PREAL.

World Bank. (2008). *Costa Rica* (World Development Indicators Data Bank). Retrieved from http://data.worldbank.org/country/costa-rica

Yapu, M. (2008). *Jóvenes aymaras, sus movimientos, demandas y políticas públicas* [Aymara youth, their movements, demands and public policies]. La Paz, Bolivia: PIEB.

Zavala, V. (2004). Literacidad y desarrollo: Los discursos del Programa Nacional de Alfabetización en el Perú [Literacy and development: Discourses of the National Literacy Program in Peru]. In V. Zavala, M. Niño-Murcia, & P. Ames (Eds.), *Escritura y sociedad: Nuevas perspectivas teóricas y etnográficas* (pp. 437–459). Lima: Red para el desarrollo de las ciencias sociales en el Perú.

Chapter 8

Deference, Denial, and Beyond: A Repertoire Approach to Mass Media and Schooling

BETSY RYMES

University of Pennsylvania

Taking the time to learn what our youth are thinking and why they create the art they do demands a capacity for deferred justification that most adults lack.

—Michael Eric Dyson (2001, p. 118)

The youthy expressions "be real," "it's all good," "you feelin' me?" or "whatever!" often strike adult-types as slippery and meaningless. But such phrases are supremely functional in youth peer culture because they encapsulate shared experience and deference to complex, collective social understandings that neither young people nor their adult critics may yet be able to articulate. Often, apparent imprecision of these phrases indicates not that their speakers are vacuous but that these words encapsulate ambiguities too complex or localized to express explicitly.

Peers, when they use these phrases, indicate they know each other well enough that they need not explain. "You feelin' me?" for example, might have the same propositional content as "Do you understand what I am saying?" However, the phrase also accomplishes interactional functions that "Do you understand what I am saying?" may not: Because it is distributionally more common in the African American community, it indexes that sociohistorical tie; because it uses the word "feel" rather than "understand," it may indicate greater intimacy between the speaker and the addressee or the personal nature of the exchange; also, because it is short and compact and not referentially transparent, it suggests that the speaker and the addressee have enough in common that total articulation of each thought is not necessary. Each of the "youthy" phrases listed—"be real," "it's all good," or "whatever"—similarly efficiently zips up a set of interactionally relevant values that usually go unquestioned in conversation, despite being referentially opaque. When

Review of Research in Education
March 2011, Vol. 35, pp. 208–238
DOI: 10.3102/0091732X10389428
© 2011 AERA. http://rre.aera.net

youth use these phrases and adults do not, adults may feel a need for clarification, where, for the youth, this denial on the part of adults of the valuable interactional elements of these phrases, itself indicates that those adults will simply never "get it."

Mass-mediated youth cultural signs (a rap lyric, a pop singer's signature hairstyle, or the theme song of a TV show) also can take on this same role: inscrutable for adults, crucial for kids. Similar to recognizably youthy ways of speaking, many other signs of youth culture are originally circulated via the mass media. Though brought to life locally, phrases with vastly different sociocultural genealogies, such as "whatever!" or "you feelin me?" and other signs of popular culture, such as Justin Bieber's hair, a "thug life" tattoo, or hip-hop style "bling," are recognizable globally and perpetuated through mass media such as the Web, TV, and global merchandising. Contemporary popular cultural formations such as hip-hop, music videos, social networking sites, movies, and video and online gaming encourage repetition and quotation on a massive scale, providing more source material for local-seeming, yet massively circulating forms of communication.

However, just as phrases such as "you feelin' me" take on different social value in different social contexts, mass-mediated popular cultural forms can function in critically different ways, depending on what new social formation they are embedded within. A hip-hop lyric, for example, only becomes a meaningful sign when it is embedded in a set of recognizable social practices: The social practices that contextualize that lyric as it emanates from a car in North Philadelphia, or a club in Los Angeles, may be very different from those surrounding that lyric as it is recontextualized in a 10th-grade English classroom in the Midwest. Similarly, educational researchers have taken very different approaches to understanding youth and their relationship with mass media.

In this chapter, I outline two general research approaches, within the education world, to these mass-mediated formations: *Deference* and *Denial*. Researchers who recognize the social practices that give local meaning to mass media formations and ways of speaking do not attempt to recontextualize youth media in their own social formations (of "critical" academia or "best practices" recommendations for teachers, for example). Rather, they enter into those words and worlds—the ambiguity of verbs such as "to be real," or the situated practices surrounding youth cultural text—through ethnographic study and/or long-term, intense involvement. These researchers investigate the *deference* involved in fully embracing mass-mediated youth cultural practices in situ, themselves deferring to initially inscrutable youth behaviors and explanations.

Another group of research on mass-mediated youth literacies takes a different approach. Rather than investigating the complex of situated practices involved in youth cultural formations, this research pulls signs of youth culture from the context of youth practices to make links to more mainstream, institutionalized educational goals. I have labeled this the *denial* approach—suggesting that these applications may often be in *denial* of the necessity of the complex web of practices that characterize youth media consumption. This body of research often takes one of two approaches:

One set of denial research (the "critical" kind) critiques certain decontextualized source texts of mass-mediated culture, doing formal analysis or pinpointing irrational leaps that are ideologically or economically motivated and developing pedagogical techniques to illustrate that critique for students. Another approach circumvents such critique but, instead, uses the decontextualized source texts or genres to bolster preexistent curricular goals by, for example, using hip-hop to develop an appreciation of Shakespeare or rap techniques to remember math formulas.

After exemplifying work within *deference* and *denial* approaches (and some researchers engage in both types of work), I argue for the development of a new approach to mass media and schooling research that facilitates research into and talk across *repertoires of deference*. A *repertoire* approach accounts for the reality that all mass-mediated signs are only humanly meaningful when embedded in social practices. Often, these practices are complex, highly localized, and unexamined even (perhaps especially) by those who participate in them. (The *denial* research, of course, is another form of social practice rife with unexamined forms of cultural deference.) In addition, these signs are often recognized across social groupings, but used differently by those different social groups. For example, when a teacher uses a familiar hip-hop beat (a mass-mediated youth cultural sign) to teach a math formula (a different practice), the sign takes on a new role. The sign may still be recognizable to youth, but the meaning it holds in a teacher's repertoire is very different. Even when some signs of teacher and student repertoires overlap, the complex practices surrounding them may not.

Paradoxically, the more widely circulated a sign is (and mass-mediated signs circulate very widely, by definition), the more diverse the practices are within which that sign will be embedded. By learning about repertoires of deference, students, teachers, and researchers can learn not only about circulating words, phrases, lyrics, music, movies, novels, or other cultural signs, but also about how they are recontextualized differently in different social formations—across different peer groups, age groups, professions, and so forth. From this perspective, education research into mass-mediated youth cultural formations need not deny the youth practices within which signs are embedded, nor need it entirely defer to youth practices surrounding those signs. Instead, a repertoire approach investigates the possibility for productive heterogeneity across diverse social domains. The goal of a repertoire approach to mass media is neither simply to defer to an "other's" repertoire (e.g., as in an ethnography of a youth clique) nor to appropriate mass-mediated signs into one's "own" repertoire (as when youth signs are put to "educational" use), but to build on whatever repertoire overlap exists across groups, expanding possibilities for the understanding of and access to multiple possible social roles, relationships, and opportunities.

To summarize, there is one body of research on mass media and schooling that investigates complex sets of practices surrounding youth mass media consumption, respecting the forms of *deference* involved in that youth cultural behavior. Another body of research largely ignores such contextualization, in effect, *denying* the relevance of such peer group–bound practices and positing new practices for making use of mass media in the context of schooling. Finally, I suggest a third possible line of research and practical inquiry, in which the study of mass media and schooling involves studying *repertoires of deference*, that is, the study of how mass-mediated signs are recontextualized in new social practices, differently, by social groups with wide-ranging commitments. Below, I begin by defining and exemplifying *deference* approaches in current literature.

DEFERENCE

As cultural anthropologist Maurice Bloch (2005) explains, when asked about their rituals, individuals often have a hard time giving rationales that make sense. Cultural insiders often struggle to explain rituals to outsiders (like anthropologists), Bloch speculates, because the point of ritual is not to understand, but to *not* understand. Rituals are acts of deference. Deference is, in Bloch's definition, a form of *not* knowing, of displaying respect by *not* needing explanation. In religious rituals, for example, people often speak in languages they do not understand, saying words and phrases that mean nothing to them in a literal, informational sense. Yet there is a trust in the collective knowledge and history of practice that make this behavior meaningful.

Bloch (2005) extends his argument beyond religious ritual to any collective and specialized form of knowledge and behavior. Humans engage in countless day-to-day activities that rely on knowledge about which they have no direct evidence, and work gets done because we defer to the expertise of others. He likens these kinds of deference to what Hutchins (1995) calls the "distributed cognition" needed, for example, by a team of sailors operating an enormous marine vessel. These forms of knowledge become shared through activities and practices in which that knowledge is deeply embedded, so that, after a while, it may be literally impossible to articulate why things work the way they do and why we take up certain roles or behaviors. Individuals defer to tradition and history and the knowledge of others when they hang a holiday wreath on the door or serve turkey on Thanksgiving or collectively navigate a ship—but also when they enact mass-mediated personas or ways of speaking, tell personal narratives, or share a sense of common history through a rap song, a graffiti tag, an online game, or a fanfiction website.

Deferring to often-untraceable sources of knowledge also sustains "digital literacy" activities such as building or using a Wikipedia entry or a thematic photo collection on Flickr (Knobel & Lankshear, 2007) or writing an "authors note" before an online fanfiction (Black, 2008b). Participation in many of these practices requires trust in the knowledge and behaviors of others to perform competently as an "individual." Paradoxically, deference simultaneously is a way of *not understanding* and of *knowing* a form of life through collaborative activity.

DENIAL

An alternative to deference would be denial of precedents, traditions, heritage, repetition, quotation, others' knowledge, and even one's own memory. One could think of this as *total originality*. If attempted in its extreme form, this might result in something difficult to recognize culturally—for example, the music of John Cage. Cage was himself a denier of tradition and a seeker of artistic freedom. A musician and composer, he preferred "organization of sound" to the term *music*. In his own compositions, Cage sought to avoid repetition and quotation: He certainly did not want Mozart motifs showing up in his music. He did not even want to hear sounds one would recognize as emanating from familiar instruments, as illustrated by his compositions for *prepared* piano. To create original sounds from a concert grand, he would carefully alter it, using bolts, strings, pieces of wire, and other objects. The resulting effect: sound that audiences would not expect from a piano. Cage believed this enabled audiences to listen anew, without the remnants of the old dragging down their understanding and experience of the moment. By preparing the piano, he believed he freed audiences of their memories of what it should sound like (Pritchett, 1993). Cage represents, then, a very pure form of denial of deference. As he has said, "We don't have to have tradition if we somehow free ourselves from our memories. Then, each thing that we see is new" (Lohner, 1993).

Although refreshing and innocent-seeming coming from Cage, the anthropologist Renato Rosaldo (1989/1993) calls this perspective on perception the illusion of "brute reality" (p. 196). Rosaldo insists that no matter how much we desire to see with fresh eyes, stretch our ears, or take the "view from nowhere" (Nagel, 1989), we are always situated culturally. Living the illusion of brute reality involves living in denial that "deference is a common aspect of human life" (Bloch, 2005, p. 135). Moreover, living in denial of the interdependence of our understandings can be isolating. Most people find Cage's compositions—built on chance and rejection of tradition—difficult to listen to or understand. Yet many embrace John Cage for the freedom of expression he models. Paradoxically, Cage's demonstration of artistic freedom feels freeing because his audiences (arguably, an elite intelligentsia) recognize its contrast to traditional perceptions. Even rejection of tradition requires tradition.

These days, Cage's denial of history, memory, and tradition may seem endearingly naïve. And, following Rosaldo's (1989/1993) critique of anthropology, many anthropologists fully recognize that their own cultural positionality enters into any analysis of social relations. Both Cage and Rosaldo illuminate cultural deference by highlighting its denial; and each, by doing so, has inspired generations to expand how they view art and culture. Unlike John Cage, most kids have little desire to deny the deference involved in their cultural aesthetics. Youth generally want to embrace the traditions and collective knowledge of their peers. And, given the multiple and wildly heterogeneous variation of practices across peer groups, localities, age groups, and so on, the collective knowledge of a peer group also becomes a form of distinction—just as a subtle secret handshake. Often affiliation with peers involves displaying familiarity with common cultural precedents through unquestioning deference to them or, perhaps, in same cases, through ironic knowingness. However, such layered understandings of the role of cultural deference in building social formations have not permeated everyday understandings of mass-mediated youth culture. Instead, a naïve denial of cultural deference—denial of a need for tradition, repetition, quotation, and connectedness of a deferential sort—characterizes widely circulating approaches to youth consumption of mass media today.

Rather than entering into the worlds of youth cultural consumption, some research implicitly adapts a widely circulating view of youth media consumption as vacuous and uncritical. Instead of recognizing this view as itself situated, some educational researchers assume that their critique of youth culture originates in a "view from nowhere" (Nagel, 1989). Such approaches deny their own positionality by characterizing texts formally (Is "rap" poetry?), critiquing their logic (You are being duped!), or arguing for their merit on the basis of what these forms of cultural consumption can "get" kids (e.g., 21st-century skills or appreciation of Shakespeare).

To summarize, *denial* approaches contrast to *deference* approaches in the following way: *Deference* approaches build on the assumption that those mass-mediated signs that youth use and care about are embedded in peer-group-based, highly localized sets of practices and values that educational researchers do not know much about and need to understand. These researchers enter into the world of youth mass media consumption by researching how youth themselves engage with mass-mediated signs by *deferring* to shared practices and commitments and collective forms of knowing. In contrast, in *denial* approaches, researchers themselves *deny* (or at least bracket) the situated nature of mass-mediated youth cultural forms. Denial researchers focus primarily on the media texts or genres themselves, in isolation, bracketing both the situated nature of youth enjoyment of mass media and the researchers' situated perspective as they recontextualize mass media in their own institutional concerns and commitments.

REPERTOIRES OF DEFERENCE

A *repertoires of deference* approach differs from a simple *deference* approach (privileging one positionality or field of deference) or a view from nowhere *denial* approach (denying there is positionality at all), by examining the co-presence of different mass media allegiances. A classroom interaction in which the Tupac Shakur lyric "Dear Mama" is being discussed illustrates what a repertoire approach might look like in action (Hill, 2009, p. 70). In this excerpt, the teacher is attempting to discuss the literary term *mood* (as distinct from "tone") by addressing the mood in Shakur's lyric:

Teacher: So what is the **mood** of **this piece?**
Joe: Sad.
Teacher: Why?
Joe: After all . . . he went through with his moms, he had to be sad.
Teacher: But isn't he thanking her for being a good mom in spite of everything?
Joe: Yeah but you gotta be sad going through that. *Me and mom and my brother went through the same shit.*

Jay: Me too. More me than my brother but *my pop wasn't there so shit gonna be sad. But you still happy 'cause you made it through.*

Teacher: I know he might've been sad thinking about everything they went through. *Just like y'all probably did.* But if you made it and everybody was listening to your story, how you think they would feel?

Joe: I think they would feel better. Like "Joe went through that and became a rapper or whatever so *it don't gotta turn out f'ed up.*"

Jay: Exactly. Like *"y'all could learn from my pain."*

Teacher: OK. OK. That's what **mood** is all about. **Not so much what the writer is feeling, but how might the reader feel when he reads it.**

As the interaction winds up, the class agrees on the word "hopeful," rather than "sad," to describe the mood of this lyric. In this case, the teacher (who is also the researcher and author, Marc Lamont Hill) gently navigates at least two repertoires: a youth repertoire, indicated in ***bold italics*** (in which Tupac is highly revered as a sensitive martyr and talented artist, but also is recognizable as "one of us," in a home life with an absent father and troubled mother), and a teacher repertoire, indicated in **boldface**, in which terms such as *mood* and *tone* are important emblems of literary practice. These intermingling repertoires are clearly traceable in the talk, and in this instance, whereas the students are drawing primarily from the youth repertoire, identifying with Tupac and his fatherless home, the teacher both accepts and draws from both this repertoire (Tupac went through a lot, ***"just like y'all probably did"***) as well as his literary repertoire, both beginning the discussion with a question about mood ("what is the **mood** of this **piece?**") and bringing their reflections on the "piece" back to his literary terminology ("that's what **mood** is all about").

As this example further indicates, the content of the talk is not all that is involved in working across repertoires. In this excerpt (and in the examples throughout Hill's book), the teacher also modulates the way he speaks, usually using school-based English (**"what is the mood of this piece?"**), but never sanctioning student departures from this register or even the occasional mild profanity ("my brother and I went through *the same shit*") and often departing from school-based normative formal English grammar himself ("just like *y'all* probably did"). Navigating multiple repertoires, then, involves not only knowing the content and context of students' associations but also recognizing and not quashing students' established ways of talking about those associations.

Hill's (2009) research design created a situation in which rap lyrics were made into objects of analysis in an English class. As such, this excerpt also illustrates what can happen when emblems of mass-mediated youth culture are "recontextualized" (Bauman, 2004; Bauman & Briggs, 1990), that is, extracted from the pervious context of their production and re-embedded in a new interactional setting. By design, Hill (2009) recontextualized a mass-mediated youth genre in a situation in which this genre rarely occurs, certainly not as an object of literary analysis. But each new context, each "recontextualization," involves different fields of deference. In this interaction, Hill manages to deftly negotiate those fields by expanding his "teacher repertoire" (in which terms such as *mood* and *tone* are important) to include a particular youth repertoire, drawing on his own empathy with the concerns of the youth who listen to and identify with Tupac's lyrics (in which themes of fatherlessness and hope within struggle are important) and his own verbal repertoire that includes multiple ways of speaking.

Any time texts are recontextualized, new fields of deference are prioritized, and old affordances of the same texts may no longer operate, unless participants expand their repertoire to include deference to new behaviors and collective knowledge. In the interaction above, when Hill (2009) deftly brings his teacherly and youthful repertoires to bear on the same interaction, the results on the students' repertoires are not clear. There is a delicate tension in this interaction between teacher and student knowledge that Hill never fully follows through on in his ethnography, nor, to be fair, is it his primary concern. However, this example does illustrate an important potential of the classroom to be a place where multiple repertoires and their relationships to one another can be developed.

Hill (2009) shows that for repertoires to coexist in a productive tension, youth cultural texts cannot simply be taken up in ways that extract them from the practices and concerns—the field of deference—through which youth construe these forms as meaningful. Using Tupac's lyric to teach about "mood" and "tone" would be impossible if the student's stories and identifications with Tupac were never aired. Similarly, institutionally sanctioned school-based knowledge is also situated within a field of deference. The descriptive value of the terms *mood* and *tone* may be taken for granted by an English teacher, who unthinkingly defers to them as important literary knowledge, but for students who do not share these associations, bridging work needs to be done to ensure that teacher and student repertoires begin to overlap. In such situations, teaching necessarily becomes a process of repertoire expansion for both teachers and students.

By researching *repertoires of deference,* investigating mass-mediated youth cultural formations goes beyond describing a genealogy of a text or set of texts to investigating how that cultural form is taken up within new fields of cultural deference (as any widely circulating text inevitably is). A *repertoires of deference* perspective may thus be able to accommodate the observation that the relevance attached to mass-mediated youth cultural forms is reconstructed to varying degrees and in qualitatively different ways within new social formations and participation frameworks. Sometimes, this reconfiguration is minimal; so the form is easy to recognize (as when Hill extracts hip-hop lyrics from songs to use as curriculum in an English class). In other cases, recontextualization transforms popular cultural emblems maximally, leaving them barely recognizable. (Imagine, e.g., "Tupac" being used as a name in a multiple-choice grammar test or a Rolling Stones melody piped in on an elevator.)

To work toward a *repertoire* approach to research on mass media and schooling, I first review literature, below, that examines the *deference* involved in mass-mediated youth cultural consumption and production. Next, I look at that research that has attempted to isolate texts—both their formal qualities and their purposes—from those contexts of deference. Then, I return to address this third way, a *repertoires of deference* approach.

STUDIES THAT FOREGROUND DEFERENCE

Studies that foreground deference investigate youth cultural landscapes that teachers may only see glimpses of in the ordinary classroom. Every day, in schools, notes may be passed, text messages written, fanfiction websites visited, and distant vibrations of hip-hop lyrics may be emanating through earphones, but youth cultural research, rather than sending out the alarm, confiscating graffiti notebooks, or crying in dismay, "What's that noise?!" seeks to understand what drives people to engage in these cultural practices and what forms of life such engagement is building.

Some features that characterize and enliven this study of youth culture, discussed in the sections that follow, include these investigators' *acceptance and exploration of ambiguity,* their blurring of the *global/local* distinction, their foregrounding of the *collective weaving of individual experiences;* and their own tendency to joyously *join in,* through their writing styles and rhetoric, in their adoption of students' perspectives, and, sometimes, by offering up their own narratives as part of the research process. In the sections below, I discuss these categories as they emerge in slightly different ways in the largely ethnographic research on hip-hop and in similar research on digital literacies.

Ethnographic Research on Hip-Hop

Hip-hop is arguably the most widely circulating and recognized youth cultural form in the world today. Certainly, a review of "mass media and schooling" would be impossible without recognizing the insistent and energizing flow of hip-hop through schools, classrooms, after-school programs, family life, neighborhoods, and probably the car idling nearby or an open window down the street. Although there is no shortage of fear and loathing surrounding "rap" in the United States, anthropologically and sociologically informed education research on youth hip-hop social formations describes the commitments and values that youth themselves develop through participation in this mass-mediated cultural form.

Taken collectively, hip-hop researchers illustrate the emergence of ethnography—here defined as substantially participating in and observing the forms of social life under study—as a favored methodology for understanding how youth are taking up this mass-mediated form and what varied forms their participation takes. The term *hiphopography,* or "the ethnography of hip hop culture and communication" (Alim, 2007, p. 24) seems appropriate here for obvious reasons, and I will use it throughout when describing these ethnographies of hip-hop.

Acceptance and Exploration of Ambiguity

Marc Lamont Hill's (2009) *Beats, Rhymes, and Classroom Life* (excerpted briefly, above) takes an ethnographic perspective on hip-hop that begins with a first chapter flashback on his own life history as a hip-hop head. As Hill writes, hip-hop gave him a way of understanding the inexplicable and sometimes threatening elements of his neighborhood. He reflects on his first awakening to the music of KRS-One, suddenly having the words and the medium to express his world in ways that stories and talk had never before been able to clarify for him:

Up to this point, I had heard stories about violence in the neighborhood, but they always seemed distant or surreal. Suddenly, I was able to attach names, faces, and stories to the fuzziest parts of my life. In many ways, hip-hop became my window into a world that was at once familiar and foreign. (Hill, 2009, p. xvi)

Through his ethnographic research, Hill's (2009) goal was to document how hip-hop culture could be integrated into public school curriculum in ways that he never experienced in the exegesis of hip-hop culture he consumed in graduate school.

Hill (2009) was intent on doing "applied ethnography"—work on the lived realities of students in Philadelphia that might somehow change their lives and possibly schooling for the better. But his research rarely takes on a "What's it good for?" perspective. Instead, he delves into the lived social worlds that Bloch (2005) identifies as critical to ritual. As a volunteer teacher of kids in a Philadelphia "twilight program" (after-hours high school equivalency), discussing hip-hop lyrics, he pushes his students for explanations just as an anthropologist might push a "native informant." Hill will probe for a decisive definition of the word "real" or trouble their distinction between hip-hop (authentic, according to his students) and rap (not so much). These conversations, he remarks, often contained a "curious mixture of ambiguity, specificity, and certainty" that he calls "a signpost of conversations among members of the Hip-Hop Lit class" (p. 32).

Greg Dimitriadis (2009) also captures the ambiguities of hip-hop as "lived practice" in his ethnography of youth participating in hip-hop culture after school at a community center. He explicitly acknowledges, in introducing his second edition (2009), that he is not attempting to show this work is "good for" something else. That type of research, he writes, "has not relegated or given up control in the way that is often necessary for breakthrough forms of understanding" (2009, p. xv). Too often, adults "inscribe our own agendas on the lives of youth" (p. xix). Dimitriadis's ethnography achieves breakthrough understanding precisely by recognizing that "understanding" (rather than rational explanation, exegesis, politicization, connections to pedagogies, etc.) comes through dwelling intimately within the lifeworld of those who consume hip-hop.

These hip-hopographers often highlight moments in their research that resist explanation, inevitably entering into the ambiguities of the lifeworlds sustained by and sustaining hip-hop culture. Discussions of "authenticity" and "keeping it real," the ambiguity of "local" knowledge, the anachronisms within proposed histories of their subjects' commitments, and the "imagined" nature of their communities are common in these ethnographic descriptions. Both Hill's (2009) and Dimitriadis's (2009) research illustrates the *deference* approach—consistently investigating youth commitments by building on the assumption that those mass-mediated signs that youth use and care about are embedded in peer-group-based, highly localized sets of practices and collective knowledge. Instead of imposing his own interpretation of phrases such as "authenticity" or lyrics such as Tupac's "Dear Mama," both of these researchers carefully explore how youth themselves engage with mass-mediated signs by *deferring* to shared practices and commitments and collective forms of knowing.

The ability to sustain unresolved ambiguity that characterizes both Hill's (2009) and Dimitriadis's (2009) research is most vividly illustrated in the way both research-ers investigate how youth build on the knowledge/legend that their hip-hop hero, Tupac Shakur, is still alive, despite mainstream media reports of his murder in 1996. The "urban legend" that Tupac Shakur is still alive (or the "myth" of his death, depending on your perspective) emerges in both Dimitriadis's and Hill's research as emblematic of deference involved in participating in mass-mediated social forma-tions. Consistent with Bloch's (2005) assertion that anthropologists need to probe ambiguity, not "clarify" it, no amount of exegesis will satisfy a researcher looking for logical explanations for the belief that Tupac lives. Neither researcher, however, attempts to debunk the narrative of Tupac's continued presence. Instead, they inves-tigate how this narrative fits within the complex context of practices and collective knowledge of the hip-hop youth they are working with.

Hill and Dimitriadis both use this epistemic break with their own view of reality to demonstrate that complex relationships and shared stories build forms of life that are recognizable and admirable in the peer networks built through hip-hop media. Hill (2009) quotes one of his students on Tupac:

Most niggas just get locked up or die. But that's what make Pac so hot, y'ah mean? He did shit what nig-gas dream about but can't do. (Jay, p. 48)

Readers of this quote might be thinking that Jay's logic is seriously flawed here. After all, it is widely known that Tupac *did* get locked up *and* die in his twenties. But as Hill (2009) writes (Dimitriadis, 2009, and Dyson, 2001, have similar analyses), these beliefs about Tupac are neither "naïve nor uncritical." Instead, fans use the Tupac narrative (and the cunning twist that he has never died—clearly, in many respects he hasn't!) to "imagine and perform" (p. 48) their own lives meaningfully and collectively.

Dimitriadis (2009) stresses, additionally, that the legend of Tupac crystallizes some transcendent, moral values for the kids he worked with. Tupac's lyrics were relentlessly "real," reflective of his own life story, and, Dimitriadis points out, bring-ing up the now-classic lyric, youth identify deeply with the unadulterated, uncondi-tional gratitude and love in Tupac articulates in "Dear Mama." The way in which Tupac "lives" today, it seems, may not be so different from the way Shakespeare lives on in English departments, or the way the bard's words enhance some peoples' per-ceptions of the world and echo through even the most casual conversations. As Dyson (2001) writes of Tupac, with words that might equally describe adoration for Shakespeare: "His spirit may be restless, but his heart is a haven for many who feel lost without his words. His future and legacy depend on their constant, unfolding adoration" (p. 268).

These researchers, with empathy and an ability to sustain ambiguity even as they carefully engage youth in discussions questioning some of their commitments, exemplify how ethnography can uncover the layers of collectively agreed-on knowledge and practices that undergird the youth appeal of mass-mediated forms such as hip-hop. Rather than insisting that their understandings come from a disinterested "view from nowhere" that might privilege a critique of youth commitments (like the belief that Tupac is still alive), these researchers investigate the forms of deference among the youth they are working with, asking about practices, beliefs, local distinctions, and ways of speaking that are not immediately transparent to an outsider. In this way, they illustrate how even such widely circulated mass-mediated youth cultural signs, like a Tupac lyric, become locally valid only through shared practices. Tupac must live, for many youth, because he is a beacon of hope for individuals who experience, in their own particular ways, much of the hardship he puts into words for them.

Blurring of the Global/Local Distinction Through Hip-Hop

Although both Hill (2009) and Dimitriadis (2009) deftly illustrate how much of the commitment youth display to hip-hop comes from the highly localized and personal connections they make to hip-hop-youth culture, hip-hop has also emerged as a global cultural form. Alim, Ibrahim, and Pennycook's (2009) edited volume, *Global Linguistic Flows* most deftly illuminates how the signature and attractive localness of hip-hop paradoxically affords its spread as a virally globalizing art form (see also Alim, this volume). Focusing in particular on how these global hip-hop movements build life forms sociolinguistically, the authors collectively aim, as Alim states in the introduction, to "listen fully, with both ears, and to pay close attention to the languages, styles, ideologies, and cultures of global Hip Hops" (p. 18). Although several of the chapters in this volume address the spread of English as intertwined with global hip-hop movements, the emphasis, overall, is not on the unidirectional spread of U.S.-based hip-hop, but on how hip-hop cultures develop around the world as "translocal" or "glocal" (global + local) forms of social life in large part, through widely ranging sociolinguistic resources.

As Alim (2009) illustrates in his chapter in that volume, speakers justify their choices about "ways of speaking" not logically, but in "just because" ways, as when Latasha talks to Alim about how she speaks with her two best girlfriends:

Alim: And how is the way y'all talk different from the way you talk to the teacher?
Latasha: Well, it's like, you know that rapper, Nelly?
Alim: Yeah, yeah.
Latasha: How he say everything like "urrrr," like for "here" he'll be like ""hurrrr"?
Alim: Yeah! [Laughing] "I ain't from round hurrrrr!"

Latasha: [Laughing] That's how we try to talk!
Alim: Why, though?!
Latasha: Cuz we like it!

Alim (2009) goes on to describe Latasha's phonological choices as arising from regional affiliations, allowing her peer group to fashion themselves as "multiregional and multilectal Hip Hop heads" (Alim, 2009, p. 216). This may or may not be their intention. In this excerpt, Latasha says nothing explicitly about regional affiliation; rather, what seems to be important for her is the collective pleasure involved in speaking that way. Within her peer group, Midwestern "hurrrr!" creates deeper affiliation. However, Latasha's conversation with Alim illustrates a point woven throughout the volume: Linguistic features spread translocally and are used, whether speakers are aware of it or not, to build local affiliations.

These collected authors (see also Dimitriadis's, 2009, extended discussion of "place") are inevitably drawn into the worlds of those *translocal* hip-hop communities they are documenting and every chapter in this book documents with detail and respect the lifeworlds of glocalizing rap communities. Those lifeworlds emerge and sustain themselves through linguistic choices that are simultaneously expressive of local affiliations and a globalizing hip-hop community. This glocalization process is largely possible because through hip-hop lyrics youth imagine themselves as simultaneously part of global hip-hop movements and a hyperlocal in-group.

Collective Weaving of Individual Experiences in Hip-Hop

Just as people in Alim et al.s (2009) volume use hip-hop lyrics, languages, diction, or phonology to see themselves as participants in a translocal movement, students in Hill's Hip-Hop Lit class were able to mingle their own stories with discussion of hip-hop narratives to "see themselves as individuals worthy of representation within the public sphere" (p. 41). As one of the students in Hill's Hip-Hop Lit class explained, "That shit is so real because sometimes you be like 'why this had to happen to me?' Then you realize that it happens to everybody" (Hill, 2009, p. 76). Ethnographic accounts of collective storytelling surrounding rap lyrics illustrate how this art form builds invaluable meanings and collective senses of the import, joy, and pain of living.

All hiphopographers touch on this issue of "making it real," and this process inevitably happens, in part, through forms of collective storytelling infused by hip-hop media. Dimitriadis (2009), for example, discusses the Ku Klux Klan with students at the community center and illustrates how students relate to history not only through hip-hop lyric representations and films he presents (*Panther* in particular) but also through talking about their own stories, discussions with relatives, and the juxtaposition of multiple media representations of Klan incidents. Similarly, Hill (2009) illustrates that only when students recognize their own stories in hip-hop lyrics do the messages ring true, as two of Hill's students discuss (p. 42):

Khaleef: Exactly, like when Cee-Lo talk about trying to eat but not wanting to work at McDonald's, I could feel that because I been through that.

Maggie: And that makes it easier to take they advice.

Empathy achieved through collaborative storytelling also builds knowledge in these hip-hop centered discussions. Brown's (2009) hip-hop "girlhood celebration," takes Hill's (2009) discussion of shared narratives and Dimitriadis's (2009) notion of "performance"-based understandings into practice, encouraging girls to simultaneously connect and interrogate their relationship to hip-hop and to go public with their collective storytelling.

So, to summarize this section so far, researchers who take an ethnographic perspective on hip-hop dig deep into the local and experienced connections that youth make with hip-hop media. One way they do this is by withholding judgment and living with the ambiguities in youth rationales for their commitments. By studying hip-hop practices, in situ researchers have also illustrated how widely circulating "global" hip-hop always becomes imbued with local affiliations and meanings. One of the processes through which these local instantiations are sustained is through collective storytelling that is fostered through hip-hop media, and the sense, among hip-hop heads, that hip-hop media articulate emotions and experiences of their own lives. In all these ways, hiphopography probes the layers of shared practices and collective knowledge in which signs of hip-hop culture are embedded, that is, the forms of *deference* that sustain youth engagement with this media. As the next section describes, by using these ethnographic approaches, researchers may also become insiders in these worlds, fostering local forms of *deference* within themselves, as they study and describe them.

Joining In: Going Native in Hip-Hop Worlds

Ethnographic approaches to hip-hop are also marked by a tendency to lean toward the "participant" side of the "participant/observer" dialectic. I call this the "joining in" tendency of hiphopography, and it is evident in obvious, conscious, and usually joyous ways throughout this research.

One of the most obvious ways hiphopographers indicate their involvement in the communities they are studying is through their own writing style and rhetoric. Merging the prose style of their staid, academic volume with the artistry of the hip-hop genre, Alim et al. (2009) call the chapters in their book "Tracks" rather than "Chapters" and organize them into two "Discs" (sections of the book). Rather than acknowledgements, they include "Shoutouts" (see also Hill, 2009) and when listing the authors in the volume, they title this section, "Hip-Hop Headz aka List of Contributors." Hill (2009) includes an appendix to his book that he labels "Bonus Tracks" and parenthetically labels his final chapter, "The Remix."

In the front and back matter, authors also take on the voice of hip-hop by mingling recognizably hip-hop ways of speaking. In shoutouts, especially, the authors tend to break with academic diction: "We been rollin *deep* for the last coupla years, straight *grindin"* (Alim, 2009) or ". . . the Hip Hop Nation in da house, BIG TIME" (Ibrahim, 2009). In chapter epigraphs or section headings, authors also indicate their embrace of hip-hop through quotes from hip-hop artists (Alim, 2007; Hill, 2009; Lin, 2009), though, in Hill's case, they are almost always paired with a social theorist canonized in academia. What these overt genre departures say implicitly is something Alim says explicitly elsewhere, "We need to take the language of the HHNSC [Hip Hop Nation Speech Community] seriously" (Alim, 2007, p. 28).

Within the texts themselves, most authors (with the notable exception of Brown, 2009) stick strictly to academic diction, but their "joining in" is still pervasive in their self-representations in transcripts and their language within those dialogues. Alim (2009) and Hill (2009), for example, often display themselves in dialogue with students, with Alim referring to himself as "Alim" or "A," and Hill calling himself "me." In these transcripts, the authors are not simply drawing information from students, but also sharing information about their own background or ways of speaking and at times, confessing deeply personal stories from their own lives, building their connection with hip-hop or hip-hop narratives (see especially Hill, 2009, p. 86).

Aside from their writing styles, and self-representations in print and transcripts, these researchers also describe their research as representing a level of involvement that is highly personal and sympathetic to student perspectives. In part, they do this by describing the quantity and quality of time spent around their research site and within the community. Dimitriadis worked as a volunteer, a staff member, and a researcher in the community center where he conducted his research for 4 years. He describes his apartment as between the students' school and the community center, a place where research participants would drop by to see him if they were in trouble or just to relax or talk. Hill began his research teaching at a school in which he was already known and where he already had a rapport with the students. He prefaces his ethnography with a description of his own familiarity with life in North Philadelphia (having grown up there). Brown (2009) describes herself as experiencing precisely the same struggles as a woman that she sees the Black girls in her program engaging in through hip-hop performance. Even Pennycook (in press) describes the joy he feels in his global hip-hop research pursuit, describing his own enviable research position as "getting" to go to music clubs, live the life, and delve into fascinating youth cultural ephemera. These researchers also either implicitly or explicitly end up siding with students over teachers, who, if represented at all, usually come off as ignorant, clueless, or just "vacant" (Alim, 2009; Dimitriadis, 2009; Hill, 2009).

Digital Literacies

Although I would personally include hip-hop in a list of new literacies relevant to youth mass-mediated culture today, in today's educational literature, hip-hop and youth engagement with digital literacies are as highly segregated as most urban schools. However, these mass-mediated forms share a common enemy: Both are often driven underground by teachers and ever-standardizing educational policy. Just as hip-hop lyrics and the discussions they generate may be seen as inappropriate for traditional classrooms, graphic novels, online writing, or social networking websites may not function within the educational policy machine as legitimate forms of literate behavior in the classroom.

Moreover, there is a group of researchers studying digital literacies, who, just like the hiphopographers, are entering into the culture of those who participate in digital literacies. While there, they are making many of the same methodological and epistemic choices that the hiphopographers are making, and many of the same discoveries. Just as the hip-hop researchers, new literacy research is marked by *acceptance and exploration of ambiguity* involved in these communities (in particular, the valuing of individual subjectivities and collective knowledge over verifiable "facts"), *blurring of the global/local distinction,* the *collective weaving of individual experiences;* and researchers' own tendency to joyously *join in* or go native within the communities they are researching.

Digital literacies include "video gaming, fanfiction writing, weblogging, using websites to participate in affinity practices, and social practices involving mobile computing" (Knobel & Lankshear, 2007, p. 1). The raw materials for digital literacies have also been called "participatory media," a term that makes explicit the inherently collaborative and active involvement of participants in fan and game cultures or other forms of new media socializing (Buckingham, 2009). Media production (including writing, photography, video and audio and combinations of all of these) in these new literacy environments involves new ways of negotiating relationships through technologically mediated space. As the listing above suggests, digital literacies are a constantly expanding, wildly uncontainable genre; however, there are some common features. I summarize and exemplify a few of those in the review that follows, while focusing primarily on fanfiction websites. Just as hip-hop researchers have used ethnography to enter into the lifeworlds of hip-hop youth, researchers on digital literacies have used a sociocultural approach to enter into the lifeworlds of youth who participate on fanfiction writing sites.

Acceptance and Exploration of Ambiguity: A Sociocultural Approach

The term *fanfiction* describes writing based on already existent texts. Although fanfictions have been around for a long time—arguably Milton's *Paradise Lost* could be considered a bible-based fanfiction (Black, 2008b)—Thomas (2007) dates the origin to the periodical *Fanzines,* published in the 1930s. Unlike these old paper-based fanfictions, digital fanfictions are mediated by Internet technology and are written on websites designed to facilitate collaborative writing. On these sites, fanfiction writers draw on characters and settings from myriad stories and media to weave new stories, sometimes even blending characters from wide-ranging source material. Similar to hip-hop artists, fanfiction writers troll widely circulating media and, blending that with their own inspiration and uniquely local source material, they create.

To enter into the world of fanfiction, researchers take the role of "participant/observers." This form of participant observation, however, looks quite different than hiphopography—rather than engaging in discussions of lyrics or spending nights in clubs with battling hip-hoppers, participant/observation of fanfiction writing involves logging on to a website, reading and writing stories, and providing feedback. Black (2008b), for example, spent 3 years participating/observing on the Fanfiction .net (FFN) website to conduct her research. Thomas (2007) spent 4 years on her ethnography of online youth literacies. By doing so, just as hiphopographers enter into the youth's collaborative understandings of history or their sense of the "real," these fanfiction researchers gradually are able to make sense of what might seem like incoherent text to outsiders.

To understand how youth inhabit new literacy environments, consider the simple example of this "Author's Note" (A/N) below, written by Nanako, a native-Mandarin-speaking high school–aged English Language Learner in Canada (Black, 2007). Despite speaking Mandarin as her native language, and English in school, she begins her Author's Note with a Japanese greeting:

A/N: Kinichiwa minna-san! This is my new story ☺. Please excuse my grammar and spelling mistakes. Because English is my second language. Also, I'm still trying to improve my writing skills . . . so this story might be really sucks . . .

As the Author's Note above suggests, and Black (2008a) stresses in her analysis, digital literacies involve a weaving of both technical knowledge (how to navigate online fanfiction sites, make profiles, use Author's Notes, and links to reviewers) and social knowledge about how to meet your communicative goals through the medium. These two kinds of knowledge are frequently distinguished in the literature on new literacies. Knobel and Lankshear (2007), for example, stress the importance of sociocultural understandings of new literacies by describing new literacies as involving not only "new technical stuff" but also the crucial "new ethos stuff."

Buckingham (2007) makes a similar point, emphasizing that "access" to new literacies "needs to be seen not merely in terms of access to technology or to technical skills, but also to *cultural forms of expression and communication*" (p. 170). Thus, just as "ethnography" affords an investigation of the contexts and cultural fabric of hip-hop, a "sociocultural approach" makes it possible for researchers of digital literacies to understand not simply the textual or technical aspects of these new forms, but the relational values they accrue in use.

Despite the shared interest in examining the social worlds of hip-hop and new literacies, across the new literacies literature, there is more expressed anxiety about ambiguity and the foregrounding of "individual subjective experience at the expense of more general truth claims" (Buckingham, 2009). Authors seem more worried about the "narrowly celebratory" approach of new literacies research (Buckingham, 2007) than they are in the hiphopography reviewed above. However, usually the sociocultural approach (see especially, the collected chapters in Knobel & Lankshear, 2007) pushes researchers to examine the pleasure students feel from participating in these forms. Gee's (2007) research into video gaming, for example, begins with the questions, "What is the deep pleasure human beings take from video games? What is the relationship between video games and real life?" (p. 95). He goes on to ask questions about these games' relationship to learning and even schooling, but these are largely incidental to his methods and analysis. He lets his phrase "real life" remain ambiguous.

Researchers of fanfiction sites also generally tend to downplay the anxieties about the "point" of these new literacies in favor of deference to the obvious pleasure and creative energy involved in writing, responding to, and editing fanfictions. Just as teachers might worry about "African American English" in their classrooms, some English teachers might worry a bit about the grammar or language choices used on fanfiction websites. Nanako's comment, "Also, I'm still trying to improve my writing skills . . . so this story might be really sucks . . ." might trouble an English teacher because of several language "problems"; however, in the social context of the fanfiction website, this formulation elicits precisely the kinds of reviews Nanako wants. Indeed, her story elicited comments from 1,700 reviewers(!), "most of whom assured her that her writing does not 'suck'" (Black, 2008a, p. 135).

Blurring of the Global/Local Distinction Through Digital Literacies

Fanfiction websites also trouble the distinction between global and local, illustrating the *glocalization* made possible through online literacies. Alim et al.'s (2009) volume illustrated how local hip-hop forms are built out of globally circulating cultural forms and ways of speaking. Similarly, the affinity groups (loosely knit networks of affiliation around a common interest; Gee, 2004) that come together in online fanfiction spaces create a sense of a local community, but are simultaneously built out of globally circulating ways of speaking and using media. Nanako, for example, quoted in the Author's Note above, is contributing her stories to a small subsection of the larger website, fanfiction.net. Her story is part of an archive of stories about the Japanese anime series *Card Captor Sakura*. This site includes native and nonnative English speakers from Canada, the United States, the Philippines, Mexico, and the United Kingdom, among other countries. In this space, Nanako's use of Japanese "Kinichiwa minna-san!" marks her transnational position as a devotee of anime, and later, use of her native Mandarin becomes a global form of cultural capital "localized" on this website, within this affinity group (Black, 2008b).

Collective Weaving of Individual Experiences in Digital Literacies

In general, digital literacies are characterized in the research as highly collaborative endeavors. Buckingham (2009) describes new media production as "distinctly public and collective, and it depends upon a shared knowledge of social norms and cultural conventions" (p. 47). Speaking specifically about "do-it-yourself" video media, Buckingham describes this "vernacular" culture as "a networked culture, which is creating new forms of *collective intelligence*" (p. 42). Burgess (2006), researching digital storytelling, describes how these multimedia presentations facilitate collaboration. Knobel and Lankshear (2007) highlight the collaborative nature of new literacies as key component of "New Ethos Stuff" (p. 9). The research on fanfiction also explicitly discusses the collaborative work on these websites, often comparing it to the goals of "peer editing" recommended for writing in schools (Atwell, 1998), but emphasizing that peer editing on fanfiction sites goes far beyond, in both quantity and content of commentary, anything possible in a traditional writing class (Black, 2008a).

The design of fanfiction websites promotes this collaboration, and Black (2007) argues that the best writers craft their author's notes (both before and after their fictional texts) strategically to receive the kind of feedback they want. In this way, reviewers take a substantial, formative role in stories as they unfold, often influencing choices in how material is presented (or whether it is presented) in subsequent segments. Because participants in the websites come from a range of backgrounds, native languages, homelands, and age groups, fanfiction reviews contribute to the translocal and sometimes even transgenerational appeal of the stories. As Nanako becomes more fluent in her storytelling (and learns more from her Japanese classes at school), she begins to insert more Japanese as well as her native Mandarin into her stories, using both Romanized forms and Chinese characters. Whereas a teacher or traditional peer editor might be confounded by this multilingualism, Nanako's fanfiction reviewers admired and encouraged this range of expression: "I'm learning so much Chinese and Japanese everytime I read" or "you are so very smart to know so much about these languages" (Thorne & Black, in press).

Thorne and Black (in press) also point out that this highly collaborative nature of writing on fanfiction sites complicates the notion of individual "identity" of authors. As Thomas (2007) illustrates further, the medium encourages not just formative feedback on a single author's fiction but also coauthorship. In the process of coauthoring and working with a huge range of source material, character journals and auxiliary role-playing sites in which characters can develop in dialog, two female coauthors she follows, Tiana and Jandalf, create hauntingly expressive prose, none of which could be directly attributed to either one of them as an individual.

Joining In: Going Native With New Literacies

As the multiple accounts of the pleasure and joy involved in new literacies suggest, researchers of new literacies often seem to be joining in these affinity spaces, just as the hiphopographers seem to revel in their own hip-hop knowledge and participation. Sometimes, this takes the form of confessional testimonials to authors' own history of pop cultural involvement (Alvermann, Moon, & Hagood, 1999). Black (2008b) joins in more implicitly, highlighting fanfiction excerpts as epigraphs and labeling sections of her work using online acronyms such as "The OMG Standard."

Despite the professed admiration for the joy participants take in their affinity spaces, and the obvious need to join in to even begin to understand how complex media such as videogames work and MMR (massively multiplayer role-playing) games are played, what fanfiction acronyms mean, or how DIY anime is produced through Machinima, there are still noticeably fewer instances of "joining in" in this research than there is in the research of the hiphopographers. Perhaps these modes of expression may still be something of a guilty pleasure for these academics.

Deference Literature: Summary and Critique

All these studies, although deeply reflective and respectful descriptions of youth participation in hip-hop or new literacies, still present portraits of hip-hop and digital literacies on their own terms. Researchers are more apt to join in or "go native" than to maintain critical distance. The disturbing disconnect between these two bodies of literature makes this even more clear. Although Alim et al.'s (2009) volume brilliantly surveys hip-hop's global influence(s), none of the researchers discussed above have ventured more fully into its superbly mass-mediated circulation out of recognizable hip-hop circles and forms of repetition. Hip-hop, for example, has been recontextualized massively commercially and has become a critical means for marketing nearly every kind of merchandise from shoes to cars to clothes to school supplies. Likewise, digital literacies researchers seldom discuss hip-hop production and circulation as a new literacy, thought it is arguably the quintessential cultural instantiation of both "new technical" and "new ethos" characteristics. Hip-hop authors are more concerned with documenting singular community instantiations of hip-hop than how the hip-hop repertoire is re-embedded in other contexts of mass-mediated consumption and youth sociality. Digital literacy researchers rarely troll the cultural surface beyond the limited social networks of those they are studying. (See however, one notable exception: Morrell, 2002, who embeds his discussion of hip-hop within a new literacies framework.)

The isolated quality of these two bodies of literature may be a reflection of the deference embodied by these two groups of researchers. Digging deep may sacrifice a view of the bigger picture. What all the deferent ways of paying attention to mass-mediated culture share, however, is that although they are deferring to unstated and perhaps unconscious fields of deference, they are also inherently limiting ways of perceiving. Ultimately, these forms of deference limit anyone's worldview and isolate people from other perspectives.

So there are some problems with overly deferent joining-in perspectives when it comes to mass media and schooling. Some scholars accordingly try to deny, or at least bracket, the highly contextual social quality of youth mass media participation and skim off those aspects of these cultural forms that might be transferable, less ambiguous, and more recognizable within school contexts, arguably with the goal of building student knowledge in the classroom. It is to these studies that I now turn.

STUDIES THAT FOREGROUND DENIAL (OR AT LEAST BRACKET DEFERENCE)

Researchers who ignore the deferent aspects of youth cultural formations are, at their best, taking a John Cage–like stance: They do not want children's world views to be limited by overly deferential, unquestioning approaches to peer-based cultural canons. These approaches risk, however, being ignorant of their own forms of deference. This dance between denying the deferent positionality of the youth culture they are critiquing (or admiring) and recognizing their own positionality can take infinite forms. I discuss and exemplify three below, first by foregrounding the widely circulating mass-mediated stances these ostensibly a-contextual approaches are reacting to.

"Is This Poetry?!!" Forms of Denial

"Is this poetry?!!" forms of denial focus on the perceived formal textual vacuity of popular media. In this form of denial, adults openly recognize and celebrate their own (superior) forms of culture. Their lives are enriched by these cultural forms, but they believe that children are in a cultural vacuum, devoid of valid forms of cultural deference. Speaking from this perspective, adults listen to "music," kids listen to "noise," rap scarcely resembles poetry, and anything done "online" is not a form of literacy. Youth cultural forms are seen as degradations of superior forms—real music, poetry, and "standard" forms of writing. In this way, adults position themselves as purveyors of legitimate forms of culture, not recognizing that their own powerful footing is based on a history of repetition and quotation, but not necessarily an articulate understanding of what makes that important to them. Insistence that youth join adults in this field of deference, or that youth themselves are in a cultural vacuum denies the forms of deference that make it possible for us to understand one another, experience mass-mediated culture deeply, and even to feel joy and pain together. Ironically, well-intentioned adults from the "what's that noise" perspective may wish for nothing more than to introduce youth to truth and beauty through "real" art and legitimate traditions.

Research on youth mass media that directly reacts to this perspective attempts to argue for youth culture on the basis that it *is legitimate in these terms if you just look closely.* Sometimes, this research highlights crucial aspects of youth cultural forms, which otherwise might go overlooked. In these cases, some researchers, in efforts to translate their more ethnographic research into *deference*, end up bracketing that ethnographic knowledge to make decontextualized points about their findings. Alim (2003), for example, in response to the perspective that rap is not real poetry, outlines the "Hip Hop poetics" of artists whose lyrics obviously use complex poetic devices, and he labels extensively the kinds of rhyming you might find in this art form—"*chain rhymes, back-to-back-rhymes, compound internal rhymes, primary and secondary internal rhymes, secondary internal rhymes,* and *polysyllabic rhyme* strings of *octuple rhymes* . . . creating a *multirhyme matrix* unparalleled in American poetics" (Alim, 2007, p. 28).

Adam Bradley's (2009) book-length study on the poetics of hip-hop brilliantly engages this perspective that rap must be connected to a legitimate "poetics" to be meaningful. He describes not only the complex rhyme schemes of rap, but also the ways rhyme, rhythm, and wordplay coordinate in hip-hop lyrics, illustrating how over the years, hip-hop artists have taken full advantage of the form and its lyrical possibilities. Geneva Smitherman (2007) also emphasizes the formal quality of hip-hop texts, calling rap the "New Black Poetry." Smitherman focuses less on the canonical qualities that English teachers might already know about, drawing attention to distinctly Black stylistic features that have their origins in traditional Black speech events as the dozens, the toast, call-response, and signification. These writers are in part justifying hip-hop's legitimacy in terms of recognizable poetic traditions (This is poetry!), but in doing so they also celebrate its unique form and expressive qualities. Still, their descriptions stand apart from those more deferent hiphopographers' illustrations of youth social formations and focus on legitimizing more strictly textual elements.

"You Are Being Duped!" Forms of Denial

"You are being duped!" forms of denial highlight concerns about the textual messages youth are assumed to be "receiving" mindlessly. From this perspective, youth act counter to adult practices, not because they have bad taste or lack respect for tradition, but simply because they do not clearly understand what they are doing. Adults rail against teens with "unformed brains" (Ahmed-Ullah, 2010) vulnerable to dangerous Internet-mediated messages or peer pressure, as if adults are seeing them from positions untouched by the mass media or forms of cultural deference. This cultural denial perspective can lead to simplistic forms of critical pedagogy in which students are positioned as if they need more critical-thinking skills, so they can more rationally understand messages they are consuming, rather than be controlled by them. Even this well-meaning form of pedagogy, however, denies the role of deference involved in media consumption. As Rosaldo (1989/1993) observed, anthropologists defer to ritual just as much as the individuals in the communities they study; similarly, critical pedagogues often pay uncritical deference to their own mass-mediated forms of speaking, writing, and behaving, while insisting students take a more critical stance on their own mass-mediated social formations.

Still, researchers on youth mass media formations often legitimate their role by lifting up the development of a "critical perspective" as the goal. From this perspective, students' knowledge of mass media is often positioned as suspect. Students themselves are seen as tools, manipulated by giant media conglomerates (Giroux, 2000) or the military industrial complex (Giroux, 2008).

Most classroom-oriented researchers in the "critical" vein are slightly more even-handed and often struggle with a tension between validating student practices and urging them to critique the art forms they love. These researchers argue with themselves in print about how it is possible to develop a critical faculty in students while simultaneously preserving the pleasure and joy students experience in mass media participation (Alvermann et al., 1999; Leard & Lashua, 2006; Mahiri, 2001). Dierdre Glenn Paul (2000) describes a slightly different struggle, one she faced as a teacher educator trying to encourage teachers to use hip-hop lyrics in their classrooms as a tool for "cultural synchronization." She describes these teachers as resistant to the messages in popular media and doubtful about their legitimate place in the classroom at all.

These attempts at engaging students in critique, and developing a teacher corps who feels competent doing this, are challenging and ongoing. Sometimes, however, researchers of critical pedagogy tend to be overly sanguine in judging their critical efficacy. Morrell and Duncan-Andrade (2002), for example, paired popular hip-hop lyrics with canonical literature from the English curriculum both to build on students' knowledge and expertise and to encourage sociopolitical critique. They concluded that

[t]he students were not only engaged and able to use this expertise and positionality as subjects of the post-industrial world to make powerful connections to canonical texts, they were also able to have fun learning about a culture and a genre of music with which they had great familiarity. (p. 91)

Such generalizing descriptions do not manage to capture the ways in which mass media are bound up in students' collective knowledge and activities, as depicted in ethnographies of their mass-mediated practices that are able to explore layers of deference. And, as Paul's (2000) descriptions of her teacher education classes suggest, such blithe descriptions of critical pedagogy also underrepresent the struggles teachers have in accepting new mass-mediated forms in their classrooms. Furthermore, students already have well-developed critical faculties that may be easily turned on teachers they do not see as "real." As Rice (2003) writes, "the potential for critical understanding always contrasts with the potential for student cynicism" (p. 469).

So, although both the "Is this poetry?!!" and "You are being duped!" forms of denial attempt to bring mass media into the classroom, they do so by removing it from the context within which it becomes meaningful for students. Similarly, a third type of denial research, "what's it good for?" type, discussed below, decontextualizes mass-mediate youth culture and attempts to laminate it onto institutionally sanctioned practices and forms of knowledge.

"What's It Good For?" Forms of Denial

The "What's it good for?" views attempt to find ways to usefully channel youth media enthusiasms into more seemingly legitimate adult goals such as "21st-Century Skills," "Academic Literacies," or "Understanding Shakespeare." From this perspective, adults take it as a given and even accept that young people take pleasure in mass-mediated youth culture, but insist that it must be good for *something else*. Just as administrators argue for more funding for "The Arts" in schools, by citing evidence that art education increases test scores, or chances for getting into a top-level college, educators often discuss youth culture for what additional perks it can *get* those who enjoy it. In each case, this "what does it get me" stance can inhibit deeper exploration into what and how "the arts" or popular youth culture build forms of life and webs of human connection in the context of their localized use.

Arguing for what youth mass media is *good for* is a common refrain, even in research that is more generally deferent to youthy pleasures. New media researchers often frame their research by making connections to 21st-century skills or more egalitarian economic advancement. Buckingham (2009), for example, frequently describes "the crucial question," as ". . . the extent to which any of this amounts to a form of empowerment" (p. 43). Mahiri (2001) also emphasizes the possibility of empowering students by using new literacies and hip-hop studies to develop skills that students will need in the new "digital economy." Even Gee (2000), while paying deference to the inherent pleasures of new media, makes connections to their important role in helping students into the economy of "fast capitalism."

Hip-hop researchers have also bracketed the pleasures of hip-hop sociality to probe the uses of "rap" in the classroom. In this vein, Baker (1991) describes his own process of making classroom connections between Shakespeare's *Henry V* and Public Enemy's "Don't Believe the Hype," having the class illustrate by a show of hands if they thought "patriotism" in the form of dying for England ("once more into the breach!") was a form of "hype." As Baker describes himself lecturing to the English students—"Henry V was a rapper—a cold dissing, def con man, tougher than leather and smoother than ice, an artisan of words" (p. 227)—the class (where he was a guest) loved it. He concludes, "I gained pedagogical entrée by playing in the new and very, very sound game of rap" (p. 228).

Baker's (1991) infusion of Public Enemy into a British English Literature classroom was a radical move more than 30 years ago! Today, largely because of Carol Lee's (1995) groundbreaking work in high school English classrooms, and as evidenced by Marc Lamont Hill's (2009) Hip-Hop Lit class and Morrell and Duncan-Andrade's (2002) curricular juxtapositions of hip-hop and English Lit standards, using hip-hop to build a bridge to classics is far more common. Today's English teachers also juxtapose other media with the classics, and researchers write about these media as not only useful pedagogical hooks but also tools for adding depth to students' understandings of otherwise arid-seeming classics (Trier, 2006).

With differing degrees of depth and self-consciousness, these "what's it good for" approaches all extract mass-mediated signs such as rap lyrics or movies or popular novels from one field of social relations in which they accrue social value (the neighborhood, the online fanfiction site), and embed them in a new field of deference in which economic advancement or different forms of cultural capital are being distributed.

SUMMARY AND IMPLICATIONS: FROM DEFERENCE AND DENIAL TO REPERTOIRES OF DEFERENCE

Denial critiques of youth culture, while often problematic in their decontextualized treatment of mass-mediated texts, potentially illuminate problems with overly *deference*-focused approaches. Although deference can be comforting, research that focuses on this aspect of cultural consumption can be "narrowly celebratory" (Buckingham, 2007, p. 143) or, much worse, dangerous and limiting. As Bloch (2005) points out,

When one is in trouble, and one does not know what to do, one allows oneself to be taken over by the knowledge and the authority of others; it is only sensible, and there is nothing much else that one can do. (pp. 135–136)

Indulging deference from a position of weakness, one can lose consciousness of the way cultural forms position their consumers. What all the ethnographic approaches to mass-mediated culture share is that although they illuminate unstated and perhaps unconscious fields of deference and carefully document forms of deference that hold people together, very little, if anything, is ever mentioned about how these are potentially limiting ways of perceiving. This is why John Cage is an inspiration to so many artists. He wanted people to relate to tradition not by critiquing it or finding its flaws, but in rejecting its limitations to our own perceptions.

Unfortunately, however, *denial*-focused perspectives, even those that foster appreciation for the value of youth cultural forms such as hip-hop or new literacies, rarely take a freeing, Cageian perspective. Instead, these approaches often reduce the value of these forms to their textual qualities (rap is a poetic form or lyrics are manipulative) or their "good-for-something-else" possibilities (new literacies are an entrée to fast capitalism, rap fosters a love of Shakespeare). Despite the impulse of well-meaning, rational adults and teachers to interrogate our children ("What makes this poetry?" "Don't you understand you're being manipulated?" "What's it good for?"), these sorts of attempts at rational dialog rarely have much of an impact.

So, both the ethnographically contextualized as well as the decontextualized accounts of mass-mediated youth culture have limitations. As researchers of mass media in education, the goal is neither to achieve a view from nowhere (impossible) nor to prioritize (or defer to) some ritual forms as better than others (inevitably myopic). Instead, we need to reconceptualize our object of study and our methods for researching it. As discussed in the following section, this entails building methods for researching *repertoires* of deference, first by reconceptualizing "mass media" as an object of study, and then, by researching its location in *repertoires of deference*.

Reconceptualizing the Object of Study: Mass Media and Schooling

Bloch (2005) crucially reminds us that "rituals are acts of repetition" (p. 126). When words, music, or any cultural forms are mass produced, they are most readily repeated. But, as all these studies illustrate, each repetition is also inevitably a *recontextualization*. A word, a phrase, a form of pronunciation, or a hip-hop lyric that circulates globally takes on local distinction, and has unique meaning in a local social performance. The Japanese greeting *kinichiwa* has highly different relational value on an anime fanfiction site than it does on a street in Tokyo. Tupac's "Dear Mama" lyric has highly different relational value in Hill's (2009) hip-hop lit class than it does as background music for a YouTube video made by a White MIT student.

The Mass Media, then, must be defined not as an object that exists separately from social interaction but as this process of endless repetition and recontextualization. These are two forces that work to balance each other. Repetition suggests boring sameness; recontextualization suggests renewal. Instead of mass media being repetitive and homogenizing, the more widely distributed something is, the more highly diverse are its recontextualizations, and the more possibilities for its involvement in new fields of ritual deference. Our object of study, then, need not be a single genre like "hip-hop" or "fan fiction," but the acts of repetition and recontextualization that make up the fabric of lives in and out of schools.

Reconceptualizing Methodology: Developing and Documenting Repertoires of Deference

Mass media have been shown to be a driving life force for students outside of school, and teachers have struggled with how to pull this creative energy into the classroom. We now need new methodological resources for understanding this recursive process of recontextualization with the depth of ethnographic studies, but with the practical goals of more applied research. The research questions need to move from "What do these forms mean to kids?" or "How can these be mobilized in schools?" to "How can educators and students learn together and from each other about these processes?"

Each profession, each form of life, has different ways of recontextualizing the meaning of a rap lyric or a piece of language. A district attorney may use rap lyrics uttered by a defendant as grounds for prosecution. A public school administrator may use one individual's hip-hop style as grounds for moving that kid to a different school. But the editor of a scholarly volume may consider a list of contributors labeled "hip-hop headz" a sign of collegial affiliation and respect. A teacher may see an overly modest "author's note" on an essay as a sign of minimal competence, while that same note on a work of fanfiction may elicit maximally productive feedback. These are the kinds of repetitions and recontextualizations in new fields of deference that new forms of research on mass media and schooling can explore.

There are hints of this new approach in some of the studies I have reviewed here. Dimitriadis (2009) calls this approach "re-articulation," writing of the ways that rap is recontextualized:

. . . the prevalence of rap, and gangsta rap in particular, points *for many* [italics added] to the broad overall decay of an out-of-control generation of youth. *For me* [italics added], after working for four years in the complex world of youth, rap's multiple uses show us all the ways young people are creatively coping with the vicissitudes of their increasingly difficult and dangerous lives—and the ways we as teachers must rise to this challenge. Indeed, if texts and practices are always in performance, they are open to re-articulation by interested educators. (p. 163)

Dimitriadis (2009) crucially notes different repertoires of deference: one *for many* and a very different one *for me*. Bringing more of these contrasts to light seems the next important goal for research on mass media and schooling.

Researchers and educators need not turn away from media forms such as "gangsta rap" because they are showing our children dangerous things! Sexist things! Racist things! Profanity! As Brown (2009) eloquently pointed out to an auntie who visited her hip-hop group for girls and worried about the occasional profanity spoken there, "This is not 'Character Education.'" What is much more worrisome is the fact that, after hearing profanity at the hip-hop group, this auntie and her niece never returned. Researchers need to develop repertoires of deference that circumvent this kind of communication breakdown and to share this kind of exploration with teachers and students. A research approach that examines multiple repertoires of deference can avoid simply dismissing either the Auntie's perspective or the radial educators.

By way of summative illustration, let us return to an expanded excerpt from Hill's (2009) Hip-Hop English classroom. As I commented earlier, a repertoire approach involves looking at the content of people's media engagement as well as the communicative techniques they use. In Hill's classroom, kids are not sanctioned for their use of mild profanity and are encouraged to relate to the lyrics under discussion by bringing in their own, very personal stories. In turn, the teacher shows a fluidity in the way he traverses both ways of speaking and the content of the talk, linking Tupac's lyrics and raw student commentaries to English curriculum words, such as "tone" and "mood." However, although Hill (2009) impressively negotiates multiple repertoires, it is unclear whether his coteacher or his students do the same, as illustrated here, in the extended-play version of the transcript. The transcript gets drawn to an end when the coteacher supplies the word "hopeful" to describe the "mood" of Tupac's lyric. Hill, the teacher, agrees immediately and goes on to a new topic, "tone."

Teacher: So what is the **mood** of **this piece?**
Joe: Sad.
Teacher: Why?
Joe: After all . . . he went through with his moms, he had to be sad.
Teacher: But isn't he thanking her for being a good mom in spite of everything?
Joe: Yeah but you gotta be sad going through that. *Me and mom and my brother went through the same shit.*
Jay: Me too. More me than my brother but *my pop wasn't there so shit gonna be sad. But you still happy 'cause you made it through.*
Teacher: I know he might've been sad thinking about everything they went through. *Just like y'all probably did.* But if you made it and everybody was listening to your story, how you think they would feel?
Joe: I think they would feel better. Like "Joe went through that and became a rapper or whatever so *it don't gotta turn out f'ed up.*"
Jay: Exactly. Like "*y'all could learn from my pain.*"
Teacher: OK. OK. That's what **mood** is all about. **Not so much what the writer is feeling, but how might the reader feel when he reads it.** So what would be a good word to describe how you might feel when you read this?
Jay: Better.
Kenef: Happy. Like y'all said, you might feel better knowing it ain't gotta end up all crazy.

Teacher: What might be a good word for that?

Coteacher: **How about hopeful?**

Teacher: **Hopeful! That sounds good. Let's say the mood is hopeful.** Now, y'all really answered this but what would you say is the tone of the piece?

Whereas Hill seems initially to be engaged in multiple repertoires, deftly moving between rap lyrics, student stories, English literature terms of art, and formal school-based (indicated in **boldface**) and informal registers (indicated in ***bold italics***), as this extension of the excerpt illustrates, the coteacher seems in this instance (and by Hill's description of his activities throughout the year, this is consistent with his overall "clueless" participation) to be limited to the "English Teacher" repertoire, supplying a "right answer" to Hill's query for an adjective of "mood." The students give no evidence of agreeing with this description or of the relevance of Hill's distinction between "mood" and "tone" to what they had just been discussing. Instead, as this interaction draws to a close, only the teacher and coteacher are participating in supplying the "right" answer. Although Hill (2009) seems to model fluent movement between repertoires of deference, even mediating between the students and his coteacher, there is little evidence that his students or the coteacher have such flexibility. Clearly, however, such flexibility is an asset in negotiating this highly complex interaction, and Hill does so quite admirably.

As this extended excerpt illustrates, talking across repertoires is subtle and difficult. Research into *repertoires of deference* would probe more deeply into how such flexibility is built and how to foster such repertoire shifting abilities not only among teachers but also among youth in today's schools. This would involve balancing long-term ethnographic study into youth cultural practices with classroom studies that examine how such practices become recontextualized in schools and in the lives of teachers. Through such study, we can begin to document how mass-mediated signs are recontextualized in new social practices, differently, by social groups with wide-ranging commitments. The study of teaching and learning then becomes the study of how teachers and students expand their repertoires to develop more overlapping communicative territory.

CONCLUSION: HANGING ACROSS THE SPECTRUM

What is the future of research on mass media and schooling? Schools are not supposed to be limiting. Ideally, they are here to expand horizons, not to cut them back. Unfortunately, however, many of the new literacy researchers point to a "new digital divide" (Buckingham, 2007; Mahiri, 2001) not between socioeconomic statuses, but between what youth do in and out of school. Obviously, the same divide exists for hip-hop. Unfortunately, the massively pleasurable and productive ways of learning documented by scholars of hip-hop and new literacies—the expanding horizons—are rarely seen in the classroom.

When researchers discount the kinds of ambiguity and deference involved in creative mass-mediated practice, their work is seen as something more classroom-like. Thus, the "denial" approaches tend to proliferate, seeking the essence of these youth cultural forms that might be skimmed off and used in schools. Research on mass media and schooling today can benefit by changing the focus from lamenting this divide, to understanding both (or all) of its sides and expanding the forms of deference and respect so that students, teachers, and researchers all more ably and deftly traverse cultural boundaries. Before this new in-school/out-of-school divide had solidified, Kalantzis and Cope (2000) encouraged a repertoire approach to schooling in the conclusion of their volume on new literacies (10 years ago!), writing the following:

Learning is not a matter of "development" in which you leave your old selves behind; leaving behind lifeworlds which would otherwise have been framed by education as more or less inadequate to the task of modern life. Rather, learning is a matter of repertoire; starting with a recognition of lifeworld experience and using that experience as a basis for extending what one knows and what one can do. (p. 124)

The repertoire approach itself seems to take on recognizable value across diverse lifeworlds. Shifting now from new literacies to Tupac, kids from Dimitriadis's (2009) study praised Tupac's ability to "hang across the spectrum," Tupac variously being "a Crip, a Blood, a Gangster Disciple, a Vice Lord, and a Black P Stone" (p. 146). Dimitriadis mentions this in the context of Tupac's moral authority. Despite claiming affiliations with these rival gangs, he was not viewed as a turncoat. He was not "flipping." His hanging across the spectrum was not cowardly, but evidence of his transcendence. This might also be a good metaphor for *repertoires of deference.* Tupac himself also hung with a much broader spectrum of gangs than those listed in that quote. He was highly involved in a literary gang, a theater gang, and even a feminist gang. As Dyson (2001) documents, Tupac listened to Kate Bush and Sarah McLachlan, and his huge personal library included Shakespeare, Richard Wright, and even *Our Bodies, Ourselves.* He was fascinated with feminism. Tupac's intellectualism allowed him to hang across the spectrum—an ideal model for researchers, teachers, and students of the mass media.

REFERENCES

Ahmed-Ullah, N. S. (2010, March 17). Parents U. offers courses in today's teen. *Philadelphia Inquirer*, p. E4.
Alim, H. S. (2003). On some serious next millennium rap ishhh: Pharoahe Monch, hip hop poetics and the internal rhymes of internal affairs. *Journal of English Linguistics, 31,* 60–84.
Alim, H. (2007). The whig party don't exist in my hood: Knowledge, reality, and education in the hip hop nation. In H. S. Alim & J. Baugh (Eds.), *Talkin black talk* (pp. 15–29). New York, NY: Teachers College Press.
Alim, H. S. (2009). Creating an empire within an empire: Critical hip hop language pedagogies and the role of sociolinguistics. In H. S. Alim, A. Ibrahim, & A. Pennycook (Eds.), *Global linguistic flows: Hip hop cultures, youth identities, and the politics of language* (pp. 213–230). New York, NY: Routledge.
Alim, H. S., Ibrahim, A., & Pennycook, A. (Eds.). (2009). *Global linguistic flows: Hip hop cultures, youth identities, and the politics of language.* New York, NY: Routledge.

Alvermann, D., Moon, J., & Hagood, M. (1999). *Popular culture in the classroom: Teaching and researching critical media literacy.* Newark, DE: International Reading Association.

Atwell, N. (1998). *In the middle: New understandings about writing, reading, and learning.* Portsmouth, NH: Boynton/Cook.

Baker, H. A., Jr. (1991). Hybridity, the rap race, and pedagogy for the 1990s. *Black Music Research Journal, 11,* 217–228.

Bauman, R. (2004). *A world of others' words: Cross-cultural perspectives on intertextuality.* Malden, MA: Blackwell.

Bauman, R., & Briggs, C. L. (1990). Poetics and performance as critical perspectives on language and social life. *Annual Review of Anthropology, 19,* 59–88.

Black, R. W. (2007). Digital design: English language learners and reader reviews in online fanfiction. In M. Knobel & C. Lankshear (Eds.), *A new literacies sampler* (pp. 115–136). New York, NY: Peter Lang.

Black, R. W. (2008a). Convergence and divergence, informal learning in online fanfiction communities and formal writing pedagogy. In D. Silberman-Keller, Z. Bekerman, H. A. Giroux, & N. Burbules (Eds.), *Mirror images: Popular culture and education* (pp. 125–144). New York, NY: Peter Lang.

Black, R. W. (2008b). *Adolescents and online fan fiction.* New York, NY: Peter Lang.

Bloch, M. (2005). Ritual and deference. In M. Bloch (Ed.), *Essays on cultural transmission* (pp. 123–137). New York, NY: Berg.

Bradley, A. (2009). *Book of rhymes: The poetics of hip hop.* New York, NY: Basic Books.

Brown, R. N. (2009). *Black girlhood celebration: Toward a hip-hop feminist pedagogy.* New York, NY: Peter Lang.

Buckingham, D. (2007). *Beyond technology: Children's learning in the age of digital culture.* Cambridge, England: Polity.

Buckingham, D. (2009). A commonplace art? Understanding amateur media production. In D. Buckingham & R. Willett (Eds.), *Video cultures: Media technology and everyday creativity* (pp. 23–50). London, England: Palgrave.

Burgess, J. (2006). Hearing ordinary voices: Cultural studies, vernacular creativity and digital storytelling. *Continuum: Journal of Media & Cultural Studies, 20,* 201–214.

Dimitriadis, G. (2009). *Performing identity/performing culture: Hip hop as text, pedagogy, and lived practice* (Rev. ed.). New York, NY: Peter Lang.

Dyson, M. E. (2001). *Holler if you hear me: Searching for Tupac Shakur.* New York, NY: Basic Books.

Gee, J. P. (2000). New people in new worlds: Networks, the new capitalism, and schools. In B. Cope & M. Kalantzis (Eds.), *Multiliteracies: Literacy learning and the design of social futures* (pp. 43–68). London, England: Routledge.

Gee, J. P. (2004). *Situated language and learning: A critique of traditional schooling.* New York, NY: Routledge.

Gee, J. B. (2007). Pleasure, learning, video games, and life: The projective stance. In M. Knobel & C. Lankshear (Eds.), *A new literacies sampler* (pp. 95–114). New York, NY: Peter Lang.

Giroux, H. A. (2000). *Stealing innocence: Corporate culture's war on children.* New York, NY: Palgrave.

Giroux, H. A. (2008). Militarization, public pedagogy, and the biopolitics of popular culture. In D. Silberman-Keller, Z. Bekerman, H. A. Giroux, & N. Burbules (Eds.), *Mirror images: Popular culture and education* (pp. 39–54). New York, NY: Peter Lang.

Hill, M. L. (2009). *Beats, rhymes, and classroom life: Hip-hop pedagogy and the politics of identity.* New York, NY: Teachers College Press.

Hutchins, E. (1995). *Cognition in the wild.* Cambridge, MA: MIT Press.

Ibrahim, A. (2009). Taking hip hop to a whole nother level: Métissage, affect, and pedagogy in a global hip hop nation. In H. S. Alim, A. Ibrahim, & A. Pennycook (Eds.), *Global linguistic flows: Hip hop cultures, youth identities, and the politics of language* (pp. 231–246). New York, NY: Routledge.

Kalantzis, M., & Cope, B. (2000). Changing the role of schools. In B. Cope & M. Kalantzis (Eds.), *Multiliteracies: Literacy learning and the design of social futures* (pp. 121–148). London, England: Routledge.

Knobel, M., & Lankshear, C. (2007). Sampling "the new" in new literacies. In M. Knobel & C. Lankshear (Eds.), *A new literacies sampler* (pp. 1–24). New York, NY: Peter Lang.

Leard, D. W., & Lashua, B. (2006). Popular media, critical pedagogy, and inner city youth. *Canadian Journal of Education, 29,* 244–264.

Lee, C. D. (1995). A culturally based cognitive apprenticeship: Teaching African American high school students skills in literary interpretation. *Reading Research Quarterly, 30,* 608–631.

Lin, A. (2009). Respect for da chopstick hip hop: The politics, poetics, and pedagogy of Cantonese verbal art in Hong Kong. In H. S. Alim, A. Ibrahim, & A. Pennycook (Eds.), *Global linguistic flows: Hip hop cultures, youth identities, and the politics of language* (pp. 159–177). New York, NY: Routledge.

Lohner, H. (Director). (1993). *John Cage: The revenge of the dead Indians* [Documentary film].

Mahiri, J. (2001). Pop culture pedagogy and the end(s) of school. *Journal of Adolescent & Adult Literacy, 44,* 382–385.

Morrell, E. (2002). Toward a critical pedagogy of popular culture: Literacy development among urban youth. *Journal of Adolescent & Adult Literacy, 46,* 72–77.

Morrell, E., & Duncan-Andrade, J. M. R. (2002). Promoting academic literacy with urban youth through engaging hip-hop culture. *The English Journal, 91,* 88–92.

Nagel, T. (1989). *The view from nowhere.* London, England: Oxford.

Paul, D. G. (2000). Rap and orality: Critical media literacy, pedagogy, and cultural synchronization. *Journal of Adolescent & Adult Literacy, 44,* 246–252.

Pennycook, A. (in press). Nationalism, identity, and popular culture. In N. Hornberger & S. McKay (Eds.), *Sociolinguistics and language teaching.* Tonawanda, NY: Multilingual Matters.

Pritchett, J. (1993). *The music of John Cage.* Cambridge, England: Cambridge University Press.

Rice, J. (2003). The 1963 hip-hop machine: Hip-hop pedagogy as composition. *College Composition and Communication, 54,* 453–471.

Rosaldo, R. (1993). *Culture and truth: The remaking of social analysis.* Boston, MA: Beacon. (Original work published 1989)

Smitherman, G. (2007). The power of rap: The black idiom and the new black poetry. In H. S. Alim & J. Baugh (Eds.), *Talkin black talk* (pp. 77–91). New York, NY: Teachers College Press.

Thomas, A. (2007). Blurring and breaking through the boundaries of narrative, literacy, and identity in adolescent fan fiction. In M. Knobel & C. Lankshear (Eds.), *A new literacies sampler* (pp. 137–165). New York, NY: Peter Lang.

Thorne, S., & Black, R. (in press). Identity and interaction in internet-mediated contexts. In C. Higgins (Ed.), *Negotiating the self in another language: Identity formation in a globalizing world.* Berlin, Germany: De Gruyter Mouton.

Trier, J. (2006). Teaching with media and popular culture. *Journal of Adolescent and Adult Literacy, 49,* 434–438.

About the Editor

Stanton Wortham is Judy and Howard Berkowitz Professor and Associate Dean for Academic Affairs at the University of Pennsylvania Graduate School of Education. He also has appointments in Anthropology, Communications, and Folklore. His research applies techniques from linguistic anthropology to study interaction, learning, and identity development in classrooms and organizations. Some of his work applies concepts and methods from linguistic anthropology to uncover social positioning in apparently neutral talk. His books *Acting Out Participant Examples in the Classroom* (John Benjamins, 1994), *Linguistic Anthropology of Education* (Praeger, 2003; coedited with Betsy Rymes), and *Learning Identity* (Cambridge University Press, 2006), together with various articles and chapters, explore interrelations between the official curriculum and covert interactional patterns in classroom discourse. He has also studied interactional positioning in media discourse and autobiographical narrative, and he has developed methodological techniques for analyzing narrative, media, and other everyday discourse. His book *Narratives in Action* (Teachers College Press, 2001) offers concrete guidance on how to uncover and document meaningful patterns in transcribed talk. More recently, he has begun research in areas of the United States that have only recently become home to large numbers of Latinos. This work is represented in *Education in the New Latino Diaspora* (Ablex, 2002; coedited with Enrique Murillo and Edmund Hamann), together with various articles. This research explores the challenges and opportunities facing both Latino newcomers and host communities, in places where models of newcomers' identities and practices for dealing with them are often more fluid than in areas with long-standing Latino populations. In addition to his work on education, he has also written about learning and development within organizations, as reported in *Bullish on Uncertainty* (Cambridge University Press, 2009, with Alexandra Michel). More information about his work can be found at http://www.gse.upenn.edu/~stantonw.

Review of Research in Education
March 2011, Vol. 35, p. 239
DOI: 10.3102/0091732X10391736
© 2011 AERA. http://rre.aera.net

About the Contributors

Thea Renda Abu El-Haj is an associate professor in the Graduate School of Education at Rutgers, The State University of New Jersey. Her current research explores new questions about youth citizenship raised by globalization, transnational migration, and the "war on terror." This ethnographic research focuses on how young Arab Americans grapple with questions of belonging and citizenship in the wake of September 11, 2001. Her publications about this study have appeared in *Anthropology and Education Quarterly*, *Harvard Educational Review*, and *Educational Policy*. Her first book, *Elusive Justice: Wrestling with Difference and Educational Equity in Everyday Practice*, offers a critical account of the range of justice claims at play inside real schools, exploring several different, important dimensions of educational equity that often are ignored in contemporary educational policy debates.

H. Samy Alim is an associate professor of education and (by courtesy) linguistics at Stanford University. His research explores the relationships between language, race, and ethnicity across a wide range of social, cultural, and educational contexts, both locally and globally. He has a specific interest in language, literacy, and youth culture, particularly Hip Hop Culture, and critical language awareness for socially and linguistically marginalized groups. His most recent book is *Global Linguistic Flows: Hip Hop Cultures, Youth Identities, and the Politics of Language* (Routledge, 2009, with Ibrahim & Pennycook). Other recent books include *Roc the Mic Right: The Language of Hip Hop Culture* (Routledge, 2006), *Tha Global Cipha: Hip Hop Culture and Consciousness* (with Spady & Meghelli, Black History Museum, 2006), *You Know My Steez* (Duke, 2004), and *Talkin Black Talk: Language, Education, and Social Change* (with Baugh, Teachers College Press, 2007).

Lesley Bartlett is an associate professor at Teachers College, Columbia University. Her research interests include multilingual literacies in Latin America, the Caribbean, and the United States. She is the author of *The Word and the World: The Cultural Politics of Literacy in Brazil* and coauthor of the forthcoming book *Additive Schooling in Subtractive Times*.

Review of Research in Education
March 2011, Vol. 35, pp. 240–243
DOI: 10.3102/0091732X10397908
© 2011 AERA. http://rre.aera.net

Nadia Behizadeh is a third-year doctoral student in language, literacy, and culture at Emory University in Atlanta, Georgia. She is a George W. Woodruff Scholar and former Piedmont Fellow. Her past experience includes teaching English language arts, being a school advisory coach, leading a science and technology club for girls, being a member of a design team for a small school, and leading professional development sessions using Critical Friends Groups. Her research interests include writing achievement and assessment, authentic writing instruction, culturally relevant pedagogy, and problem-based learning. Using cultural–historical activity theory (CHAT) and Critical Text Production as theoretical frameworks, her research examines classroom systems and the outcomes resulting from context-specific instructional interactions between teachers and students as they create a community of learners. Her mixed methods work draws on contextualized student voices as a central data source.

Sally Wesley Bonet is a doctoral student at the Graduate School of Education at Rutgers, The State University of New Jersey. A former elementary school teacher, she has extensive experience teaching in U.S. and Egyptian schools. Her research interests include the educational experiences of refugee, immigrant, and migrant students, particularly of youth from regions afflicted by war and conflict.

Jennifer Cole is a professor of anthropology in the Department of Comparative Human Development at the University of Chicago. Drawing from her long-term fieldwork in Madagascar, her work takes topics such as memory, youth, or migration as sites through which to investigate the intersection between everyday lived experience and broader historical change. In addition to several edited volumes on youth and globalization, she has recently published *Sex and Salvation: Imagining the Future in Madagascar* with the University of Chicago Press. She is currently conducting fieldwork on marriage migration from Madagascar to rural France.

Yasmin B. Kafai is a professor of learning sciences at the Graduate School of Education at the University of Pennsylvania. Her research on children's learning as designers of games, simulations, and virtual worlds has received generous funding from the National Science Foundation, the Spencer Foundation, and the MacArthur Foundation. She has edited several books, among them *Beyond Barbie and Mortal Kombat: New Perspectives on Gender and Gaming* (2008) and *The Computer Clubhouse: Constructionism and Creativity in Youth Communities* (2009), and worked on the recent National Educational Technology Plan for the U.S. Department of Education. She undertook her studies on learning theories and technologies in France and Germany, and received a doctorate from Harvard University while working with Seymour Papert at the MIT Media Laboratory.

Dina López is a doctoral candidate in the International Educational Development program at Teachers College, Columbia University. Her research interests include immigration and education, sociocultural approaches to language and literacy, and the relationship between identity and language learning processes.

Erika Mein is an assistant professor of literacy education at the University of Texas at El Paso. Her research looks at adolescent and adult literacies across educational contexts, with a particular focus on community-based organizations in Latin America and on the U.S.–Mexico border.

Kylie A. Peppler is an assistant professor in the Learning Sciences Program at Indiana University, Bloomington. An artist by training, Peppler engages in research that focuses on the intersection of arts and computer science education. A Dissertation-Year Fellowship from the Spencer Foundation as well as a UC Presidential Postdoctoral Fellowship has supported her early work in this area. Peppler's current work is supported by two recent grants from the National Science Foundation to study creativity in youth online communities as well as a recent grant from the John D. and Catherine T. MacArthur Foundation. Peppler's research has or will be published by *Teachers College Record*; *Mind, Culture, and Activity*; the *International Journal of Learning and Media*; and the *Cambridge Journal of Education,* among others. In addition, Peppler has coedited a book with Yasmin Kafai and Robbin Chapman titled *The Computer Clubhouse: Constructionism and Creativity in Youth Communities*, published by Teachers College Press (2009).

Betsy Rymes is an associate professor of educational linguistics in the Graduate School of Education at the University of Pennsylvania. Her discourse analytic research on talk and social formations in schools has been published widely in journals that include *Harvard Educational Review, Language in Society, Linguistics & Education, Research on the Teaching of English* (*RTE*), and *Anthropology and Education Quarterly* (*AEQ*). She is also the author of two books, *Conversational Borderlands* (2001) and *Classroom Discourse Analysis* (2009), and coeditor (with Stanton Wortham) of *The Linguistic Anthropology of Education* (2003). Her current research examines the intersecting roles of multilingualism, transnationalism, and mass-mediated culture in schools and society.

Shalini Shankar is an associate professor of anthropology and Asian American studies at Northwestern University, Evanston, Illinois. Her research interests span cultural and linguistic anthropology and include race, ethnicity, language use, youth, media, advertising, and consumption in Asian American communities. She is interested in issues of language use and schools, youth and media, and the creation and circulation of racial imagery. Her book *Desi Land: Teen Culture, Class, and Success in Silicon Valley* (Duke University Press, 2008) examines how youth of different immigration histories and class backgrounds negotiate social and linguistic dimensions of their education and community lives, and the ways in which they come of age in the midst of a rapidly transforming high-tech industry. Further developing linkages between youth, media, and consumption, her current research explores the production of media stereotypes and imagery of Asian Americans. She is conducting NSF-funded fieldwork and archival work on verbal and visual representations of Asian

Americans in niche and general market advertising agencies. She is additionally coediting two volumes, one on youth, race, and power, and another on the concept of the "postracial" in an age of Obama.

Laura A. Valdiviezo is an assistant professor of language, literacy, culture, and society in the School of Education at the University of Massachusetts Amherst. Her research interests include language policy and teacher practices in indigenous language revitalization programs in the Americas.

Maisha T. Winn (formerly Maisha T. Fisher) is an associate professor of language, literacy, and culture in the Division of Educational Studies at Emory University, where she teaches graduate courses in literacy theory and research as well as curriculum and instruction courses in English for preservice teachers. She was named the American Educational Research Association Division K Early Career Award in Research recipient in 2008 as well as the National Council on Research in Language and Literacy (NCRLL) Early Career Award in Research recipient in the same year. Her program of research examines the ways in which youth perform writing in school and in out-of-school contexts. She has published extensively in journals, such as *Harvard Educational Review, Anthropology and Education Quarterly, Research in the Teaching of English, English Education, Written Communication*, and *Race, Ethnicity, and Education*. She is the author of *Writing in Rhythm: Spoken Word Poetry in Urban Classrooms, Black Literate Lives: Historical and Contemporary Perspectives*, and the forthcoming *Girl Time: Gendering Youth Justice*.